PRESENTED
SOP
Jan04

D0808168

THE INTERNATIONAL DIRECTORY OF

Voluntary
Work

DERBY COLLEGE LIBRARY
WITHDRAWN
FOR REFERENCE ONLY

DERBY COLLEGE LIBRARY

THE INTERNATIONAL DIRECTORY OF

Voluntary Work

DERBY COLLEGE LIBRARY

BROOMFIELD LIBRARY

29

MORLEY, DERBY

WITHDRAWN

331

FOR REFERENCE ONLY

Editor
VICTORIA PYBUS

Distributed in the U.S.A. by
PETERSON'S GUIDES, INC
202 Carnegie Center
Princeton, N.J. 08543-2123

Published by
VACATION WORK
9 Park End Street, Oxford

First published 1979
Second Edition 1982
Third Edition 1985
Fourth Edition 1989
Fifth Edition 1993
Sixth Edition 1997

THE INTERNATIONAL DIRECTORY OF
VOLUNTARY WORK

Copyright © Vacation Work 1997

No part of this publication may be reproduced or transmitted in any
form or by any means without prior written permission
of the publisher

ISBN 1 85458 164 3 (softback)
ISBN 1 85458 165 1 (hardback)
ISSN 0143 — 3474

Cover design by the Miller Craig and Cocking Design Partnership.

Imageset and Printed by **Unwin Bros Ltd**, Old Woking, Surrey

Contents

PART ONE

Residential Work Throughout the World

PART TWO

Non-Residential Work in the United Kingdom 193

Introduction

It is difficult to forsee a time when volunteers will not be needed. Wherever you look it seems there are organisations looking for someone to give of their time and services. Not all such organisations are of the social, medical or international relief type, though it is these that usually have the highest profiles. In between there are hundreds, if not thousands of local and specialised organisations whose aims may include anything from conserving local wildlife habitats to uniting and supporting sufferers of a rare disease or syndrome. Your time, sometimes expertise, particular qualities of personality or understanding of particular problems, are some of the things that volunteer organisations look for in a volunteer. Sometimes even less is called for; a pair of willing hands may be sufficient. In other words, anyone can be a volunteer, at almost any time of their lives.

This book sets out to cover the full range of voluntary work. At one extreme are the long-term positions away from home lasting for over a year, in which the participant may almost lose contact with their old way of life; at the other are opportunities such as helping a charity with a door-to-door collection that may require only an occasional commitment and can be done even by most people with full-time jobs and families to look after. In between the two are those placements lasting for a few weeks or months that can be done by those taking a year off between school and university and students with a few weeks or months to fill during their year. It is also possible for working people with generous holiday entitlements or sympathetic employers to make temporary interruptions to the normal direction of their life. There are also organisations where you can combine a holiday, often in an exotic location such as a rainforest, with voluntary research work for an educational or conservational foundation.

This book contains opportunities to suit all types of people, from those with highly specialised skills or qualifications such as a surgical specialty or a pilot's licence, to those with none. Different types of work call for volunteers of different abilities, sometimes on the same premises: for example a Romanian orphanage may need people with experience in child care, fully-qualified medical personnel and experienced decorators and plumbers. All types of volunteer can make a valuable contribution. When you mention volunteer work, many people still have a mental image of a volunteer for an international aid organisation riding in the back of a Land Cruiser laden with sacks of food supplies across inhospitable terrain. This is only a very small part of the picture. One of the largest relief charities, Oxfam, does not send volunteers abroad, but relies on over 28,000 of them working part-time in their charity shops across the UK, not to mention in their central and regional offices. Without these volunteers Oxfam would not be able to raise the funds necessary for its work.

Another common misconception is that volunteers are not paid. This is not universally true, particularly where long-term, full-time volunteering is involved. No organisation could expect someone to spend perhaps two years of their life totally without an income, however dedicated they may be: even the most self-denying of volunteers may wear out their last pair of socks, or need to pay to have their spectacles mended. In practice, pocket money is often paid to volunteers who commit themselves to working for more than a few weeks on a project such as a long-term archaeological excavation. Long-term volunteers in developing countries will often receive a wage in the local currency, which is adequate for the location but which would be a pittance back home.

Most volunteers are prepared to work hard for little or no material gain and free board and lodging of the most basic kind. There are however, a growing number of charitable organisations whose short-term volunteers are expected to work hard and pay for the privilege. These include archaeological digs and research or community projects. Many of these paying volunteer projects are in South America and Mexico and the volunteers are often North American students who can gain university credits or tax advantages by doing a paying volunteer programme.

It is generally accepted by volunteers that there are few material benefits to be derived from volunteering. There are other benefits though, some of them are subjective and hard to quantify as some form of personal development is usually involved. For instance a student working on an archaeological dig in Israel or France may find their history studies gain added depth; a dentist may gain a new perspective on his or her profession by practising in India, as might a surveyor working in Africa. Other benefits are more tangible such as enabling a future employer to spot a team worker, a good organiser or someone with resourcefulness and adaptability. For an unemployed person, working on a local community project or for the National Trust can lead to the acquisition of new skills most likely in craftsmanship or horticulture which they can use as the basis of CV to show a future employer. Retirement may be a time to relax, but it is also a time to try new ventures: retired people of all ages can take on a range of responsibilities from teaching English to Polish university students in Kraków or driving a mini-bus part-time for handicapped children; to keep them active and full participants in their community.

This sixth edition of *The International Directory of Voluntary Work* contains the widest ever range of opportunities around the world for all types of people with all types of experience or none at all. As you will see, voluntary work can involve far more than just helping to meet basic human needs at home or abroad: tackling human deprivation in all its forms is just one of its manifestations. The volunteer is more than a human sticking plaster to apply to the wounds that the state does not bandage. To volunteer means simply to give your time and energies freely to help some project or cause. Some volunteers may choose an area or cause that they feel strongly about to provide the source of their motivation. This may mean fighting starvation in Africa or helping to get the population and infrastructure of a war weary nation back on its feet and functioning; it could be less heroic like helping the campaign against smoking in Britain, or menial like acting as an unpaid labourer on an organic farm in Belgium, or improving the standard of housing for the poor in Latin America. Some volunteers may wish for a complete contrast to the materialism inherent in most of our daily lives. Some may want to boost their CV and some may want to feel useful and involved in their community. Whatever your wishes and motivations there is almost certainly an organisation in this book that needs you.

Victoria Pybus
December 1996

*This edition is dedicated
to the memory of
Colin Pybus who for
many years devoted
his time and energy
to providing caring
homes for the homeless
and the needy.*

While every effort has been made to ensure that the information contained in this book was accurate at the time of going to press, some details are bound to change within the lifetime of this edition. Costs, pocket money/ stipends and the policies and details of individual organisations are particularly liable to change as are political situations. Some parts of the world are particularly prone to upheavals and have ongoing internal problems. Readers are therefore strongly urged to check facts, credentials and current political situations for themselves.

If in the course of your volunteer work you come across something that might be of interest to readers of the next edition, please write to: The Editor, International Directory of Voluntary Work, 9 Park End Street, Oxford OX1 1HJ; fax 01865 790885). A free copy of the next edition will be sent to anyone whose contribution or suggestion is used.

PART ONE

Residential Work Throughout the World

This section of the Directory examines the different types of voluntary work for which the volunteer is required to live and work away from home. This usually means a full time commitment, ranging from a weekend to several years.

For the purposes of classification, organisations requiring resident volunteers have been divided between long term and short term. The organisations classed as 'long term' require volunteers for periods of a year or more; 'short term' denotes residential work for anything up to a year. The short term organisations are further sub-divided geographically.

Obviously the dividing line between short and long term is indistinct and arbitrary and there are many organisations which fall into both categories. In such cases these organisations will be fully described under the category in which they are most active. Cross references will then be found at the end of the chapter on the other relevant category.

Applicants for voluntary work outside their own country are reminded that visas and work permits are sometimes necessary. The fact that voluntary work is unpaid does not always exempt them from these requirements. Regulations around the world change frequently, so volunteers going abroad are advised to check with the appropriate embassy before departure.

Long Term

A dividing line has to be drawn between short term residential voluntary work, which many people can take part in without unduly disturbing the flow of their lives, and long term voluntary work, which involves a clear break with normal routine. Most working people could go on a two week voluntary placement as part of their annual holiday allowance, and many students, teachers and academics could manage to spare a couple of months or more during the long summer vacation for a slightly longer stay: some students also take a year off before or after going to, or while studying at, college.

Even now, at a time when many people feel that their jobs are less than totally secure, there can be found sympathetic employers who will allow their workers to go on sabbatical for six months or up to a year; over a year, however, and even the most generous employer may begin to have doubts about the worker's loyalty to his job. In many cases, therefore, long term volunteers must face the possibility of their job not being held open for them when they return from their placement; even where this does not happen, they risk losing the chance of climbing a rung or two on the career ladder while away.

It is, of course, not only the volunteer who is placing a lot at stake by taking up a long-term post; the organisation that recruits him or her is also taking a chance. Sending a volunteer abroad for a period of a year or more involves a major investment of both time and money: in the initial screening of applicants to make sure they are suitable, in training them, which may well involve teaching them a new language, and finally in all the direct costs involved in a placement, such as air fares, insurance etc. Even when the organisation or government that actually is making use of the volunteer covers the cost of housing and living allowances as, for example, happens with VSO, this still comes to a considerable sum. And a glance through this section will reveal that the type of people that recruiters are looking for to invest all this time and money in are, in most cases, people with some definite profession, skill or qualification to offer.

For the long term volunteer is, in general, no longer someone who goes to work in a developing country for a year or two with nothing specific to offer except energy and a wish to help. The emphasis with most of the large placement organisations now is to help developing countries to help themselves by sending experienced professionals abroad not only to do a specific job, but also to train a local worker to take over the job from them when the placement finishes. The range of skills needed is wide and includes people with a background in education at almost any level, mechanics, trained doctors, dentists, opticians and nursing staff, engineers, horticulturalists, foresters, builders, librarians, and administrators, among many others.

By sending professionals of these types voluntary organisations can provide a country with a level of expertise that it would never be able to afford by paying the going commercial wage. There are several reasons why it is best that people with these skills should be placed for periods of one or two years, or even longer: the first is to spread the investment over as long a period as possible. It costs the same to fly a surgeon to the Sudan whether they stay for a week or a year, but obviously it makes more economic sense to keep them there for the longer period. When they reach their placement the volunteer will need time to adjust to the new way of life, perhaps to become familiar with a new language or dialect, and to come to terms with the job they have been sent to do: then, once they have become familiar with their task, they may well have to help select the local worker who they will in due course train to replace them.

Volunteers who devote a year or more of their lives to helping others require a considerable amount of dedication to the particular cause for which they are working. It is hardly surprising therefore, that many of the organisations requiring long term volunteers are religious foundations. Some of these, like the Missions to Seamen are overtly Christian and evangelistic in outlook, and their need is therefore for committed Christians. Other Christian organisations, like the Catholic Medical Mission Board, are less interested in the evangelical side of missionary work, and more interested in providing practical help (in this case, medical) to the third world.

Not all long term work is in the developing countries, and not all projects are concerned with long-term development programmes. For example ATD Fourth World Voluntariat specialises in the developed nations of the 'first world', and the Tear Fund is an organisation that handles disaster relief programmes rather than the mainstream of development.

Long term volunteers stand to gain more from their period of service than their short term counterparts. To begin with, they are likely to have had all their travel and living expenses paid. More significantly, the deeper involvement gives a greater insight into both the project and the country in which the work is done, and it may be found that abilities may be stretched further and responsabilities greater than they would be when working back home. Thus a recently qualified teacher may find him or herself confronting a whole class of adults in a teacher training college, or a young staff nurse may be appointed chief nursing officer in a brand new hospital. Anyone who survives such challenges is likely to return more confident, more skilled, and with a completely new outlook on life. But not everyone is capable of bearing such pressure, and so applicants for long term voluntary work must be prepared to undergo a rigorous selection process by the recruiting organisation.

The main organisations needing long term volunteers are described in the following pages. A number of the organisations concentrating on short term opportunities also offer varying amounts of long term work. These organisations are listed at the end of this chapter, but are described in full in the various sub-sections of the *Short Term* chapter, which follows.

Action Health

Unit 10, 25 Gwydir Street, Cambridge CB1 2LG; (tel 01223 460853; fax 01223 461787).

Action Health works to help people improve the quality of their lives, through improving basic health care, by sending volunteer health workers to share their skills with local partners and communities in Africa and Asia.

Action Health aims to bring people who are very poor, marginalised, under privileged, denied access to skills or resources, to improve their basic health care, where it can be done effectively.

Action Health's work also brings benefits to the professional volunteers themselves, to the people they serve in the UK and to a broader public, through greater awareness and understanding of different cultures.

Volunteers working with Action Health form a link between communities here and in the developing world. Each volunteer makes an individual contribution to a continuing programme of assistance which passes on the skills local communities have identified for effective primary health care.

Volunteers need to be flexible, adaptable, resourceful and resilient. They are guests of the local community and must be willing to respect and accommodate local culture. They must be prepared to work as part of a local team with people whose skills may be different to your own. They will need the ability to work with local officials and represent their project and Action Health at organisational and governmental levels if necessary.

Action Health recruits fully qualified health professionals (doctors, physiotherapists, midwives, health visitors, occupational therapists, dentists and speech and language therapists) with a minimum of two years' post qualification experience. Applications from individuals, couples, families, mature individuals and those with no previous experience of working overseas will all be considered. Contracts range from six months to two years.

Further details from Pam Evans, Administrator at the above address.

Africa Inland Mission
2 Vorley Road, Archway, London N19 5HE; (0171-281 1184; fax 0171-281 4479).

Africa Inland Mission is a Christian organisation that sends volunteers with a strong Christian commitment to teach in rural secondary schools in East Africa (mainly Kenya, Uganda and Zaire. Periodically, there are also opportunities for qualified teachers, secretaries and medical doctors. Usually 30-35 volunteers are taken on annually and the minimum period of stay is 12 months. The age limits are 18-70 years and good health is essential. Vacancies arise all year round, but for teaching applicants the deadline for applications is the end of March. Volunteers raise all their own finances and though accommodation is usually provided, rent may have to be paid. The costs for 12 months range from £4000 to £5,500 depending on the country. Africa Inland Mission produces a quarterly magazine. French is needed for Zaire and A-levels or above for teaching in rural schools. Work permits are required.

Applicants should apply directly to the Personnel Officer at the above address.

Annunciation House
1003 East San Antonio, El Paso, Texas 79901, USA (tel +1 915 545-4509).

Annunciation House sponsors three large houses, known as houses of hospitality, for the homeless poor, intended in particular for the those without documentation, who are largely immigrants from Mexico and refugees from Central America. The hospitality offered in the houses includes everything to do with food, shelter, clothing, social needs and networking with immigration asylum counsellors. Annuniciation house is an independent organisation supported by individual contributions and donations and by an all volunteer staff. Working for the organisation is a way of life that requires a complete commitment and openness to doing whatever needs to be done.

Volunteers are needed as hospitality shelter staff, for social services, work with Hispanics (especially Central and South Americans and Mexicans), immigration/ refugee services, basic health care, border education and research, office and computer work, accounting and bookkeeping, building maintenance and construction trades, community development and Christian based communities. Annunciation House is located at the border between El Paso, Texas and Juarez, Mexico.

Volunteers must make a minimum commitment of one year. Shorter term and special skills (e.g. research interns, construction trades, building maintenance, computer, accounting etc) are handled on a case by case basis. There is a ten-week summer Internship Programme available. At any one time there are 15 full-time volunteers serving at the houses operated by the organisation.

Volunteers should be aged 20+ and single or married without dependants, and religious (though not necessarily Catholic as the organisation is). A college education and Spanish are helpful. International volunteers must speak be able to speak English and should arrange the required visa that allows them to do voluntary work in the USA.

Volunteers receive room and board but no pocket money. Laundry facilities are provided. Minor medical expenses are covered at a local clinic. Volunteer accommodation is in the hospitality houses or in adjacent housing in shared rooms. Transportation allowance home after one year's complete service.

A week-long volunteer training programme is provided on site, plus ongoing training and in-service. Volunteers meet regularly for staff discussions, prayers and reflection.

Application should be completed at least three weeks prior to proposed arrival date. Intakes are in January, March, June, August and November; for the ten-week internship 1 June.

Applications to Ruben Garcia or Margaret Schroeder at the above address.

L'Arche
10 Brigatte, Silsdon, Heighley, West Yorkshire; (tel 01535-656186; fax 01535-656426).

L'Arche Communities are places where people with and without learning disabilities live and work together as a family in a simple way. The lifestyle is non-competitive and based on the Christian belief that everyone, whether disabled or not, is of unique value. In the UK, L'Arche comprises a network of seven communities, most of which have several work projects including workshops for weaving, candlemaking and horticulture.

Volunteers are known as assistants and share the life and work with people with learning disabilities in an ecumenical, Christian-based community. Any nationality may apply but visas are required by anyone coming from outside the EU or EEA. Volunteers must be aged 18+ and able to stay for at least a year. Three month summer vacation work is also sometimes available. Assistants are given about £25 weekly pocket money and free board and lodging. Explanatory videos and tapes are available.

Anyone interested should apply to the above address.

The Agency for Personal Service Abroad (APSO)
29-30 Fitzwilliam Square, Dublin 2, Ireland; (tel +353-1 661 4411; +353-1 661 4202). E-mail apso@iol.ie

APSO is the state sponsored organisation which recruits, trains and funds Irish development workers to work in developing countries. In 1995, APSO supported

1,200 volunteers in development projects in over 60 countries in Africa, Asia, Latin America and European countries in transition.

Approximately 1000 Irish volunteers are recruited annually for a vast range of projects. All volunteers must have some skill or qualification that is appropriate to the project. The main categories of programmes are: health, engineering, administration and business, social, technical and trades. Volunteers will always be involved in passing on their skills to others.

Only Irish passport holders are eligible. Language training will be given but a driving licence is an advantage. The minimum age is 21 and good health is essential. APSO currently has some volunteers in their 70s. The average period of commitment is two years but shorter or longer terms are possible. APSO provides monthly living allowances in line with local salaries, accommodation, flights, insurance. Also provided are start-up, mid and end of assignment grants.

APSO publications include a quarterly newsletter for volunteers *The APSO Post*. APSO also has Ireland's most comprehensive resource centre on living and working in developing countries with written and audio-visual materials.

Applicants should apply directly to the above address.

ATD Fourth World
48 Addington Square, London SE5 7LB (tel 0171-703 3231; fax 0171-252 4276).

ATD Fourth World is an international organisation working in Europe, the USA, Canada, Asia, Africa and Central America.

The movement is concerned with the 'Fourth World', a term referring to the part of any national population at the bottom of the social scale which is excluded from social, economic, and political life. Through long-term involvement with the most disadvantaged communities, the purpose of ATD Fourth World's work is to demonstrate the will and capacity of the very poorest individuals and families to fulfill their role as parents and citizens. Practical projects established with the poor include family centres, children's street libraries and learning clubs, youth clubs, literacy programmes, training workshops, family holidays and community programmes that reinforce co-operation between very disadvantaged families and the community they live in. Fourth World families are involved in the planning, implementation, and evaluation of these projects.

The core of the movement is formed by an international voluntariat, whose members are full time workers from different professions and backgrounds who are concerned by the suffering of persistently disadvantaged families.

Applicants undergo a three-month training programme in their country of origin before entering the voluntariat. The minimum age for participation in the voluntariat is 18. Good health and references are required and previous work experience is desirable, but no specific qualifications are needed.

Food, accommodation and pocket money are offered during the first year. General health insurance should be obtained by the volunteers themselves for the first three months, except for cover for accidents while at work. After the first year, minimum wage and National Insurance contributions are paid for by ATD Fourth World. Normal visa requirements apply.

ATD Fourth World also organises working weekends in the UK and summer work camps in the UK and France. They provide an opportunity to find out more about the organisation, to contribute practically to the development of ATD Fourth World and to discover how people can work together to change the situation of these families.

Associate Missionaries of the Assumption

227 North Bowman Avenue, Merion, PA 19066, USA (tel +1 610 664 1284; fax +1 610-664 7328).

A lay missionary association, Associate Missionaries of the Assumption operate religious communities in Third World countries or their equivalent, which help the local people through education and self-development programmes. Communities currently exist in Africa, the United States, Japan and countries in Europe. Around 15 volunteers a year are required for one to two years service as parish ministry workers, health or child care workers or teachers.

Volunteers must be single Catholics aged 23 to 40 who have a college degree and are fluent in the language of the country they intend to visit. Training consists of a one week orientation course in Merion. Board and lodging within the religious community and a monthly stipend are provided. The volunteer pays for medical expenses and insurance, and must obtain a visa for their period of stay as a lay missionary.

British applicants should apply to Sister Jessica, 23 Kensington Square, London W8 before March of each year.

Benedictine Lay Volunteers

Mother of God Monastery, 120 S.E. Avenue, Watertown, SD 57201 USA (tel +1 605-886-6777; fax +1 605-886-2108).

Sponsored by the Mother of God Benedictine Monastery this programme provides volunteers with the opportunity to live in a monastic setting and serve American people. Volunteers provide the community with whatever skills they have — teaching children, cooking, gardening, health care, recreation/camp services, maintenance etc.

Approximately five one year placements are available yearly to single people who are aged at least 21 years, in good health and who speak English. Board, lodging, and local transportation are provided. Depending on the site, short-term placements of from two weeks to two months are also possible in June and July.

Apply to the Director at the above address for further information.

Boys Hope/Girls Hope

National Offices: 12120 Bridgeton Sq. Dr. Bridgeton, Missouri 63044-2607; (tel +1 414-298 1250). E-mail at: BoysHope-GirlsHope@charitiesusa.com

Boys Hope/Girls Hope helps children who are hurt and at risk, yet academically capable, to realise their potential by providing value-centred, family-like homes and quality education through college. Founded in St. Louis, Missouri, in 1975, Boys Hope/Girls Hope operates 25 homes in 14 US cities and three foreign countries. Programmes are under development in additional cities as well.

Each year, approximately 25 volunteers are needed to work in the BH/GH homes, the national offices and a summer camp in Canada. Full-time volunteers make a one year commitment, living and working with the youth and staff in a group residence. These volunteers serve as assistants to the paid houseparents, provide a positive influence as a 'big brother', or 'big sister' role model, and contribute to providing tutoring and academic support for the children in the programme. Summer volunteers fill a variety of roles in staffing an outdoor wilderness camp in Canada.

Room and board and a small stipend are provided. Volunteers from outside the United States must be able to provide their own transportation to the US and have appropriate visa status. The volunteer year runs from August to August, although mid-year placements are also possible. Contact: Bruce B Bradley, Director of Personnel and Training at the above address.

Brethren Service
15O Route de Ferney, 1211 Geneva 2, Switzerland (tel +41 22 791-6330).

Brethren service is an American based organisation, sponsored by the Church of the Brethren, whose primary activity relates to the exchange of personnel between America and other countries. After a brief period of orientation volunteers are assigned to a project related to social work, community development, youth leadership in churches etc. Most of those taking part in the scheme are American, but Brethren Service in Geneva does also send Europeans to projects in America.

Most volunteers are in their twenties, but the scheme is open to anyone aged 20+ who is in good health. Although Brethren Service is a church sponsored agency, applicants need not be Christian in the orthodox sense but they must be motivated primarily by spiritual and humanitarian concern. The more skills the applicant has the better, although none are essential. However, most projects request persons with some training, experience or interest in 'social-type' work. A knowledge of foreign languages, for example, may increase the applicant's chances of being accepted. Volunteers going to the USA must pay for their own travel, but once there room, board and pocket money are provided. The normal term of service is one year.

Those interested should write to the Co-ordinator at the above address for further details.

Brethren Volunteer Service
1451 Dundee Avenue, Elgin, Illinois 60120, USA (tel +1 847 742-5100; fax +1 847-742 6103).

The goals of the BVS programme are making peace, advocating social justice, meeting human needs and maintaining the integrity of the environment. Volunteers serve in community-based organisations or national offices working on grass-roots needs as well as on systemic structural changes leading towards these goals. Projects include counselling delinquent youth, community development work, care of the elderly and people with AIDS, office work and refugee work. Volunteers serve a minimum of one year in the USA.

Volunteers must be at least 20 and in good health. Specific requirements may apply to some placements. The volunteers' experience begins with three weeks of orientation in preparation for service. Participants receive living expenses and $45.00 per month pocket money, as well as medical and accidental death insurance.

Contact the Recruitment Officer at the above address for further information.

Britain-Vietnam Friendship Society
Flat 2, 26 Tomlins Grove, London E3 4NX; (tel/fax 0181-980 7146).

The aim of the BVFS is to build and develop friendship, support and understanding between the peoples of Britain and Vietnam. As part of this aim a project called 'Teachers for Vietnam was set up in conjunction with the Highland Education Development Organisation in Vietnam. The Highland people of

Vietnam are amongst the poorest in the country and need all the support they can get.

The Britain-Vietnam Friendship Society needs four to five volunteers a year to teach English in the provinces of Vietnam for a year. Possibility to stay longer.

Please contact the above address for further details.

British Red Cross
National Headquarters, 9 Grosvenor Crescent, London SW1X 7EJ; (tel 0171-235 5454; fax 0171-245 6315).

The International Red Cross and the Red Crescent Movement founded in 1863 is the largest aid agency in the world. It has 120 million volunteers, 250,000 paid staff and spends around 20 billion US dollars a year. It has 163 national societies of which the British Red Cross is one. The national societies are all equal partners in the International Federation of Red Cross and Red Crescent societies whose headquarters is in Geneva. When any National Society is faced with a development or relief need beyond its resources it will ask the Federation Secretariat to issue an appeal on its behalf. The Federation is separate from the International Committee of the Red Cross (ICRC) whose programmes are primarily in war zones which the Federation's are not.

The British Red Cross operates primarily in Africa, Asia, eastern Europe and the Russian Federation. It runs a register for recruitment purposes and holds selection days to identify suitable candidates for this register. The professions invited to join the register include medical, accountancy/finance, relief workers/ logistics experts, water/sanitation engineers, warehouse/workshop managers, development specialists, information/press officers, programme managers, tracing and dissemination experts and telecommunications specialists.

Candidates must be aged 25+ and have the relevant professional experience and qualifications. Previous experience of working in a developing country is also normally required. Contracts are from three months to two years. Salaries from £15,000+. Local daily allowance, accommodation, transportation and insurance are also paid. A one-week residential course is provided for briefing prior to taking up residence overseas.

Camphill Special Schools Inc
Beaver Run, 1784 Fairview Road, Glenmoore, PA 19343, United States of America; (tel +1 610-469 9236; fax +1 610-469 9758.

The Camphill organisation spans many countries in Europe and South America as well as the USA. They provide communities for disabled adults and children. The Beaver Run school is for children and young adults from age five to 19 years. Volunteers are needed to spend at least a year taking care of a group of two or three disabled children under supervision. Also, to help with the house, the grounds and assisting the teacher in school. For those who wish to commit themselves to a full training there is a three year seminar course leading to a certificate. Sometimes, it is possible to stay for a period of several weeks or months rather than a year. There is an orientation course for which attendance is compulsory. The Beaver Run School has an annual contingent of 25-30 volunteers. Applicants should be proficient in English, and if possible have experience of children. They must be aged 19+. The organisation provides room and board, insurance and pocket money ($130 per month and $500 bonus for the summer vacation), and six weeks' holiday per year. Working at Beaver Run is an intensive process living and working together for 24-hours a day. Free time is limited to about two hours per day and four evenings a week (after the children are in bed) and a full day off every week))

Useful publications about the Camphill organisation include *Village Life* and *Candle on the Hill* at $25 each. Other literature is available on request.

Catholic Medical Mission Board (CMMB)

10 West 17th Street, New York 10011-5765, USA (tel +1 212 242-7757; fax +1 212 807-9161).

The Placement Services Department of the CMMB facilitates the placement of health care volunteers in independent medical missions in Latin America, the Caribbean, Africa, India, Asia and Eastern Europe. The Board reviews the credentials, licences, registration and letters of recommendation of prospective licensed physicians, surgeons, nurses, dentists, optometrists and other registered ancillary health care workers who are seeking placement as volunteers. Instructors, in any healthcare discipline are especially asked to contact the CMMB. We are seeking to design educational programmes for local populations, and are in need of qualified instructors. Limited funds are available to reimburse the travel expenses of volunteer instructors. Students of any discipline, who provide a licensed preceptor to monitor their efforts can be placed in select clinical facilities. Students will not be accepted for any placement without a preceptor.

Each mission has its own requirements, and makes its own contract with the applicant. Many missions seek one to two years (with allowance) service commitment. Some short term tours of duty lasting from two weeks are also available. Missions provide room and board. Applicants must pay their own travel costs to the mission.

Applicants should contact Michael P Maguire, Co-ordinator, Program Services, at the above address.

Catholic Network of Volunteer Service (CNVS)

4121 Harewood Road N.E., Washington, D.C. 20017, USA (tel +1 202-529 1100; fax +1 202-26-1094). E-mail cnvs@ari.net

CNVS acts as a reference centre for various agencies and programmes and potential volunteer personnel. Lay volunteers from all walks of life with many different skills and qualifications are referred to organisations which then send them on programmes which take place all over the world. Volunteers are usually aged between 25 and 65, but some are younger. Most programmes last for one to three years, but a few are for the summer only.

Those interested should contact CNVS at the above address, who will send the RESPONSE, a directory of lay mission programmes, and offer assistance for finding an agency that suits their interests and qualifications.

Christians Abroad

1 Stockwell Green, London SW9 9HP (tel 0171-737 7811; fax 0171-737-3237).

Christians Abroad (World Service Enquiry) provides information and advice on working overseas on a short or long-term basis for both unskilled and professionally-skilled volunteers. One-to-one careers guidance interviews are available to anyone, regardless of age or experience, seeking work overseas. *Opportunities Abroad*, a monthly bulletin with a range of overseas (and UK) jobs for professionally skilled people with the main volunteer-sending agencies is also available.

World Service Projects recruits skilled personnel with a Christian commitment for teaching, health and administration posts on behalf of overseas employers.

Further information can be obtained by contacting Christians Abroad at the above address. For details of unskilled voluntary opportunities send a SAE.

Christian Foundation for Children and Ageing

1 Elmwood Avenue, Kansas City, KS 66103, USA (tel +1 913 384-6500; fax +1 913 384-2211).

The Foundation is an organisation founded and directed by Catholic lay people to work with poor and abandoned children and ageing people through person-to-person assistance programmes. Volunteers are a vital link in their service as they form part of a local mission team. Motivated by love, their goal is to embrace the poor and to serve, recognizing their dignity, and work with them towards self-sufficiency. At present the Foundation has teams working in Central and South America, India, Africa and the Philippines.

Project co-ordinators request long term volunteers every year of varying skills and backgrounds, from agriculturalists to child care workers, nurses, building tradesmen, social workers etc. The Foundation cannot place medical doctors in a clinical or surgical setting, but there is a need for health care professionals who wish to provide more basic health care. Posts are for a year or longer. Fluency in Spanish is required for Latin American placements.

All volunteers must fund themselves, but room and board is provided at the project sites. Applicants need not be US citizens but all applicants must come to Kansas City for a four-day orientation, although this does not mean that a commitment to service has been made by either party. Due to travel expenses this may be difficult for applicants outside the USA. The minimum age is 21 years.

Those interested should contact Holly A Neff at the above address.

Christian Outreach

1 New Street, Leamington Spa, Warwickshire CV31 1HP (tel 01926-315301; fax 01926). E-mail 100656.1612@Compuserve. com.

Christian Outreach is a relief and development organisation committed to helping children, refugees and vulnerable people, both at times of crisis and post-emergency. Operations exist in Thailand, Cambodia, Vietnam, Sudan, Eritrea, Mozambique, Tanzania, India, the Philippines and Rwanda. Projects include healthcare, construction and community development. Personnel requirements include health workers, engineers, community development workers and administrators. All team members must be committed Christians, over 22 years of age and preferably single. Appointments are for a minimum of one year and all expenses are paid including air fares, accommodation, food, some pocket money and a resettlement allowance in the UK depending on previous experience.

Those interested should contact Kay Bugg, Personnel Officer at the above address.

Christian Welfare and Social Relief Organisation

Box 981, 39 Soldier Street, Freetown, Sierra Leone, West Africa (tel +232 224096/224781; fax +232 22 224439).

The Organisation provides an array of much-needed services in Sierra Leone including adult literacy programmes, camp programmes, agricultural and relief work, community health programmes, rural water projects, tree planting, environmental programmes and work with the handicapped.

About 700 volunteers of any nationality are needed every year to help with teaching, construction, voluntary relief work and agricultural work. Volunteers can be aged between nine and 45, and no special qualifications or skills are needed. Short-term volunteers can stay for one month, others can stay for up to three years. Accommodation is provided, but there is no pocket money. Volunteers pay registration and orientation fees.

All applications to Rudolph Hill, the Director, at the above adress.

Concern Worldwide

52-55 Camden Street, **Dublin**, Ireland (tel +353 1 4754162; fax +353 1 4754649); 47 Frederick Street, **Belfast** BT1 2LW, Northern Ireland (tel 01232 331100; fax 01232 331111); 248-250 Lavender Hill, **London** SW11 1LJ (tel 0171-7381033; fax 0171-7381032); Level 2, 80 Buchanan Street, **Glasgow** G1 3HA; (tel 0141 2213610; fax 0141-2213708).

Concern is a non-denominational organisation devoted to the relief, assistance and advancement of people in need in less developed areas of the world. It has over 140 international volunteers and staff working alongside 6,000 local staff on contracts lasting from six months to three years in 11 countries throughout Asia, Africa and Central America.

Volunteers are recruited from a broad skills base and include nurses, midwives, agriculturists, civil engineers, environmental health officers, foresters, teachers, social and community development workers, accountants, mechanics, administrators and logisticians. First-time volunteers commit for a two-year period, and food, accommodation, travel, monthly allowances, medicals and insurance are provided by Concern Worldwide. Volunteers must be aged 21+, in good health and, in the majority of cases have a minimum of 18 months' post qualification experience.

For further information contact the Overseas Application Section at one of the addresses above.

Crosslinks

251 Lewisham Way, London SE4 1XF; (tel 0181-691 6111; fax 0181-694 8023). E-mail 10163.623@compuserve.com

Crosslinks is an evangelical mission agency of the Church of England, working in partnership with the Anglican Church in different parts of the world. It seeks to recruit people who are willing to use both their professional skills and spiritual gifts in Christian service in another culture. The minimum period of service is two years.

Crosslinks looks for people who are committed Christians, believe in the inspiration and authority of the Bible, are actively involved in their local church and have a commitment to service. There are vacancies for bible teachers, doctors and medical workers, engineers, evangelists, ordained ministers, teachers, theological tutors and youth workers. The minimum age for service is 21 years. Candidates are expected to go through a selection process that could take eight to 12 months, and participate in further training if necessary.

Enquiries should be made to Mrs. Bukola Akinkugbe, PA to the International Secretary at the above address.

CUSO

2255 Carling Avenue, Suite 400, Ottawa, Ontario, Canada K2B 1A6; (tel +1 613-829 7445; fax +1 613-829 7996. E-mail: cusocan@web.apc.org

CUSO is a Canadian international development organisation which works in partnership with people to foster equality and freedom, safeguard their cultures and communities, and protect the environment. CUSO has partners in Africa, Asia, Latin America, the Caribbean and the South Pacific, as well as in Canada.

Only Canadian citizens and Canadian landed immigrants are recruited and placed. CUSO has 200+ volunteers at any one time working in 30 countries around the world sharing their skills.

Applicants must be suitably qualified and in good health. Age limits depend on individual countries. Contracts are for two years. Salaries are modest by Canadian standards but are sufficient to cover living costs. CUSO also pays for travel to and from posting and medical, dental and disability insurance and cash benefits to assist with departure and resettlement costs. Couples and families can be accommodated on some postings depending on what facilities are available locally. CUSO provides an orientation prior to departure and immediately upon arrival overseas. Ongoing support is provided by field offices.

CUSO has 14 offices throughout Canada which handle recruitment and selection. Applicants should send a copy of their resumé (and that of any adult who will accompany them) to the CUSO office nearest to them. Applicants residing outside Canada may send their resumé to the above address.

The Daneford Trust

18 Cheverell House, Pritchards Road, London E2 9BN (tel 0171 729-1928).

The Trust supports group and individual exchanges between young people in inner-city areas of the UK, particularly inner London, and young people in Africa, Asia and the Caribbean; the main placement areas overseas are Botswana, Zimbabwe, Nambia and Bangladesh.

The Trust helps about 20 individual participants a year. Applicants must live within the above areas and be aged between 17 and 25 years, keen to do much work themselves and willing to maintain interest and do follow-up work in the wider community after placement. Any skills, such as typing, experience of working with children, driving licence etc. would be useful. Placements last between three months and a year. Accommodation is provided, but most participants have to share full costs (with help from the Trust).

Applications should be sent to Tony Stevens at the above address.

East European Partnership

Carlton House, 27A Carlton Drive, London SW15 2BS; (tel 0181-780 2841; fax 0181-780 9592).

The East European Partnership (EEP) was set up by Voluntary Service Overseas with the objectives of posting skilled volunteers to countries in eastern and central Europe in response to requests from these countries. It currently sends around 150 volunteers a year to Albania, Bulgaria, Czech Republic, Estonia, Hungary, Latvia, Lithuania, Macedonia, Poland, Romania, Russia, Slovakia and Slovenia. Volunteers are needed to work as teachers of TEFL/ESP in schools and colleges, social workers and specialist nurses in the field of learning disability and NGO/business advisors. There are also opportunities for volunteers interested in agriculture, tourism and the environment.

Volunteers must have relevant qualifications and work experience and should be aged between 20 and 70, without dependants. Placements are normally for two years, but there are opportunities for one year. For further details, please contact the above address.

Eirene, International Christian Service for Peace
Engerser Strasse 74b, 56564 Neuwied, Germany; (tel +49 2631 8379-0; fax +49 2631 31160). E-mail EIRENE-INT@OLN.comlink.apc.org

Eirene organises three voluntary programmes which are complementary to each other: the north programme is operating in Europe and USA, the south programme in Nicaragua, Nigeria and Chad and the solidarity and learning programme in Africa, Latin America and Asia. In the north programme young and older volunteers, especially conscientious objectors, work together with minority groups such as migrant workers and handicapped people: in the south programme professionally qualified and experienced volunteers collaborate with projects in agriculture, irrigation, handicrafts, community development, co-operatives, health and vocational training: and in the solidarity and learning programme volunteers are invited to propose to Eirene a project in the Third World in which they want to collaborate. This scheme is financially and morally supported by basis groups in Europe: it provides a real link on the grassroot level between the Third World and Europe.

Approximately 30 volunteers are needed yearly; most of them are recruited from Germany. Those wishing to work in Europe and the USA must be at least 20 and those going to Africa or Latin America must be at least 21. All volunteers are expected to know the language of the country to which they are being sent, and to have some previous involvement in social and non-violent activities. In the north programme the minimum duration of service is one year, in the south programme it is from one to three years. Board, lodging, a monthly allowance, insurance and travel costs are all paid for, although volunteers are asked to find a support group to give some financial contribution as well as to support the service of the volunteer.

Applications should be made to the above address.

Food for the Hungry — Hunger Corps Program
UK: 58 Beulah Road, Tunbridge Wells, Kent TN1 2NR (tel 01892 534410).
US:7729 East Greenway Road, Scottsdale, Arizona 85260 USA (tel +1 602 998-3100).
Canada: 33283 Century Court, Abbotsford BC V2S 5Y2, Canada ; (tel +1 604 855 0202).

The Hunger Corps Ministry of Food for the Hungry offers overseas opportunities for Christians who desire to help meet the two hungers — physical and spiritual. The Hunger Corps offers invaluable experience which can open the door to a lifetime of cross-cultural ministry or employment. For people who are just beginning, as well as those with prior overseas experience, Hunger Corps offers assignments of two to three years' commitment, as well as opportunities to serve as a career.

Most overseas positions currently involve skills in agriculture/animal husbandry, primary health care/nutrition, engineering/water resources, physical or occupational therapy, community development or administrative/logistics/office skills. No special linguistic knowledge or previous overseas experience are required. The minimum age limit is 18 years. Benefits include a cost of living allowance, transportation, training, pension, health/life insurance, and a return from field allowance. Those desiring to serve with Food for the Hungry must be able and willing to contribute actively to the physical and spiritual 'Vision of a Community'. Contact the appropriate address above for further details.

Fundación Golondrinas
Isabel La Catolica 1559, Casilla 1211-Suc. 17-21, attn Maria-Eliza W Manteca, Quito, Ecuador; (tel +593-2-226602; fax +593-2-222390.

The Foundation works both in the conservation of highland cloudforest (the Cerro Golondrinas Cloudforest Conservation Project) and in the implementation of permaculture/agroforestry in deforested areas under agriculture.

The project was established in 1992 on the western slopes of the Andes in the north of the country and is seeking to conservice this area with its exceptionally rich biodiversity and high levels of endemism. Fundación Golondrinas has been implementing small scale activities in several parts of the area; i.e. tree nurseries and three demonstration sites where permaculture and agroforestry techniques are applied in order to teach local farmers sustainable productive methods.

Four long-term volunteers are also needed for a minimum of a year to further develop eight acres agro-forestry, permaculture demonstration site (*centro productivo y educativo agroforestal*). Tree nursery, bamboo, fruit and nut trees, nitrogen fixing trees, alley cropping, tree planting. And/or scientists or students (as part of their studies for which credit is granted or as a practice for their career) to assist and carry out research on sustainable agriculture, forest resource management, flora and fauna. Room and board are provided. No salary. Location: Gallupe and the Golondrinas Reserve. Bilingual Spanish necessary. Candidates with agro-forestry/permaculture certificate or degrees and wide knowledge in an environmental science preferred.

Applications to the President of the Foundation, Maria-Eliza W Manteca at the above address.

GOAL
PO Box 19, Dun Laoire, Co. Dublin, Ireland/9 Northumberland Ave, Dun Laiore, Co. Dublin, Ireland (tel +353 1 2809779; fax +353 1 2809215).

GOAL is a non-denominational relief and development agency whose principal aim is to alleviate poverty amongst the poorest of the poor, and believes every human being has the right to food, water, shelter, medical attention and literacy.

GOAL has approximately 100 volunteers in 17 countries in the developing world in Africa and Asia and also in Bosnia at any one time. These countries include Vietnam, Rwanda, Angola, Sudan, Cambodia, India, Ethiopia and the Philippines.

GOAL also supports a variety of projects in over 20 countries throughout the developing world.

Nurses, doctors, administrators and accountants are always in demand. Applicants of all nationalities are welcome to apply, but overseas volunteers should be available for pre-departure orientation courses. A full driving licence and excellent health are essential. GOAL covers expenses, including travel to the programme area and accommodation. Applicants must be at least 21 years of age. Applicants should write to the above address at any time of the year.

Habitat for Humanity International
121 Habitat Street, Americus, GA 31709, USA (tel +1 912 924 6935).

Habitat for Humanity International is an ecumenical Christian housing ministry whose objective is to eliminate sub-standard housing from the world. Habitat has 1,200 house building affiliates in the United States and also has affiliates in 48 countries worldwide. Habitat's international work covers the following areas: Africa and the Middle East, Europe and the NIS, Asia-Pacific, Latin America and the Caribbean. Habitat's philosophy is to engage and empower people in partnership in grass-roots community development to address housing needs.

International Partners (IPs) serve at international assigments for three-year terms. IPs receive a living allowance, accommodation, transport to and from the location, insurance, re-settlement bonus and an escrow account. IPs have a modest living standard similar to that which the prospective Habitat home-owners aspire to.

Applicants with skill and experience in resource development, accounting and project management are required to spend part of their assignment at the Habitat National Office. All appliants have to attend an eight-week training course at the International HQ.

Further information can be obtained from the International Rectruiter at the above address or e-mail IPP@habitat.org.

Additionally, there are many volunteer opportunities at International HQ: accounting, information systems, public relations, graphic design, photography and countruction coupled with internships are just some of the potential volunteer positions. Habitat provides an allowance, accommodation and health insurance. Further information can be obtained from the Volunteer Service Dept. at the above address or from e-mail VSD@habitat.org

House of Hospitality Ltd
Holy Cross Priory, Cross-in-Hand, Heathfield, East Sussex TN21 OTS (tel 01435-863808; fax 01435-867843).

The House of Hospitality is an interdenominational charity running homes for the elderly based in a Catholic religious institution. It has six residential homes, a nursing unit and sheltered flats. Volunteers are invited to join the life of prayer and charity work of this lay community (Shalom). Shalom members are usually aged between 18 and 55, but age limits are flexible; a satisfactory medical report is normally required, however.

Members of the lay community work full-time hours, with one free day per week. They must have a desire to share in the work and prayer life of the community of Sisters. The minimum length of placement is one year. Full board and lodging are provided, together with pocket money of approximately £30 per week.

Those interested in joining Shalom should contact Sister Patricia at the above address.

ICYE-UK
Argyll House, 1A All Saints Passage, London SW18 1EP; (tel 0181-877 9393).

ICYE is an international exchange programme. Volunteers receive a work placement in the host country as part of a cultural exchange. Countries participating are: Ghana, Kenya, Nigeria, India, Taiwan, Japan, New Zealand, South Korea, Mexico, Honduras, Costa Rica, Columbia, Bolivia, Poland, Brazil, USA and most European countries. Volunteers all over the world work in a variety of fields including: conservation, drug rehabilitation, with street children and homeless people, AIDS prevention, teaching and the elderly. Opportunities vary according to the country and the type of work in which the volunteer is interested. ICYE is open to all nationalities.

ICYE-UK sends ten volunteers abroad annually and takes ten to spend a year in the UK. The minimum period is a year, but shorter periods may be arranged. Qualifications and experience are not required. ICYE values, maturity and open-mindedness are more important. The age limits are 18-28. The programme is also open to people with disabilities.

Applicants have to be self-financing. A fee is payable for travel, insurance, administration, board and lodging (with the host family) and pocket money in the host country.

Applications have to be in by the 31st December and all volunteers depart from the UK at the end of July every year. Late applications can be accepted if places remain.

Contact the above address for further information.

Innisfree Village
Route 2, Box 506, Crozet, Va. 22932, USA (tel +1 804 823-5400; fax +1 804 823-5027).

Volunteers are needed to join the life-sharing community living and working with adults with mental disabilities. Volunteers are house parents, sharing cooking, cleaning and informal counselling. They also participate in the weavery, woodshop, garden, bakery or community centre kitchen.

Applicants should be at least 21, possess an interest in living with people with disabilities, have patience, common sense, ability to empathise and a sense of humour. Interest in community process and living are also essential.

Board and lodging are provided as are medical expenses and $160 a month pocket money. Volunteers are required to stay for one year including three weeks' holiday with $30 daily spending money. They also accumulate $45 a month for severance. Anyone interested should write to the above address for further information.

International Co-operation for Development (ICD)
Unit 3, Canonbury Yard, 190a New North Road, London N1 7BJ (tel 0171-354 0883; fax 0171-359 0017).

ICD which is the overseas technical cooperation department of the Catholic Institute for International Relations, recruits professionally qualified people with a minimum of two years' work experience to share their skills with communities in developing countries. ICD has development workers in South and Central America, the Caribbean, Africa and Yemen to implement pro-grammes that challenge poverty and promote development.

ICD recruits people in response to requests from partners overseas. These partners are usually community organisations, peasant federations, women's groups, co-operatives, local development associations or government minstries. ICD development workers are employed in various capacities: as advisers in agricultural co-operatives, as health workers in urban and rural health care programmes, as trainers in peasant-run education programmes or as teacher trainers and university lecturers. ICD offers a minimum two-year contract, a salary based on local rates, a UK allowance, accommodation and essential household equipment, return flights, a pre-departure grant, comprehensive insurance cover, language training and extensive briefings.

Write to the Recruitment Officer at the above address for a copy of the current vacancy list.

International Health Exchange (IHE)
8-10 Dryden Street, London WC2E 9NA (tel 0171-836 5833; fax 0171 379 1239).

IHE is a clearing house for information on jobs and courses in health and developing countries. IHE maintains a register of health professionals, publishes *The Health Exchange Magazine* and its *Job Supplement* and runs information workshops to prepare health professionals for work in developing countries.

For further information contact the Information Worker at the above address.

International Office for Asia — YMCA of the USA
101 N. Wacker Drive, Chicago, IL 60606, USA.

Volunteers are required to teach conversational English in community-based YMCAs throughout Taiwan. The OSCY program is more than a language program, it is a cultural learning opportunity for both the teacher and the student. Approximately 20-25 people are placed annually. Due to visa restrictions, teachers must be US or Canadian citizens, or have successfully completed twelve years of teaching English language learning.

In Taiwan, teachers are expected to work a thirty hour week, with up to 15 of these spent in the classroom. Applicants must speak English fluently, be flexible in adjusting to new situations and be interested in participating in extra-curricular activities that strengthen personal relationships and a sense of community. It must be emphasised that the length of placement for teaching in Taiwan is one year. Applicants must have a four-year degree. Teaching experience and training are desirable.

The deadline is April 15 for the autumn placement. Accommodation is provided in addition to a return airfare (to the US), monthly allowance, health insurance, allowance to study Mandarin Chinese, paid vacation and financial bonuses.

Write to the Taiwan OSCY Program Administrator at the above address for brochures and application forms.

Irish Missionary Union
IMU, Orwell Park, Rathgar, Dublin 6, Ireland (tel +353 1 4965433/4971770; fax +353 1 4965029).

The IMU was founded to promote co-operation between missionary, mission-sending and mission-aid organisations, thereby helping them to make the best and most efficient use of their personnel and other resources. Its principal aim is to assist the Bishops in the task of spreading the Gospel and therefore the IMU works in close collaboration with the Irish Hierarchy. It also acts as a liaison between missionary bodies and national or international organisations involved in evangelization and development.

The IMU recruits volunteers to work in the following areas in African and Latin American countries; medicine, education, trade, agriculture and pastoral and community development. Qualified and experienced doctors, nurses, laboratory technicians, teachers, paramedics, builders, plumbers and social workers are all needed. It is essential that all volunteers should derive their motivation from Christian values, and be in good health and at least 21 years of age. The minimum length of placement is two years. A monthly allowance, accommodation, resettlement allowance, insurance and return airfare are all provided.

Those interested should contact the Overseas Personnel Liaison Officer at the above address at any time of the year.

Jesuit Volunteer Community: Britain

St. Wilfrid's Enterprise Centre, Royce Road, Hulme, Manchester M15 5BJ; (tel 0161-226 6717; fax 0161-226 7114). E-mail STAFFjvc.u-net.com

JVC Britain offers voluntary work in areas such as homeless hostels, learning difficulty projects, alcohol and drug abuse centres, disability centres, church projects and credit unions.

About 20-25 volunteers are taken on annually. Good English is essential. If coming from abroad volunteers must arrange their own visa if required. JVC will supply a covering letter. Volunteer age should be in the range of 18-35 years and good health is essential with no history of drug or alcohol problems. A minimum commitment of 12 months is required starting at any time of year. Volunteers receive £38 weekly pocket money plus £9 towards household bills. Accommodation is provided. JVC publishes a free newsletter published three times annually.

Anyone interested should contact Shelagh Fawcett, Team Leader at the above address.

Jesuit Volunteer Corps: California-Southwest

PO Box 3266, Berkeley CA 94703-0266 USA; (tel +1 510-653-8564; fax +1 510-653-5145).

The Jesuit Volunteer Corps is a service organisation which offers women and men an opportunity to work full time for justice and peace. Jesuit Volunteers work in the United States by serving the poor directly and working for structural change. The challenge for the volunteer is to integrate Christian faith by working and living among the poor and those on the margins of society by living simply and in community with other Jesuit Volunteers and by examining the causes of social injustice. Since 1956 Volunteers have worked in collaboration with Jesuits whose spirituality they incorporate in their work, community lives, and prayer. The JVC seeks to develop persons whose year or more of service challenges them to live always conscious of the poor, devoted to the promotion of justice and service of faith.

Applicants should be 21 years or older, or have a college education and have a firm Christian outlook, be in good physical condition, adaptable and have a good sense of humour. A one year commitment beginning in August is expected; room and board are provided, plus a small monthly stipend.

Applications should be made to the above address.

JVC Britain

St Wilfrid's Enterprise Centre, Royce Road, Hulme, Manchester M15 5BJ; (tel 0161-226 6717; fax 0161-227 9972).

The Jesuit Volunteer Community offers young adults the opportunity to develop themselves through living in the community while working in areas of social need. The volunteers live together in small groups of five or six and work as full-time volunteers in a variety of placements. JVC has communities in Glasgow,

Liverpool, Birmingham and Manchester. JVC offers a structured development programme which consists of a series of workshops/retreats during the course of the year. Approximately 24 to 30 volunteers are taken on each year.

Current placements include work with the homeless, with refugees, with people with learning difficulties, with victims of crime, with people with drug and alcohol addictions and at advice centres. New placements are being developed on a regular basis. The emphasis is on working with people who are marginalized or discriminated against by society. Each work placement provides any necessary training and each volunteer has regular supervision. Applicants of any nationality are accepted, but applicants must be fluent in English and must be able to pay for travel to and from Britain for interviews, and start and end of placement. Only three or four applicants from overseas can be accepted at any one time. Final acceptance is dependent on being accepted by a work placement.

Volunteers must be aged between 18 and 35, in good health, available for a full year and have Christian motivation. The usual length of a placement is one year. The JVC year begins in late August and interviews take place from January onwards. Accommodation is provided, and each work placement provides the rent, bills and food allowance, pocket money and travel expenses to and from work.

Those interested should contact The Administrator at the above address.

Lalmba Association

7685 Quartz Street, Arvado, CO 80007, USA (tel +1 303 420 1810; fax +1 303 467 1232).

The Lalmba Association operates medical clinics and other health programmes in Sudan, Kenya and Mexico. Between 20 and 40 volunteers are needed annually to staff these projects. Most opportunities are for medical staff, (physicians, nurses, and midwives), but occasionally volunteers with managerial or administrative skills are needed to act as project directors. Placements in Sudan are for one year while placements in Kenya and Mexico are for two years.

Applicants must be at least 25 years old, qualified in either the USA or certain European countries, and have some experience in their field. Round trip transportation, board, lodging, health and life insurance and pocket money are provided.

Contact the Medical Director at the above address for more information.

Lutheran Volunteer Corps

1226 Vermont Ave, NW Washington, DC 20005 USA (tel +1 202 387-3222; fax +1 202 667 0037). E-mail LVC DC.parti@ecunet.org

The Lutheran Volunteer Corps operates a one to two-year volunteer service programme. 75-85 volunteers per year work for social justice full-time in agencies ranging from shelters and health clinics to environmental and public policy agencies. Volunteers live simply in Christian communities of four to seven volunteers, located in six different urban areas in the United States. The areas in which help is needed include community organising, environmental work, hunger relief, emergency social services, health care, housing, legal assistance, neighbourhood centres, public policy advocacy, shelters, youth/education, women's issues and more.

Non-US citizens need a work permit. Volunteers must be at least 21 years of age and without dependants. Skills needed vary depending on the placement agency; for all volunteers, flexibility, dependability and commitment are essential. The usual length of placement is one to two years. The application process runs from January to July; the programmes begin at the end of August. Volunteers receive room and board plus $85 per month personal allowance. Travel to the placement, health insurance and two weeks of vacation are also provided.

Those interested should contact Dawn Longenecker at the above address.

Mansfield Outdoor Centre
Manor Road, Lambourne End, Essex RM4 1NB (tel 0181 500-3047; fax 0181-559-8481).

This Outdoor Centre and Farm in Essex is a charity catering for able-bodied and handicapped children and young people from Newham and surrounding areas. The Centre provides a range of activities including archery, climbing, canoeing, orienteering and also a small farm unit for 'hands-on' experience. The Centre aims to help young people in their personal development using outdoor activities.
Six volunteers per year work at the centre as trainee activity instructors and/or farm assistants. The Centre sometimes accepts volunteers from abroad. Applicants must have some previous experience of outdoor activities and/or farming knowledge. Volunteers are needed all the year round; long-term volunteers stay for a year, while short-term volunteers are needed in the summer for one month or more. Volunteers receive an allowance of £45 per week; accommodation is provided in caravans.
Those interested should contact Mrs Irene Lock or the Centre Manager at the above address.

Marianist Voluntary Service Communities (MVSC)
PO Box 9224, Wright Bros. Branch, Dayton, OH 45409 USA (tel +1 513 229-4630; fax +1 513 229-2772). E-mail MVSC@saber.udayton.edu

MVSC is a lay volunteer programme dedicated to service among disadvantaged people in urban areas of the United States. Volunteers provide services through existing social agencies. MVSC offers the opportunity for mature Christian men and women, single or married but without dependents, to develop personally and spiritually through experiences of service, a simple lifestyle and Christian community. Volunteers share household expenses, meals and group prayer. 15 to 20 volunteers are engaged by MVSC every year to participate in a wide variety of activities including business, clerical, building or child-care work, healthcare, law and legal advice, group home-work, youth advocacy, counselling, social work and senior citizen outreach.

Applicants of any nationality are welcome to apply but they must be able to speak English fluently. Applicants must not be using the programme as a way to get into the USA, and it is preferable that applicants have had some cultural understanding of the USA and/or previous service or volunteer experience, particularly in cities or urban areas. A driving licence and a knowledge of Spanish are useful. Those who have had a secondary education are preferred. The ability to live with others is essential. Applicants should between 20 and 70, with no pre-existing health problems; please note that MVSC is not able or equipped to handle severe disability. The minimum length of placement is one year with an option for renewal for a second year (if approved).

Accommodation is provided and volunteers receive a monthly allowance which adequately covers food, rent and other expenses, but MVSC does not pay for travel to and from the mission site in the USA.

Applicants should contact Laura Libertore at the above address; the deadline for applications is May 1st each year.

Maryknoll Mission Association of the Faithful (MMAF)
P O Box 307, Maryknoll, NY 10545-0307; (tel +1 914-762 6364; +1 914-762 7031).

Maryknoll is a Catholic missionary organisation dedicated to evangelising and joining forces and skills with the marginalised people in communities worldwide. Volunteers must share the vision and vocation of the organisation. About 130 volunteers work worldwide and have a variety of professions and skills including doctors and other health workers, educationalists for education and formation at grass roots level, social workers for community development and environmentalists for environmental issues. There are also pastoral ministries, justice and peace, human rights, vocational instruction fields among others.

Volunteers must have legal resident US status in order to qualify for missionary visas. Language training is provided. The expected term of service is three and a half years. Volunteers receive a stipend and expenses and accommodation is provided.

For further details contact the above address.

The Medical Missionary Association
157 Waterloo Road, London SE1 8XN; tel 0171-928 4694; fax 620 2453).

The MMA acts as an agent channelling young doctors, nurses, dentists and paramedical workers to various mission and church organisations in many countries of the world. It does not have any voluntary work of its own overseas but recruits for most of the Protestant mission societies of the UK.

The conditions of service vary, according to the usual practice of the society concerned. A magazine, *Saving Health*, is published depicting medical mission work in the world, and listing present openings in the various Protestant mission and church hospitals.

Applicants should apply to the Secretary at the above address for information on openings.

Mennonite Central Committee
21 South 12th Street, PO Box 500, Akron, Pennsylvania 17501-0500, USA. (tel +1 717-859 1151; fax +1 717-859 2171). E-mail mailbox@mcc.org

The Mennonite Central Committee is the relief and development agency of the North American Mennonite and Brethren in Christ churches. MCC has more than 900 personnel in 50 countries in Asia, Africa, Europe, Latin America and North America, usually in conjunction with other agencies to which they often second personnel.

MCC assignments include agricultural development, water conservation, health, formal and informal education, economic and technical projects, church-related programmes, relief administration, social services and peace-making. Language training is provided for work in non English-speaking areas. A small monthly allowance is paid, and all expenses, including round trip transportation, are met in full. Accommodation is also provided. North American assignments are two years in length; overseas assignments are three years.

Applicants must be members of a Christian church and committed to non-violent peace-making. Most applications come from North America and Europe, but applications are also accepted from Mennonite or Brethren in Christ church members from other continents.

Inquiries and applications should be sent to the Personnel Officer at the above address.

Mercy Corps
Gwynned Mercy College,Gwynned Valley, PA 19437, USA (tel +1 215 641-5535; fax +1 215 641-5503).

Mercy Corps, committed to a more merciful and just world, invites women and men to join with the Sisters of Mercy of the Americas in giving service to the poor, sick, and uneducated throughout the USA. Mercy Corps empowers the laity through opportunities for compassionate service, community and spiritual growth.

Volunteer placements through Mercy Corps include, but are not limited to: nursing, social work, physical and occupational therapy, AIDS ministry, administrative, and education at all levels.

Applicants need not be US citizens and the minimum age limit is 21 years. Volunteers must be in good health and possess flexibility, a sense of humour and the ability to get along with others. Length of placement is for a year with an option for a second. Volunteers receive room and board, a small stipend, medical insurance and transportation. Volunteers must pay their own travel costs to and from the USA.

Application deadline is May 1. The volunteer year starts in August. Those interested should contact Sr. Eileen Campbell, the Director, at the above address.

Mission Aviation Fellowship
Ingles Manor, Castle Hill Avenue, Folkestone, Kent CT20 2TN (tel 01303-851155 & 850950; fax 01303-251958).

Mission Aviation Fellowship is a Christian organisation which provides an air service for churches, missions and development agencies working in remote areas. The United Kingdom branch currently has bases in Chad, Ethiopia, Kenya, Madagascar, Tanzania and Uganda and also flies into other neighbouring countries. Commercially qualified pilots and engineers are needed, as well as administrators, builders and teachers. Terms of service are normally for a minimum of three years.

MAF workers must be committed Christians, fit, in good health and have appropriate experience. MAF staff usually raise their own support, which includes cost of accommodation and other relevant expenses. MAF obtains any visas or work permits and provides pre-field training.

Further information can be obtained from the Chief Executive Officer at the above address.

Missions to Seamen
St. Michael Paternoster Royal, College Hill, London EC4R 2RL (tel 0171-248 52O2).

The Missions to Seamen is the Anglican Church working for the practical and spiritual welfare of seafarers of all races and creeds in ports throughout the world.

The scheme offers 16-18 one year placements (usually to coincide with the academic year) for people aged 21-26, assisting full-time chaplains in seafarers' centres in seaports in the UK and overseas. Duties may include ship visiting, serving in the bar and shop, driving, assisting with worship, and practical tasks such as cleaning and gardening. A driving licence is necessary. Board, lodging, travel costs and pocket money are paid.

Volunteers should be committed Christians, prepared to participate in Anglican ministry and worship. Further details from the Ministry Secretary at the above address.

Mission Volunteers USA & International
The Presbyterian Church (USA), 100 Witherspoon Street, Louisville, Kentucky 40202-1396,USA.

The Mission Volunteers USA and Mission Volunteers International Programmes of the Presbyterian Church in the USA give participants a variety of opportunities to enter the world serving communities locally or globally. Various positions include teaching, health care, agricultural development, youth work, community service and more. Volunteers must be active members of their church communities and be willing to live simple lifestyles. Room and board may be provided; volunteers may need to work with their church communities to raise funding. Service terms from three months to two years.
Further information can be obtained from the above address.

Overseas Training Programme
145 Islingword Road, Brighton, Sussex BN2 2SH; (tel 01273-621446; fax 01273-621446).

The Overseas Training Programme was started in December 1992 as a VSO initiative though it receives separate funding from the Overseas Development Agency. The programme exists to provide worthwhile and relevant work experience for students who may be interested in longer term involvement (ten to 12 months) in development work either in the UK or overseas. Strictly speaking, it is a training rather than a volunteer programme.

Applicants should be under 25 and studying at a UK academic instituton (details of courses and institutions acceptable can be obtained from the above address). Applicants arrange their own placement in collaboration with their departmental tutors. They are supervised by their academic institution and the host partner organisation overseas. Sometimes trainees work in countries where VSO does not operate. Over 150 trainees have gone overseas in the first four years of the programme.

Paradise House Community
Paradise House, Painswick, Stroud, Glos. GL6 6TN (tel 01452-813276).

Paradise House is a long-term home for 29 adults suffering from a wide range of mental disabilities who are in need of special care. Its activities are based on the work of Rudolf Steiner. The residents' time is divided into training, work, adult education and recreation. Between 12 and 15 volunteers work as full members of staff for periods of at least a year helping to organise the activities, which include teaching the basics of housekeeping, gardening, farming, craft work etc.

Although specific skills in crafts, cooking, gardening or farming would be useful, it is more important that the volunteers should be enthusiastic and genuinely interested in this demanding work. There are no strict age limits, but applicants aged over 20 are preferred. Volunteers are provided with free board and lodging and pocket money of around £28 per week.

Applications should be made to the Principal at the above address.

Peace Brigades International
83 Margaret Street, London W1N 7HB; (tel 0171-636-5564; fax 0171-436-1129). E-mail pbiuk@pbicol.gn.apc.org

Peace Brigades International sends unarmed peace teams when invited into areas of violent repression or conflict; these teams can flexibly pursue avenues not open to governments or political groups. Their work is to reduce the violence and support local social injustice initiatives through protective accompaniment of those whose lives are threatened, fostering reconciliation and dialogue for peace among conflicting parties, and educating and training in non-violence and human rights. The organisation has its main international office in London, but has support groups which liaise with potential volunteers in 17 countries.

Volunteers of all nationalities work with PBI every year; they can join the peace teams in Colombia, Sri Lanka, Haiti, North America, Guatemala or the Balkans, or assist with administrative work in PBI offices in Britain and Canada, or work with the regional support groups — of which there are 12 in Europe, two in North America, two in the South Pacific and one in Central Asia. The projects use the official languages of the states in which they are based; volunteers must have knowledge of these.

The minimum age for volunteers is 25 years, but younger applicants will be considered depending on experience and suitability. The minimum length of placement for projects is six months, but longer is desirable; for office work this varies. Accommodation is provided; the peace team members have their living costs covered and receive some pocket money. They usually have to pay their own travel costs but PBI groups are able to advise on possible sources of bursary aid for this.

There are PBI groups in Aotearoa/New Zealand, Australia, Austria, Belgium, Britain, Canada, France, Germany, Ireland, Italy, The Netherlands, Norway, Outer Mongolia, Switzerland, Sweden, Spain and the USA. Their addresses may be obtained from the co-ordinator at the above address.

Applicants in the USA, Australia or Canada should write to the relevant address below:

PBI-USA, C/O Kara Hooper & Ken Maclean 2642 College Ave. Berkeley CA 94704 (tel 510-540-0749; fax 510 849-1247). E-mail pbuisa@igc.apc.org

PBI-Australia, Michael Salla, Dept. of Political Science, The Faculties, Australian National University ACT 0200 (tel 06-2494697; fax 06-2495054. E-mail michael. salla@anu.edu.au

PBI-Canada, 192 Spadina Avenue, Toronto Ont. M5T 2C2; (tel 416-504-4429; fax 416-504-4430). E-mail pbi@web.apc.org

British volunteers wanting more information should contact PBI-Britain at the address above.

Peace Corps of the United States
1990 K Street, NW, Washington, DC 20526, USA (tel 800-424 8580; extension 2293).

The Peace Corps was established by President J F Kennedy in 1961 since when over 140,000 Americans have offered their services abroad. The goals of the

Peace Corps are to help promote world peace and friendship, assist developing countries to meet their needs for skilled personnel and to promote mutual understanding between people of the United States and those of developing countries. There are close to 6,000 Peace Corps volunteers and trainees in 90 nations in Latin America, Africa, Asia, the Pacific and Eastern Europe. Placements normally last for two years plus three months training time.

The Peace Corps is looking for people with practical experience. Specialists are needed in the areas of agriculture, business, engineering, forestry, fishing, health, maths and sciences and skilled trades such as masonry, carpentry, plumbing and education.

Volunteers must be US citizens and at least 18 years old. The volunteers receive a monthly allowance for rent, food, travel and medical costs, transportation to and from training sites and overseas placements and a readjustment allowance of US$200 per month, paid on completion of service.

Those interested should contact the above address.

Personnel Programme Team
Church Mission Society, 157 Waterloo Road, London SE1 8UU (tel 0171-928 8681).

The Society sends mission partners to 26 countries in Africa and Asia. Such people go in response to requests from churches overseas for assistance in particular areas. A wide range of ages and occupations is represented by mission partners and all have a particular skill or occupation. There is a particular need for people to offer themselves for long service of six years or more although the minimum is two years' service. There are also some openings for short-term service; these too require a professional qualification or practical skill (see below).

All mission partners must be practising Christians though not neccessarily Anglican. All should have technical or professional training and be qualified in their field. Mission partners receive an allowance related to the cost of living in the country they work in, fares are paid and there is a pension scheme. Visa and work permit requirements vary from country to country.

The Society also organises two programmes for young people aged 18 to 30. These are: Project Experiences for groups which last about five weeks; and Experience Placements which are for individuals and enable young Christians to gain cross-cultural experience of mission through being placed in an appropriate location six to eighteen months. These placements are either overseas or in Britain and are task-based. Applicants are responsible for most of their own costs.

For further information about any of these schemes write to the Overseas Service Department at the above address.

Pestalozzi Children's Village Trust
Sedlescombe, Battle, East Sussex TN33 0RR (tel 01424-87044; fax 01424-870655).

The Village is devoted to the education and training of children from developing countries, who all live within the Village community. From 1997 the Trust intends to extend the education offered to students aged 16+ to do further education (International Baccalaureate.) Volunteers of different nationalities are engaged annually to help in many areas. These volunteers can work as research assistants (researching into trusts that provide financial support for education), or in public relations and marketing, or on the farm and estate. They can also assist with holiday activities with the children or sports and hobbies.

Volunteers are also required to work as EFL teachers and as assistant/trainer houseparents.

Volunteers must be aged between 25 and 65. There is no fixed duration for a placement; some people stay for three months, some for three years. Food, single accommodation and some pocket money are provided.

Those interested should contact Val Winslade, Director, at the above address.

Ponape Agriculture and Trade School
PO Box
39, Pohnpei, Federated States of Micronesia 96941; (tel +691 320-2991; fax +691 320-6046). E-mail: 103676/1667@compuserve.com

Ponape Agriculture and Trade School (PATS) is a four-year vocational High School run as a a residential boarding school for young men from all over Micronesia. Volunteer teachers, especially specialists in agriculture/life sciences, mechanics and construction are always needed. There is also a need for high school-standard teachers to teach academic subjects. Students work in the classrooms in the mornings and work at their trades under supervision in the afternoons. Volunteers are also needed to give secretarial help, and to act as administration personnel. The School usually has about 15 volunteers on its staff.

Applicants of any nationality are welcome but they should note that the School is in a remote area 23 miles from Pohnpei town, on a very isolated island. The School has a strong Christian focus, in which all volunteers are expected to share. Volunteers should have a university degree or extensive experience in one of the trades and are only taken on for two or three year commitments. Other qualities necessary include an ability to live in a very close-knit community, respect for others and Christian commitment. The desire to quietly pass this sense of commitment on to others is also required. Applicants should be in fairly good health, as the Micronesian Health Services are not particularly good. For this reason, it is very difficult for the School to accept handicapped people. The School needs help all the year round. Two weeks vacation per year are granted to volunteers, as well as an allowance of 60 US$ per month. Room and board are provided along with some other modest perks. Volunteers must pay for their own travel costs to and from Pohnpei, although help can sometimes be given.

Those interested should contact Fr. Joseph E Billotti, the Director, at the above address.

Project Trust
The Hebridean Centre, Isle of Coll, Scotland, PA78 6TB (tel 018793-230444; fax 018793-230357).

Project aims to further the education of school leavers who have taken A Levels or Highers by sending them to live and work overseas for a year. Project has 28 years' experience in sending young people to work in projects in South Africa, Botswana, Zimbabwe, Namibia, Uganda, China, Japan, Thailand, Vietnam, Hong Kong, Indonesia, Malaysia, Guyana, Chile, Peru, Brazil, Honduras, Cuba, Pakistan, Jordan, Egypt and Sri Lanka.

Volunteers are mainly involved in social service, English teaching, outdoor activity and community development projects. Each volunteer, assisted by the Project Trust, raises through fund-raising activities, a portion of the total costs of going overseas. People who can apply are young people in full-time education, studying for qualifications acceptable for university entrance. They should be between the ages of 17 and 19 when going overseas. It is necessary to have a

British passport and be in excellent health. While overseas, volunteers receive living expenses and are provided with a accommodation and food.

Applications are usually accepted January to December each year but early application is recommended.

Quaker Peace and Service
Friends House, Euston Road, London NW1 2BJ, UK. (tel 0171-387 3601; fax 0171 388 1977). E-mail qps1@gn.apc.org

This organisation is engaged in a variety of activities around the world, all of which are committed to practical peacemaking. QPS supports long term projects for experienced representatives (on two-year or longer assignments) in working on the tasks of reconsiliated at all levels including the victims of wars or violence. There are QPS workers in Africa, Asia, the Middle East and Europe, including Northern Ireland and at the Quaker UN office in Geneva. In addition there is a programme of four to eight one-year placements with suitable peacemaking agencies abroad and at home.

QPS also organises educational and experimental programmes in the promotion of non-violent alternatives to creating change in schools, and amongst concerned groups of adults. QPS works with secular as well as the church-based peace movements, particularly on disarmament issues. Lastly, QPS cooperates with decision-makers, whether diplomats, politicians or financiers in non-official ways as intermediaries to encourage the peaceful resolution of conflict.

Formal membership of the Society of Friends is not essential, but understanding of and sympathy with Quaker objectives is. Food and accommodation are always provided and pension rights, etc, are safeguarded. All transportation expenses are paid.

Applications and enquiries should be sent to the Personnel Department at the above address.

Queen Louise Home for Children/Lutheran Social Services
PO Box 866, Frederiksted, St. Croix, US Virgin Islands 00841.

The Home provides temporary care for abused, abandoned, neglected and developmentally retarded children, regardless of race, religion or national origin, while permanent placement plans for them are processed. The Virgin Islands Department of Human Services relies heavily upon the Home to meet a large part of the evergrowing need for institutional childcare. The Home takes in approximately six volunteers annually to work as cottage parents. Cottage parents serve as live-in caretakers for eight to ten children, aged between three and twelve. Responsibilities include caring for each child's emotional, physical, educational and spiritual needs; developing creative, social, educational, recreational and cultural programmes for them; and maintaining the cottages, grounds, clothes and vehicles. Applicants may either be married with no dependants or two single people who work as a team. They must have experience with children, be flexible, patient and be culturally adaptable, as well as professional and objective in judgement and attitude. They must be team workers and willing to work under supervision.

Applicants of any nationality are welcome, but they must have had two years of college training (preferably in child development but this is not essential). They must possess a strong personal Christian commitment and have had experience of childcare in or out of a job setting. A valid driving licence is essential. The Home is wheelchair-accessible, but disabled applicants should note that the role of cottage parent demands a high level of energy and physical capabilities. Cottage parents applying as a couple are contracted to spend a total of 18 months at the home;single cottage parents are contracted to spend one year.

The Queen Louise Home is part of the Americorp programme and volunteers are eligible for the same benefits of other participants in their programme. Eligibility is limited to US citizens only.

Enquiries should be sent to the Director at the above address.

Returned Volunteer Action (RVA)

1 Amwell Street, London EC1R 1UL (tel 0171-278 0804).

RVA is an independent membership organisation of and for serving overseas volunteers and development workers, and those interested or active in development work. RVA does not send volunteers to work abroad.

RVA's aims are: to press for improvements in overseas programmes, especially in training, support and project evaluation; to help returned workers evaluate their overseas experience and feed it into action in this country; to encourage those seeking placements overseas to examine their personal and political motivations and expectations. The membership database enables returned workers to be in touch on a cross-agency basis, and enables prospective volunteers to learn from their knowledge.

RVA is a small organisation and much of its work is done through its regular newsletter and its publications and training resources. RVA urges anyone considering working overseas to buy *Thinking About Volunteering* and *Volunteering and Overseas Development: A Guide to Opportunities*, which are available from RVA as a joint pack for £3.50 plus 36p SAE. A full Resources List or Membership Form is available from the above address.

Richmond Fellowship International

Clyde House, 109 Strawberry Vale, Twickenham, London TW1 4SJ; (tel 0181-744 9585; fax 0181-891 0500.

The Richmond Fellowship International exists to help its sister organisations in countries overseas (mainly the United States) to improve the condition of the mentally ill, generally by helping them to set up therapeutic communities to be used as a model for the future extension of mental health work in each country, and by providing training courses for practitioners. RFI has vacancies from time to time for volunteers who are given placements in one of the RFI therapeutic communities around the world where they work alongside the regular staff. One of their main tasks is to help people to take their place in society after a breakdown; this might include home-making, administrative work and public relations. Applicants are required to have qualifications in social work, psychology, nursing or previous volunteer experience.

Applicants may be of any nationality, but they should be at least 22 years of age, able to speak fluent English and to deal with stress and have a mature outlook. A driving licence is an advantage. Special ethnic and language preferences depend on overseas placements but within the UK RFI is committed to equal opportunities. Ex-drug users are accepted to work on drug rehabilitation projects. The usual length of placement is one year; the minimum is six months and volunteers are required all the year round. Board, lodging, insurance, 28 days annual leave and a weekly allowance of £30 (or equivalent in other currencies) are all provided.

Those interested should contact the above address.

Services for Open Learning
North Devon Professional Centre, Vicarage Street, Barnstaple, Devon EX32 7HB; (tel 01271-327319; fax 01271-76650).

SOL is concerned with the recruitment of graduates, preferably with teaching or language degrees and TEFL qualification, to teach in schools in eastern central Europe (Belarus, Croatia, Czech Republic, Hungary, Romania, Slovakia).

About 75 teachers are needed annually. Candidates must be native-speakers of English and available for interview in Britain (or eastern central Europe) in spring. As well as being certified fit to undertake the work by their doctor, volunteers must be prepared to stay a minimum of one academic year. Partial financial support is provided for Romania and Belarus because of the additional expenses involved.

Anyone interested should contact SOL at the above address.

Skillshare Africa
3 Belvoir Street, Leicester LE1 6SL (tel 0116-2540517; fax 0116-2542614).

Skillshare Africa sends skilled and qualified personnel to work in support of development in Botswana, Lesotho, Mozambique and Swaziland. Its objective is to tackle the causes of deprivation and underdevelopment by promoting self-reliance and reducing dependency. Volunteers are recruited in response to specific requests from the governments, NGOs and local communities of the countries.

Placements are very diverse and have included dress designing, boat building, public relations, tropical agriculture, business advice, community development and many other skill areas. Placements are for two years and flights, national insurance payments, modest living allowance/salary, small home savings allowance, rent-free accommodation, health insurance and equipment grants are all provided. Applicants should have relevant qualifications and at least two years' post-qualification experience. It is also essential that volunteers are flexible, mature, able to perform under stress and respond to a challenge.

Information packs and application forms are available by phoning the above number and leaving your name and address.

St. Ebba's
Hook Road, Epsom, Surrey KT19 8JQ (tel 01372-734140).

St. Ebba's is part of Surrey Heartlands NHS Trust. It is a home for for 360 mentally and/or physically handicapped adults. Volunteers are welcomed to help with sports and other day services departments and in all areas of work that require training of the home's residents. Applicants may be of any nationality but must be fit, interested in working with the handicapped and able to speak good English. The minimum age limit is 18 years, and volunteers must be in good health. The length of placement is one year. No pocket money is provided and only volunteers who can come on a daily basis (i.e. no accommodation) are acceptable at present.

Those interested should contact E M Cathcart at the above address.

Tear Fund
100 Church Road, Teddington, Middlesex TW11 8QE (tel 0181-977 9144; fax 0181-943 3594).E-mail enquiry@tearfund.dircon.co.uk

Tear Fund is an evangelical relief and development charity, working in partnership with Christians around the world to tackle the causes and effects of poverty and to bring Jesus Christ's message to the poor. Tear Fund is currently active in the UK and in over 90 countries in Africa, Asia, South America and Eastern Europe.

One of the ways in which Tear Fund supports its partners is by sending UK-based personnel for a variety of short to medium-term assignments in the UK and overseas. Applicants need to be committed Christians, with strong links with a home church.

For further information, please contact the Enquiry Unit at the above address.

United Nations Association International Service (UNAIS)
Suite 3a, Hunter House, 57 Goodramgate, York YO1 2L5 (tel 01904-647799; fax 01904-652353. E-mail: unaisuk@geo.2.poptel.org.uk

UNAIS recruits skilled and motivated people to work in West Africa, Latin America and the Middle East. With them it helps selected organisations which aim to strengthen local groups struggling to improve their situation, and to gain a fairer share of resources. UNAIS have about 60 volunteers in the field in three main categories: health, agriculture and water engineering but other possible projects include human rights and forestry. The countries in which they work are: Bolivia, Brazil, Mali, Burkina Faso, and the Palestinian Territories of the West Bank and Gaza.

Applicants must have at least two years' relevant experience. Volunteers are paid a monthly allowance calculated in relation to the local cost of living which is very adequate for a single person. Their accommodation is also covered and there are a variety of grants paid during the period of service. Flights and insurance are also provided.

For further information contact the Recruitment Administrator at the above address.

United Nations Volunteers (UNV)
Headquarters mailing address: Postfach 260111, D53153 Bonn, Germany. Internet: enquiry@unv.org or http://www.unv.org.
Address for offers of service: P.O. Box 5605, Nicosia, Cyprus.

Established by a 1970 resolution of the UN General Assembly, UNV partners UN agencies and field operations, governments, NGOs and community-based organisations. It assigns only fully qualified and experienced men and women from some 115 fields: their average age is 40. They work in technical cooperation for development, particularly in seeking to facilitate the initiatives of local communities; in humanitarian relief work; in promotion of human rights and democracy; in conflict resolution; and in advice for private and public enterprise. More than 2000 UNVs are at work at any given time, some three to four thousand in the average year. Approximately 52% serve in Africa, 21% in Asia/Pacific, 16% in Latin America/Caribbean, 6% in Arab States and 5% in Europe/CIS..

UNVs are drawn from more than 125 nationalities. In longer term development work, two-year contracts offer a monthly allowance adequate for necessities, rather than a salary at market rate. Assignments can be shorter, although not less than three months, in the humanitarian relief, democracy/electoral, and enterprise advice areas. Airfares are met, together with insurance cover. UNV does not offer short-term overseas workcamps, 'gap years' or practical assignments for students.

Persons with a minimum of university degree and several years' working experience who wish to be candidates should write enclosing a two-page cv to the UNV Cyprus address given above. The assignments of UNVs who are UK nationals are normally co-sponsored by VSO, to whom candidates may also write, mentioning UN Volunteers.

United Society for the Propagation of the Gospel (USPG) Experience Exchange Programme
Partnership House, 157 Waterloo Road, London SE1 8XA (tel 0171-928 8681; fax 0171-928 2371.

The Experience Exchange Programme enables people of all ages over 18 to spend six to 12 months living and working in Africa, Asia or Latin America. Participants work alongside local people in church-based projects such as schools, community development programmes or hostels.

No specific skills are required although applicants should be flexible, adaptable and open to new ideas. Through living in another culture, participants 'learn to see the world and God's interaction with the world through others' eyes. Participants are strongly encouraged on their return to share what they have learned from their experience with church groups in the UK.

United Society for the Propagation of the Gospel (USPG) Root Groups
Partnership House, 157 Waterloo Road, London SE1 8XA (tel 0171-928 8681; fax 0171-928 2371.

Root groups are for people aged 18-30, who are looking for a challenge as they try to discover how Christianity should affect their lifestyle and attitudes. Three or four people live together, supporting one another as they look for ways to get involved in their local community. Activities vary widely according to personality and placements: they often include elements of youth work, befriending the lonely and disadvantaged, worship and bible study, and volunteering at community centres. In all their work, Root Groups are building relationships with their local community and developing links between church and community.

Viatores Christi
38/39 Upper Gardiner Street, Dublin 1, Ireland (tel +352 1 8749346/8728027; fax +353 1 8745731).

A lay missionary association founded in Dublin in 1960, Viatores Christi has its headquarters and training programme in Ireland. It recruits, trains and helps place volunteers overseas wherever there is need for them. Besides offering their own skills in such fields as medicine, teaching, carpentry, mechanical engineering, secretarial work, etc. volunteers, as lay missionaries, should be prepared to participate actively in the work of the local Church.

Volunteers must undertake a part-time training course held at weekends in Ireland for a minimum period of nine months. To be assigned overseas they should be practising Catholics, at least 21, in good health and possess some professional qualification or skill. All assignments are for a minimum period of one year but most volunteers stay for at least two years.

Applications should be made to the Secretary at the above address. Since it is necessary to be in Ireland in order to undertake the part-time training course, residents in the UK may prefer to contact the Volunteer Missionary Movement.

Visions in Action
3637 Fulton Street, NW, Washington, DC 20007, USA (tel +1 202-625 7402; fax +1 202-625 2353). E-mail: africajob@aol.com

Visions in Action is an international non-profit organisation founded in 1988 out of the conviction that there is much that individuals can learn from, and contribute to, the developing world by working as part of a community of volunteers committed to achieving social justice in an urban setting. Visions volunteers work side-by-side with host country nationals, allowing a genuine understanding of the country's needs to emerge. The Development Volunteer programme aims to work towards social and economic justice in the developing world by providing overseas volunteer opportunities with non-profit organisations, working as partners in the development process.

60-80 volunteers per year work in indigenous or expatriate organisations as development journalists, community workers, project managers, low-income housing facilitators and healthcare assistants, etc. Placements are available in the following sectors: agriculture, appropriate technology, children, communications/journalism, education, environment/natural resources, food/nutrition, family planning, health, housing, human rights/law, mental or physical disabilities, natural science, refugees/relief, small business, social science, women and youth in South Africa, Zimbabwe, Kenya, Uganda, Burkina Faso, Tanzania, Mexico and the Dominican Republic. All programs last for one year, with the exception of South Africa, which has a six-month or one-year option. Applicants may be of any nationality, but they must have two years' college experience or equivalent. Programmes begin at various times in the year. The total cost of participating in a program is $5,000. Volunteers must pay for all their costs. The programme fee includes accommodation.

Those interested should apply at the above address.

VSO
317 Putney Bridge Road, London SW15 2PN (tel 0181-780 2266).

VSO is a registered charity which works for economic and social justice by giving practical aid through a volunteer programme and so assisting individual development and the alleviation of poverty. It is committed to sharing skills with the peoples of developing countries. There are over 2000 volunteers in the field at any one time in 55 developing countries contributing to improvements in education, health and food production as well as in the use of appropriate technology, social development and the growth of business.

Historically VSO has provided volunteer teachers and about 40 per cent of its volunteers are working in educational posts; however a great many of these are now technical, vocational and teacher training posts within community development projects and are not confined to the formal education sector.

Posts are for a minimum of two years. Volunteers aged between 20 and 70 must all have qualifications and usually relevant work experience in their respective fields, although VSO does post some people soon after qualifying if they have studied sciences and/or languages and are prepared to teach.

VSO pays air fares, national insurance contributions, grants towards equipment and re-settlement and arranges language courses where necessary. Accommodation and salary, which is paid at the local rate for the job, are provided by the overseas employer.

For further details contact the Enquiries Unit on the above number.

World Education Forum
P O Box 383-4005, San Antonio de Belén, Heredia, Costa Rica (tel +506 223 9413; fax +506 233 1909/+506 223 9413)

WEF is an international, educational, non-profit organisation with headquarters in Costa Rica, that sponsors exchange programmes between the USA and Mexico, western Europe and Costa Rica. Programmes offer North-American and European students and educators an opportunity to be voluntary, part-time teachers who themselves receive Spanish tuition while living with a host family in Mexico or Costa Rica. Volunteers participate as English language, mathematics, science, biology or pre-elementary/elementary education teachers or teacher assistants.

For English teaching positions, a minimum of two years of higher education in any field are required. For other positions, a minimum of a bachelor's degree in the specific field is required. Positions are normally for one academic year or longer and start by March 1, though applications are welcome all year round.

WEF will mail participants a certificate of eligibility for visa purposes. Applicants should apply direct to the above address.

World Exchange
121 George Street, Edinburgh EH2 4YN (tel 0131-225 8115).

World Exchange is organised by a number of Scottish and British Churches acting together. It offers volunteer work overseas ranging from one to two years for people with a wide variety of skills. In 1995 volunteers were placed in Asia, the Middle East, Europe, Africa and Central America. World Exchange considers candidates who come straight from school or university as well as people who come with skills and experience.

Candidates can be of any age between 17 and 70. A local allowance is paid and food and accommodation are provided. A travel pool operates on the basis that candidates are expected to do fundraising before departure of roughly £2,000.

World Exchange is always pleased to give more information about working abroad as a volunteer. For more information contact the address above.

WorldTeach, Inc.
Harvard Institute for International Development, One Eliot Street, Cambridge, MA 02138-5705, USA (tel +1 617 495-5527; fax 617 495-1599). E-mail worldteach@hiid.harvard.edu

WorldTeach is a small, private, non-profit organisation which contributes to educational development and cultural exchange by placing volunteers to teach in developing countries in China, Costa Rica, Ecuador, Mexico, Namibia, Poland, South Africa, Thailand and Vietnam. Over 275 volunteers a year teach English, maths, science and environmental education to students of all ages. Teachers must have a bachelor's degree for all programmes except the summer programme in Shanghai, China. As volunteers, the teachers pay or fundraise a fee to cover the cost of international airfare, health insurance, field support, training and administration. Training includes pre-departure literature and briefing, a three to four-week orientation (in-country) and a mid-service and end-of-service conference (both in-country). Deadlines for applications vary depending on the country. Volunteers are provided with room and board; there is a modest stipend for the full-year programmes.

Youth With a Mission (YWAM)
13 Highfield Oval, Ambrose Lane, Harpenden, Herts AL5 4BX (tel 01581-463300; fax 01581-463305).

YWAM is an international charitable organisation which is interdenominational in character and undertakes evangelical, training and relief ministries in about 100 countries. All tasks are undertaken by volunteers and are financially supported by their home church, fellowship, friends or family.

Volunteers are needed in whatever field they wish to offer their service, and they can serve from two weeks to a lifetime. Those wishing to serve for a long term must be willing to attend a basic training course with YWAM. Volunteers must be committed Christians with their own financial support (£200 per month is a rough average, depending on the location).

For more information apply to the Director of Personnel Services at the above address.

Other Long Term Opportunities

The following organisations have been included in the various sub sections of the *Short Term* chapter, but also require a number of volunteers for periods of a year or longer.

Worldwide
Action Health
Christian Medical Fellowship
Global Outreach UK
Institute of Cultural Affairs
Mission Aviation Fellowship
UNIPAL
WEC International

North, Central and South America
Los Ninos

United Kingdom
Camphill Rudolph Steiner School
Paradise House Association

Europe
Share Operation Mobilisation
Camphill am Bodensee

Short Term

There is a far wider range of short rather than long term opportunities available to the volunteer; there are also far more people who may be free to leave home to volunteer for a few weeks or months than could spare a period to be measured in years. Some of the schemes described in the next few chapters could be fitted into a worker's or student's holiday entitlement, and there are others that could be fitted into a pre-arranged short-term leave of absence.

It is not possible to make the same broad generalisations about short term voluntary work as can be made about the long term version. Some of the organisations below have needs for professional workers that are every bit as specific as those in the long term section: for example, HCJB UK is looking for, among others, audio and broadcasting engineers, scriptwriters and announcers for work in Ecuador for periods of from one to three months: but to spend the same length of time working on a Kibbutz in Israel you need just be able-bodied and aged between 18 and 30.

Some of the schemes below require dedication from the volunteer as great as any in the long term section , but others require little more than enthusiasm. The latter applies in particular to many of the large number of workcamps that are are organised every year; they are aimed primarily at volunteers aged under thirty, but some organisers will consider older applicants if asked. While most of the short term opportunities described below are pretty self-explanatory, a note of introduction is advisable about workcamps.

A workcamp is a project that sets out to accomplish some specific goal over the course of one or more seasons with the help of groups of volunteers who arrive to help for periods of perhaps two or three weeks. This project may involve conservation work, forestry, restoring an ancient monument, building some community amenity, or one of many other types of job that would not be done if volunteers were not prepared to undertake it. Workcamps take place all over east and west Europe, North America, North Africa and sometimes further afield. While each camp will have some specific objective, such as clearing a derelict pond and the surrounding woodland and converting it into public parkland or restoring an ancient building, they also achieve something by their very existence. Many organisations select the participants on a camp to represent as many nationalities as possible, in order to give those taking part the opportunity to meet and work alongside people from different cultures and backgrounds.

Many volunteers on short term assignments — and this applies particularly to students on workcamps, archaeological digs and kibbutzim — see their involvement principally as a working holiday or a means of staying somewhere rather more cheaply than would otherwise be possible. Indeed in some eastern European countries short term voluntary work may be the only way of getting more than a tourist's view of the way of life. And, although English is the standard language in most international workcamps, the environment can provide invaluable practise for students of other languages. The hours of work expected of volunteers on a workcamp can be light, perhaps just involving working in the mornings: at least part of the remainder of the time may be filled with organised 'educational' activities such as outings, lectures etc., intended to give participants a taste of the local culture.

It is not possible to generalise about the financial arrangements for short-term voluntary work. In some cases pocket money is paid in addition to travel expenses and free accommodation. In other cases no money changes hands at all, or volunteers may find themselves making a contribution towards the cost of food and accommodation. It all depends on the source and extent of available funds. Officially sponsored organisations, like Community Service Volunteers, usually have the funds to provide at least the bare necessities. As another example, kibbutzim, by their very nature, are expected to provide volunteers with free board and accomodation, but could not reasonably be expected to meet everyone's travel expenses, particularly when applicants literally come from all over the globe. Stays on kibbutzim therefore tend to be marketed as 'working holidays', as do many archaeological digs for the same reason — no funds are available to cover all costs. Indeed, participants in many archaeological digs have to pay for their own board and lodging as well.

Because of the great number of organisations requiring short term volunteers, it has been necessary to sub-divide them geographically. One or two organisations thus fall into more than one classification and will therefore be listed more than once. However, the organisations which are truly international in their recruitment policies and activities have been listed separately under the heading *Worldwide*.

As there is a preponderance of British and European organisations, the sections on the United Kingdom and Europe have been further subdivided, the UK by types of work, and Europe by country. These divisions are far from clear cut, especially in the UK chapter. Many of the entries under *Religious Projects*, for instance, cut across several of the other classifications: and there is a great deal of overlap between child care and work with the sick and disabled, as jobs involving sick and disabled children tend to be listed in the former category. The subheadings are therefore to be considered as a rough guide only. Entries are otherwise listed in simple alphabetical order within their respective sections or sub-divisions.

Worldwide

Archaeology Abroad
31-34 Gordon Square, London WC1H OPY; (tel 0171-387-7050 ext. 4750).

This organisation provides three information bulletins annually about forthcoming opportunities for archaeological fieldwork and excavations abroad. Publications are available by subscription. Enquiries should be sent to the Secretary at the above address enclosing a stamped and self-addressed envelope.

British Executive Service Overseas (BESO)
164 Vauxhall Bridge Road, London SW1V 2RB (tel 0171-630 0644; fax 0171-630 0624).

BESO is an independent charity founded in 1972 with the support of the Institute of Directors, the Confederation of British Industry and Corporate and individual sponsors.

Its mission is to send senior volunteers with skills and expertise to help developing and emerging economies in countries overseas. It has a database of 3,000 skilled and professional people who undertake assignments of two weeks to six months in nearly 100 countries from Azerbaijan to Zimbabwe.

BESO's assistance is only available to clients who cannot afford commercial fees. While on assignment advisors work as unpaid volunteers. Travel expenses are met by BESO, overseas accommodation and living expenses are provided by the client.

BESO always welcomes properly qualified senior volunteers who want to help others. Accountancy, banking, bee-keeping, information technology, justice, management skills, picture framing, retailing, surveying and experience with other voluntary bodies, are just some of the skills on the current BESO register.

If you would like to know more about BESO and its work please contact: Meg Viner, Registrar at the above address.

BTCV International Working Holidays
36 St Mary's Street, Wallingford, Oxon OX10 0EU (tel 01491-39766; fax 01491-39646).

BTCV is the UK's leading practical conservation charity for improving and protecting the environment. The Trust aims to harness people's energies and talents to protect the environment by practical action. To this end the Trust organises international working holidays for over 500 volunteers a year lasting from one to three weeks throughout Europe, North America and Japan.

There is a variety of sometimes unusual assignments from drystone walling in Japan to creating a bird reserve in the grounds of a Belgian château. The working day is 9am to 5.30pm and the evenings are free. The average cost is about £70 a week inclusive of basic accommodation and food. Whilst undertaking traditional conservation projects, it is hoped that volunteers will adapt to local life-styles as well as participate in community affairs.

Those interested should write to the International Development Unit at the above address for further details enclosing a large stamped addressed envelope.

Canadian Crossroads International
31 Madison Avenue, Toronto, Ontario, M5R 2S2, Canada (tel +1 416 967 0801).

Canadian Crossroads International is a non-profit making organisation of volunteers in Canada and 31 other countries in Africa, the South Pacific, South and Central America and the Caribbean. Volunteers take part in short term work placements: about 200 Canadians are sent overseas, about 60 Third World volunteers are brought to Canada and over 800 volunteers help run the programmes. Volunteers live and work with host families and agencies. The work undertaken varies but could include community development, health care, education, agriculture, construction, etc. Placements are from four to six months.

All volunteers must be at least 19 years old. Volunteers are accepted from all countries in which Canadian Crossroads International operates but to qualify for placements in a developing country applicants must be Canadian citizens or landed immigrants.

Further information can be obtained from the Administrative Assistant at the above address.

Christian Medical Fellowship
157 Waterloo Road, London SE1 8XN (tel 0171-928 4694; fax 0171-620 2453)

The Fellowship offers advice for Christian doctors and medical students. There is a list of about 40 medical misssionary organisations with vacancies for doctors to work in the developing world, for periods of six months and longer. There is a similar list for medical student electives of two to three months.

For further information contact the General Secretary at the above address.

Concordia (Youth Service Volunteers) Ltd.
Heversham House, 20/22 Boundary Road, Hove, East Sussex BN3 4ET.

Concordia is a small charity which organises the placement of UK volunteers on International Voluntary Workcamps in the following countries: Albania, Armenia, Belarus, Belgium, Bulgaria, Spain, Czech Republic, Denmark, Estonia, Finland, France, Germany, Hungary, Italy, Japan, Lithuania, Morocco, The Netherlands, Poland, Russia, Slovakia, Tunisia, Turkey, Ukraine and the USA. Volunteers must be aged 18-30 except for Tunisia, Turkey and Morocco where the age limit is 20+. The camp language is English, unless otherwise stated and for some camps language skills are a prerequisite.

Camps last two to three weeks from June to September. Concordia can also arrange longer term placements on farm work schemes in Switzerland and Norway. Pocket money is provided on these as well as board and lodgings. The voluntary projects include: archaeological digs, building work, restoration of castles and other monuments, ground maintenance in parks and gardens, nature conservation, social work and work in children's camps. Pocket money is not paid on these camps, although some trips/social activities are provided.

Volunteers must pay their own travel costs and make their own arrangements. Once at camp, board and lodging and usually insurance are provided free. However all volunteers are strongly advised to take out their own insurance before travelling so they are covered at all times.

Finally, a registration fee of £65 must be paid. This goes towards any exchange fees charged by partner organisations, administration costs as well as the costs of running International Voluntary workcamps in the UK for overseas volunteers to participate in and, for which UK volunteers are needed to act as group leaders (aged 20+ with previous workcamp or leadership experience).

For more details write to the Overseas Coordinator at the above address enclosing a SAE.

Council on International Educational Exchange (CIEE)
in the UK: 52 Poland Street, London W1V 4JQ; (tel 0171-478 2000; fax 0171 734 7322). In the USA:
205 East 42nd Street, New York, NY 10017, USA (tel +1 212-661 1414; fax +1 212-8222089). Internet: http://www.ciee.org/

The Council on International Educational Exchange is a non-profit organisation that, in affiliation with co-operating organisations throughout Europe, sponsors voluntary service projects for young people in the USA and abroad. Participants have the chance to explore, in a cross-cultural setting, international perspectives on global issues such as environmental protection, cultural preservation and development while working closely with 15 to 20 other volunteers from many countries. The minimum age for participants is 18.

The work, generally lasting for three weeks, involves manual labour or social service and is of great value to the communities in need. There is a wide range of project possibilities in the summer, including forest conservation in eastern Europe, archaeological digs in Kentucky and Spain, care for the elderly in Germany, and construction of a water trench in Turkey. Participants' costs are minimal, being around $195 application fee plus transportation. Room and board are provided by the workcamp sponsor.

For further information please contact the International Workcamps Co-ordinator, at the above addresses. (Please note: that the CIEE in the USA is involved with placing American citizens only. Other nationalities should contact a voluntary service organisation in their home country. A list of cooperant organisations in other countries can be obtained from the above addresses.

Crusaders
2 Romeland Hill, St Albans, Herts, AL3 4ET (tel 01727-855422).

Crusaders runs Christian young people's groups and adventure holidays where the emphasis is on evangelism and Bible teaching. Volunteers are needed to help with young people's holidays and expeditions in Britain and abroad.

Around 300 holiday helpers are needed during the summer vacation to help with young people's holidays and houseparties at over 50 sites in Britain. Camps may be for a week or a weekend. The children are aged from eight to 16 years old and the group size varies between 15 to 70 children. Helpers supervise and organise all of the group's activities, which include sports, crafts, Bible studies, etc. Applications should be made to the Crusader Holidays Manager at the above address.

The number of expeditions undertaken changes from year to year. In 1995 there were expeditions to Brazil, Bolivia, Zimbabwe and South Africa. Only two to four leaders are needed on each trip as the group size is usually just ten to 20 young people, aged 16 to 21 years old. Expeditions last for three to four weeks.

All leaders must be aged 18 or over, speak English, have a Christian commitment and leadership qualities. Skills in specialist sports and outdoor activities are desirable but not necessary. Applicants must pay for all their own expenses.

Applications should be made to the CRUSOE at the above address.

Earthwatch
Belsyre Court, 57 Woodstock Road, Oxford, OX2 6HJ (tel 01865-311600; fax 01865-311383). E-mail ewoxford@vax.oxford.ac.uk

Earthwatch recruits paying volunteers to help research scientists in fields from archaeology to zoology on short term research projects in over 40 countries and 27 states of America, around the year. The scholars who request Earthwatch volunteers are based at universities and museums worldwide. Around 3,400 volunteers each year take part in the projects which last for two or three weeks. Team volunteers may learn to excavate, map, photograph, observe animal behaviour, survey flora and fauna, gather ethnographic data, make collections, conduct oral history interviews, measure astronomical alignments, assist in diving operations, lend mechanical or electrical expertise, record natural sounds, and share all other field chores associated with professional expedition research.

All English speaking volunteers aged 17 and over are welcome although some projects may require special skills such as languages and sporting or practical skills. Some projects may also have health restrictions as they take place in remote areas or at high altitudes, etc. Volunteers pay a share of the project costs, ranging from £375 to £2,000 which includes accommodation costs but not travel.

Those interested should apply to the above address. US applicants should contact: Earthwatch, 680 Mount Auburn Street, Box 403N, Watertown, MA 02272, USA (tel 800-776 0188).

Education for Development
Woodmans, Westwood Row, Tilehurst, Reading R63 6LT (tel 01734-426772; fax 01734-352080).

This organisation provides a small number of training visits to adult education, non-formal education, and extension in development programmes in countries including India, China, Namibia, Bangladesh, Sri Lanka etc. Volunteers, who must be qualified and experienced in adult education, are needed all the year round to help with all the above areas. Placements vary in duration , but usually last between 2-3 months. No expenses (including travel) are paid and volunteers must also pay for their accommodation.

Applications to Professor Alan Rogers at the above address.

Emmaus International
183 bis, rue Vaillant-Couturier, 94140 Alfortville, France (tel +33 0 1-48 93 29 50).

The Emmaus movement started in Paris in 1949 and there are now some 340 Emmaus communities in 35 countries, mainly in Europe but also in Africa, Asia and North and South America. These communities try to provide a meaning in life for those without one — that meaning being to help others in need. Each community is autonomous and independent of race, sex, religion, politics, age etc. Living conditions are usually simple and the work hard.

One community accepts long-term volunteers: GIVE (Groupement International des Volontaires d'Emmaus, 21 Ave. de la Gare, 31750 Escalquens, France). Other Emmaus communities in Europe organise workcamps for volunteers during the summer. Volunteers must usually speak English or the language of the country being visited, be over 17 years old and able to work at least two weeks. Accommodation and food are provided but volunteers pay all other costs.

Those interested in long term or summer voluntary positions should apply to the Secretary at the above address for more information on individual communities.

Europe Conservation Italy
Via Bertini 34, 20154 Milan, Italy; (tel +39 2 33103344; fax +39 2 23104068). E-mail ecomil@imiucca.asi.unimi.it

Europe Conservation in Italy arranges eco-volunteer programmes in Italy and worldwide. Projects include: the study and conservation of whales, dolphins (Mediterranean), sea turtles (Mexico and Turkey), wolves, ibex and many other animals.

Eco-volunteers help the researchers in the field and pay a participation fee which goes directly to funding the project.

No special skills are required but for some projects, volunteers must fill in a form to test their attitude towards the type of work.

The minimum age for volunteers is 18 years but some projects are not suitable for elderly people (Kenya, Yucatan). The minimum period is one week. There are projects all year round except for projects on cetaceans (sea turtles) which are in summer only.

Further information from the above address on request.

The Experiment in International Living

Otesega, West Malvern Road, Malvern, Worcs WR14 4EN (tel 01684-562577; fax 01684-562212).

The Experiment in International Living (EIL) is a non-profit, non-political, non-religious organisation existing to promote international understanding and has been involved in international education and exchange since 1932, working mainly through the homestay principle, sending and receiving people to and from more than 50 countries worldwide, either in groups or as individuals. As well as its main programme of individual homestays, EIL can arrange youth exchanges, including Young Worker and Disabled and Disadvantaged programmes with EU and East European countries and Language Aquisition programmes in many countries.

The Au Pair Homestay USA is aimed at British young British men and women. Participants spend a year with an American host family on a legal basis. All host families are screened and interviewed before being matched with a suitable au pair. Applicants for the au pair homestay must be aged 18-26, have appropriate child care experience, have completed secondary education, be non-smokers and in possession of a valid driving licence. For details call 0345 626984.

Fill the Gap

World Challenge, Black Arrow House, 2 Chandos Road, London NW10 6NF (tel 0181-961 1122; fax 0181-961 1551).

World Challenge is well established in the area of organising school expeditions to remote parts of the world. As a complementary activity they also offer three to sixth month work placements for volunteers who are in their gap year to give them an opportunity for independent travel and personal growth before starting university. Placements are available in Asia, Africa and South America. Volunteers teach basic English and other subjects in secondary schools, work on conservation projects and care for the disabled depending on where they are sent. There are also opportunities for paid work. Volunteer numbers are approximately 150 for each of two annual departures in January and September. Applicants are required to attend a one-day Induction Course prior to departure.

Participants have to raise their own placement costs which average £1,300 which includes, the training course, return flight, transfer cost to the accommodation and support in the country of placement from trained representatives.

Frontier

77 Leonard Street, London, EC2 4QS; (tel 0171-613-2422; fax 0171-613 2992). E-mail enquiries@frontier.mailbox.co.uk

Frontier is an environmental organisation that recruits about 250 volunteers a year to participate in conservation expeditions in remote and unexplored areas of the world. The projects address high priority resource management and habitat conservation issues in Tanzania, Uganda, Mozambique and Vietnam. Volunteers work on coral reefs, in rainforests and game reserves.

Work includes collecting data (both biological and socio-economic). The work could involve diving surveys on coral reefs, large mammal surveys in game reserves or the collection of biological information in rainforests. The techniques are simple and full training is given so no previous experience is necessary although it would obviously be useful.

Volunteers must be aged 17+, are expected to stay ten weeks and must raise £2,850 towards their costs. Comprehensive fundraising advice will be given by Frontier. The contribution covers food and basic lodging, equipment, staff costs etc.

Frontier publishes papers in scientific journals and have prepared a book on the forests of Tanzania.

Prospective volunteers should write to Frontier for an information pack at any time of year.

Gap Activity Projects (GAP) Limited
GAP House, 44 Queen's Road, Reading, Berkshire RG1 4BB (tel 01734 594914; fax 01734 576634).

GAP arranges voluntary work overseas for over 1,200 school leavers a year. If you are interested in living and working in another country during your year out, rather than just being a visitor or tourist, GAP may have just the project. With placements in 33 different countries, GAP offers something for just about everyone: voluntary work (including kibbutz work), teaching English as a foreign language, conservation work, and caring for the disadvantaged are some of the possibilities. GAP placements last from three to nine months, giving the participants time to travel before or after their placement, and/or to work to raise funds towards the costs.

GAP projects cost from £800, with costs rising with distance and increased airfares. GAP can help you with suggestions about how to raise the necessary funds and encourages volunteers to work and contribute to their own placement costs. Most GAP placements provide accommodation and food and some pay a small allowance of pocket-money, so once you are in the country everyday costs are kept to the minimum.

Applicants should want to learn about another culture and language, be able to work hard and be in possession of a sense of humour. Application is simple: send a stamped addressed envelope (36p) to the above address as early as possible in your last year of school for a brochure and application form. Applicants will have to be interviewed before being offered a placement. The earlier you apply, the wider the choice of placements is likely to be.

Global Citizens Network
1931 Iglehart Ave, St Paul, Minnesota 55104, United States of America; (tel +1 612-644 0960). E-mail gcn@mtn.org

GCN is a non-profit organisation that sends teams of volunteers to rural communities around the world including Belize, Guatemala, Kenya, the Yucatan and New Mexico. Projects ae determined by the villages that GCN is in partnership with and are aimed to promote cross-cultural understanding. The projects vary but have included building a health clinic, teaching in a primary school, developing eco-tourism or renovating a youth centre.

Volunteers are not required to have special skills but a knowledge of Spanish would be helpful for Guatemala and the Yucatan. The minimum age is 18 unless accompanied by a parent. Trips last one or two weeks only all year round. Volunteers pay a contribution which ranges from US$ 400 to US$ 1300 depending on the programme. The cost of transportation to the programme is also at the volunteer's expense. Accommodation is provided. A small number of partial scholarships are available.

GCN publishes a free quarterly newletter which is available on request. Applicants for trips should apply directly to the above address. Ex-volunteers who are interested can also apply to be team leaders for other GCN trips. Potential team leaders have to be recommended by their own team leader and attend a training session in Minnesota. Team leaders can be any nationality and although the the position is unpaid airfares and most in-country expenses will be paid.

Global Outreach Mission UK

108 Sweetbriar Lane, Exeter, Devon EX1 3AR (tel 01392-59673; fax 01392 491176).

Global Outreach UK is a Christian evangelical missionary society with representatives in 26 countries. Christian camps, Bible courses, radio broadcasting and in particular establishing churches are all methods used to propagate the Gospel. Opportunities exist for volunteers as career and short term missionaries, members of summer outreach teams and itinerant evangelists. A whole-hearted agreement with Outreach's Statement of Faith is required and volunteers must be over 18 years old. Volunteers must supply a doctor's certificate of good health and are responsible for raising their own funds.

A short term missionary programme is designed for young graduates of Bible school, single or married couples, who require 'in service' training. The volunteers are attached to a local church for periods of 12 to 24 months and work with the pastor on all aspects of the church's programme.

Career missionaries are placed in churches financially unable to support a full time pastor, but able to provide accomodation and if possible, part salary, with the balance coming from interested churches and individuals.

For further details on volunteer requirements, financial information and other facts, contact the General Secretary at the above address.

Global Volunteers

375E Little Canada Road, St. Paul, MN 55117, USA (tel +1 612 482-1074; +1 fax 612 482-0915; toll free US 800-487-1074). E-mail @globalvlntrs.org

Global Volunteers is a non-profit US Corporation founded in 1984 with the goal of establishing a foundation for peace through mutual international understanding. The programme centres around one, two, or three-week volunteer work experience placements in rural communities fifteen countries: China, Vietnam, Tanzania, Indonesia, Costa Rica, Jamaica, Mexico, Poland, Russia, Spain, Italy, Greece, Ecuador, Turkey and the southern United States. About 1000 volunteers are engaged per year on these projects. At the request of local leaders and indigenous host organisations, Global Volunteers' teams live with and work alongside local people on human and economic development projects identified by the community as important to their long-term development. In this way, the volunteers' energy, creativity and labour are put to use and at the same time they gain a genuine, first-hand understanding of how the vast majority of the world's people live day-to-day.

Projects vary from site to site, and from one season to the next. Most volunteers work in one of three areas. There are voluntary opportunities in the area of education such as teaching English, providing training in business, maths or basic sciences in the classroom, or tutoring small children. Volunteers are also needed in the area of community infrastructure to help with the construction of community centres and health clinics, the establishment of portable water systems, repairing classrooms and roads, and building houses. Finally, volunteers are also required to share their professional services such as dentistry, assisting rural health-care providers, identifying crop diseases and helping to establish small businesses. Sometimes volunteers are asked to simply assist with painting, planting or other beautification projects, for which specialised skills are not necessary. Everyone is welcome to apply, but minors must travel with a parent, guardian or adult group leader. Team members must be in good physical and mental health. Most teams' placements last for 1-3 weeks; about 90 teams are recruited each year. Volunteers must pay for their own trip. Costs range from $450 to $2,100 excluding air fare. All trip-related costs are tax deductible to US tax payers and cover ground transportation, on-site food and lodging, administrative fees, and all project related costs. Volunteers are provided with accommodation in the community where they work.

Those interested should contact Global Volunteers at the above address.

HCJB UK
131 Grattan Road, Bradford, West Yorkshire BD1 2HS (tel 01274-721 810; fax 01274 741302).

HCJB undertakes media and medical ministries in Ecuador, South America, and the United Kingdom. Around 50 volunteers are needed each year to help with various projects. Audio and broadcasting engineers, announcers, scriptwriters and other volunteers with experience in communications are needed for media ministries; nurses and laboratory technicians are required for the medical ministries in Ecuador, and youth workers, printers, secretaries, office helpers, etc. are needed for each. Placements vary from one to three months or longer, all year round.

All volunteers are welcome but they must be committed Christians and in agreement with this organisation's Statement of Faith. Only medical volunteers must speak Spanish but it is an advantage to speak Spanish or Italian if wishing to serve in Equador or Italy. Volunteers must raise their own financial support and accommodation on a rental basis is provided. No visas are required for periods of less than three months.

For more details contact the Personnel Secretary at the above address.

Health Volunteers Overseas (HVO)
c/o Washington Station, PO Box 65157, Washington DC 20035-5157, USA (tel +1 202 296-0928; fax +1 202 296-8018). E-mail hvo@aol.com

HVO is a private non-profit organisation committed to improving health care in developing countries through training and education. HVO currently recruits about 200 fully trained and qualified medical profressionals per year to partici-pate in programmes in the following specialities; anaesthesia, dentistry, oral and maxillofacial surgery, orthopaedics, paediatrics, internal medicine and physical therapy. Programme sites are in Africa, Asia, the Caribbean and South America.

Although each programme is different in goals and content, the principal concept remains the same — that volunteers should teach rather than provide service. Applicants of any nationality are accepted; most programmes require Board Certified or Board Eligible physicians, dentists, oral surgeons or physical therapists, RNs and CRNAs. Volunteer requirements vary according to programme site. Usual length of placement is two to four weeks. A few sites provide housing for volunteers, but at other sites housing arrangements are made for the volunteers but the volunteers absorb the cost. A one month assignment costs a volunteer on average $3,500 (for transportation, room, board etc) in personal expense.

Those interested should contact Kate Skillman at the above address.

HELP (Scotland)
60 The Pleasance, Edinburgh EH8 9TJ; tel 0131 650 1000; fax 0131 667 9780).
E-mail Library@UK.AC.EDINBURGH

HELP Scotland is a humanitarian and education long-term project organiser that takes on short-term volunteers for teaching, construction and conservation projects. Volunteers are taken on for four to six weeks during July and August. It is preferable they return every year in order to maintain good contact with the community they are working with in Asia, Africa and South America. About 170 volunteers work for the organisation in one year.

Opportunities for volunteers include building work (anything from building schools to drilling wells). Also English teaching in schools and conservation work which may include tree planting, fencing and path building. A knowledge of Spanish is useful for South America but otherwise languages are not essential. Applicants must be aged 18-25 and pays a contribution which pays for all the materials required on the workcamp and for board and accommodation whilst on the workcamp.

Application forms are available from early January and selection takes place in late January.

The Institute of Cultural Affairs
PO Box 133, Bristol BS99 IHR.

The Institute of Cultural Affairs, a registered charity, is affiliated to ICA Development Trust. ICA:UK is part of a worldwide network of organisations whose common focus is the empowering of people involved in world development through educational methods and participatory approaches. Some overseas ICA projects offer volunteer placements.

ICA:UK runs Volunteer Orientation Weekends (VOW) designed for people seeking to address the personal as well as global issues in volunteering. These are run throughout the year and in various locations. Through a varied programme of workshops, group discussions, personal reflection and games, it offers an alternative way of looking at the volunteering opportunities available with ICA and other organisations.

For further details, please send a SAE to the Volunteer Programme Coordinator, at the above address.

International Christian Youth Exchange (ICYE)
International Office of ICYE, Georgenkirchstrasse 70, 10249 Berlin, Germany; (tel +49 30 24063-214; fax +49 30 24063-215); E-mail icyeio@igc.apc.org

ICYE is an international organisation composed of autonomous national committees in over 30 countries which offers young people over 16 years old the chance to live overseas for six months or one year. The volunteers are hosted by a family or in an alternative living situation and attend high school and perform voluntary service work in the community in which they are living. Only volunteers aged over 18 years perform voluntary service work. This work may include work with children or the aged, involvement with rehabilitation, women's or disabled programmes, teaching, etc. ICYE is present in countries in Africa, Asia, Europe, Latin America, the Pacific and the United States of America. Departure to the host country takes place in July of each year.

Age limits vary for different countries but no special skills are required. Volunteers should supply a health certificate. There are scholarships available but usually a volunteer pays a participation fee to the sending committee, which covers administration, travel and insurance costs.

Volunteers should apply through the ICYE National Committee in their country. Where ICYE does not have such a committee the nearest committee suffices. Further information can be obtained from the Programme Executive at the above address, which can supply contact addresses for ICYE National Committees.

International Voluntary Service (Northern Ireland)
122 Great Victoria Street, Belfast BT2 7BG; (tel 01232 238147; fax 01232-244356). E-mail georget@ivsni.dnet.co.uk

IVS-NI is the northern Irish branch of Service Civil International (ISCI) an international network of organisations dedicated to the promotion of international understanding through the exchange of volunteers. About 100-150 incoming volunteers are placed in N. Ireland and 70-100 volunteers are sent abroad annually.

IVS-NI organises international workcamps lasting 2-3 weeks; also teenage workcamps on an exchange basis, for 4 weeks and some weekend ones; also volunteer posts for 3 months to a year or longer. There is an Africa/Asia exchange of 6-8 weeks. In addition there are special programmes e.g. conflict resolution, training; study tours and so on.

Volunteers wishing to come to Northern Ireland from abroad should apply through a branch of SCI or a recognised partner in their own country. English is the working language on all camps. Ages: for teenage workcamps 16-18 years; International Workcamps 18+; longer posts 18 or older depending on the scheme. Asia/Africa programme 21+. Opportunities are available all year round but mainly June to September. Only teenage workcamps are subsidised on other schemes volunteer pay for their own travel. Pocket money provided on longer term schemes.

An International Workcamps brochure is available every mid-April for £2.50. For further details contact the above address.

International Volunteer Expeditions (IVEX)
PO Box 13309, Oakland, California 94661-0309, United States of America; (tel +1 510 339-7770; fax +1 510 339-3749). E-mail oakland2@ix.netcom.com

IVEX conducts short-term international workcamps all year round and typically lasting two weeks in California, East Africa, Mexico and the Caribbean with an emphasis on environmentalism and nature. Skilled and unskilled volunteers of all nationalities are welcome. Work projects include building and restoring affordable housing, environmental and conservation projects and counsellors at youth camps.

Workcamps are very nature-oriented and many are camping trips. All involve strenuous hiking, hard work and outdoor recreation. Tasks include painting, planting, weeding, digging, building, youth counselling, cleaning.

Participants must be aged 18+ unless accompanied by an adult. All must be open-minded, flexible, enthusiastic, have a spirit of adventure and a desire to make a difference.

Participants pay for their own transportation and a fee (Dominica and the Caribbean US$695; Kenya US$650-1,250; California US$290). Meals and lodging are provided. Participants may be any nationality subject to visa requirements. References available from past participants in most European countries and the USA.

Applications to the above address.

Involvement Volunteers Association Inc.

PO Box 218, Port Melbourne, Victoria 3207, Australia (tel/fax +61-3 646-5504).

Involvement Volunteers exists to give people the opportunity to participate in volunteer activities related to environmental research, archaeology, history, or social welfare. Individual placements or Team Task placements run for 2-12 weeks, some with free accommodation and food, others costing up to £40 per week. Volunteers need to understand and speak some English. Individual and/or Team Task placements are available in Australia, California, Fiji, Germany, Hawaii, India, New Zealand and Thailand.

Involvement Volunteers is a non profit-making organisation which charges a fee of approximately £220 to cover administration costs. For volunteers coming to Australia, this fee includes travel and visa advice, meeting the volunteer on arrival at Melbourne airport, initial accommodation, paid work introductions for volunteers with suitable work permits, advice on taxation and banking as well as a communication base for the visit. However, volunteers from overseas would have to pay for their own travel costs. Volunteers in Australia have access to discounted special coach travel·passes and scuba diver training on the Great Barrier Reef.

For further information please contact the above address.

European applicants can contact Involvement Volunteers-Deutschland, Giebethweg 27, 91056 Erlangen, Goettingen, Germany (tel/fax +49 91 35 80 75).

The Lisle Fellowship, Inc

433 West Sterns Road, Temperence, MI 48182, USA (tel +1 313 847-7126; fax +1 419-530-1245; toll free USA 1-800-477-1583). E-mail mkinney@utnet.utoledo.edu

The Lisle Fellowship is an educational organisation which seeks to improve the quality of human life through human understanding among people of diverse cultures. The foundation of Lisle is aimed at creating an education for 'world mindedness'. Since the Fellowship's work began in 1936, over 11,000 persons have participated in its programme. Lisle offers programmes of up to six weeks in such places as Alaska, Columbia, India, Bali, Uganda and Japan. Programmes emphasize personal development, inter-cultural group living experiences, small group field work assignments in the local community, and group times to integrate learning and usually take place in the spring and summer. Orientation takes place in a 'home-centre' prior to field visits. Volunteers might find themselves working in an Indian rural village, an Inuit (Eskimo) community, or a Japanese school. Each programme is primarily designed as a personal learning experience.

Programmes are open to students, teachers and others over 18 years of age. Lisle looks for people from diverse cultural backgrounds who have an ability to get along with and work with others. Programme fees are offered at the lowest possible cost, in order to provide for people of all economic resources. Limited financial aid is available to participants who demonstrate a need for assistance. Participants in the Fellowship's programme may be eligible for college credits.

There is a programme fee, which covers board, lodging and travel related to the programme. Applications should be made to The Lisle Fellowship at the above address.

Médecins Sans Frontiéres

124-132 Clerkenwell Road, London EC1R 5DL (tel 0171-713 5600; fax 0171-713 5004). E-mail: office@london.msf.org

The charity Médecins Sans Frontiéres provides medical assistance throughout the world to the victims of war and disaster without discrimination of any kind. Every year the organisation sends out 2000 volunteers to 70 countries. Volunteers are contracted for a minimum of nine months, but some take on longer assignments. MSF is the world's largest independent aid agency of its kind, and has developed a detailed understanding of the best ways to bring effective relief to the victims of conflicts and natural disasters, constantly improving methods of emergency aid.

As well as qualified doctors, nurses (R.G.N.), anaesthetists, midwives, lab technicians and surgeons with at least two years post qualification experience, MSF also recruits qualified administrators, engineers and accountants with substantial working experience. For medical staff, a diploma in tropical medicine is preferred. For all categories of staff, previous travel and work experience in developing countries is an asset.

The selection process is rather lengthy involving a number of interviews, tests and pre-departure courses. The UK address above only accepts applications from UK residents. MSF has offices worldwide including:

USA: 11 East 26th Street, suite 1904, New York NY 10010.

CANADA: 355 Adelaide Street, W 5B Toronto.

AUSTRALIA: P.O. Box 51411, Sydney 2001.

JAPAN: Takadanobaba 3-28-1, Shinjuku-Ku, Tokyo 169.

MERLIN (Medical Emergency Relief International)

1A Rede Place, Chepstow Place, London W2 4TU; (tel 0171-229 4560; fax 0171-243 1442). E-mail merlin@gn.apc.org

MERLIN is a humanitarian organisation set up in 1993 to provide medical relief in the first phase of international emergencies, when the local infrastructure has broken down and people are at their most vulnerable. Past countries of operation have included Afghanistan, Chechnya, Rwanda, Siberia, Sierra Leone and Sri Lanka.

The number of volunteers is rising steadily. A range of professional medical expertise is needed but primarily it is for surgeons, doctors, nurses and support personnel which are people with logistical and/or administrative skills and experience.

Volunteers of all nationalities can apply but as there is no fund to pay for trips to interview in Britain, the applicants tend to be British-based. Merlin can arrange visas but not work permits. At least two years post-registration experience is required for most medical personnel. Previous overseas experience is not essential but desirable. Volunteers are continually being recruited onto the register and are generally contracted for six months. Travel expenses are paid for the second interview, a volunteer allowance is paid in the UK for work overseas and flights, visas, insurance, accommodation are all covered by the Organisation.

Applications to Lucy Markby, Human Resources Department, at the above address.

Mobility International USA (MIUSA)

PO Box 10767, Eugene, Oregon 97440, USA (tel +1 503 343 1284; fax +1 503 343 6812).

MIUSA is a non-profit making organisation that exists to increase the opportunities for educational exchange and travel for people with disabilities. MIUSA's programmes include organizing international educational exchange programmes which include disabled and non-disabled people working together in the USA and overseas. MIUSA programmes have been in Italy, Mexico, England, Germany, Costa Rica, China, and the Russian Federation. Themes of the exchanges vary but the goals are to increase international understanding through contact between people, and to improve the lives of disabled people around the world by sharing information and strategies for independent living. The exchange experiences last three to four weeks, and usually include a community service component and a stay with a family in the host country.

Persons with disabilities and able-bodied persons are encouraged to apply. Applicants must have an interest in independent living and an international understanding. Fees and specific requirements vary depending on the programme.

For further information regarding MIUSA contact the Director at the above address. Enclose an International Reply coupon and a self-addressed envelope.

Nothelfergemeinschaft der Freunde e.V

Auf der Kornerwiese 5, 6000 Frankfurt 1, Germany (tel +49 69-599557).

This organisation recruits about 800 volunteers each year to work on workcamps in Germany, Israel, Ghana, Togo, Kenya, India and Tanzania. Activities include co-operation in non-profit institutions, construction work, path construction, painting etc, and domestic and social work. Food, accommodation and insurance are provided, but volunteers must be prepared to finance their own transportation and incidental expenses.

The camps, which are either for those aged 16-17 or for those 18 years and over, are of about a month's duration, but volunteers may attend two or three camps consecutively. The camps generally run from the end of June to the end of October although occasionally there are camps in March/April. Applications for work outside Germany are open to Germans only.

Although applicants need have no special qualifications, manual skills are very useful. A knowledge of English or French is necessary.

Enquiries may be sent to the above address.

Operation Mobilisation
Quinta, Weston Rhyn, Oswestry, Shropshire, SY10 07L (tel 01691-773388; fax 01691-778378). E-mail info@omuk.om.org

Operation Mobilisation is an international mission organisation. It is now in more than 70 countries and has 2,800+ workers who have joined for a year or longer. The main emphases of their work are evangelism with local churches and training of young Christians so that they are better equipped to share their faith. In addition, Operation Mobilisation has two ships, *Doulos* and *Logos II* which give similar evangelism and training opportunities to the land-based teams. The minimum age for the year programme is 17 years in the UK and 18 years abroad. There are opportunities for people with practical work experience and skills. Applicants of any nationality are welcome. Most are sponsored by their churches.

Short term options in 1996 comprised mainly summer programmes, but over the coming years more opportunities are likely to be available on a year-round basis. These comprise an initial week of training then volunteers/participants go out in evangelistic teams in the country of their choice for one to eight weeks. The cost is dependent on duration and location.

For further information please contact the Personnel Department at the above address.

OPTIONS, A Service of Project Concern International
3550 Afton Road, San Diego, CA 92123, USA (tel +1 619 279-9690; fax +1 619 294-0294). E-mail patty@projcon.cts.com

OPTIONS is an international health care professional recruitment and referral service providing hundreds of volunteer opportunities per year that link health care professionals with hospitals, clinics and medical teams worldwide. Positions are listed for every area of the health care field including: primary care, nurses, physicians assistants, therapists, ophthalmologists, psychologists, surgeons, anaesthetists and so on. Volunteers provide direct patient care, health education and training of local community health workers for local programmes.

Applicants of all nationalities are accepted, as long as they are certified in their field of expertise, but OPTIONS can only place volunteers in the US who have a US licence. Students are accepted through a programme called Med-Serve International, which is a collaborative programme between OPTIONS and the American Medical Student Association (AMSA). Students must contact AMSA in the first instance for an application details.

Language requirements depend on the placement location. Volunteers are normally recruited for between two weeks and two years. Each individual location sets the standards for compensation. Most facilities provide room and board with all other expenses assumed by the volunteer. Longer term volunteers can sometimes negotiate a small stipend.   Applications should be made to Patty Brown, OPTIONS Program Manager, at the above address.

Project HOPE
Health Sciences Education Centre, Millwood, VA 22646, USA (tel +1 540 837-2100; fax 540-837-1813) E-mail stardino@projhope.org

Project HOPE provides assistance in establishing or upgrading existing health personnel training programmes in developing countries. Around 300 volunteers are needed each year to act as educators in this project. Placements are for two months or more all year round as academic years differ from country to country.

Volunteers must have teaching experience within a health care profession, the ability to educate other trainers and a professional licence. Transportation, housing and a daily meal allowance are provided.

Those interested should apply to the International Recruitment Section for further information.

Quaker International Social Projects (QISP)

Friends House, Euston Road, London NW1 2BJ; (tel 0171-387 3601).

The aims of QISP are to promote co-operation and international understanding between people and to support communities.

Volunteer Opportunities in the UK: QISP organises 25-30 volunteer projects lasting two to four weeks in Britain and Northern Ireland. They take place in spring and summer. Typical projects include playschemes, work with adults or children who have mental or physical disabilities, manual projects like decorating shelters for the homeless, youth work, community arts projects and more.

A volunteer team comprises eight to 15 people coming from all walks of life and nationalities. The age minimum for volunteers is 18 years (16 for some youth projects). Volunteers with disabilities are welcome to apply. No special skills or qualifications are needed but motivation, enthusiasm and commitment to living and working with a group are.

Volunteer Opportunities Abroad: QISP's projects abroad are similar in scope and are arranged through exchange agreements with volunteer organisations abroad including those in eastern Europe, Turkey and the USA. Most projects run in summer and last one to four weeks.

The minimum age for projects is 18 years. Applicants aged 18-24 should have completed a project in the UK *or* had similar residential volunteering experience *or* should have lived abroad. Applicants must be aged 24+.

For projects in the UK and abroad, simple food and accommodation are provided but volunteers pay a registration fee of £17-£44 depending on means, and travel expenses.

Applications (from UK only) requre a large SAE and a covering letter giving age and previous volunteer experience. To go on the QISP mailing list send a £5 cheque or postal order to 'Britain Yearly Meeting' at the above address.

Applicants outside the UK should apply through an organisation in their own country.

Raleigh International

Raleigh House, 27 Parsons Green Lane, London SW6 4HZ; (tel 0171 371 8585; fax 0171 371 5116).

Raleigh International is a youth development charity that carries out demanding environmental and community projects at home and abroad. During three months in remote areas volunteers, known as 'venturers', develop self-confidence and new skills which they are then encouraged to use on their return home. Over the years, Raleigh International has run expeditions in Zimbabwe, Chile, Malaysia, Brunei, Namibia, Mongolia, Guyana and Mauritius. About 1,000 venturers every year go abroad, but a further 1-2,000 ex-venturers work at home.

Venturers may find themselves helping with scientific research in tropical rain forests, building health centres and schools in remote villages, constructing bridges for the benefit of local communities or helping eye surgeons with cataract operations. All work is done with local venturers and volunteers. Applicants of all nationalities are welcome, but the ability to speak some English, as well as the ability to swim, is important. Voluntary staff are also needed to run projects, such as engineers, diving instructors, doctors and nurses.

Venturers must be aged between 17 and 25, while skilled staff must be over 26. The length of placement is always three months, and there are about ten expeditions throughout the year. Venturers have to raise their own funds, but many national fundraising events are arranged and they also receive plenty of local support. Venturers don't have to carry tents although they often camp, or sleep in cabins etc. where possible.

Those interested should contact the above address.

Service Civil International /International Voluntary Service
Old Hall, East Bergholt, Colchester C07 6TQ.

International Voluntary Service (IVS) is the British branch of Service Civil International (SCI), an international voluntary movement which was begun in 1920 by Pierre Ceresole, a Swiss pacifist, with the aim of furthering reconciliation between participants in the Great War. Its objectives are to promote peace, international co-operation and friendship through the means of voluntary work. The 'Service Civil' in its name describes its role as an alternative to military service; for example during the Second World War International Voluntary Service, the British branch of the organisation, was able to provide alternative service for conscientious objectors. There are now SCI branches in 25 countries and partner organisations in 20 more, which organize annually about 350 short term projects lasting for two or three weeks in Asia, Europe and the USA, involving up to 6,500 volunteers.

The national programme in each country is autonomous and develops its programme according to its special needs and possibilities. All volunteers accepted must appreciate the aims and objectives of SCI, and be prepared to work as a team in basic conditions.

An international workcamp consists of a group between 10 and 20 people from many different countries who live and work together for two to four weeks on a community project. Volunteers not only participate in the work, but also take part in discussions and the team life of the group. The projects undertaken vary from manual work with rural communities to helping with a playscheme for children in an inner-city area, or work and study on such subjects as ecology, conscientious objection, or solidarity with oppressed groups.

Service Civil International stress that a workcamp is not just a cheap holiday; volunteers are normally expected to work an unpaid 40 hours a week. Meals and basic accommodation are provided, but participants cover all other expenses themselves (including travel). Volunteers should be at least 18 years old. Applications are welcomed from people of all racial, cultural and social backgrounds and from people with physical disabilities.

For further information about Service Civil International projects British applicants should contact the address in their country listed below: where there is no address contact the International Secretariat at 73, 7th Main, 3rd Block, IV Stage, Basaveshara Nagor, Bangalore 560079, India.

Austria:	SCI, Schottengasse 3a/1/4/59, 1010 Vienna
Belgium:	SCI, Rue Van Elewyck 35, B 1050, Brussels
Belgium:	VIA Draakstraat 37, 2018 Antwerp

Finland:	KVT Rauhanasema, Veturitori, 00520 Helsinki 52
France:	SCI, 2 rue Eugene Fourniere, 75018 Paris
Germany:	SCI, Blucherstrasse 14, 5300 Bonn 1
Greece:	SCI 43 Arlonos Street, 10443 Athens
Ireland:	VSI, 37 North Great Georges Street, Dublin
Italy:	SCI, Via dei Laterani 28, 00184 Rome
Netherlands:	VIA Pesthuislaan 25, 1054 Amsterdam
Northern Ireland:	IVS 122 Gt. Victoria Street, Belfast
Norway:	ID Langesgate 6, 0165, Oslo 1
Spain:	SCCT Rambla de Catalunya, 5 pral.2.a.08007 Barcelona
Sweden:	IAL Barnangsgatan 23, 11641 Stockholm
Switzerland:	SCI, Postfach 228, CH-300 Bern 9
USA:	SCI, Innisfree Village Rte 2, Box 506, Crozet Virginia 22932

Other organisations co-operating with Service Civil International:

Czechoslovakia:	KMC Malostraske nabrezi 1, 111800 Prague
Denmark:	MS Bordergade 10-14, 1300 Copenhagen
Hungary:	SCI Olajliget utca 28, 1103 Budapest
Netherlands:	SIW Willemstaat 7, Utrecht
Poland:	SCI ul. Stefans-kiego 43, Poznan, Warsaw
Portugal: Lisbon	Instituto da Juventude, Avenida da Liberdade, 1200
Turkey:	Genctur Cad 15-3 Sultenahmed Yerabatan Istanbul
Slovenia:	MOST Breg 12, PP279, Ljubljana
USA:	Volunteers for Peace, Tiffany Road, Belmont, Vermont 05370

Schools Partnership Worldwide
17 Dean's Yard, Westminster, London SW1P 3PB; (tel 0171-222 0138; fax 0171-963-1006).

Schools Partnership Worldwide offers opportunities for school leavers and graduates to work as teaching assistants or to participate in practical and educational environmental programmes in Tanzania, Zimbabwe, Uganda, Namibia, India and Nepal. SPW was set up in 1985 with the aim of offering challenging experiences outside formal education and to focus on developing countries where educational and social services are poor. This aim is activated through:
Teaching and social programmes where the volunteer works as a teaching assistant providing language teaching support, and organising extra curricular activities.
Environmental programmes where a group of volunteers from the North is matched with a group of young people from the country being targeted and they spend their time learning about and acting upon important environmental issues. These programmes generally involve working with a local non-governmental organisation.
During the programmes volunteers are also involved in spending funds raised in the West, on mini-projects to benefit the schools and local communities where they are working. Examples of projects include: levelling and equipping playing fields, setting up poultry, pig and bee-keeping and library creation.
Volunteers are aged 18-25. Local African and Nepali volunteers are recruited on the same basis as their European counterparts. Thre is an optional schools

sponsorship scheme through which schools agree to provide financial support for their pupils who wish to go away with SPW.

The volunteers' expenses for a teaching programme include £1000 for travel, insurance, innoculations and £750 sponsorship which provides a basic living allowance, training and administration overseas. Any money remaining is put into a Project fund.

Expenses for an environmental programme are about £2250.

In addition all volunteers are asked to raise extra money to contribute towards mini development projects which they carry out while abroad.

Details about the application procedure and about school sponsorship schemes can be obtained from the Director at the above address. There are obligatory pre-departure and in-country training sessions. For teaching programmes basic language and TEFL training is given.

Scottish Churches World Exchange

121 George Street, Edinburgh EH2 4YN, Scotland (tel 0131-225 5722).

World Exchange is organised by a number of Scottish churches acting together. It offers volunteer opportunities ranging from six to 18 months for people with a wide variety of skills. In the past volunteers have been placed in Asia, the Middle East, Africa and Central America. While teachers and medical staff are the easiest to place, World Exchange will also consider candidates who come straight from university or with other more practical skills.

Candidates can be of any age between 18 and 80. A small local allowance is paid and food and accommodation are provided. A travel pool operates on the basis that candidates are expected to do a considerable amount of fundraising before departure. Applicants should be Scottish and be a member of any Christian Church in Scotland. Scottish candidates resident elsewhere in the UK may also apply.

Those interested should write to the Director at the above address.

Teaching English Abroad

46 Beech View, Angmering, Sussex BN16 4DE (tel 01903-859911; fax 01903 785779). E-mail: teaching — abroad@garlands.uk.com
Internet: http//www.garlands.uk.com/ta

Volunteer teachers of English as a foreign language needed to teach in Poland, India, Ukraine, Ghana and Russia (Moscow and Siberia). No TEFL qualifications required. Dates are by arrangement (summer posts and up to a year possible). Full range of back-up services in each country.

Other types of voluntary work also available in India and Ukraine: business placements, hotel and tourism work, medical experience and observation and placements in accountancy, finance, law, environment, conservation and research.

Prices without travel: from £425 (Poland) to £1595 (Ghana). Prices with travel: from £495 (Poland) to £2295 (Ghana).

The above costs cover a home and all meals with a local family or in a comfortable hostel for teachers.

Trekforce Expeditions

134 Buckingham Palace Road, London SW1W 9SA (tel 0171-824 8890; fax 0171-824 8892).

Trekforce is a charity that organises expeditions in remote areas of the world, particularly Belize and Indonesia. It is the part of the International Scientific

Support Trust which organises expeditions in support of scientific research and environmental conservation. Volunteers work alongside leading scientists. Expeditions involve adventurous trekking in remote national parks with spartan living conditions and hard physical labour for up to eight hours a day. Inspite of these apparent disincentives, people are queueing for a chance to go on them. Two-day 'jungle' training courses to 'test their initiative and ability to work in teams' are held for prospective volunteers in the UK. Training courses cost £25. In addition, successful applicants have to raise up to £2,700 towards the cost of the expedition. Projects include working with animals: orang-u-tans in Borneo and elephants in Sumatra.

Most volunteers tend to be aged 17-23 but there is no upper age limit.

United Nations Association (Wales) International Youth Service
Welsh Centre for International Affairs, Temple of Peace, Cathays Park, Cardiff, CF1 3AP (tel 01222-223088).

The UNA (Wales) International Youth Service offers facilities for people from Great Britain to attend international volunteer projects within Wales and in most countries in Western and Eastern Europe, the United States, Canada, India Japan, South America as well as certain African countries. These projects usually last between two and four weeks during the summer and involve work on a variety of schemes including hospital and social work, playschemes, and environmental work. The aim of these projects is the encouragement of international understanding, and development of community projects. The projects normally consist of between 10 and 15 volunteers aged over 18. There are also projects for volunteers aged 15-17.

Volunteers are required to meet their own travelling expenses to the projects, but once there they are provided with free board and accommodation. On acceptance, volunteers have to pay a registration fee, which is £45 for projects in Wales, and £70-100 for projects abroad.

Those interested should write to the IYS officer at the above address, enclosing an SAE, to receive membership details.

United Society for the Propagation of the Gospel(USPG) Exchange Programme
Partnership House, 157 Waterloo Road, London SE1 8XA (tel 0171-928 8681; fax 0171-928 2371).

The Society organises church-related projects in Britain, Africa, Asia, South America, the Middle East and the Caribbean. 50 volunteers per year are involved in a wide range of activities including root groups dedicated to parish work and community living in Britain, an experience exchange programme which organises various overseas placements, overseas sabbaticals and overseas pastoral placements for theological students. Applicants of any nationality may apply, but most placements are only open to British citizens living in Britain. There exist some places in the root groups for 18-30 year olds from overseas, and these are recruited only through churches in partnership with the Society. Specialist skills are occasionally needed depending on placement.

Volunteers for the root groups are aged between 18 and 30, for all other placements the minimum age is 18 and there is no upper limit. Good health is essential. The length of time for which volunteers are normally recruited varies from three months to a year. The selection process takes place from November to May each year, with placements beginning in the autumn.

Participants are expected to raise as much as possible towards costs and USPG can give grants in cases of need. Accommodation is usually available, depending on placement.

For further information please contact Nicki Donovan at the above address.

WEC International

Bulstrode, Gerrards Cross, Bucks SL9 8SZ (tel 01753-884631). E-mail Compuserve 100546, 1550

WEC International seeks to evangelise the remaining unevangelised areas of the world in the shortest possible time. As well as spreading the Gospel, WEC volunteers also give practical help with community development projects. Small numbers of volunteers are needed to help full-time WEC volunteers in over 60 countries of the world. Unskilled volunteers or students can give service during the summer to help with building work, looking after children and other practical work. For those with specific skills or training, (secretaries, teachers, mechanics, nurses, doctors, builders, etc), there are more opportunities and placements are for one or two years.

All volunteers must be evangelical Christians. Volunteers are responsible for their fares to and from the field and their living costs whilst there, although in some situations board and lodging will be provided.   Those interested should contact Francis Blackmore at the above address.

World Council of Churches — Youth Sub-Unit

P O Box, 150 Route de Ferney, PO Box 66, 1211 Geneva 20, Switzerland (tel +41 22-916 065).

The Youth Sub-Unit has a programme called Ecumenical Youth Action which sponsors workcamps in Africa, Asia, Latin America and the Middle East. Volunteers from all nationalities and faiths share in work and live in a local community. Theological discussions and manual work such as agricultural, construction and renovation projects form an important part of the programme. Workcamps are held between April and September with the length being from one to three weeks.

Volunteers should be aged 18 to 30 years. They must arrange and pay for their own travel and insurance. Around £3 per day is expected to be contributed towards the camp's expenses.

Those interested should write to the above address for a workcamp programme but should then apply directly to the individual camps.

World Horizons

Glanmor Road, Llanelli, Dyfed, Wales SA15 2LU (tel 0116-2230001/2; fax 0116-2230003). E-mail admin@whorizons.org

World Horizons is a modern missionary movement offering committed Christians the opportunity to be involved in expeditions and short-term placements, as well as long-term, with its full-time teams in Britain, Europe, the Middle East, Asia, Africa, Australia and the Americas.

No particular skills are required although administrative, secretarial, building or mechanical skills are always helpful. Most opportunities are between Easter and October; the minimum age for Europe is 17, and 18 for the rest of the world. There are also some specific expeditions for the 14-17 age range. Volunteers are responsible for raising their own finances. Accommodation is provided but must be paid for by the volunteer.

Write to the Perrie Lewis of the Personnel Team at the above address for further details.

WORLDTEACH, Inc.
Harvard Institution for International Development, One Eliot Street, Cambridge, MA 02138-5705, USA (tel +1 617 495-5527; fax +1 617 495-1599). E-mail worldteach@hiid,harvard.edu (Web-site http://www.hiid.harvard.edu/)

WorldTeach is a non-profit educational development and cultural exchange organisation which places volunteers to teach in countries abroad. Most programmes are for a full year (see page 45), but there is a summer programme in Shanghai, China. Volunteers pay or fundraise a fee to cover the cost of airfares, health insurance, field support, training and administration. Training includes pre-departure literature and briefing. Volunteers are provided with room and board.

Applicants may be of any nationality but they must speak English with native fluency. Volunteers must have accquired at least 25 hours training or experience in Teaching English as a Foreign Language before they depart. For the summer programme in Shanghai volunteers must be college or graduate students. Volunteers must be in good health and able to live and work under rigorous conditions. The summer programme in China lasts for two months

Further details from the above address.

World Vision
599 Avebury Boulevard, Milton Keynes MK9 3PG; (01908-841000; fax 01908-841014).

World Vision has occasional vacancies (about five a year) for volunteers overseas in agriculture and health, construction and logistics in areas of Africa and south east Asia. Applicants should have a degree or relevant experience in the field for which they are applying. The period of service is usually three months. Expenses for the trip must be borne by the volunteer. World Vision publish a monthly job update available from the above address.

WWOOF Willing Workers on Organic Farms

WWOOF exists to give people the opportunity of gaining first hand experience of organic farming and gardening in return for spending a weekend or longer working on a farm. Since WWOOF began in England in 1971, similar schemes have developed in other countries around the world.

Each of the groups listed below is an independent group with its own aims, system, fees and rules. They are all similar in that they offer volunteers the chance to learn in a practical way the growing methods of their host. The minimum age for Wwoofing in the UK is 16 and abroad it is 18 years. Volunteers must pay their own travel expenses but food and accommodation is provided. Each group will supply a worklist booklet to members from which volunteers can choose a farm; send International Reply Coupons when writing to an overseas group.
WWOOF schemes:

Australia:	WWOOF (Aus), Lionel Pollard, Mt Murrindal Co-op, Buchan, Victoria 3885.
Canada:	WWOOF (Canada), John Vanden Heuvel, RR2, Carlson

	Road S18 C9, Blewett, Nelson, British Columbia VIL 5P5.
Denmark:	VHH, c/o Bent & Inga Nielsen, Asenjev 35, 9881 Bindslev.
Ireland:	WWOOF(Ireland), Harpoonstown, Drinagh, Co Wexford, Ireland.
Germany:	WWOOF e.V. Thalhauser Fussweg 30, 85354 Freising, Germany.
Netherlands:	NVEL, Willemsvaart 1-304; 8019 AA Zwolle, The Netherlands.
New Zealand:	WWOOF (NZ), Jane Bryan-Strange, PO Box 10-037, Palmerston North.
Norway:	ATLANTIS, Rolf Hofmogst, 18, N-O655 Oslo 6 and APøG c/o Noll, Langvevn 18, 5003 Bergen.
UK:	WWOOF(UK), Don Pynches, 19 Bradford Road, Lewes, BN17 1RB, Sussex.
USA:	FRIENDS OF THE TREES, PO Box 1064, Tonasket, WA 98855, USA.
USA:	NEWOOF, New England Small Farms Institute, PO Box 937 Belchertown, MA 01007, USA.

Youth Action for Peace (YAP)

Methold House, North Street, Worthing BN1 1DU; (tel 01903/528 619; fax 01903-528611).

The main activity of YAP is organising summer voluntary work. Each year YAP sends volunteers to hundreds of projects in Europe, the Middle East, India, North Africa and Latin America. The work undertaken is diverse: it may be manual, social work or include action around social issues. Projects provide volunteers with an opportunity to live in a multicultural environment helping those in need. The majority of workcamps take place from June to September and last two to six weeks. Food and accommodation are provided but not travel costs. The minimum age is 18 (except in Teenagers' Projects). The complete list is available on request annually in April.

YAP also organises longer term projects lasting six months. These involve working directly with people or in one of the YAP national offices. Volunteers are given board, accommodation, pocket money and 75% travel reimbursement. Support is given and language courses are available.

YAP's other activities revolve around organising International Seminars and Training Courses on human rights, peace and multicultural issues. Travel subsidies are available for seminars.

United Kingdom

Archaeology

Arbeia Roman Fort & Museum

Baring Street, South Shields, Tyne and Wear, NE33 2BB; (tel 0191-454 4093; fax 0191-427 6862).

Archaeology and museum work includes excavation, site recording, drawing, finds processing, museum interpretation. No experience of archaeology necessary but volunteers must understand basic English. Age limit 16+. Volunteer period lasts from July to September and usual period is two to four weeks. Accommodation can be arranged in local guest houses and camp sites at the volunteers' expense.

Useful publication *Guide to South Shields Roman Fort* available at the site for £1.95. Volunteers get a 'volunteer pack' on arrival.

Applications to Elizabeth Elliott at the above address.

Council for British Archaeology
Bowes Morrell House, 111 Walmgate, York YO1 2UA; (tel 01904-671417; fax 01904-671384). E-mail 100271.456@compuserve.com

The Council publishes *CBA Briefing*, an information supplement to its magazine *British Archaeology*. *CBA Briefing*, which appears in the first week of March, May, July, September and November each year, carries announcements of forthcoming fieldwork opportunities on archaeological sites in Britain. An annual subscription for the magazine and *CBA Briefing* is £17.00 for the UK, £22 for Europe and £29.00 for airmail outside Europe. US$ payments also accepted. Send an International Reply Coupon for details.

Department of Continuing Education, University of Wales
Newtown, Powys SY16 3PW; (tel 01686-650715; fax 01686-650656).

The Department of Continuing Education of the University of Wales organises archaeological excavations lasting up to three weeks in Wales during July and August. Up to 20 volunteers are required to help. No experience is necessary as volunteers are introduced to all aspects of work, digging, recording, surveying, artefact processing and so on.

Volunteers pay £40 per week towards the cost of food. Accommodation is provided on a campsite with shower.

Applicants should apply to C J Arnold, at the above address.

Sedgeford Hall Archaeological Research Project
Institute of Archaeology, 31-34 Gordon Square, London WC1H OPY.

Volunteer archaeological excavators (20-30) are needed mid-July to the end of August. The hours of work are from 8.45am to 5.15pm, six days a week with Saturdays free. The charge is £48 a week for students/unwaged and £95 for non-students to cover basic accommodation and food. It is recommended that students stay for at least two weeks. Volunteers must be at least 16 years old, (those under 18 years need parental consent). No professional qualifications or experience needed.

Upper Nene Archaeological Society
Toad Hall, 86 Main Road, Hackleton, Northampton NN7 2AD (tel 01604-870312).

The Society oversees the excavation of a Romano-British villa and underlying Iron Age settlement. Volunteers are required to help with trowelling and a variety of excavation and post-excavation procedures. Volunteers may be of any nationality but they must be able to speak English. The lower age limit is normally 16; there is no upper limit. Applicants should consider themselves physically capable of carrying buckets of soil, pushing wheelbarrows and kneeling to work.

Volunteers are required for a minimum of two weeks in August, but anyone within daily travelling distance is welcome to come and help on Sundays throughout the year. Pocket money is not provided, but volunteers must pay a specified contribution towards the everyday expenses of running the excavation. Accommodation is available in the form of a basic campsite, or bed and breakfast accommodation at reasonable rates can be arranged locally. This must be paid for by the volunteer.

Those interested should contact Mrs D E Friendship-Taylor at the above address.

Child Care

AFASIC, overcoming speech impairments
347 Central Markets, Smithfield, London EC1 (tel 0171-236 3632; fax 0171-236-8115).

Each summer AFASIC organises outdoor Activity Weeks at various outdoor pursuit centres, hostels and guest houses in Britain. Each child is attached to a 'Young person helper' (Link), a volunteer who acts as a friend and support for the week.

Volunteers should be over 18 years and in good health. No experience is required and a briefing is given. Board and lodging is provided. Volunteers must provide their own travel expenses though every effort is made to cut this cost by linking helpers to share transport or to use Association vehicles which are being taken for use on Activity Weeks.

Those interested should apply to the above address.

Birmingham Phab Camps
52 Green Lanes, Sutton Coldfield, Birmingham B73 5JW; (tel 0121-382-7218).

This organisation runs holiday camps each summer for equal numbers of physically disabled and able-bodied young people, enabling the disabled young people to integrate with their able-bodied contemporaries. There are six camps a year, four of which cater for different age groups; Junior (7-10), Senior (11-13), Teenage (14-16), and 16 plus. The first two camps take 25 young people, the third 20 and the fourth 12-15. The two camps are run for severely (i.e. multiply-disabled) young people of various ages. 20 volunteers are needed for this holiday.

Many young people who are physically disabled have little opportunity to mix and form friendships with their peers and the camps are designed to remedy this isolation and overcome prejudice. There is a wide range of activities from swimming and discos to seaside and camping trips, in which all the young people take part. The camps are run entirely by unpaid volunteers, of whom 80 are needed each year. The volunteer will work at a camp for up to ten days with a team including an experienced leader, two cooks, and a qualified nurse. The Camps are held at a variety of activity centres which provide good accommodation.

Volunteers should be aged between 17 and 30, and speak recognisable English. Obviously the ability to communicate with young people is important. Skills in sport, music, art and so on are valuable, as is previous experience. Energy, dependability, a capacity for hard work and an ability to enthuse young people and win their confidence are essential.

There is a limited number of places for disabled volunteers. Training days are held before each camp, where medical staff from special schools give advice on special needs, and the team plans the camp programme. Accommodation is provided, but expenses and pocket money are not. Transport from Birmingham to the camp and back is paid.

Volunteers should apply to the Volunteer Recruitment Officer at the above address.

Birmingham Young Volunteers

BYV Association, 4th Floor, Smithfield House, Digbeth, Birmingham B5 6BS; (tel 0121-622 2888).

This organisation needs volunteers to help on its activity holidays (BYV Adventure Camps) for disadvantaged children during the school summer holidays. Each volunteer would help for one week only. Four camping holidays are run in Tywyn (mid-Wales) during July and August for children aged 10-16 years and four residential holidays run in the Midlands during August for children aged five to ten years.

Volunteers will look after two or three children on trips, take part in group activities, swimming, games, craft sessions etc. The holiday for the oldest age range (14-16) is very much an 'outward-bound' type. The work is very demanding being with the children 24 hours a day and also very rewarding. Volunteers with clean licences and driving experience are also needed as are people interested in cooking for groups of up to 60.

Travel expenses to and from Birmingham may be paid, but personal expenses on the holiday are not. Accommodation and food are provided. Training weekends for volunteers are arranged and volunteers are police-checked. Applications are accepted from people aged 17 and over and resident in the UK. We are particularly keen to hear from people living in the Birmingham/West Midlands area. Volunteers should apply to to the coordinator at the above address.

Break

7a Church Street, Sheringham, Norfolk NR26 8QR (tel 01263-822161); fax 01263-822181).

Volunteers aged 18-25 are needed for care work at BREAK's six centres in Norfolk. Expenses are paid for travel within the British Isles. Food, accommodation and pocket money of £23 per week are provided. Volunteers work alongside permanent staff and must be able to understand and speak English capably. Preference is given to volunteers who can stay nine to twelve months except for the Rainbow and Sandcastle homes (see below) where commitments of six weeks to six months are possible.

The centres for which volunteers are required are:

Rainbow in Sheringham and *The Sandcastle* in Hunstanton which provide holidays for adults and children with learning disabilities. A wide spectrum of guests with special needs are accepted, some requiring considerable help with meals, dresssing, toiletting and mobility. Each week is challenging and very different from the previous week.

Family Group Home in Sheringham cares for six mildly disturbed children from disrupted families whose need for a family-like atmosphere is paramount. Volunteers live with the children and give them companionship and support. One volunteer is required at a time.

Residential Family & Assessment Unit in Sheringham provides residential assessments and interventions for a broad range of families. The unit runs programmes designed to assess parental skills and family dynamics. Up to two volunteers are required at a time.

Leaving Care Unit in Sheringham provides accommodation for up to four young people, aged 16+, and is designed to prepare them for independent living. One volunteer is required at a time.

There is also a non-residential post for one volunteer to work five days a week at *Day Break in Sheringham* looking after adults with learning disabilities.

Caldecott Community
Mersham-le-Hatch, Ashford, Kent; (tel 01233-503954; fax 01233-502650).

The community is a residential treatment centre and special school for about 80 children between the ages of 5 and 18. The children are taken into care, which is provided around the year, after suffering complete breakdowns due to stresses at home. Contact is maintained with home as much as possible especially during the holidays. There is a primary school within the community which prepares the younger children for entry into secondary schools in the area. A few volunteers are taken on to assist the 70 adults in the community, living with family-type groups of 10 children.

There are no special skills required, but the volunteers should enjoy being with children and have some ability in sports, music, arts and crafts or possession of a driving licence would be an asset. Volunteers are usually taken on for between three months and a year. Board, lodging, travelling expenses and £44 per week are provided.

Those interested should apply to Liz Fisher at the above address.

Camphill Loch Arthur Community
Beeswing, Dumfries, DG2 8JQ; (tel 01387 760687; fax 01387 760618).

Loch Arthur is one of the worldwide Camphill communities living and working with mentally disabled adults. Thirteen volunteers are taken on annually for a variety of tasks in the community including: housework, gardening, farming, cheesemaking, cooking, weaving, care etc. The community's life also revolves around a busy social and cultural life. Applicants should check in their own country whether they need visas to enter Britain. The community will send a letter of invitation if required. Volunteers should be prepared to stay a minimum of six months and preferably twelve. Applications are accepted at any time of year. Board and lodging and a small amount of pocket money are provided.

Applicants should apply directly to the above address.

Camphill Rudolf Steiner School
Murtle Estate, Bieldside, Aberdeen AB1 9EP (tel 01224-867 935).

This is a residential school for children and adolescents in need of special care. Volunteers are needed to live-in and help care for the young people in a home and teach in the school setting. A full time commitment is required with volunteers expected to join in the community life as fully as possible, and emphasis is placed on Christian ideals, social responsibility and the development of the individual. Duties include caring for the young people both physically and emotionally in houses, teaching in classrooms, general domestic tasks, arranging sports and craft activities and working on the land. Around 80 volunteers of any nationality are needed all year round. Placements are usually for at least a year, but in some cases may only be for six months.

Applicants must be willing to live with and fully involve themselves in the community activities with the young people, physically fit, mentally stable, aged over 19 years and have respect for Christian ideals. Exceptions are made for people with certain medical conditions but otherwise no-one with drug habits is accepted. Board, lodging and weekly pocket money are provided. Volunteers who stay for the entire agreed period have their return fare home paid.

Apply to the Staff Committee at the above address.

Camp Windermere
Low Wray, Ambleside, Cumbria; (tel 015394-32163).

Camp Windermere is a charitable outdoor education camp for young people between the ages of ten and 17 from schools and youth organisations. Volunteer instructors and assistant instructors for outdoor pursuits are needed for sailing, canoeing, climbing and hill walking. Applicants need to have previous experience of this kind of activity. Free board and lodging is provided in return for hard work. Overseas applicants welcome if they have reasonable English.

Children's Community Holidays
P O Box 463, Belfast BT7 IPQ; (tel 01232-833753).

Children's Community Holidays is a non-profit organisation involved primarily with cross community work in Northern Ireland. The winter programme consists of running youth clubs and playgroups in various cities and organising some residential weekend camps for children. Volunteers are required during July and August to help run residential holidays for about 800 children aged from eight to sixteen who are taken on seven-day holidays. Positions offered include mini-bus drivers, caterers, domestics, matrons, clerical staff, supervisors and directors of holidays. Recruitment is for seven-day periods but volunteers may work for three consecutive weeks. While the majority of positions are available during the summer, some volunteers are needed during winter.

All applicants are required to agree to the DSS pre-employment vetting scheme which includes a scrutiny of police and statutory agency disciplinary records. Applicants for the summer camps must be able to attend a training course in the first week of July. Overseas applicants with reasonable English are welcome. The minimum age is 17 years.

Applicants should contact the Administrator at the above address.

Children's Country Holidays Fund
First Floor (Rear), 42-43 Lower Marsh, London SE1 7RG (tel 0171-928 6522).

Every year the Fund provides holidays in the country, at the seaside, in private homes or established camps, for almost 3,500 disadvantaged London children. The arrangements for the children's holidays are undertaken by voluntary workers, under the umbrella of a small administrative staff in Head Office. Volunteers are also needed to act as train marshals supervising the children's travel to and from London.

There are no special requirements for camp supervisors, beyond a minimum age of 18, good health, and the ability to supervise children aged between nine and thirteen. The holiday periods vary between ten to fourteen days, and holidays always take place during the six weeks of the school summer holidays. The Fund very much regrets that owing to administrative procedures it can only accept applications from England and Wales. It can therefore no longer accept applications from outside the UK.

Those interested should write to the Director at the above address to find out how they can help.

The Children's Trust
Tadworth Court, Tadworth, Surrey, KT20 5RU (tel 01737-357171).

Requires volunteers to work on residential summer scheme for profoundly disabled and exceptional needs children, who normally live at home. The services are provided in a children's hospital and at a residential school. The work involves acting as a friend to the children, carrying out basic personal care, organising games, encouraging them to take an active part in daily activities, escorting them to outings and organising evening activities. Previous experience with children or handicapped children is preferable, but not essential. Only those wishing to go into the 'caring professions' should apply. Creative skills, handicraft or musical ability welcomed. The work is very rewarding but can also be physically and emotionally tiring. 15 volunteers are appointed each year. Ages 18+. 37½ hours a week. Two days off a week. Mid-July to the first week in September. Students are expected to stay for the duration of the scheme. Accommodation is provided free of charge and an allowance of £42 per week is paid. Travel expenses from mainland England will be paid. Apply to Rachel Turner before 31 March.

The Residential School requires volunteers for six to 12 months to assist with the daily routine of physical care and education of the children in both the residential home and school. Under the guidance of teachers, therapists and senior care staff, work as part of an interdisciplinary team on the individual planned programmes for the children. Same ages, hours, days off and pocket money as above. Travel expenses in the UK can be reimbursed.

Cities in Schools (CiS)
60-61 Trafalgar Square, London WC2N 5DS; (tel 0171-839 2899; fax 0171-839 6186).

CiS is an organisation that helps children who have difficulties at school school to build their confidence and self-image. Volunteers are needed to help such children and young people in local projects. There is free training provided. The organisation's projects are usually small-scale but there are larger programmes run during vacations. Apart from the above address those interested may contact two other regional addresses:
CiS Tower Hamlets: 91 Brick Lane, London E1 6QN (tel 0171-247 9489) and CiS Gwent: c/o K Block, British Steel, Strip Products, Llanwern Works, Newport, Gwent NP9 OXN; (tel 01633-290011 ext. 4441).

CLAN
54 Eva Road, Winson Green, Birmingham, B18 4NQ; (tel 0121-523 3156).

This organisation provides short holiday breaks for children aged from 7 to 13 who would not normally be able to visit the countryside. The camps may be up to a week long and are held during the summer vacation at attractive sites in the West Midlands during July and August.

Around 10 volunteers a year are need to help look after the children and organise leisure activities. No special requirements are expected of volunteers other than that they be mobile and aged over 16. Board, lodging and reasonable travelling expenses within the UK are provided.

Applicants should contact the above address, enclosing a stamped addressed envelope or an international replly coupon.

Community Action Projects (C.A.P.)
Students' Union, Goodricke College, University of York, Heslington, York. YO1 5DD (tel 01904-433133).

CAP runs two types of holiday for a total of 200 children who would not normally get a holiday; most have special needs because they come from low income, broken or unsettled family backgrounds. Easter and summer camps for 6 to 13 year olds consist of site-based drama, craft, sport activities and day trips. Venture Weeks in August for 14 and 15 year olds are more adventurous outdoor pursuit holidays, including hill walking and abseiling.

Around 100 volunteers are needed to help with the general running of the camps as well as participating in and initiating activities. Anyone over 18 years with enthusiasm would be welcomed, but people with specific skills including first-aid, driving and walking experience are also required. Accommodation is provided.

For further information contact the Community Action Officer at the above address.

The Cotswold Community
Ashton Keynes, Nr. Swindon, Wiltshire SN6 6QU (tel 01285-861239; fax 01285-860114).

This community provides care, treatment and education for 40 severely emotionally deprived and abused boys aged from nine to 18. The community consists of four separate households, a school and a farm. Around four volunteers are needed each year to teach and care for the boys. Placements are approximately six months. Volunteers may be of any nationality provided that they are at least 20 years old, speak English well and are in good health. Full board and lodging and about £22.50 pocket money per week are provided.

For further information contact the Principal at the above address.

Glen River YMCA National Centre
143 Central Promenage, Newcastle, Co. Down BT33 OHN, Northern Ireland (tel 013967-24488).

The Centre is an outdoor education centre which needs volunteers to act as domestic staff and cooks, instructors in outdoor pursuits such as canoeing, hill walking, archery, etc, and tutors in personal development. Around 14 volunteers are required for eight or nine weeks during summer and in winter two or three volunteers are needed. An interest in community relations would be an advantage.

Volunteers should be physically and mentally fit, aged 18 years or older and fluent in English. Volunteers for instructor positions should be skilled in the relevant activity and for volunteers older than 25, a driving licence is useful. Board, lodging and pocket money are provided.

Applications should be made to the Programme Manager at the above address.

Leicester Childrens Centre
Quebec Road, Mablethorpe, Lincs. LN12 1QX (tel 01507-472444).

This Centre provides summer holidays for groups of 40 girls and 40 boys from socially deprived backgrounds in the Leicester area. The two week-long camps are held from the beginning of May to the end of August each year. The centre requires about 15 volunteers to act as leaders organising, instructing, and supervising children aged seven to 12 on an outdoor activities programme. Energy, enthusiasm and a sense of humour are essential. Board, accommodation and a weekly wage are provided. Preference is given to applicants able to work the entire season. The minimum age is 18 years.

Write (enclosing a s.a.e.) to H Eagle, Warden at the above address from January.

Liverpool Children's Holiday Organisation (LCHO)
Wellington Road School, Wellington Road, Dingle, Liverpool L8 4TX (tel 0151-727 7330).

LCHO provides residential holidays for Merseyside children who would not normally get a holiday away from home. Volunteers are needed to act as supervisors and will be responsible for a small group of children 24 hours a day. Applicants must be over 18 and fit. Prior to working on the holidays, volunteers must be interviewed and complete a week-long residential training course run by LCHO. Qualified first-aiders and mini-bus drivers are also needed.

Recruitment usually takes place between January and March for that year's summer holiday period. Accommodation is provided and expenses paid. Due to the interviews and training course the voluntary work is only really suitable for UK residents.

Applicants should contact the above address.

Mansfield Outdoor Centre
Manor Road, Lambourne End, Essex RM4 1NB; (tel 0181-500 3047; fax 0181-559 8481).

Mansfield Outdoor Centre is situated in 60 acres of open country. As well as organising leisure activities, it aims to encourage social interaction amongst the young, disabled and disadvantaged within a Christian framework.

Volunteers are needed to work $37\frac{1}{2}$ hours/five days a week, including some weekends. The work includes helping lead outdoor activities and play sessions, grounds and general maintenance and farm work. Experience of outdoor activities such as climbing, canoeing, archery, farmwork etc are required, as well as experience of working with young people. Travel and expenses to be negotiated. Free board and lodging are available. Volunteers can stay a minimum of two weeks (1 year maximum). The period of highest demand is however, April to September. Activity and youth work training will be given. Applicants must be aged 18+ and available for interview.

Applications to the Manager, at the above address.

Nansen Society (UK) Ltd
Redcastle Station, Muir of Ord, Ross-shire IV6 7RX; (tel 01463-871255; fax 01463-870258).

The Nansen Society is a charitable organisation offering training and support to young people with special needs which range from behavioural problems to learning difficulties. The Society places a strong emphasis on environmental awareness and outdoor activities, within an international community and tries as far as practicable to maintain a staff to trainee ratio of one-to-one by making use of trained and experienced volunteers, many of whom come from other countries.

Nansen UK has six volunteers who stay about six months, three part-time local ones and ten or more for residential two-week workcamps in summer.

The sixth month volunteers participate fully in the training and care aspects of the Society's work with young people. This includes some evening and weekend work and holiday expeditions and community activities (such as beach clean-ups). The training week includes one-to-one formal training in life, personal and vocational skills, according to the trainees' needs; one day working on the Nature Trail as a group activity, one afternoon taking part in sports and perhaps some maintenance or farming work, usually with a trainee. Volunteers participate in the weekly training meetings, weekly staff meetings and monthly community meetings (for all staff and trainees). Work is varied but demanding and being adaptable is an essential requirement for the job.

Volunteers should be aged 23+ and in good health with good spoken English. A driving licence is very useful and experience with special needs essential. Some outdoor/sports experience useful.

Volunteers get board and lodging, plus £25 weekly pocket money. No travel expenses are provided.

Anyone interested should contact the above address.

The National Autistic Society
276 Willesden Lane, London NW2 5RB (tel 0181-451 1114; fax 0181-451 5865).

There are limited opportunities for volunteers to work with children with autism on special projects lasting a week or a fortnight during the school vacations or on a longer term basis. Most of this work is in special schools.

Applicants who send their enquiries to the National Society office in London will be sent a list of the special schools and units around the country.

Phoenix YCP Ltd
16 Alexander Square, Lurgan, Craigavon, Northern Ireland (tel 01762 325927).

Phoenix YCP organises youth work with children aged seven to 13 years such as games, drama and art and crafts through a summer scheme programme in Northern Ireland. It also recruits volunteers for Fellowship of Reconciliation in Belfast and Pacem-in-Terris in Delaware, USA.

Volunteers are needed for the summer scheme to act as Volunteer Leaders with the seven to thirteen year olds. Applicants of any nationality may apply, though all applicants must have previously worked with children, and have a fair knowledge of English. The minimum age is 18 years. Volunteers are required for one month between July and August. They must pay for their own travel expenses, as well as £50 for accommodation, food and a social programme.

Enquiries should be made to Pearl Snowden at the above address.

Conservation, the Environment & Heritage

Alford and District Civic Trust Ltd

Manor House, West Street, Alford, Lincolnshire LN13 9DJ; (tel 01507-463073/462127).

Alford Civic Trust is a volunteer-led organisation which derives its main income from a museum and providing refreshments. Volunteer positions offered are as a curatorial assistant and horticulturist to work Monday to Friday from 10am to 5pm. Accommodation is provided free of charge. Volunteers should be prepared to stay at least a month between May and September.

Applicants should have experience or qualifications relevant to the post and the curatorial assistant would probably suite a second year student (must be aged 20+). All applicants should be available for interview but this may be waived if distance creates difficulty.

Enquiries to John Needham, Secretary at the above address.

Berrington Hall

Near Leominster, Herefordshire HR6 ODW; (tel 01568-615721).

Berrington Hall is a National Trust Property which requires volunteer room stewards every day from April to October. Also needed are volunteer car park attendants to work on Bank Holidays. Volunteers must be aged 18+. No accommodation is provided but travel costs are provided (up to 20 miles round trip) and those who offer 40 hours of service get a volunteer card entitling them to free entry to National Trust Properties in the UK and 10% discount in the shops. Overseas applicants are welcome.

Anyone interested should apply to the House Steward at the the above address.

British Trust for Conservation Volunteers

36 St Mary's Street, Wallingford, Oxfordshire OX10 OEU (tel 01491-39766).

BTCV is the country's leading charity protecting the environment through practical action. A network of over 80 field offices allows some 60,000 volunteers of all ages and from all sections of the community to train and take part in a wide range of environmental projects. These include planting trees and hedges, repairing footpaths and drystone walls, improving access to the countryside and creating urban wildlife sanctuaries.

BTCV's Natural Break programme of conservation working holidays enables nearly 6,000 volunteers between the ages of 16 and 75 to spend a week in a spectacular setting, learning new and challenging conservation skills from the repair of drystone walls to the construction of steps and stiles. Around 600 holidays take place throughout the country all year round offering the perfect opportunity for individuals to make a practical contribution to the protection of the environment. Volunteers from overseas must be over 18 and speak good English. Prices start at around £32 a week including food, accommodation and all training.

A free brochure is available from the above address (2 x 2nd class stamps appreciated).

Cathedral Camps
16 Glebe Avenue, Flitwick, Bedfordshire MK45 1HS (tel 01525-716237).

Cathedral Camps invite young people to undertake maintenance and conservation work in Cathedrals and their environments, and major parish churches in Britain.

Volunteers join a group of 15-25 young people to work on these buildings of high architectural importance at different venues. Hours of work are normally 8.30am to 5.30pm four and a half days a week. Camps take place from July to September and each one lasts for a week.

A contribution of £40 is requested towards the cost of the camp, board and lodging. The minimum age is 16 and most volunteers are aged 17-25: the upper age is 35. Applicants from outside the British Isles are welcome to apply.

For further details and an application form, contact Mrs. Shelley Bent, Administrator, at the above address.

The Centre for Alternative Technology
Machynlleth, Powys SY20 9AZ (tel 01654-702400; fax 01654-702872).

Established in 1974, the Centre for Alternative Technology is an internationally renowned display and education centre promoting practical ideas and information on technologies which sustain rather than damage the environment.

The Centre runs a short-term volunteer programme, from March to August inclusive, for stays of one or two weeks. There is also a long-term volunteer programme for individuals to help in specific work departments for up to 6 months. Short term volunteers help with gardening, landscaping, site maintenance and preparation for courses. Long term jobs for volunteers include engineering, gardening, information and site maintenance.

Applicants for the long-term programme should have relevant experience. Applicants for either programme can be of any nationality; long-term volunteers must be eligible for British state benefit payments, or be able to fund themselves. Accommodation is basic, in youth-hostel style, shared with other volunteers; food, drinks, soap, toothpaste, shampoo, tampons etc. are all provided.

Applicants for the 60 short-term places and the 12 long-term places available annually should contact Rick Dance at the above address.

Conservation Volunteers Northern Ireland
159 Ravenhill Road, Belfast BT6 0BP; (tel 01232-645169; fax 01232-644409).
E-mail: cvni@btcv.org.uk

The Northern Ireland branch of the British Trust for Conservation Volunteers takes on some 7000 people a year for week long working holidays and a further 2000 on weekend projects. Most of the projects involve conservation/environmental work. However, some are combined with special interest activities such as caving or canoeing. Volunteers aged 16 to 80 are needed year round but the majority are needed during the summer. Groups of ten to twelve participants carry out various conservation tasks including drystone walling, building kissing gates, footpath construction and repair, pond building, tree planting and woodland management. Sites for the work may be urban or rural — from the Mourne Mountains to the sand dunes of Portrush to Belfast's urban wildlife reserve at Beersbridge Nature Walk. Costs around £35-£65 per week and £12 per weekend break which includes comfortable accommodation and meals.

Training programmes are offered all year round on a day, two/three day or six-day basis.

Derbyshire International Youth Camp

Derby Youth House, Mill Street, Derby DE1 1DY; (tel 01332-206027; fax 01332 345760).

Derbyshire International Youth Camp operates for four weeks during the summer holidays (July and August). About 250 volunteers aged 16 to 24 take part annually on projects involving conservation work, children's summer playschemes and community based projects. There is also a programme of freetime activities including swimming and sports, canoeing and rock climbing and music, art and cultural activities. UK volunteers stay for one week and volunteers from abroad stay two weeks. All accommodation and food is provided.

Applications should be sent anytime before June, the earlier the better and applicants will be informed as soon as possible if they have been accepted. In the case of UK applicants preference initially will be given to young people from the Derbyshire area who have not attended a camp before.

Dyfed Wildlife Trust

The Welsh Wildlife Centre, Cilgerran, Cardigan, Dyfed SA43 (tel 01239 621600).

Volunteers welcome all year round for a maximum stay of two weeks at this unique nature reserve. Varied habitats include: woodland, slate waste, reedbeds, meadow and estuarine. Up to four volunteers can be accommodated at a time in bunk house, self-catering style.

Applicants must be aged 16 up to any age. An interest in natural history would be an obvious advantage. Tasks would include footpath and general maintenance work, surveys etc. Contact the Centre Manager direct.

Farming and Wildlife Advisory Group (FWAG)

National Agriculture Centre, Stoneleigh, Kenilworth, Warks. CV8 2RX; (tel 01203 696699; fax 01203 696760).

FWAG is a registered national charity whose aim is to promote greater integration of landscape and nature conservation with modern farming through the provision of advice to landowners, farmers and other land managers.

FWAGS are organised on a county basis and there are 64 farm conservation advisors who are employed by the Farming and Wildlife Advisory Group but who are directly responsible to the county-based FWAGS.

There are both salaried and voluntary student placements. For a list of FWAGs nationally and further details contact Jane Hampson, Administration Officer, at the above address.

Festiniog Railway Company

Harbour Station, Porthmadog, Gwynedd, North Wales (tel 01766-512340; fax 01766-514576).

Hundreds of volunteers are needed throughout the year to help in the operation and maintenance of a 150-year-old narrow gauge railway between Porthmadog and Blaenau Ffestiniog. The work done by individual volunteers depends on their skills many of which are built up over a period of regular commitment to the railway which provides on-the-job training. The railway is divided into departments: trains and stations operation, workshops for the maintenance of rolling stock and engines, civil engineering dealing with track and structures, buildings, parks and gardens, sales and catering and signals and telecommunications. Thus jobs range from selling tickets and souvenirs to the 'elite' task of driving the engines.

Railway enthusiasts and non-enthusiasts of any nationality may apply provided they speak good English. The minimum age is 16 years. Limited self-catering accommodation is provided for regular volunteers, for which a small charge is made; food is extra. Camping space and a list of local accommodation is also available.

Further information may be obtained from the Volunteer Officer, Festiniog Railway Company.

Forest School Camps
110 Burbage Road, London SE24 9HD or 7 Park Crescent, London N3 2NL.

Forest School Camps, a national organisation for young people, aims to give young people the opportunity to live in a rural camp for one or two weeks, learning to live in a community and learning about their surroundings. The numbers on camps vary but can be up to 65 children and 20 leaders. Some camps are mobile travelling by cycle, foot and canoe but cater for smaller groups.

Volunteers are needed to act as leaders and should be over 18 and preferably have been on one of the camps themselves. There are also Forest School Conservation Camps where volunteers undertake voluntary work in different communities with work to be done. Volunteers will probably have to contribute towards the expenses of food and accommodation depending on the arrangements made with the work sponsors.

Lake District Art Gallery and Museum Trust
Abbott Hall Art Gallery, Kendal, Cumbria LA9 5AL; (tel 01539-722464; fax 01539-722494).

Volunteer research assistants, reception staff, events helpers and coffee shop staff are needed to work in the Kendal Museum, Abbot Hall Art Gallery and the Museum of Lakelank Life and Industry. Hours are from 9am to 5pm Monday to Friday and weekends in July, August and September. Accommodation may be available free of charge.

Volunteers should be undergraduates or graduates wishing to gain museum experience. All applicants must be available for interview.

Enquiries should be addressed to Mr Edward King at the above address.

The Monkey Sanctuary
Murrayton, Nr. Looe, Cornwall PL13 1NZ (tel 01503-262532).

The Monkey Sanctuary was established in 1964 near Looe in Cornwall. As the first place where the Woolly Monkey has survived and bred outside of its natural habitat in the South American rain forests, it serves as a conservation centre and is open to the public at Easter and during the summer months.

Most of the several dozen volunteers taken on every year are needed during these periods to help with various duties including preparing food for the monkeys, performing domestic tasks and attending to the public. During the winter volunteers are still needed mainly for maintenance work, gardening and cleaning the monkey enclosures. Volunteers stay for periods of two to four weeks depending on availability but only volunteers staying for long periods or making repeated visits would be asked to take on more responsible tasks with the monkeys.

Applicants must be fluent in English, in good health and over 18 years old. Board and lodging are provided.

For further information contact the Volunteer Co-ordinator at the above address sending a s.a.e.

National Trust, East Midlands Region
Stableyard, Clumber Park, Worksop, Nottinghamshire S80 3BE; (tel 01909-486411; fax 01909-486377).

East Midlands National Trust needs about 3000 volunteers annually to perform a variety of indoor and outdoor jobs. Hours of work vary, depending on the project available. The minimum period of service is normally four weeks and the minimum age is 16 years. No remuneration is provided by volunteers receive travel expenses and other benefits, such as free entry to National Trust properties. Accommodation is provided on week-long working holidays at a charge of £50 with full board.

The National Trust Volunteers Office: Working Holidays
33 Sheep Street, Cirencester, GL7 1ZP (tel 01285 651818;brochure line: 0891-517751; calls cost 39p per minute cheap rate/ 49p other times; fax 01285 657935).

The National Trust organises Conservation working holidays throughout England, Wales and Northern Ireland on two, three or seven day projects all year round. Projects vary in size from 12 to 20 volunteers and there are 450 to choose from. About 4,000 volunteers participate annually and can join join two or more projects. These include dry stone walling, woodland path construction, downland management, botanical surveys, building construction and archaeology. Prices average about £42-£50 a week including accommodation and food. The minimum age for participants is 17 years or for overseas visitors 18 years. Volunteers must pay their own travel expenses. Accommodation is provided but volunteers must bring their own sleeping bags, suitable footwear and water-proofs. Individuals and pairs may apply. No experience is needed as tuition will be given.

Application forms and further details can be obtained from Sue Green at the above address. All requests should be accompanied by a 50p stamp (or 5 international reply coupons, if applicable). Early application is advisable.

There are also possibilities of longer-term volunteering (six months or longer) for unemployed people which include on-the-job training. Long-term volunteers ar helping in many regions with wardening and countryside conservation work, archaeological research, interpretation of sites for educational purposes, custodial duties and indoor conservation. Details of longer-term vacancies can be obtained by sending a stamped addressed envelope to Maggie Burton, Co-ordinator, Long-Term Volunteers, at the above address.

The National Trust (Northern Ireland Region)
Northern Ireland Regional Office, Rowallane House, Saintfield, Ballynahinch, Co. Down, Northern Ireland BT24 7LH (tel 01238-510721; fax 01238-511242).

The National Trust in Northern Ireland offers hundreds of volunteers per year many opportunities for voluntary work, mainly of a practical nature, at National Trust properties (houses, gardens and countryside) in the area. Short-term volunteers can participate in week-long residential camps in which activities for volunteers are centred around practical conservation including tasks such as path,pond or scrub clearance, general garden work and fencing. There is a limited range of other activities such as event management/stewarding and office work.

Volunteers must be over 16 years of age and in good health; the minimum age limit for those from overseas is 18 years. Most volunteers join the one week Acorn Camps in the summer; accommodation is provided. Those resident in the area work on a more regular basis. Travel expenses that occur on the job will be reimbursed, but volunteers must pay their own travel costs to the Camps.

General enquiries should be sent to William McNamara at the above address, while those interested in the Acorn Camps should contact Beryl Sims, The National Trust Working Holidays, P O Box 538 Melksham, Wiltshire SN12 8SU (tel 01225-790290).

National Trust for Scotland (Thistle Camps)
5 Charlotte Square, Edinburgh EH2 4DU (tel 0131-226 9470; fax 0131-243 9444).

The National Trust for Scotland, founded in 1931 is Scotland's leading conservation organisation. In its care are over 100 properties and 180,000 acres of some of the finest countryside in Scotland.

Thistle Camps are residential voluntary work projects organised by the Trust to help in the conservation and management of the properties in its care. Camps last one to three weeks and take place at locations all over Scotland, often in remote areas.

Work is always of a practical nature and can vary from upland footpath repair to drystane dyking and fencing to encourage woodland regeneration.

Applicants must be aged 16+, understand English and be reasonably fit. There is an administration charge of between £37 and £82 depending on the camp. Accommodation and food are provided.

Apply or telephone the above address for further details.

Pilgrim Adventure
120 Bromley Heath Road, Downend, Bristol, BS16 6JJ; (tel 0117-9586525).

Pilgrim Adventure is an ecumenical Christian organisation based in Bristol which organises 'pilgrim journeys' to the remoter parts of the UK (e.g. Iona); also Ireland. Each journey caters for an average of 20 pilgrims.

About half a dozen volunteers are needed to to assist the Pilgrim Adventure staff with: camp chores, guiding pilgrims, arranging worship and catering. Minibus drivers are also required. Volunteers should enjoy hill walking, island hopping, arranging worship and the 'pilgrimage experience'. The period of service is one to three months in summer. A small pocket money allowance is provided and accommodation is free. *Shoreline — Journal of Pilgrim Adventure* is produced twice a year and costs £2.50 per year including postage.

For further details, please contact David Gleed, Chair, at the above address.

Royal Society for the Protection of Birds (RSPB)
The Lodge, Sandy, Bedfordshire SG19 2DL (tel 01767-680551).

Volunteers are needed to take part in the RSPB's Voluntary Wardening Scheme which operates on 25 of their nature reserves throughout England, Scotland and

Wales. Duties vary but may include basic management such as building paths, digging ditches, or dealing with visitors, as well as bird monitoring.

The scheme operates throughout the year, and volunteers aged 16 years or over and in good general health are welcome to take part. An interest in natural history is desirable. Accommodation is provided free but volunteers are responsible for their own travelling expenses and food during their stay. The minimum stay is one week and the maximum is a month.

Further information and application forms may be obtained from the Residential Voluntary Wardening Scheme at the above address.

The Scottish Conservation Projects Trust

Balallan House, 24 Allan Park, Stirling, FK8 2QG (tel 01786-465359).

The Scottish Conservation Projects Trust was founded specifically to support and promote practical outdoor conservation in Scotland. Conservation tasks include the management of nature reserves and other places of wildlife interest, the improvement of public amenities and access to the countryside, the environmental renewal of Scottish towns and cities and educating the public to appreciate Scotland's natural heritage.

Around 8,000 volunteers are needed annually to help with all aspects of practical outdoor conservation work on residential and non-residential projects, fund-raising and publicity. Training in tree-planting, dry-stone dyking, fencing and habitat management is given. Long term volunteers are recruited for several months while residential projects normally run for seven to 14 days. Most volunteers are needed between March and October but some projects are undertaken during winter.

A working knowledge of English is desirable. The minimum age of volunteers accepted is 16 years and volunteers must be aware that some tasks are physically demanding. Accommodation and food are provided at a cost of £4.00 per night.

Those interested should apply to the Programmes Administrator at the above address.

Strathspey Railway Co Ltd

Aviemore (Speyside) Station, Dalfaler Road, Aviemore PH22 1PY; (tel 01479-810725; fax 01479-811022).

Volunteers are needed to help run a small private railway in Scotland. Tasks include guard, ticket inspector, booking clerk, and also railway maintenance (including track, locomotives and rolling stock). No pay is given but free, very basic accommodation in a sleeping car at Boat of Garter, a hostel for members who work at Aviemore is provided for £2 a night. The minimum age for volunteers is 16 and training is given on the job. A reasonable degree of fitness is required for some jobs.

Applications to L M Grant, Commercial Manager at the above address.

St George's Island Craft Centre

Looe, Cornwall PL13 2AB; (tel 01836-522919).

The private island of St George's or Looe lies a mile off the Cornish Coast and comprises $22\frac{1}{2}$ acres and is one mile in circumference and rises to 150 feet at its highest point. The present owners have opened the island to day visitors in a non-profit project in which the landing fees and income generated are poured back into the island's conservation and to provide uncommercialised visitor facilities. The island's conservation projects are encourage by the National Trust and the British Trust for Conservation Volunteers in the form of voluntary working holidays which last one or two weeks from April to October.

Volunteers live in shared, self-catering cottages for which there is a charge of £15 per person per week to cover calor gas and electricity. Volunteers carry out tasks according to their enthusiasms and skills: gardening, general DIY, decorating, wood and track clearing, fencing, log cutting, general conservation and arts and crafts. Volunteers will also be required to meet and assist day visitors.

As post is only delivered to and collected from the island once a week please allow at least two to three weeks for a reply to enquiries.

Waterway Recovery Group
114 Regent's Park Road, London NW1 8UQ; (tel 0171-586 2510; fax 0171-722 7213).

Waterway Recovery Group was formed in 1970 to formalise voluntary restoration work by enthusiasts that had been carried out since the 1960s. The aim of the group is to be a coordinating force, not centred on any individual project, but backing up and assisting local restoration groups with publicity, the loan of tools and plant, technical advice, visiting work parties and Canal Camps.

Canal Camps can be joined by anyone aged 17 to 20 who has a week to spare helping to restore one of Britain's derelict canals. Jobs on the camps can include restoring industrial archaeology, demolishing old brickwork, bricklaying and pouring concrete, driving a dumper truck, clearing silt, helping to run a waterways festival, cooking for other volunteers, clearing vegetation and trees. The working day is roughly 9am to 5pm and volunteers pay about £35 towards the cost of food and basic accommodation. Volunteers also need to bring their own spending money for social activities. Camps take place almost year round from February to December.

Contact the above address for details and an application form.

Welshpool & Llanfair Railway
The Station, Pool Road, Llanfair, Caereinon, Welshpool, Powys SY21 OSF; (tel 01938-810441); fax 01938-810861).

The Welshpool and Llanfair Railway is a narrow gauge steam operated railway which needs volunteer maintenance staff at any time of time for varied duties from engine operation through trackwork to administration and the clearing of vegetation. The railway has a volunteer taskforce of about 200, about 25 of whom are active at a time. No pocket money is paid but accommodation is available at cheap rates. Volunteers should be aged 16+, fit and enthusiastic. Membership of the Welshpool & Llanfair Railway Preservation Society costs £12.50 per year.

Enquiries to David Moseley, at the above address.

Wildfowl and Wetlands Trust (W&WT)
Slimbridge, Gloucester GL2 7BT; (tel 01453-890333; fax 01453-890827).

The Wildfowl and Wetlands Trust is a registered charity whose aim is to preserve and protect wetlands around the UK through programmes of scientific study, education and the operation of eight visitor centres around the UK. Volunteers are needed at the visitor centres to help with a variety of practical conservation tasks including grounds maintenance (planting, weeding, trimming etc) and also as visitor centre staff working on the information desk, helping with school parties, envelope stuffing. There is also the opportunity to learn a lot about the unique environments of the wetlands themselves.

The regional centres are in Cambridgeshire, Co Down, Dumfriesshire, Dyfed, Lancashire, Tyne and Wear and West Sussex. Contact the National Centre at the above address in the first instance for further details.

Religious Projects

Amitabha Buddhist Centre
St Audries House, West Quantoxhead, nr Taunton TA4 4DU (tel 01984-633200; fax 01984-633807).

The Amitabha Buddhist Centre is a Buddhist community of ordained monks and nuns, and lay people living together in a large mansion set in 60 acres of parkland amongst the beautiful surroundings of the Quantock Hills and Somerset coast. Volunteers are welcome to go there on working holidays all year round. Stays of one to four weeks are usual but longer stays are possible in some circumstances. Volunteers help with gardening, cooking, sewing, clerical work, painting and decorating, carpentry, general building and maintenance work. Accommodation and food are provided but volunteers are asked to bring their own sleeping bag.

Working holidays provide an ideal opportunity to sample life in a Buddhist community and volunteers can attend teachings and meditations in their free time if they wish.

Careforce
c/o Scripture Union, 577 Kingston Road, London SW20 8SA; (tel 0181-543 8671).

Careforce is a scheme set up by four Evangelical Christian bodies in which young Christians are placed in inner-city churches and organisations caring for the needy throughout the UK and the Irish Republic. Around 130 volunteers are needed annually to undertake practical work such as cooking, cleaning, administration, visiting, youth and community work, etc., and when suitable assume varying degrees of responsibility and leadership in spiritual work. Placements begin in September and last for ten to twelve months.

Volunteers must be committed Christians with an above average degree of maturity, aged 18 to 25 years old and in good health. Board, lodging and a small weekly allowance are provided and pastoral and work support are provided within each placement and there is additional support from the Careforce staff.

Those interested should apply to the Organising Secretary at the above address. For practical reasons careforce is unable to accept applications from abroad.

The Corrymeela Community
Ballycastle, Co. Antrim, BT54 6QU, Northern Ireland (tel 012657-62626; fax 012657-62770).

Corrymeela is an ecumenical Christian community working for reconciliation in Northern Ireland and the world at large. It runs an administrative centre in Belfast and a residential centre at Ballycastle on the North Antrim coast where people from all backgrounds can come together and meet in an easy relaxed atmosphere.

Opportunities exist at the Ballycastle centre for volunteer helpers on both a long and short term basis. The commitment of the long term volunteers is generally for 12 months commencing in September of each year, and the volunteers receive their room and board plus a small weekly allowance. During the months of July and August, a number of additional volunteers are welcomed for periods of one to two weeks, to assist with family groups and projects or as summer staff helpers, assisting with recreation, arts and crafts, cooking, laundry etc. The lower age limit for all volunteers is 18 years.

Those interested in long term volunteer work should contact the Volunteer Co-ordinator at the above address. A leaflet, *Summer Opportunities*, which details all possible involvement during July and August is published in December of each year and those interested should apply to the above address. In England, further information about Corrymeela is available from the Corrymeela Link, P.O.Box 118, Reading, Berks. RG1 ISL.

The Grail

125 Waxwell Lane, Pinner, Middlesex HA5 3ER (tel 0181-866 2195/0505; fax 0181-866 1408).

The Grail Centre in North London hosts courses, conferences and workshops. Subjects range across prayer, spirituality, arts and ecology and complementary therapies. Grail Volunteers help the resident community of women with domestic tasks, cooking, gardening, office duties and all aspects of hospitality. No special qualifications are required, but skills are appreciated.

Applicants should be 20+, in good health and with a functional grasp of English. It is also important that they can withstand a communal lifestyle and the constant pressure of visitors.

The minimum stay is three months though an occasional exception is made for students on a limited summer vacation. Board, lodging and pocket money (£16 per week) are provided. Applicants should apply five to six months ahead of their intended date of arrival. Religious observance is not a requirement.

Apply by letter to the Volunteer Coordinator, include a photo and CV (resumé). UK applicants should enclose a S.A.E. and overseas ones an international reply coupon. The Grail is not a vast organisation and accepts only about 15/20 volunteers annually.

Hothorpe Hall

Theddingworth, Lutterworth, Leicestershire LE17 6QX (tel 01858-880257).

Hothorpe Hall is a Christian conference and retreat centre which needs volunteers throughout the year to look after its guests as well as maintain its facilities. The wide range of jobs includes kitchen work, housekeeping, maintenance, and gardening.

Volunteers should have a firmly rooted commitment to the Christian faith, although participants are accepted from many different denominational backgrounds. Participation in community worship, devotions and discussions will be expected. Applicants must be over 18 years and in good health. The centre endeavours to create an international mixture among its staff, although all must conform to British immigration regulations and a good standard of English is necessary.

Applications and information may be obtained by writing to the Secretary at the above address.

Madhyamaka Centre
Kilnwick Percy Hall, Pocklington, York Y04 2UF.

The Centre, established in 1979 is a residential Buddhist Centre with about 50 residents and room for many visitors. It is situated in an elegant Georgian mansion surrounded by spacious and peaceful grounds. As well as running evening classes, day courses and retreats the Centre welcomes volunteers who would like to come and work 35 hours a week in exchange for free dormitory accommodation and vegetarian food. On weekends and evenings, volunteers are free to exlore the area and attend teachings and meditations if they wish.

The kind of work is generally building, decorating, gardening and sewing though it varies from week to week. Most volunteers stay one week and find the combination of being away from the daily rush of life amongst friendly people and stimulating conversation very relaxing. Special skills are not necessary.

Pilgrim Adventure
120 Bromley Heath Road, Downend, Bristol BS16 6JJ; (tel 0117-958 6525).

Pilgrim Adventures organises an annual programme of Pilgrim Journeys within the UK and Ireland. Duties include assisting with worship and camp chores. Volunteers receive full board, lodging and travel. The period of work is from early May to mid-October. Each pilgrim journey lasts between five and 15 days, with usually, two or three days off between trips.

Applicants must be aged at least 18, with an interest in outdoor activities. Overseas applicants welcome. Applications to the above address.

Quaker International Social Projects (QISP)
Friends House, Euston Road, London NW1 2BJ; (tel 0171-387 3601).

The aims of QISP are to promote co-operation and international understanding between people and to support communities.

Volunteer Opportunities in the UK: QISP organises 25-30 volunteer projects lasting two to four weeks in Britain and Northern Ireland. They take place in spring and summer. Typical projects include playschemes, work with adults or children who have mental or physical disabilities, manual projects like decorating shelters for the homeless, youth work, community arts projects and more.

A volunteer team comprises eight to 15 people coming from all walks of life and nationalities. The age minimum for volunteers is 18 years (16 for some youth projects). Volunteers with disabilities are welcome to apply. No special skills or qualifications are needed but motivation, enthusiasm and commitment to living and working with a group are.

Simple food and accommodation are provided but volunteers pay a registration fee of £17+ depending on means.

Applications (from UK only) require a large SAE and a covering letter giving age and previous volunteer experience. To go on the QISP mailing list send a £5 cheque or postal order to 'Britain Yearly Meeting' at the above address.

Applicants outside the UK should apply through an organisation in their own country.

Tara Buddhist Centre
Ashe Hall, Ash Lane, Etwall, Derbyshire DE65 6HT (tel 01283-732338; fax 01283-733416). E-mail: tara@rmplc.co.uk

Tara Centre is a residential meditation centre situated in a large Jacobean mansion in 38 acres of wooded grounds. The Centre operates a 'working holiday' scheme whereby volunteers can help with all aspects of the centre's activities in exchange for full board and accommodation and any classes they wish to attend. As many as a 100 such volunteers are taken on annually. The work may include any of the following: DIY, joinery, building work, gardening, sewing, cooking, cleaning, plumbing, electrics, graphic display work and decorating. The usual period of stay is one week though people coming from abroad can stay longer. A basic knowledge of English is essential.

Time for God
2 Chester House, Pages Lane, London. N10 1PR (tel 0181-883 1504; fax 0181-365 2471). E-mail 100675.2702.compuserve.com

This is a scheme which provides an opportunity for the applicant to serve between nine months and one year in a church-based placement. The scheme is sponsored by the Methodist, Anglican, Baptist, Catholic, Congregational, and United Reformed Churches, the National Council of YMCA's and the Church Army.

Every year some 150 volunteers are needed to care for children, the elderly, the homeless or the disabled in organisations such as the National Children's Home, YMCA, or to help with work of all kinds in local churches or community centres. Full board and lodging is provided during the placement. Volunteers receive weekly pocket money, and travel expenses are paid for the journey to the placement for an exploratory visit and on start of service. Volunteers are entitled to a week's holiday, with pocket money and fares home, for each three months of service (volunteers from overseas should be given fares for a reasonable journey in Britain). Christian applicants of any nationality or denomination are welcomed, provided that they speak fluent English and are between 17 and 25 (or between 18 and 25 for overseas applicants).

Those interested should write to the above address for more information.

Social and Community Schemes

Ashram Community Service Project
23-25 Crantham Road, Sparkbrook, Birmingham B11 1LU (tel 0121 773-7061; fax 0121 766-7503).

There are four projects based at the above address in the multi-racial and inner city area of Sparkbrook which seek to respond to poverty, unemployment and racism in the district. The Community Service Project is an employment project, developing small business and self-employment initiatives. Ashram Acres is a land reclamation project, using the farming skills of local people. Ashram Volunteers Project is specifically for integrating volunteers from other sections of the projects and also developing other activities. Volunteers have the chance to live as members of a radical Christian community and so share in the social life and household tasks. Ashram Community House is deeply involved in the life of the neighbourhood, and gives volunteers a fantastic opportunity to meet and learn from people of different cultures. The local population is predominantly Muslim/Pakistani in origin.

About 100 volunteers are involved in the Project, participating mainly in back-up work; cleaning, gardening, building, animal husbandry, cooking and decorating. The range of activities grows according to the length of the volunteer's stay. A volunteer might eventually take responsibility for one particular area, organize social events and become involved in publicity. Applicants of all nationalities are welcome but some degree of commitment and a basic level of maturity are essential. No particular skill is essential, but the following are particularly welcomed; horticulture, animal care, driving, office skills, Asian languages. The minimum age limit is 20 years. Disabled people are welcome, but the building is not suitable for wheelchairs.

The minimum length of time for which volunteers are recruited is two weeks but volunteers come for varying lengths of time — from one month to over a year. Volunteers are expected to contribute what they can towards expenses and the amount due is worked out according to the financial situation of each volunteer. Accommodation is provided in either Ashram Community House or connected accommodation in Sparkbrook. Volunteers are required throughout the year.

Those interested can obtain further information from the above address.

Bondway Night Shelter
35-40 Bondway, PO Box 374, London SW8 1SJ.

Bondway provides emergency accommodation for 120 homeless people and operates a soup run for these forced to sleep out. 14 full-time volunteers assist a salaried staff group with practical work, administration and supervision of the shelter. Volunteers work throughout the week with shifts covering the full 24 hours. They must be prepared to stay for 6 months. In exchange they receive accommodation, travel expenses to the project and weekly allowance.

Applicants need to be available for interview and aged over 19. For more information contact the volunteer co-ordinator at the above address.

Camphill Village Trust
19 South Road, Stourbridge, West Midlands; (tel 01562-700350; 01384-372122).

One of the worldwide Camphill Villages that care for people with learning disabilities in a community setting. This takes the form of extended family households with work on the land, craft workshops and service industries. There are nine CVT communities in rural and urban areas of England and Scotland.

The Stourbridge community takes on 25 to 40 volunteers annually to help in the house communities, working in the workshop, farm and gardens, serving in the cafeteria/catering/food processing and working alongside people with special needs. Volunteers should be aged 17+. The work period is summer (June to September) but there are also positions for a year. The Community provides board, lodging and pocket money. A useful publication *Camphill Villages* is available from Botton Bookshop, Danby, Whitby, N Yorks YO21 2NH for £3.99 plus 50p postage and packing.

Community Service Volunteers
237 Pentonville Road, London N1 9NJ (tel 0171-278 6601; fax 0171-837 9621).
E-mail 100631.1720@compuserve.com
Freephone volunteer recruitment line: 0800 374 991

CSV offers anyone aged 16-35 the chance to do something different and challenging which benefits people in need. All volunteers work full-time and away from home for between four months and a year. CSV offers more 'gap year' volunteer opportunities than any other UK agency.

Every year 3,000 volunteers work throughout the UK with elderly or homeless people, people living with disabilities and other young people. They work alongside professional staff in hostels, day centres, hospitals and in the community. Volunteers work hard, have fun and gain valuable experience and life skills. Placements range from working on an organic farm for adults with learning difficulties in rural Wales, to working on the streets of Glasgow with homeless young people.

Volunteers are provided with accommodation, food, a weekly allowance and supervision. No specific skills are required, just energy, enthusiasm and a willingness to give. Applications are welcome throughout the year. No application is rejected.

Edinburgh Cyrenian Trust
20 Broughton Place, Edinburgh EH1 3RX (tel 0131-556 4971).

The Edinburgh Cyrenian Trust runs two communities for single, homeless men and women aged 18 to 30 years old; one in Edinburgh and another on a smallholding outside Edinburgh. Around 22 volunteers are needed each year to live with the residents and befriend them. Other tasks include performing various housekeeping and book-keeping tasks. Placements are for 6 months at a time.

Volunteers must be fluent in English, 18 to 30 years old, energetic and have initiative. Applicants with a full driving licence are preferred. Travel expenses to attend an interview are paid. Successful applicants receive one-way travel to the project, accommodation, pocket money and holiday and termination grants.

Applicants should apply to Debbie Peasgood at the above address.

Great Georges Community Cultural Project
Great George Street, Liverpool L1 5EW (tel 0151-709 5109; fax/minicom 0151-709 4822).

The Project is a centre for experimental work in the arts, sports, games and education housed in the centre of Liverpool. The Centre, or the 'Blackie' as it has become known, has gained an important position in the life of the city, as it provides opportunities for local people which would otherwise not exist. Among these are work shops for photography, cooking, dance, music, film, pool, reading, writing, drawing and typing. In addition, the centre is a venue for entertainment, which has recently included original poetry, performance art, contemporary music, modern dance, and the screening of films.

At any one time there are both full time and short term volunteers on the staff. Ideally, one month is the minimum period, although there are exceptions, e.g. some volunteers join the Project specifically to work on a play scheme which last two weeks. If a volunteer wishes to stay longer than a month, this is a matter of mutual discussion and agreement between the volunteer and senior staff at the Blackie at the end of the first four weeks.

The general work of the scheme is shared as equally as possible, with everyone being prepared to do some administration, cook, sweep the floor, play with kids, talk to visitors as well as supervise the activities.

A bed and food are provided for £17.50 per week. The minimum period of voluntary work is four weeks. Although skills in arts and crafts are useful, more important are stamina and a sense of humour. Volunteers must also bring their own sleeping bag.

Request for further information should be made to the Duty Officer at the above address, enlosing a stamped addressed envelope. Overseas applicants are welcome provided they have some background in English and are willing to advance their communication level while working.

Homes for Homeless People
6 Union Street, Luton, Beds LU1 3AN (tel 01582-481426).

Homes for Homeless People, (formerly National Cyrenians) is a national federation of local housing groups running projects for single homeless people throughout the UK. Most projects are long or short-term houses but there are some emergency accommodation centres and day centres as well. The aim of the organisation is to treat the homeless as individuals with individual problems.

The local groups are legally and financially autonomous. They run over 200 projects staffed by approximately 100 temporary project workers (volunteers) and 80 permanent salaried workers.

These groups are constantly needing new workers to help in the running and day-to-day life of their projects. No experience or qualifications are needed. The work is demanding (both physically and emotionally), and involves the ability to get on with people in residential situations and often take responsibility. It is particularly relevant and rewarding to those who wish to gain experience for socal or community work courses or future work. Workers receive board and lodging, plus pocket money. There is a minimum six months commitment.

If interested contact TPW Recruitment at the above address.

Iona Community
Iona Abbey, Isle of Iona, Argyll, Scotland (tel 01681-700404; fax 01681 700603).

The Iona Community, an ecumenical Christian community, invites volunteers aged 18+ to come for six to eighteen weeks to share in a ministry of welcome and hospitality. Members of the community are scattered throughout the world. Volunteers are not members but come to the historic island of Iona to share alongside guests in a weekly programme of work, worship and recreation.

The food is mainly vegetarian (though all diets are catered for) and meal times are important times of contact with guests. Volunteers work as kitchen and housekeeping assistants; in the coffee shop, and Abbey Bookshop; and as craft workers and guides. They receive pocket money of £17 weekly and return travel expenses within the UK. Accommodation is shared with two or three others.

Applications are received throughout the year and invitations for voluntary places are sent out in January for the season, which runs from March to November. Contact the Staff Coordinator for further information.

Lothlorien (Rokpa Trust)
Corsock, Castle Douglas, Kircudbrightshire DG7 3DR; (tel 01644-440602).

Lothlorien is a supportive community for people with mental health problems which was founded in 1978. The guiding principles of the community are hospitality, care and respect for the person, and a belief that the potential of the individual can be encouraged through a communal life in which al have a contribution to make. It consists of a large log house with 14 bedrooms and communal living areas. It is set in an isolated rural area, with 17 acres of grounds which include organic vegetable gardens, woodland and outbuildings.

Volunteers at Lothlorien have an opportunity for personal growth and is especially relevant to those considering a career in the caring professions. There are four live-in volunteers who play a key role in creating a warm, accepting atmosphere through which everyone in the community feels valued.

On a practical level, volunteers along with all community members participate in domestic tasks such as cooking and cleaning, as well as working in the vegetable gardens and maintenance work on the house and in the grounds. It is not essential that volunteers have any specialist skills.

There are vacancies on a regular basis. A minimum commitment of six months is necessary. The minimum age is 21. Volunteers get free board and accommodation and pocket money of £25 weekly. Volunteers can only be considered if they are eligible for housing benefit.

Anyone interested should contact the Project Manager, at the above address.

The Ockenden Venture
Constitution Hill, Woking, Surrey GU22 7UU (tel 01483-772012; fax 01483-750774).

About a dozen volunteers are recruited to care for a group of Vietnamese and Cambodian refugees (also some British), with learning difficulties and/or a physical disability, giving volunteers the opportunity, through working as part of a team and using initiative, to learn about others and themselves in all types of situation.

Volunteers are normally recruited for a year but shorter term vacancies do occasionally occur. Volunteers receive board and lodging and £25 a week pocket money.

Further details are available from the Personnel Officer at the above address.

The Simon Community
PO Box 1187, London NW5 4HW (tel 0171-485 6639).

The Simon Community is a small registered charity working and living with homeless people. We aim to support primarily long-term rough sleepers and others for whom no provision exists, with a philosophy of acceptance and tolerance. The Community operates an emergency night shelter and three residential houses as well as participating in extensive outreach work in the city of London. Workers and residents share in the decision-making and running of the community.

Volunteers are required throughout the year and should be 19+, speak fluent English and be looking to stay for six months or more, though shorter periods are sometimes acceptable. Workers live in the project to which they are assigned; they receive full board and accommodation and £25 weekly pocket money. Every three months workers get two weeks' leave and a substantial amount of pocket money to ensure a good break. For long term workers there is a pattern of external training and internal training and support is provided for everyone throughout. Applicants attend a weekend following which their suitability as a worker is decided. Apply to the address above.

Work With the Sick and Disabled

Association Of Camphill Communities
Camphill Rudolf Steiner Schools, Murtle House, Bieldside, Aberdeen AB1 9EP.

This Association was set up in 1978 to bring together the many different interests and concerns of the 30 or so Camphill communities in the British Isles. These communities for handicapped children and adults or those with special needs are all based on anthroposophy as founded by Rudolf Steiner. Opportunities for living and working as volunteers within a Camphill community exist for longer and shorter periods. In general, one able bodied volunteer is needed for every two community members.

The Association can supply more information on individual member communities but applications to work as volunteers should be sent to the individual centres. The addresses of current member communities are given below.

Bolton Village, Danby, Whitby, North Yorks YO12 2NJ (tel 01287-60871).

Cherry Orchards Camphill Community, Canford Lane, Westbury-on-Trym, Bristol BS9 3PF (tel 0117-9503183).

The Croft, Highfield Road, Old Malton, North Yorks YO17 0EY (tel 01425-474291).

Camphill Devon Community, Hapstead Village, Buckfastleigh, South Devon TQ11 0JN (tel 01364-42631).

Delrow College and Rehabilitation Centre, Hillfield Lane, Aldenham, Watford, Herts. WD2 8DJ (tel 01923-856006).

Grange-Oaklands, Newnham-on-Severn, Gloucs. GL14 1HJ (tel 01594-516246).

Larchfield Community, Hemlington, Middlesborough, Cleveland TS8 9DY (tel 01642-593688).

Camphill Milton Keynes Community, 7 Sterling Close, Pennyland, Milton Keynes MK15 8AN (tel 01908-674856).

Mount School Community, Wadhurst, East Sussex TN5 6PT (tel 0189-288 2025).

Penine Camphill Community, Boyne Hill House, Chapelthorpe, Wakefield WF4 3JF (tel 01924-255281).

Shelling Community, Horton Road, Ashley, Ringwood, Hants. BH24 2EB (tel 01425-477488).

Camphill Houses, Heathfield Cottage, 32 Heath Street, Stourbridge, W Midlands DY8 1SB (tel 01384-372575).

William Morris Camphill Community, William Morris House, Eastington, Stonehouse, Gloucestershire GL10 3SH (tel 01453-824025).

Coleg Elidyr, Nangwyn, Rhandirmwyn, Llandovery, Dyfed SA20 0NL (tel 01550-760272).

Clanabogan Camphill Community, Omagh, Co. Tyrone, BT78 1TL (tel Omagh (01662-256100; fax 01662 256114).

Glencraig Community, Newry Road, Kilkeel, Co. Down BT34 4EX (tel 06937-62229).

Ballytobin Community, Callan, Co. Kilkenny (tel 056-25114).

Dunshane House, Brannickstown, Co. Kildare (tel 045-83628.

Duffcarrig House, Gorey, Co. Wexford (tel 055-25116).

Beannachar, Banchory-Devenick, Aberdeen AB1 5YL (tel 01224-868605).

Camphill Blair, Drummond, Blair Drummond House, By Stirling FK9 4UT (tel 01876-841341).

Corbenic College, Drumour Lodge, Torchry, Nr. Dunkeld, Perthshire PH8 0BY (tel 013505-206).

Loch Arthur Village Community, Beeswing, Dumfries DG2 9JQ (tel 01387-76224).

Newton De Village, Bielside, Aberdeen AB1 9DX (tel 01224-868701).

Ochil Tower, Auchterade, Perthshire PH3 1AD (tel 01764 662416).

Camphill Rudolf Steiner Schools, Murtle, Bieldside, Aberdeen AB1 9EP (tel 01224-867935; fax 01224-868420).

Simeon Care Communities, Cairnlee Estate, Bielside, Aberdeen AB1 9BN.
Templehill Community, Glenfarquhar Lodge, Auchilblae, Kincardine AB3 1UJ (tel 015612-230).

Beannachar
Beannachar, Banchory-Devenick, Aberdeen AB1 5YL (tel 01224-869138).

Every year the Beannachar Community takes on between 6 and 10 volunteers to live and work with young adults with special needs. Work is to be done in the kitchen, laundry, garden and on the farm; tasks also include making herbal medicines and candles and weaving. Volunteers are also expected to participate in evening and weekend leisure activities. Volunteers need not be British, but they must speak fluent English and make a minimum commitment of six months. Board and lodging will be provided, plus pocket money of £25.

Applications may be sent to Elisabeth Phethean, at the above address.

CARE-Cottage and Rural Enterprises Ltd.
9 Weir Road, Kibworth, Leicester LE8 OLQ (tel 0116-2793225; fax 0116 279 6384).

CARE provides care for adults with learning disabilities in communities in Devon, Kent, Lancashire, Leicestershire, Shrophshire, Northumberland, Sussex and Wiltshire.

Volunteers, aged 18 or over, live and work alongside residents and are expected to stay for a minimum of four weeks. Applicants must speak English and be personally interviewed at the Community they are assigned to. Accommodation is provided in single bedsits and meals are taken with the residents. Volunteers receive £25 per week pocket money and are expected to work up to 40 hours a week on a rota basis.

Those interested should apply to the Regional Director at the above address.

Churchtown Outdoor Adventure
Churchtown Farm, Lanlivery, Bodmin, Cornwall PL30 5BT (tel 01208-872148).

Churchtown Farm provides outdoor, environmental and adventurous training courses accessible to everyone, regardless of degree of special need. As well as the more traditional courses, in ecology and outdoor pursuits, a new development is the provision of personal development programmes which concentrate on personal growth, encouraging a positive image of self and promoting self-confidence. In-service courses for teachers and carers can be organized and opportunities exist for team building and development courses, suitable for all staff groups. The Centre is attractively converted and well equipped with an indoor swimming pool, farm, nature reserve and attractive grounds. Sailing and canoeing takes place on the nearby River Fowey and the Centre is only five miles from the coast. Help is available with care requirements and a qualified nurse is on call on site throughout the night.

Ten volunteers are needed at a time to support the professional staff. Accommodation is in a shared house adjacent to the main Centre. Applications are invited from anyone who feels they have an empathy with people with special needs. Whilst a background in environmental, outdoor or medical areas would be an advantage, volunteers are welcome regardless of academic qualifications. Currently an allowance of £20 per week is payable and providing volunteers stay for longer than three weeks.

Those interested should apply to the Head of Care at the above address.

The CRYPT Foundation
Forum, Stirling Road, Chichester, West Sussex PO19 2EN (tel 01243-786064).

CRYPT (Creative Young People Together) provides small group homes in the UK for young people with disabilities who wish to study any of the creative arts. A CRYPT Community Volunteer is responsible, with other CCVs, for the safety and the care of students within the project. Applicants of all nationalities are accepted, but they must be able to speak English.

Volunteers must be aged between 18 and 30. The students are often profoundly disabled and need to be lifted etc. A timetable is arranged and will generally involve twenty-four hours on duty, followed by 24 hours off duty, with alternative weekends free. Pocket money, accommodation and living allowances are all provided. Volunteers stay for 4-6 months, and are required all the year round.

Applications from inside Britain should be sent to Community Service Volunteers; others should contact the above address.

Cura Domi-Care at Home
8 North Street, Guildford, Surrey GU1 4AF; tel 01483-302275; fax 01483-304302.

Cura Domi is an organisation that arranges home care for the elderly nationwide. Assignments last two to three weeks or for much longer indefinite periods (i.e. live-in positions). Volunteers receive expenses or full pay depending on the service carried out. No particular skills or qualifications are needed but a driving licence can be useful in some cases. Volunteers from abroad must speak English. Work permits are required for non EU nationals.

Applications at any time to the above address.

The Disaway Trust
2 Charles Road, Merton Park, London SW19 3BD (tel 0181 543-3431).

The Disaway Trust is a charity which provides group holidays for physically disabled people. The organisation is run by a Committee of volunteers and is entirely supported by voluntary help and contributions. Disaway relies on voluntary help to achieve its objective of providing disabled people with holidays. Each helper is asked to look after the needs of one holidaymaker during the holiday. This will include helping with, amongst other things, needs like washing, feeding, dressing and helping in the bathroom. Most holidays last for about a week. Inexperienced helpers will be allocated a holidaymaker needing minimal care and every effort is made to match helpers and holidaymakers with similar interests. Helpers have to be reasonably fit and strong, and every applicant is required to complete a medical form; acceptance is at the discretion of the Medical Officer. Minimum age limit for volunteers is 18 years.

Helpers are asked to pay half towards the cost of the holiday including a deposit of £50-£100 to be submitted with the application form. Costs are given with holiday details. Many people enjoy this type of holiday and previous helpers will vouch for their enjoyment of a fulfilling vacation in a friendly atmosphere. There is no limit to the number of helpers needed.

For an application form, please write to the above address.

Family Investment Ltd
Greenbanks, Greenhills, Barham, Canterbury, Kent CT4 6LE; (tel 01227-831731).

Family Investment provides support for disabled adults in their daily living. Volunteers are needed as care/support workers throughout the summer months to act as escorts on outings and to take part on an instructional basis in their work placements. Duty hours are from 7.30am to 10.30pm but shifts no longer than 8 hours. Volunteers have all meals provided as well as out of pocket expenses when undertaking duties. Applicants should be aged 18+ and motivated with a sense of humour and a realistic attitude.

Contact Mrs. Stapley, Resident Housemother at the above address.

Friends for Young Deaf People
East Court Mansion Council Offices, College Lane, East Grinstead, West Sussex RH19 3LT; (tel 01342 323444; fax 01342-410232).

FYD is dedicated to helping the young deaf and hard of hearing though its annual programme of projects and courses. The aim is to further the personal development of young deaf people and to integrate them with hearing young people. Many of the projects involve outdoor activities including conservation and sailing. Volunteers are always needed to help the organisation with its work.

Help the Handicapped Holiday Fund (3H Fund)
147a Camden Road, Tunbridge Wells, Kent TN1 2RA; (tel 01892-547474; fax 01892-524703).

This charity group holidays for physically disabled children and adults. Recent holidays have been to Disneyworld, Florida, Jersey, Ibiza, Isle of Wight, Blackpool and Cornwall. Each year around 100 volunteers are required. Volunteers may apply to assist with one or more holidays.

The success of the holidays depends on a full complement of volunteers. Half board hotel accommodation is provided and in return the helper looks after the guest in his/her care. School leavers, students and anyone between the ages of 18 and 60 with a strong back and willing to give up a week of their time can really enjoy themselves in a happy and informal atmosphere whilst undertaking worthwhile voluntary work. Candidates for the Duke of Edinburgh Gold Award are particularly welcome.

The holidays will embrace a wide cross-section of disabilities many requiring considerable personal help particularly dressing, toileting, eating and the pushing of wheelchairs. In consequence the work can prove particularly physically and mentally demanding and requires great patience and a good sense of responsability but humour as well. Please note new helpers will not be given 'high care' guests to look after.

Those interested should apply to Peggie King, Holiday Organiser, at the above address.

Hertfordshire Association for the Disabled
The Woodside Centre, The Commons, Welwyn Garden City, Herts AL7 4DD; (tel 01707-324581; fax 01707-371297).

For over 30 years the HAD has aimed to meet the needs of the disabled in Hertfordshire with services including financial support, counselling, equipment exhibitions and hire and driving instruction in a fully adapted car. The Association also has its own hotel at Clacton-on-Sea.

About 100 volunteers are needed annually to assist disabled people on holiday for two-week periods from March to November. Some UK travel expenses may be paid. Free return coach travel is provided to and from the Woodside Centre to Clacton. Volunteers also receive free board and lodging. Further details (an Information Pack and Holiday Fact Sheets 1-10 can be obtained by sending a 75p postage stamp to the above address. Ages 18-70 years.

Holiday Care Service
2nd Floor, Imperial Buildings, Victoria Road, Horley, Surrey RH6 7PZ; (tel 01293-774535; fax 01293 784647).

Holiday Care Service is a national charity that advises the elderly, disabled, single parents those on low income or anyone who has special needs or problems in finding a suitable holiday. It also runs 'Tourism for All' a scheme for low-cost holidays and runs a booking service for accessible accommodation in the UK. There is always a need for volunteer helpers to accompany clients on holidays etc. Information about volunteering can be obtained from the above address.

Holidays for the Disabled
Flat 4, 62 Stuart Park, Edinburgh EH12 8YE; (tel 0131-339 8866).

Volunteers are recruited annually to help with holidays for the. Holidays for the Disabled provides a large scale annual holiday for all ages of physically handicapped people. The organisation runs a wide range of interesting holidays in the UK and abroad. In addition to holidays at fixed locations there are boating and camping trips. Activities on the holidays include discotheques, swimming, horse riding, wheelchair sports, barbecues and banquets.

No special qualifications are needed and all nationalities are recruited. The age range is 18 — 35 years, and the length of time for which helpers are needed is usually one week. Helpers are asked to pay a contribution towards 40% of the total cost of holidays abroad and 25% on holidays in the Uk.

Those interested should apply to the organisation at the above address.

Horticultural Therapy: Land Use Volunteers
Goulds Ground, Vallis Way, Frome, Somerset BA11 3DW (tel 01373-464782).

Horticultural Therapy is a charity which encourages the use of horticulture and gardening as a therapy for people with special needs of all ages. Its volunteer scheme, Land Use Volunteers, places volunteers with a wide variety of horticultural therapy projects in Britain run by other organisations. The project provides the volunteer with free board and accommodation, and a minimum of £25 per week pocket money. Once placed HT provided on going support, and a number of other benefits including attendance on HT courses. Volunteers are usually expected to work a normal full week, but exact hours and circumstances vary from project to project.

Because of the nature of the projects and the scheme volunteers must have some sound horticultural or gardening experience and/or qualifications, as well as the wish to work with people with special needs. Volunteers need to be available for a minimum of six months; most projects prefer a year. Requests for further information and application forms should be made to the Volunteer Co-ordinator at Horticultural Therapy at the above address. Allow up to three months between initial enquiry and final placement. Owing to a number of factors it is not possible to consider applications from those living outside Britain.

Independent Living Alternatives
Ashford Passage, Ashford Road, London NW2 6TP; tel 0181-450 4055; fax 0181-450 2009.

Independent Living Alternatives is an initiative which has been established to promote independence and freedom for people with supportive disabilities. The Company quite simply aims to enable people who need to use physical support to be able to live independently in the community, taking full control of their lives and thereby having individuality and spontaneity. This is achieved by recruiting and placing full-time support on a voluntary basis. The Company brings two or three people together to live on a semi-communal basis in an atmosphere of mutual inter-dependence. About 30 volunteers in all work as full-time carers each year, providing physical support to disabled people within the London area.

Volunteers help people to go to the toilet, get dressed, washed etc., and give practical support in terms of housework, shopping, cleaning, cooking, etc. Applicants may be of any nationality, but they must speak English to a very high standard. Overseas volunteers require visas; ILA does not finance visas. A driving licence would be useful. Volunteers are needed all the year round and the minimum length of placement is 4 months. Voluntary carers receive £58,99 per week. Accommodation is provided as mentioned above.

For further information and an application form contact Tracey Jannaway, Service Coordinator, at the above address.

Independent Living Schemes
Lewisham Social Services, Kingsweir House, Dartmouth Road, Forest Hill, London SE23 3YE; (tel 0181-699 0111; fax 0181-291-5720).

Special projects known as Independent Living Schemes have been set up in Lewisham with the aim of enabling people with disabilities to lead the lifestyle of their choice. About 50 Volunteer helpers are wanted to assist with these schemes. Volunteers provide care for a severely disabled person; tasks include toiletting, bathing and administering suppositories. The volunteer helper would be expected to accompany that person on social, business and cultural activities. The helper also helps with the cooking, cleaning and shopping under the direction of the disabled person. Applicants may be of any nationality, although basic English and reading skills are essential. Applicants must be willing to enable severely disabled people to regain their civil rights.

Volunteer helpers are asked to spend six months on a scheme. There is a one month trial period, which means that a helper is not bound to stay. However, most volunteers do settle and stay with the scheme; some like it so much they sign on for a further six months.

Rent-free accommodation is provided for helpers in a fully furnished two or three bedroomed flat to be shared with other helpers situated near the scheme. Heating and lighting bills as well as local telephone charges are met, and everyday household items like cleaning materials, light bulbs, bed linen etc., are supplied. A weekly allowance of £55, (£35 for food and £20 for pocket money) is paid, and is payable for up to a fortnight's sickness. There are also monthly allowances for recreation (£7) and clothing (£8). A week's paid leave is given after a helper has been with the scheme for four months. Helpers get a Saver Return Rail

Travel Warrant to any mainland UK destination, if required, or a Travel Card if they decide to stay in London. Helpers' return fares to and from their home are covered at the beginning and end of their involvement with the scheme. A social worker is available to offer guidance and advice to helpers.

Apply to Kenneth Smith at the above address when you are in the UK as no help can be given with entry visas.

Leonard Cheshire Foundation
26-29 Maunsel Street, London SW1P 2QN (tel 0171-828 1822; fax 0171-976 5704).

The Leonard Cheshire Foundation is a registered charitable trust running homes throughout the UK for people with severe disabilities, mainly physically disabled adults. Voluntary workers are needed in many homes to assist with the general care of residents who require help with washing, dressing and feeding as well as with hobbies and other recreational activities.

Volunteers cannot be aged under 18. Preference is generally given to people under 35 planning to take up medical or social work as a career. Volunteers work up to a 39 hour, five day week, with one week's paid holiday for every four month's service. The minimum period is one month, but most jobs are for between three and 12 months.

Full board, lodging and pocket money of £27.50 per week is provided, this rate being reviewed each April. Volunteers must pay their own travel costs to the home. Overseas applicants must be able to speak good English.

Applications should be sent to the Personnel Officer at the above address.

Lifestyles Independent Living Partnership
Woodside Lodge, Lark Hill Road, Worcester WR5 2EF; (tel 01905-350635; fax 01905-350684).

Volunteers are needed to enable people with a disability to lead as normal a life as possible in their own homes. Duties can include intimate personal care, cooking, housework, shopping and sharing leisure interests. Full-time work in shifts can include weekends and sleeping over. Volunteers receive free accommodation plus an allowance of £50 per week. Accommodation is shared with with other volunteers, and all heating and lighting bills are paid by social services.

Volunteers are required at all times of year. The normal minimum commitment expected is four months, but it may be possible to arrange placements during college vacations. Volunteers should be aged 18+ and be reliable and caring.

Enquiries to the above address.

MENCAP — The Royal Society for Mentally Handicapped Children and Adults
MENCAP Holiday Services Office, 119 Drake Street, Rochdale OL16 1PZ (tel 01706-54111; fax 01706-43179).

Each year the MENCAP Holiday Services Office arranges a programme of holidays for people with a learning disability, which are based in premises of many kinds — schools, farmhouses, adventure centres, holiday villages and guest houses — and covers the country from Devon to the Lake District. MENCAP also arranges holidays abroad for guests who require minimal supervision.

Some children are severely and multiply handicapped and will need almost constant care on special care holidays. Others who are less disabled may enjoy adventure or guest house holidays where the accent is placed upon enjoying outdoor activities or the 'traditional' type of seaside holiday. The success of these holidays depends upon volunteers who spend a week or two helping each year, receiving assistance towards their travelling costs with MENCAP providing for their board and lodging.

Prospective volunteers should be aged 18+, enjoy using their initiative and have a sense of fun. Flexibility is essential due to the wide range of jobs to be done.

Those interested should contact the Holidays Officer at the above address.

Otto Schiff Housing Association
Central Office, Osmond House, The Bishop's Avenue, London N2 0BG (tel 0181-209 0022; fax 0181-201 8089).

The Association provides sheltered accommodation and both residential and nursing care in London for elderly, Jewish, refugees from Nazi persecution. It runs five residential care homes and sheltered accommodation for a total of 290 elderly people, and aims to enable residents to maintain their personality and dignity by providing an ambience that makes them feel part of the community and allows them to regard their environment with affection.

A number of full-time residential volunteers are engaged by the Association at any one time. There are also approximately 50 non-residential volunteers who visit homes, help with care/domestic work, give clerical asistance, help with gardening and maintenance and befriend residents. Applicants of any nationality are welcome, and any skills a volunteer can offer will be considered. The full-time live-in volunteers must stay for a minimum of six months; they receive board and lodging, as well as £35.25 pocket money per week.

Those interested should contact Tim Inkson, General Manager at the above address.

Queen Elizabeth's Foundation for Disabled People
Lulworth Court, 25 Chalkwell Esplanade, Westcliff on Sea, Essex SS0 8JQ; (tel 01702 431725; fax 01702 433165).

Queen Elizabeth's Foundation is a registered charity and Lulworth Court is its holiday and respite centre for physically disabled adults located on the sea front, a mile from Southend. Guests come without their carers and qualified staff provide all care necessary, aided by volunteers of whom 300 are needed annually.

Volunteers help permanent staff with personal care of the guests including washing, dressing, help at mealtimes, in the toilet. Volunteers also help with all the outings to pubs, theatres, shops, river trips, football matches, dancing etc. There is a friendly and informal atmosphere and volunteers are made to feel very welcome. No experience is necessary as simple training and lots of support is given, but volunteers need to be fairly fit for heavy lifting and wheelchair pushing. Volunteers are needed for one to two weeks for all dates from late January to mid-December. Volunteers receive free board and lodging. Excellent food and warm, clean but simple accommodation. £15 is provided per week to offset travel expenses. Prospective volunteers are invited for an informal chat to find out what the work involves. Many volunteers return regularly, but new ones are always welcome.

Applicants should contact the Director at the above address.

Richard Cave Multiple Sclerosis Home
Servite Convent, Leuchie, North Berwick, East Lothian EH39 5NT (tel 01620-892864).

The Home is run by the Order of Servite Sisters as a holiday home for sufferers of multiple sclerosis of all ages.

Volunteers are taken on to assist with health care, taking patients for walks, writing postcards, and to accompany them on special outings. Vacancies might be available from mid-April to December/January. The duration of stay will depend on suitability and other factors.

Driving licences, nursing qualifications and any other skill are useful but not essential.

Applicants should be aged 17 to 25 and English-speaking. Board, lodgings and £35 weekly pocket money are provided.

Applications to the Matron, Sister Frances at the above address.

Ritchie Russell House Young Disabled Unit
The Churchill Hospital, Headington, Oxford OX3 7LJ (tel 01865 225482).

The Unit cares for disabled people aged between 16 and 65. Volunteers are required as carers on the Unit holidays for the disabled on a day-to-day basis. They are also needed to help on the Unit in Oxford. The number of volunteers engaged depends entirely on the nature of the work; for the holidays, as many as 20 carers may be required. The Unit organisers aim to take three holidays away per year for which carers over the age of 19 are needed. Help is also needed in the Unit with creative activities, gardening, table games, story groups, computers and the cooking group, as well as with outings and publicity.

Applicants of all nationalities are welcome. although perfect English is essential as the Unit's clients have hearing and communication problems. Applicants must be fit and healthy, patient and willing to work hard. They must be aged between 19 and 60. The holidays last for between one week and ten days, but helpers on the Unit will be required on occasional days for an indefinite period.

On the holidays accommodation and travel are paid for by the Unit, but a small donation towards food costs would be appreciated.

Carers must be prepared to work a 24-hour day. No accommodation is provided for regular Unit volunteers.

Enquiries should be sent to Mrs Barbara Martin at the above address.

The Royal Association for Disability and Rehabilitation (RADAR)
12 City Forum, 250 City Road, London EC1V 8AF (tel 0171-250 3222; fax 0171-250 0212).

Every year RADAR publishes a list of holiday centres for the disabled which require help from volunteers for a few weeks. These centres are run by several agencies and organisations including Social Services Departments, MENCAP, BREAK, DISAWAY TRUST, The Shaftesbury Society, The Winged Fellowship Trust, and PHAB. The list published by RADAR specifies the type of help needed. In some cases the volunteer must be fit or have medical training while in others the job may be suitable for an active pensioner. The list also mentions whether food, travel expenses and accommodation are provided.

Those interested should write to the Holidays Office at the above address.

SHAD Haringey
Winkfield Resource Centre, 33 Winkfield Road, London N22 5RP (tel 0181-365 8528).

The Shad Haringey is a registered charity which runs a scheme in which more than 35 volunteers per year work with physically disabled people in their own homes assisting with all aspects of independent living including personal care, housework, cooking and helping with leisure, work and education activities.

Applicants of EC countries are welcome and people from other countries will be considered. Good English is essential. Volunteers must be in good health and able to lift people, although training will be given. Volunteers should be aged 18 to 30 years.

The usual minimum length of placement is three months, and volunteers are required all year round. Volunteers are accommodated in shared flats with all bills paid by SHAD, and a pocket money and food allowance of £54 a week is provided. Travel expenses up to £30 will be reimbursed as will all out-of-pocket expenses.

Applications should be made to Sue Denney at the above address.

SHAD Wandsworth
c/o The Nightingale Centre, 8 Balham Hill, London SW12 9EA (tel 0181-675 6095; fax 0181-675 3542).

SHAD Wandsworth is an independent living scheme which supports ten disabled people with severe physical disabilities to enable them to live independently in their own homes. This is achieved by recruiting teams of two or three full-time volunteers who act as physical facilitators. The organisation is user-managed as it is SHAD's belief that a disabled person should have control over the decisions which affect every aspect of their lives.

Volunteers are not care-workers, they are recruited so that we can 'borrow their arms and legs' along with their time and energy. The work involves personal care, lifting and handling, escorting the person to social events, driving, cooking, housework and other tasks which are all done under the direction of the disabled user-member. SHAD user-members require 24-hour facilitation and volunteers work on a rota basis to provide the need. Support and advice are always available, the only requirement is that volunteers are enthusiastic, with a sense of humour and flexible. The minimum age is 18 years, although the majority of volunteers are aged 20-30. Volunteers must be fit and healthy. Due to the physical nature of the work, they are required to attend a one-day lifting and handling training course.

Overseas applicants are welcome, but must be able to attend an informal interview in London and we cannot always guarantee a placement even after interview. Good spoken English is essential and an international driving licence is an advantage, but otherwise no particular skills are needed.

Volunteers are asked to make a commitment of four months in the first instance. After this, a further length of stay may be negotiable. The first month with SHAD is viewed as a probationary period by all parties. SHAD pays half the cost of the interview expenses (for overseas volunteers a maximum of £25 is paid).

SHAD pays all household bills and provides basic cleaning materials. Volunteers receive an allowance of £52 per week to cover their food and other living expenses. Travel costs whilst working are re-imbursed.

Those interested should contact Sue Hiscock, Recruitment Worker, at the above address.

SHARE HOLIDAY VILLAGE
Discovery '80 Ltd. Smiths Strand, Lisnaskea, Co Fermanagh BT92 OEQ, Northern Ireland; (tel 013657-22122; fax 013657-21893).

Share is a registered charity that runs a residential centre, which through varied outdoor activities aims to encourage contact between disabled and able-bodied people. All ages from primary school children to senior citizens are welcomed at the Centre.

The Centre has a small permanent staff and relies heavily on volunteers about 300 of which are needed over the summer in one-week shifts, to assist disabled people as well as helping with domestic duties and outdoor activities. £10 pocket money is given weekly plus full board and accommodation.

Also needed are outdoor activity instructors who are waged (£40 to £80 per week) and a few volunteers to assist them leading groups in sailing etc. if they have the relevant experience in outdoor pursuits.

The minimum age for general volunteers is 16 years. There is also a senior volunteer programme for those over 55. The minimum period of work is two weeks between April and October. Applications should be sent at any time of year to the above address.

Speyside Handicapped Holiday Trust
Badguish Outdoor Centre, Aviemore, Inverness-shire PH22 1QU; (tel 01479-861285).

Volunteer care assistants are needed to work for one or two weeks in January, April and May-October. Volunteers are expected to work ten hours a day with two days off per week. In return they receive board and lodging and £20 pocket money per week.

Minimum age for all staff is 18+ and applications are accepted all year round. Some waged positions also available.

Stallcombe House
Sanctuary Lane, Woodbury, Nr. Exeter EX5 1EX (tel 01395-232373; fax 01395-233351).

Stallcombe House is a residential farm community in East Devon for mentally disabled adults. Residents of the three households are involved in all aspects of the community, 55 acre farm and small organic horticultural area. Two volunteers are needed annually to help care for the residents: cooking, cleaning and assisting the residents with their daily activities including personal hygiene, hobbies and outings. Placements are for 6 — 12 months. Other volunteers are needed seasonally to help with farm and garden work, and local volunteers who can work daily or less frequently on an on-going basis will be welcomed.

Residential care volunteers must want to work with people in a caring environment. All volunteers need a working knowledge of English and should be in good mental and physical health. Residential care workers receive accommodation and pocket money of £20 per week but assistance with travel expenses depends on the individual volunteer's circumstances.

Applicants should apply to the Principal at the above address.

Sue Ryder Foundation
Sue Ryder Home, Cavendish, Sudbury, Suffolk (tel 01787-280252).

This international foundation runs more than 20 homes in Britain for the sick, disabled and physically handicapped, as well as cancer patients and those suffering from Huntingdon's Disease.

Volunteers are needed, particularly outside the summer months, to do essential duties at Headquarters or in the Sue Ryder Homes which may include dealing with the patients, and any domestic, office or any other work that arises. Minimum period of service is normally eight weeks. Free simple accommodation, meals and pocket money are provided. Minimum age is 16.

Please apply to the above address. A stamped addressed envelope or international reply coupon with applications is appreciated.

Winged Fellowship Trust
Angel House, 20-32 Pentonville Road, London N1 9XD (tel 0171-833 2594; fax 0171-278 0370).

Every year some 4,000 helpers are needed in five holiday centres for physically disabled people located in Surrey, Essex, Lancashire, Hampshire and Nottinghamshire. The purpose of the Trust is not only to provide holidays for severely physically disabled people, but also to enable the families who normally care for them at home to take perhaps their first worry-free holiday in years. Volunteers live in the centres and are given free board and lodging, during which time they not only take care of the physical needs of the guests and help with the domestic chores, but also provide companionship for them.

All that is required of volunteers is that they be over 17 years. Those with nursing qualifications would be particularly welcome. The centres are in operation for 11 months of the year, so although travel expenses are not normally paid, there are certain times of the year when help is in short supply, and requests for assistance will be considered, especially if those who are volunteering are unemployed.

Those interested should apply to the above address.

Woodlarks Camp Site Trust
Woodlarks Camp Site, Tilford Road, Farnham, Surrey, GU10 3RN (tel 01252-716279).

Over the summer the camp site offers the opportunity for physically handicapped children and adults to have a camping holiday on a wooded camp site. Facilities include a heated outdoor swimming pool, a trampoline, and archery. The camp site is run entirely by voluntary help; every summer around 500 volunteers assist some 500 handicapped people.

Volunteers are normally taken on for the duration of one camp, lasting one week, but some stay for more than one camp. Accommodation is provided in tents, a small fee is usually paid by helpers to cover the cost of food.

Those interested should contact the Honorary Secretary at the above address, enclosing an SAE or an International Reply Coupon.

Youth Activities

Brathay Exploration Group
Brathay Hall, Ambleside, Cumbria, LA22 OHP (tel 015394-33942).

The Group organizes expeditions and leader training courses in the British Isles and overseas. Expedition members are aged from 15 — 26 years old. A variety of expeditions are organized by voluntary leaders each year, combining adventure with field study work, and volunteers are needed to participate. In some circumstances assistant leaders may be required and would have experience in the outdoors or scientific skills.

Around 100 physically fit volunteers are needed each year. To be considered for a place in an expedition leader team, applicants must be 20 to 60 years old and have expedition experience, or specific scientific or medical knowledge.

Applications should be sent to the above address.

Fellowship of Reconciliation in Ireland
224 Lisburn Road, Belfast BT9 6GA, Northern Irelend (tel 01232-660194).

The Fellowship helps recruit volunteers for playschemes in Northern Ireland for Catholic and Protestant children aged between 5 and 16. The sites chosen are usually deprived and segregated areas as the long term aims of the playschemes are understanding and reconciliation. Volunteers act as play leaders and should be older than 18 years and able to cope with tense situations.

About 30 volunteers are needed for three weeks during the summer. Volunteers receive board and lodging but must pay their own travel expenses.

Apply to the above address.

Pax Christi
9 Henry Road, London N4 2LH (tel 0181-800 4612; fax 0181-802 3223).

Pax Christi is the international peace movement of the Catholic Church. In July and August it recruits a total of 130 volunteers to help run four childrens' playschemes in Northern Ireland and temporary youth hostels in school buildings in London.

Playscheme volunteers work for a minimum of three weeks while those in youth hostels work for either two or four weeks. They are given free board and lodging. No special skills or experience are expected of volunteers but they must be aged over 18. One of the main objectives of these schemes is to further the cause of international understanding, and volunteers taking part may be of different religions and nationalities.

Those interested should contact the Workcamps Organiser at the above address for further details.

Tent City Ltd and Hackney Camping
Old Oak Common Lane, East Acton, London W3 7DP; (tel +44 (0)181-743 5708).

Tent City is a place where tourists can stay in London cheaply, and is open from June to September, 24-hours a day. It has 450 beds in 14 large tents, men's, women's and mixed. It is run by an international team and supported entirely by volunteers.

Over 60 volunteers of all nationalities are needed over the summer months to help with cleaning, reception, tent maintenance, the snack-bar and cooking. The only requirement is that volunteers should have a basic level of spoken English, and that they should stay for four to six weeks. Food, accommodation and pocket money of £33 per week are all provided.

The same team runs a normal campsite called Hackney Camping and volunteers are also required there. Conditions and benefits as above.

Those interested should contact Maxine Lambert at the above address enclosing an international reply coupon.

Trident Transnational
Saffron Court, 14b St Cross Street, London EC1N 8XA; tel 0171-242 1515; fax 0171- 430 0975). E-mail ttn@trid.demon.co.uk

Trident Transnational provides UK work placements (vocational) for young people aged 18-25 from overseas. About 500-700 students are placed annually through Trident's 70 regional offices and 72,000 employer base. All kinds of jobs are available lasting from three weeks to six months all year round. Expenses and pocket money are at the employer's discretion. Accommodation is not provided by employers but can be arranged through a host and guest service with British families for reasonable terms.

Trident also provide other services including counselling, monitoring, briefing, evaluation, certificate of work placement by the University of Cambridge Local Examinations Syndicate.

There is a possibility also of some non-vocational paid jobs via 'Camp Trident' scheme.

Further details from the above address.

Other Short Term Residential Opportunities

The following organisations have their main entry elsewhere in this book but also have some short-term possibilities:

ATD Fourth World is an international organisation concerned with the part of any national population at the bottom end of the social scale. ATD organises summer work camps in the UK.

The following organisations have been included in the *Non Residential* chapter, but under certain circumstances or on specialized projects some residential volunteers are also needed.

Human Service Alliance
Jewish Blind Society
Mansfield Outdoor Centre
Meldreth Manor School
Pestalozzi Children's Village Trust
Saturday Venture Association
Tools for Self Reliance.

Europe

Multi-National

The ACROSS Trust
Bridge House, 70-72 Bridge Road, East Molesey, Surrey KT8 9HF (tel 0181-783 1355; fax 0181-783 1622).

The Trust is a registered charity that arranges weekly pilgrimages and holidays for the sick and disabled (the unable) from March to November each year. These last 10 days. Places visited on pilgrimages include Lourdes, Rome, the Holy Land and Poland. Places visited on holidays include Belgium, France, Spain, Switzerland, Austria, Ireland and Holland. Transport is by 'jumbulance', a purpose-built jumbo ambulance, which carries all the necessary facilities for the unable.

Each group consists of two to three nurses, a doctor (if necessary), a chaplain and male and female helpers, all of whom volunteer their time and pay their own expenses to care for the ten unable in the group. ACROSS gives priority to those with terminal illness, with progressive diseases, those confined to bed or wheelchair, and people with illnesses that make other forms of travel impossible or unsuitable. The group, with a maximum of 24 or 44 persons, live together as a family throughout their holiday, with everyone devoting themselves to the needs of the group 24 hours a day. The work of caring for the unable, i.e. feeding, dressing, toileting, etc. is shared among all the group.

Volunteers need to be in good health and dedicated. Nurses and helpers pay the same as the rest of the group. Accommodation is provided in Lourdes at the Trust's purpose-built homes. Once volunteers apply, they will be offered the available dates.

Enquiries for the appropriate application form (eg doctor, nurse, chaplain, lay helper) should be sent to the Group Organisers at the above address.

APARE
41 cours Jean Jaures, 8400 Avignon, France (tel +33 490 85 51 15; fax +33 490 86 82 19).

APARE organise voluntary workcamps dedicated to the restoration of historic buildings and sites particularly in Provence (south of France) but also throughout the rest of Europe.

600 volunteers are needed in the summer to work on the sites; applicants must be aged 18+ and fit.

For Provence, no particular skills are required as each workcamp composed of about 15 people is supervised by a technical group leader.

For Europe, applicants must be high level students.

Placements last for three weeks. Accommodation is provided, although pocket money is not and participants pay a fee of 600 French francs.

For more details, please write or fax Mireille Pons (Provence) or Marie-Christine Pascal (Europe) at the above address.

ATD Fourth World
Summer Activities, Boite Postale 7726, 950 Cergy Pointoise Cedex, France.

International Workcamps, Street Workshops and Family Stays in France, Belgium, Spain and the Netherlands in July and August. Preparation weekends for Street Workshops and Family Stays are held late in April. There is a charge of FF450 for the International Work Camps to cover accommodation and food for a fortnight. ATD summer activities are aimed at young people aged 18+.

BTCV International Working Holidays
36 St Mary's Street, Wallingford, Oxon OX10 0EU (tel 01491-39766; fax 01491-39646).

BTCV is the UK's leading practical conservation charity for improving and protecting the environment. The Trust aims to harness people's energies and talents to protect the environment by practical action. To this end the Trust organizes international working holidays for over 500 volunteers a year lasting from one to three weeks throughout Europe (also North America and Japan).

There is a variety of sometimes unusual assignments e.g. creating a bird reserve in the grounds of a Belgian château. The working day is 9am to 5.30pm and the evenings are free. The average cost is about £70 a week inclusive of basic accommodation and food. Whilst undertaking traditional conservation projects, it is hoped that volunteers will adapt to local life-styles as well as participate in community affairs.

Those interested should write to the International Development Unit at the above address for further details enclosing a large stamped addressed envelope.

Box-Aid
11 Hill Top Lane, Saffron Walden, Essex CB11 4AS (tel 01799-523321).

Box-Aid makes, demonstrates and cooks with solar cookers and 'Wonderboxes' at Green Fairs in the UK, and also at Sunseed's desert technology centre in Spain. The latest solar cooker is the Anahat which has a back-up for evenings. Box-Aid also works in co-operation with Compassion and other similar organisations in southern Africa, and sometimes shares volunteers with the Sunseed Trust.

Volunteers, of any nationality, would begin by experimenting with the cookers. If keen, they could then demonstrate them in the UK or spend from one to 24 weeks at the Spanish centre cooking food in them for other volunteers. After that they might be able to go to other countries where this fuel-saving type of cooking is needed. Board and lodging is provided in Spain, but not yet in the UK. No special qualifications are necessary; a driving licence is an advantage in Spain for those aged over 27. A knowledge of any extra languages is useful but not essential.

Applications can be sent, all the year round to Anna Pearce at the above address.

Applicants may first like to read Anna Pearce's book *Simply Living* which will give them a much better idea of what would be needed from them in African countries.

Ecumenical Youth Council in Europe (EYCE)
Youth Unit, British Council of Churches, Inter-Church House, 35-41 Lower Marsh, London SE1 7RL (tel 0171-620 4444; fax 0171-928 0010).

EYCE organises work camps for study, manual labour and social development in most countries in Europe. The camps last two to three weeks throughout the summer and provide places for about 30 volunteers each. Both the activities and the studies have topical objectives, and aim to promote Christian understanding and faith. Participants must contribute towards their expenses and food costs, but accommodation is provided. Volunteers must be over 18 years of age and able to adapt to communal life in a Christian environment.

Applications may be sent to EYCE, Youth Matters, at the above address if from British citizens; the international headquarters of EYCE is PO Box 185, Fin-00161, Helsinki, Finland (+358 0 1802449). Please enclose a stamped addressed envelope or an international reply coupon with your enquiries.

Grouping of the European Campuses
41 Cours Jacques Jaures, 84000 Avignon, France (tel +33 4 90 27 08 61; fax +33 4 90 86 82 19).

The Centre organises and recruits volunteers for the European Environment and Heritage Campuses. This extensive network of academic workshops is intended for all young people interested in these fields. As training projects, but also tools of action for the benefit of local initiatives for the protection of our heritage and environment, the campuses allow the participants to become part of multidisciplinary teams working voluntarily on research/action programmes in such fields as the Gdansk local environment plan in Poland and the programme for eco-tourism in the Zagori Natural Park in Greece. These truly practical academic workshops last thee to four weeks. In 1995 the Grouping offered 30 such campuses.

To volunteer, applicants must have a university degree, with additional experience in environmental or heritage disciplines. Applicants must also speak several European languages. The groups of 15 are led by university tutors.

The Campuses are free and provide board and lodging though not the return fare. The determining factor in the choice of candidates will be their commitment to a multi-disciplinary, practical experience.

For more information on the Campuses please write to the above address.

Internationale Begegnung in Gemeinschaftsdiensten (IBG)
Schlosserstrasse 28, D-70180 Stuttgart, Germany (tel +49 711-6491128; fax +49-711-640 98 67).

IBG was founded in 1965 by the Boy Scouts' Association. International work-camps lasting three weeks are organised in Germany and Switzerland in close conjunction with local villages. Chosen projects are designed to benefit the whole community, such as the construction of children's playgrounds, hiking paths, public gardens, afforestation, etc. In exchange for 30 hours of work per week, volunteers receive food and lodging, insurance and some spare-time excursions.

Applicants between 18 and 30 from all over the world are welcome. Volunteers are advised to bring a sleeping bag and heavy footwear, as well as musical instruments, games and records from their own countries. The registration fee is 150DM (about £65) which should be submitted with an application form.

Enquirers to the above address will be sent a brochure containing dates and locations of the various workcamps.

Internationale Bouworde/International Building Companions
rue des Carmes 24, 6900 Marche-en-Famenne, Belgium.

Bouworde needs hundreds of volunteers every year to do manual work helping to improve unhealthy and unmodernised housing. These projects take place throughout the year in Flanders and also in France, Germany, Austria, Italy, Spain, Hungary, Croatia, Slovenia, Lithuania, Russia, Poland, Romania and the Czech and Slovak republics in the summer (July, August and September).

The minimum period of work is three weeks. Free board, accommodation and insurance are provided, but volunteers must pay for their own travel costs. Participants must be aged at least 18.

Applications should be sent to the above address.

International Bouworde-IBO
St Annastraat 172 6524 GT Nijmegen, The Netherlands (tel +31 80-226 074).

Internationale Bouworde (or International Building Companions) gives volunteers the opportunity to assist in socially useful building projects in Europe. British participants will be integrated in international groups, especially in Belgium, Holland, Germany and Poland.

The workcamps last for three weeks. The actual construction work provides the most important element of the camps, and volunteers are expected to treat it as such. It acts as a focus for the other aspects such as encounters with fellow participants and with the local population.

Volunteers should be aged 18+ years old and fit enough to be able to meet the physical demands of the camp which are eight hours per day of labouring work. They must also be willing to adapt to foreign attitudes and life-styles. Volunteers have to pay their own travel costs to and from Belgium and Holland. Volunteers participating in a camp in Germany or Poland will travel together with volunteers from Holland to the project. For part of this journey, organised and paid for by the Dutch branch of IBO, a contribution is asked. IBO pays the insurance and provides board and lodging. Applicants from the UK should apply to Tony McGuirk, 31 Sunbeam Road, Old Swan, Liverpool L13 5XS. Other applicants should apply to the appropriate address below.

IBO-Osterreichischer Bauorden, Hornesgasse 4, A-1031 Wien, Austria.
IBO-Bouworde, Tiensesteenweg 145, B-3200 Kessel-Lo, Belgium.
IBO-Compagnons Batisseurs, 6 Av Charles de Gaulle, F-81100 Castres, France.
IBO-Les Compagnons Batisseurs, Rue Notre-Dame de Graces 63, B-5400 Marchen-Famenne, Belgium.
IBO-Internationaler Bauorden, PO Box 1438, D-6420 Worms, Germany.
IBO-Internationale Bouworde, St Annastraat 172, NL-6524 GT Nijmegen, Holland.
IBO-Soci Costruttori, Via CBattisti 3, 1-20 071 Casalpusterlengo (MI) Italy.
IBO-Internationaler Bauorden, Kirchweg 7, CH-9438 Luchingen SG, Switzerland.
IBO-Epito Baratok, Blathy Otto u. 10, H-1089 Budapest, Hungary.

Ocean Youth Club
The Bus Station, South Street, Gosport, Hants. PO12 1EP (tel 01705-528421 ext 241).

The Ocean Youth Club needs volunteers to act as First and Second Mates on its expeditions and voyages from March to October. The aim of the club is to provide young people aged 12-24 with the opportunity to take part in adventurous offshore sailing, and so to develop their sense of awareness and responsibility and their ability to work in a team. It has bases throughout the UK. Volunteers work for weekends, weeks and occasionally longer voyages.

All Mates must be qualified to the appropriate RYA and OYC level. All volunteers must be fit and able to swim. Accommodation is provided, as are safety and foul weather equipment. First Mates are asked to make a contribution towards their upkeep, and other mates pay £15 a day towards the cost of food.

Applications should be made to the Director at the above address. Volunteers are also required to help with tasks such as fundraising, recruitment, presentations and refit work on the vessels.

La Sabranenque
Saint Victor la Coste, 30290 Laudun, France (tel +33 4 66 50 05 05).

La Sabranenque is a non-profit organisation working for the preservation of the rural habitat by restoring abandoned rural sites for present day use. Saint Victor la Coste serves as the headquarters for the organisation as the work projects are mainly in southern France, although there are three sites in Italy. Around 150 volunteers are needed for work which includes restoration of roofs, terraces, walls and paths, planting local tree species and the reconstruction of small houses. Techniques are learned on the job. Workcamps last a minimum of two or three weeks during the summer, and occasionally stays of two months or more are possible.

Volunteers must be at least 18 years old and in good health. No language skills or previous experience are required for summer workcamps, but non EC volunteers must obtain a French visa for their period of stay. Board and lodging are provided at a cost of about £200 per two-week project.

Applications to Marc Simon, the Programme Co-ordinator at the above address.

Sunseed Desert Technology
PO Box 2000, Cambridge CB3 OJF; (tel 01480-411784).

Sunseed Desert Technology is the Spanish project of the Sunseed Trust a UK registered charity.

The aim of the project is to find and spread methods that will alleviate poverty and improve the environment of people in desertified areas. Sunseed also aims to raise awareness of desertification and to promote sustainable living practices.

Skilled and/or unskilled volunteers are needed to assist in the south of Spain with arid-land tree trials, crop research, hydroponics, organic gardening, building and using solar cookers, other appropriate technologies and building and maintenance. Linguistic ability is always in great demand.

About 500 short-term volunteers are engaged annually from between one and five weeks, as are roughly 30 placements who stay from between five weeks to nine months to undertake specific projects.

Individuals of all nationalities are welcome to apply. Pocket money of about £10 a week can only be paid to staff, although volunteers are given board and accommodation.

Applicants should apply to Tim or Mary Eiloart at the above address.

TOC H
1 Forest Close, Wendover, Aylesbury, Bucks, HP22 6BT (tel 01296-623911; fax 01296-696137).

Toc H runs short-term residential projects throughout the year in Britain and Germany, usually from a weekend up to three weeks in length. Projects undertaken can include work with people with different disabilities or children in need; playschemes and camps; conservation and manual work; study and/or discussion sessions.

These projects provide those who take part with opportunities to learn more about themselves and the world. Whilst foreign applicants are welcome, a preference is held for those living in the EC. The Toc H programme is published twice yearly on the first Mondays in March and September. Whilst there is a minimum age limit of 16 years, there is no upper age limit. There is no closing date for applications but you are advised to apply early. Over 500 volunteers a year are recruited. Toc H does not offer any long-term paid employment opportunities or supervised placements.

Enquiries should be sent to the above address enclosing a stamped self-addressed envelope.

Tutmonda Esperantista Junulara Organizo — TEJO (World Organisation of Young Esperantists)
Nieuwe Binnenweg 176, NL-3015 BJ Rotterdam, Netherlands (tel +31 10 4361044; fax +31 10 4361751).

In addition to arranging Esperanto courses for workcamps organized by other organisations, TEJO also co-ordinates the recruitment of volunteers for Esperanto workcamps in several European countries. These camps include work on building sites and enhancing the environment. There is also a system of half-work, half-learning Esperanto 'camps'. Volunteers are usually recruited for 2-5 weeks, and accommodation is provided.

No prior experience is needed; although a few camps are limited to Esperanto speakers, some camps include Esperanto lessons for beginners. The camps are usually composed of people aged 16-30.

Enquiries should be sent to the above address enclosing an International Reply Coupon.

Universities and Colleges Christian Fellowship (UCCF)
38 De Montfort Street, Leicester LE1 7GP (tel 0116-2551700; fax 0116 255 5672). E-mail uccf@cix.compulink.co.uk

All of the fellowship's activities have Christian teachings and evangelical aims as their basis. Around 300 volunteers are needed to take part in evangelical teams, help with camps, community activities and church-based work in Britain, Ireland and Europe. These activities may last from one week to one month during the summer vacation.

Volunteers may be of any nationality but must be committed Christians. Languages may be required for some evangelical teams in Europe. Most activities require a contribution for board and food although some may pay expenses. The volunteer meets all travel expenses.

UCCF also publish *Vac Acts*, a directory of summer volunteer activities for Christian students. It is available each February at no cost.

Those interested in UCCF's activities or *Vac Acts* should apply to the Assistant to Head of Student Ministries at the above address.

Belgium and Holland

Annee Diaconale Belge
Service Protestant de la Jeunesse, Rue de Champ de Mars, 5, 1050 Bruxelles, Belgium (tel +32 02-513 24 01).

Part of the Service Protestant de la Jeunesse, or Protestant Youth Office, arranges for volunteers to spend between ten and 12 months in Christian or other institutions in Belgium. Around 15 volunteers a year are placed in children's homes, homes for the elderly and disabled etc. Volunteers receive free food, accommodation and laundry, their travelling expenses and pocket money of around £80 per month. Placements begin in September.

Participants should be aged between 18 and 25 and have a basic knowledge of French. Whatever their background all candidates' applications will be welcome. Possession of a driving licence and/or a teaching certificate would be advantageous.

Contact the Secretary at the above address for further details.

Association pour la Promotion de l'Archéologie de Stavelot et de sa Région
Centre Stavelotain d'Archéologie, Abbaye de Stavelot, 4970 Stavelot, Belgium; (tel +32 80 86 41 13; fax +32 80 86 41 13).

The Association exists to carry out excavations in Stavelot and the surrounding region in the province of Liège. These include excavation of an 11th century ottonian abbey church, destroyed after the French Revolution. The excavation includes an introduction to archaeological methods and fieldwork.

About 20 volunteers a week are taken on for 11 weeks during July, August and part of September. The work includes fieldwork, drawing, photography and artifacts registraton.

No fares or wages are paid, but volunteers are provided with lodging, meals and and insurance. The minimum period is one week and the minimum age for volunteers is 16 years.

The Association has a booklet on the history of the Stavelotain site available on request at BF 150.

For further information, contact Brigitte Evrard-Neuray, Administrator at the above address.

Belgian Evangelical Mission
20 Vicarage Farm Road, Hounslow, Middlesex TW3 4NW (tel 0181-5773023).

The Belgian Evangelical Mission conducts summer evangelical campaigns in a number of towns and villages in both French and Dutch speaking Belgium. Around 60 volunteers from Britain are needed to join the international campaign teams which last from two to six weeks. These teams start each September and last until the following July.

Volunteers may be of any nationality provided they are Christians and can provide a home church recommendation. Summer evangelical team members pay £9 per day and a £5 deposit. All volunteers must pay for their own travel but accommodation is provided.

Those interested should apply to Richard Martin at the above address.

Centre Stavelotain d'Archéologie
Abbaye de Stavelot, Belgium; (tel +32 80 86 41 13).

The CSA organises volunteer archaeological programmes around church and castle excavations at the above site. Experience is preferable but not essential as instruction will be given. Students of archaeology are especially welcome. Free accommodation is provided in the Abbey but volunteers must bring their own sleeping bag and air mattress. Breakfast and lunch are provided but volunteers have to make their own dinner arrangements. There is a weekly contribution by volunteers up to a maximum of BF 1000.

NATUUR 2000: The Flemish Youth Federation for the Study of Nature and for Environmental Conservation
Bervoestraat 33, 2000 Antwerpen, Belgium (tel +32 32 31 26 04; fax +32 32 33 64 99).

NATUUR 2000 organises nature study and nature conservation activities for young people aged between eight and 25 including birdwatching camps, management of nature reserves, etc. It also runs an environmental information centre for young people. About ten volunteers per year, preferably with experience in field biology, are required to help prepare and lead the study and working camps. Help is also needed in the Antwerp and Ostend based offices all year round; those with computer experience will be preferred. Applicants of any nationality will be considered, as long as they are interested and motivated. They must also have experience in field biology and computer/clerical work. An international driving licence could be helpful.

Volunteers are required for from two weeks to one month, or longer. The camps take place from mid-June until Mid-September. Camp registration fees start at BF 1,000 which includes accommodation, food and insurance.

Further information from the above address.

Universale Esperanto-Asocio
Nieuwe Binneweg 176, 3015 BJ Rotterdam, Netherlands (tel +31 10-43610444; fax +31-10 4361751). E-mail uea@inter.nl.net

Esperanto is the international language invented by Zamenhof, a Polish occulist, in 1887. It now has more than a million speakers throughout the world. The Universala Esperanto-Asocio is the world organisation for the advancement of Esperanto. Its Head Office is situated in Rotterdam, where a staff of ten to twelve workers from various parts of the world, both paid and voluntary, are involved in day-to-day administration, accounts, mail order services, congress organisation, editing and production of books and magazines, and maintaining a library. The Association has another office in New York to deal with contacts with the UN. Thus the Association needs one or two volunteers from time to time to help with its work. The minimum period of service for volunteers is nine months, the maximum one year.

Volunteers *must speak Esperanto fluently* as this is the working language of the organisation. Other qualifications may be necessary depending on the specific vacancy. Applicants must be between 18 and 29 years of age. Free accommodation is provided, and insurance and a small living allowance is paid. Residents of EC countries do not need a visa or work permit.

Volunteers from other countries will need both. A period of six to twelve months should be allowed for the acquisition of these permits.

Eastern Europe

Anglo-Polish Universities Association (APASS)
UK Northern Area, Secretariat: 93 Victoria Road, Leeds LS6 1DR.

Host organisations in Poland (universities, medical schools, colleges, sixth form colleges and individual families) invite British people through APASS to participate in the programme 'Teaching Holidays in Poland' which operates in July and August and lasts approximately three weeks. Invitees teach for 15 hours a week, mainly conversational English. There is a generous programme of holiday/leisure activities laid on.

There are also a few long-stay possibilities. Teaching experience is welcome but not essential. The upper age limit is 60 years otherwise good health is essential. Applicants must be British-educated, native speakers with clear diction and legible writing. Accepted applicants will be assisted with the passage to Poland and hospitality and transport in Poland will be provided free.

For further details contact the above address or send £2.50 to the above address for a 30-page information pack with detailed information about the cost and requirements involved.

ATM (Belorussian Association of International Youth Work)
PO Box 64, Minsk, Belarus 220199, Republic of Belarus (tel +375 17 2768662; tel +375 172 273395/278183). E-mail sergey@atm.minsk.by

This service organises and co-ordinates workcamps in Belorus in different fields including ecology and many other social issues. It acts as an advisory service for overseas volunteers coming to Belarus. It also places 150 volunteers from Belarus in workcamps throughout Europe. About 150 volunteers come to these workcamps every year to take part in activities and study programmes, or to help with office work, or to lead the camps and help with the co-ordination of the summer exchange.

Applicants of any nationality are welcome; some exchanges have only participants from one country. Volunteers from abroad are assisted with visas, etc. ATM is has also been engaged, together with 35 other non-governmental organisations from many countries, on the long-term Anti-Chernobyl Environmental Educational Project.

No special skills are needed, apart from Russian language skills for some of the programmes. The minimum age limit is 18 years and there is no upper limit. Disabled applicants are welcome, but they must contact the organisation prior to application. The usual length of placement is three or four weeks between June and September, although some volunteers can be placed for two to four months. Volunteers must pay an application fee, but during the workcamp they are provided with free food, accommodation and health insurance. Accommodation is provided in student hostels.

For further information contact the above address.

Bosnia Aid Committee of Oxford
35 Stockmore Street, Oxford OX4 1JT; (tel 01865-295049; fax 01865-243537).

The Bosnia Aid Committee fundraises in the UK though musical and sponsored events and supplies medical, building and other aid workers to Bosnia. About ten volunteers are taken on annually and those whose services are invaluable include plumbers, electricians, carpenters, psyschotherapists and medical personnel. A knowledge of the Bosnian language is preferred but not essential. Volunteers work for a minimum of ten weeks at any time of year. Transport to and from Bosnia, plus board and lodging are provided by the Organisation.

Anyone wishing to volunteer please contact Tim Winter at the above address.

Brontosaurus Movement
Bubenska 6, 17000 Prague 7, Czech Republic; (tel +42 2 667 102 45; fax +42 2 667 10245).

The Brontosaurus Movement is an environmental movement focusing on the environmental education of children and youth. They organise a large number of summer camps and working weekends around the Czech Republic and also, seminars, competitions, exhibitions etc.

Over 2000 volunteers work annually on nature conservation and restoration of historic monument projects. Most of the work involves practical tasks. Camps last approximately two weeks during July and August and board and accommodation are provided free in return for about 30 hours work weekly. The age limits are 16-30. The languages of the camps are English, German and Russian.

Applications should be sent direct to the above address.

Eastern Europe Relief Drive
A Project of The Body Shop Foundation
Watersmead, Littlehampton, West Sussex BN17 6LS (tel 01903-850906; fax 01903-859296).

The Relief Drive was founded in 1990 by Anita Roddick to alleviate the suffering of Romanian orphans in three orphanages in Halaucesti, North Eastern Romania. Today there are active projects in both Romania and Albania, where their long-term commitment includes refurbishment, medical care and child development. Qualified nurses and child development specialists (such as art Therapists and Play Therapists) are needed to volunteer their skills for three, six or 12 months. There is also an opportunity for unskilled volunteers to work on playschemes for the children or to work on refurbishment, trips or to paint institutions. The playscheme deadlines are usually in February of each year, though they accept applications all year round. Accommodation is provided, but volunteers should raise funds for their airfares and a little more, though long-term volunteers who are skilled in a trade or healthcare are sponsored.

Applicants of all nationalities may apply, and the minimum age limit is 18.

To apply, or to obtain an information pack, please contact Mandy Frith, Volunteer Co-ordinator, at the above address.

International Exchange Center
2, Republic Square, 1010 Riga, Latvia (tel +371-7027476; fax +371 7830257). E-mail iec@iec.vernet.lv.

The Center recruits volunteers of any nationality to work as counsellors in summer children's camps in Latvia and Russia in addition to arranging placements for westerners as au pairs. Placements usually last for between four and twelve weeks. A basic knowledge of Russian or Latvian is necessary, and applicants should be aged between 18 and 35.

For further details contact the above address.

Jacob's Well Appeal
2 Ladygate, Beverley HU17 8BH (tel 01482-881162; fax 01482-865452).

The Appeal is a Christian charity that organises medical aid to Eastern Europe and Asia. The Appeal sends volunteers to work in a hospital for mentally disabled children in Siret, Romania. The minimum length of placement here is two weeks, and the maximum placement can be as long as two years. Doctors, nurses, volunteer nurses, teachers, physiotherapists, pharmacists, administrators and students over 18 years are all needed to work with understimulated and unloved children. There is a great need for qualified physiotherapists as well.

In addition there are opportunities for voluntary work in the Appeal's warehouse in the UK; sorting of medicines and equipment, packing containers and collecting supplies by van or lorry. Volunteers are also required to help with the Appeal's administration. About 80 volunteers per year work for the Appeal, both abroad and in the UK. Applicants may be of any nationality, but they must be qualified in their chosen area of work, and fluent in English. A certificate of health is needed for all work in Romania and volunteers must accept the principles of the Appeal's constitution. The average length of placement in Romania is 2-3 months, at all times of the year. Accommodation is provided for volunteers working abroad at small cost. Expenses (apart from travel costs) are paid for all volunteers except for short-term workers in Romania.

For further information please contact Dr. Beryl Beynon at the above address.

MOST

Breg 12 — PP 279, 61000 Ljubljana, Slovenia (tel +38 661-1258067; fax +38 661-217208).

MOST organises voluntary work in Slovenia, particularly in areas not adequately covered by the government such as ecology, care of the disabled and refugees. MOST also organises workcamps mainly in summer, and an exchange scheme for local volunteers with organisations abroad. 200 Slovenian volunteers and 400 foreign volunteers are engaged per year.

There are opportunities for volunteers to participate in manual work such as building, painting or decorating. Ecologically-minded volunteers are needed to help with gardening and research work and also to find data and run campaigns. There are volunteer opportunities in the area of social work including work with mentally or physically disabled children, elderly people and refugees, and also to organise study sessions among marginalised groups. Applicants of all nationalities are welcome; there is no need for a visa or work permit. Volunteers must, however, be able to speak English and preferably have previous experience of voluntary work. The minimum age is 18.

Foreign volunteers usually join the summer workcamps, which last from two to four weeks, but there are also medium-term placements of six months and long-term placements of one year. Workcamp volunteers get food and accommodation free, while for the medium and long-term volunteers accommodation and pocket money are provided. On workcamps the accommodation is usually basic and communal.

Those interested in going from Britain, should contact the International Voluntary Service, British branch of Service Civil International who will forward the the application to the organisation in Slovenia.

UK IVS Offices

IVS South, Old Hall, East Bergholt, Colchester C07 6TQ.
IVS North, Castlehill House, 21 Otley Road, Headingley, Leeds LS6 3AA.
IVS Scotland: 7 Upper Bow, Edinburgh, EH1 2JN.

OHP: Voluntary Work Corps

International Workcamps, Grzybowska 79 00-844, Warsaw, Poland (tel +48-22 632 43 99; fax +48-22 632 00 10).

OHP organises international workcamps and brigades to undertake social, preservation and conservation projects within Poland. Over 350 volunteers help each year by undertaking unskilled manual work, study and social projects. The workcamps are held during the summer and last from two to four weeks.

Volunteers must be English speaking, 18-35 years old, in general good health and have obtained a Polish visa. Board and lodging are provided.

Those interested should apply through a Service Civil International member organisation in their home country as no individual applications can be accepted by this organisation.

Orfan
38 The Green, South Bar, Banbury, Oxon OX16 9AE; (tel 01295-272770; fax 01295-268790).

Orfan provides support and volunteers for a Romanian orphanage for 200 children. It supplies clothes, toys etc. and runs a permanent, classroom based teaching programme to stimulate the children who have learning difficulties and emotional problems due to neglect.

About 12 volunteers are recruited annually to work with children with ages ranging from four to seventeen years in a classroom situation with educational handicrafts to write reports on each child and to prepare activities. The volunteers also build up a good relationship with the staff and the director of the orphanage.

Volunteers should obtain their own visas from the Romanian Embassy for which they will need a letter in Romanian from a person in authority inviting them to Romania and a letter from the charity. Ideally applicants should have previous experience of children with emotional problems, basic Romanian and a clean driving licence.

Age limits are 20-35 years and strength and health essential. Coordinator positions are for six to nine months while co-worker stints are for three months at any time of year.

Volunteers have to raise their own funds for the trip though the charity wil help out if preparation time is limited. No airfares are paid.

Further details from G M Cumming at the above address.

Teaching Abroad
46 Beech View, Angmering, Sussex, BN16 4DE; (tel 01903 249888 or 859527; fax 01903 785779). E-mail 100533.26240 compuserve.com

Volunteers are needed to teach (mainly spoken) English in local schools in the Ukraine and language classes in Russia and the Ukraine and in summer camps in the Ukraine. In the summer camps in the Ukraine, volunteers may also be asked to help with sports and cultural activities. No TEFL or teaching qualifications needed. Work permits are obtained by Teaching Abroad where needed. Volunteers are needed all year round for periods of two weeks up to a year. Placements and food and accommodation for the whole stay are provided for an all inclusive charge from £445. Back-up is also provided.

A free information pack is available from the above address.

Ukrainian Orthodox Church Kiev Patriarchate in Great Britain and Ireland
Headquarters, 38 Gunton Road, London E5 9JS; (tel 0181-806 4680).

The UOCKP helps conserve, restore and maintain cathedrals and major churches in Eastern Europe. 30 volunteers are taken on annually for one month at a time during the summer. Volunteers should have some conservation experience and a knowledge of Ukrainian, Polish or Russian. Good health is essential. Visas, but not work permits are required. Volunteers will have their accommodation provided.

Applicants should apply to the Right Reverend Father Abbot Mgr. Marek Sujkowski.

Union Forum
Ternopilska 10, P O Box 10722, Luiv 290034, Ukraine; (tel +380 322 422003; fax +380 322 422003).

Union Forum organises various international workcamps in the Ukraine from June to September:
Volunteers are needed for two weeks to work from June 6th to to 5th July to teach English at a recreational centre in the countryside for 5 hours per day. Should have experience with young children.

Volunteers for renovation, painting, cleaning etc in a open-air museum for five hours daily, five days a week for two weeks in June and July. Hostel accommodation.

Volunteers to work in a national reserve on environmental tasks, renovation, painting etc. Accommodation in wooden houses. Periods of work are 2 weeks in July and September.

None of the above is paid. For further details contact Helen Klmova, Coordinator at the above address.

Eire (Ireland)

Conservation Volunteers Ireland
P O Box 3836, Ballsbridge, Dublin 4, Ireland (tel +353 1 6681844).

CVNI coordinates and promotes volunteer environmental work nationwide through its affiliations with many local conservation organisations. There is an annual membership fee which gives members details of and access to a wide range of projects lasting a weekend or longer.

Volunteers pay a contribution towards costs which start at about £15 for a weekend.

Irish Wildlife Federation Groundwork Volunteers
3 Lower Mount Street, Dublin 2, Ireland (tel +353 1 6768588; fax +353 1 676 8601).

Groundwork is a special section of The Irish Wildlife Federation dedicated to organising voluntary conservation projects. It was started in 1981 to tackle the rhododendron infestation of the Killarney Oak Woods. The *ponticum* species of rhododendron (introduced into Ireland in the nineteenth century) has a tendency to become so dense that it blocks 98 per cent of light reaching the woodland floors thus preventing any regeneration at that level. Summer camps to control the problem are now established in both the Killarney and Glenveagh National Parks. In 1995, five weeks of workcamps were run in Glenveagh. In Killarney ten weeks were worked with volunteers from 17 different countries. Volunteers pay about £10 per week to cover administration costs.

For more information on workcamps, send an International Reply Coupon and self-addressed envelope to Groundwork, at the above address.

Pilgrim Adventure
120 Bromley Heath Road, Downend, Bristol, BS16 6JJ; (tel 0117-9586525).

Pilgrim Adventure is an ecumenical Christian organisation based in Bristol which organises 'pilgrim journeys' to the remoter parts of Ireland and the UK. Each journey caters for an average of 20 pilgrims.

About half a dozen volunteers are needed to to assist the Pilgrim Adventure staff with: camp chores, guiding pilgrims, arranging worship and catering. Minibus drivers are also required. Volunteers should enjoy hill walking, island hopping, arranging worship and the 'pilgrimage experience'. The period of service is one to three months in summer. A small pocket money allowance is provided and accommodation is free. *Shoreline — Journal of Pilgrim Adventure* is produced twice a year and costs £2.50 per year including postage.

For further details, please contact David Gleed, Chair, at the above address.

The Simon Community
National Office, P O Box 1022, Dublin 1, Ireland; (tel +353 1 671 1606; fax +351 1 671 1098).

The Simon Community is a voluntary organisation which provides accommodation, food and companionship for homeless and rootless people. Full and part-time volunteers run shelters, community houses and other services for the homeless in Cork, Dublin, Dundalk and Galway.

All nationalities are welcome and no formal or special qualifications are required. Personal qualities such as compassion, sensitivity, and adaptability are most important. Fluency in English and the ability to communicate are essential. Accommodation and a weekly pocket money allowance are provided. Volunteers are expected to stay for a minimum of three months; two weeks holiday, with an allowance, are given after every three months of a stay. The minimum age is 18.

Further information can be obtained from the Recruitment Co-ordinator at the above address.

France

Amis de Pax Christi
58 Avenue de Breteuil, 75007 Paris, France; (tel +33 1 3 44 49 06 36; fax +33 1 44 49 02 15).

The French branch of Pax Christi, the international peace movement of the Catholic Church, runs a temporary youth hostel over the summer in Lourdes. The hostel is run by an international team of about 10 volunteers. Volunteers should be aged over 18 and be prepared to live together as a close Christian Community sharing the work, leisure time, etc.

For further information contact the above address.

Amis de Chevreaux-Chatel
Mairie de Chevreaux, 39190 Chevreaux, France; (tel +33 3 84 85 95 77; fax +33 3 84 85 95 77).

An international workcamp involving the rehabilitation of the Castle of Chevreaux, is organised during the first three weeks of August. Work involves clearing, reconstruction of ruins, stoneworking and topography. Volunteers are expected to work about six hours a day during five days. After work: local recreation facilities including a swimming pool and at the weekends there are discovery tours of the landscapes of the Jura. Volunteers are unpaid and will be lodged on site (castle) with camp beds. All sanitary and kitchen equipment is provided. Ages: 18-25. No special qualifications required, but must be motivated.

For further details contact Jacques Genest, President of the Association at the above address.

ARENA-Association Pour la Réinsertion de l'Enfance et de l'Adolescence
Hameau de la Pinède, Traverse Valette, 13009 Marseille, France; (tel +33 4 91 25 05 03.

ARENA has organised a summer camps for children since 1960. The camps currently take place in Switzerland and are for children aged 5-15 years from the Marseille area of France. Most of the children are of Maghrebian origin but born in France. Although their parents have lived in France for many years they are part of extended families and are strongly influenced by their country of origin. Their lives are difficult in Marseille because they fall between two cultures in an area where unemployment and delinquency are rife amongst young people and because they are often victims of racist attitudes.

The summer camp gives these children an ideal opportunity to escape from the usual pressures of their lives and to experience personal growth through outdoor adventures and where they can learn the art of communal living and how to respect others.

The camp is run by full-time ARENA staff in conjunction with volunteer activity leaders from many different countries and also from Marseille. There are two adult leaders responsible for each group of 5/6 children of the same sex and age. The leaders build up an important relationship with the children which can be immensely rewarding. The work involves also manual work, excursions and evening activities. Volunteers are provided with board and lodging and insurance for the duration of the three-week camp in Switzerland during July/August.

Applications should be sent to Hamed Benkou, at the above address. It is essential to be able to speak French.

Association Alpes de Lumiere
Prieure de Salagon, Mane, 04300-Forcalquier, France (tel +33 492 75 19 13; fax +33 4 92 75 25 14).

The Association organises several camps around Provence lasting about three weeks between June and September dedicated to the restoration of historic buildings, and the development of historic sites. These sites become recreational and cultural centres. Food and basic accommodation, but not pocket money, are provided for the volunteers. The emphasis of the camps is also on enriching the participants' awareness of the culture and customs of the area. The working day begins at 7.30am and ends at 1.30pm; the afternoons are free. Participants work a 30-hour week under the direction of a specialist and a group leader.

Applicants of all nationalities will be accepted for the 150 places available each year. The minimum age is 18 years, and applicants must be fit and not subject to any allergies.

Enquiries should be sent to Vincent Bobillier at the above address.

Association Chantiers-Histoire et Architecture Medievales (CHAM)
5 et 7, rue Guilleminot, 75014 Paris, France (tel +33 2 43 35 15 51; fax +33 2 43 20 46 82).

The Association is dedicated to the conservation and restoration of medieval buildings around France. 600 volunteers per year are needed to work in July and August for a minimum of ten days on the restoration of monuments, chateaux, bridges and abbeys.

Applicants should be enthusiastic and have a very good knowledge of French; they must also be over 16 years of age. No pocket money is provided and applicants must pay, not only for their travel expenses, but also a contribution of 150 francs, plus 60 francs per day for their board and lodging.

Those interested should apply to Francoise Blusson at the above address.

Association de Recherches et Etudes d'Histoire Rurale
Maison du Patrimonie, 21190 Saint-Romain, France (tel +33 3 80 21 28 50).

This association is conducting a long term research project on the archaeological, ethnolological and historical development of Saint-Romain village and its area.

Approximately 40 volunteers per year are needed to work during July and August for a fortnight or longer. The work consists of digging and restoration. No qualifications or experience are needed but a knowledge of French is useful. The minimum age is 18. There is a small daily charge for board and accommodation. Also a registration fee which includes insurance cover. Accommodation is at the Association's Centre or on a nearby campsite.

Applicants should write to Serge Grappin, the Director, at the above address.

Association le Mat
Le Viel Audon, 07120 Balazuc, France (tel +33 4 75 37 73 80).

This Association undertakes restoration, reconstruction, farm and agricultural activities at the village of Audon in the Ardeche region of France. Around 300 volunteers are needed each summer to assist with this work, although only groups of 80 people can be catered for at any one time. Volunteers can choose their daily task from those offered as long as they work at least five hours per day.

Volunteers should be 17 — 25 years old. Camping areas are provided and some beds are available but volunteers must pay for food (about £4 daily), £1 for insurance and a joining fee of around £5.

Those interested should contact the Co-ordinator at the above address for more information.

Association des Paralyses de France
17 Boulevard Auguste-Blanqui, 75013 Paris, France (tel +33 1-40 78 69 00; fax +33 1-40 78 69 03).

The Association needs some 1,500 volunteers each year to help in its work with people suffering from physical disabilities. Much of the work involves assisting them with mobility i.e. pushing wheelchairs, etc. and assisting when they go on holiday, usually in specially organised groups.

Volunteers may be of any nationality, but must be at least 18 years old and enjoy good health. Boys who can speak at least a little French are especially needed. Expenses and pocket money are paid. The period of work is generally 15-21 days during the summer vacation. No special qualifications are needed but applicants should be able to speak a little French.

Applications to APF Evasion at the above address.

Bardou
34390 Olargues, France; (tel +33 4 67 97 72 43).

Volunteers are required to help restore and maintain a 16th century hamlet and to help look after a flock of pedigree sheep. Free lodging is provided in a self-catering house in exchange for 16 hours of help per week. The minimum stay is one month between 1 March and 1 July and 1 September and 1 December.

Enquiries should be sent to Klaus and Jean Erhardt, enclosing an international reply coupon to the above address.

Centre Nationale de la Recherche Archeologiques
1 Place Aristide Briand, 92190 Meudon, France (tel +33-1 45 07 50 04; fax 1 45 07 58 99).

This organisation is undertaking an archaeological excavation at Verberie in France. The aim of this project is to reconstruct the everyday life and economy of the reindeer hunters who inhabited the area by excavating an open air site consisting of structures and hearths. Around fourteen volunteers are needed in July and the first half of August to assist with the diggings and to be trained in fine excavation techniques. Volunteers are normally recruited for three week periods.

This organisation only recruits EXPERIENCED DIGGERS OR ARCHAE-OLOGY STUDENTS who can speak some French. Board, lodging and insurance are provided, but special diets cannot be catered for.

Applications should be sent to Francoise Adouze at the above address.

Centre Socio-Culturel
Place de l'Hotel de Ville, 79700 Mauléon, France; tel +33 5 49 81 86 31; fax +33 5 49 81 43 13).

An international workcamp for European youth which takes place at Mauléʃon 80km south of Nantes. About sixteen volunteers between the ages of 17 and 23. The workcamp involves restoring a 12th century castle which was badly damaged during the 16th century. The work involves restoring the ramparts, cleaning the walls and clearing the land around. All work takes place under supervision and occupies the mornings. The afternoons are spent exploring the region with a guide. Participants pay a registration fee of FF 500 to cover board and lodging. Travel to the site is also at the volunteers' expense. Participants should also bring funds to cover other daily personal expenses. The camp lasts from the 12-26 August.

Further details from Isabelle Cousin, Animatrice, at the above address.

Chantiers d'Etudes Medievales
4 Rue Du Tonnelet Rouge, 67000 Strasbourg, France (tel +33 3 88 37 17 20).

These workcamps lasting between 10 and 15 days undertake to restore and maintain medieval buildings and sites. The projects include two fortified châteaux at Ottrott near Strasbourg and another castle Petit Koenigsburg near Selestat. These sites will become cultural and recreational centres. Food and basic accommodation in tents or huts will be provided for the volunteers on payment of fees which vary between £38 and £53 per session. Apart from preserving historically important buildings and converting them into places which will benefit the community the Chantiers d'Etudes Medievales also aims to provide the participants with cultural enrichment and physical exercise.

Applicants of all nationalities will be accepted for the 250 places available each year. The minimum age limit is 16 years although applicants under the age of 18 require parental permission.

Enquiries should be sent to the Secretary at the above address.

Chantiers de Jeunes: Provence/Cote d'Azur

La Ferme Giaume, 7 Ave. Pierre de Coubertin, 06150 Cannes la Bocca, France (tel +33 4 93 47 89 69; fax +33 4 93 48 12 01).

This non-profit association provides voluntary activity holidays for 13 to 17-year olds. These workcamps take place on the islands of Ste Marguerite, just off Cannes. There is a variety of camps throughout the year but mainly in summer, lasting two to 15 days. There are 15 participants at a time on each camp. Volunteers spend five hours a day working on the restoration of historic buildings. In the afternoons, and also evenings the volunteers can choose from a range of activities including sports. The camps are based on communal life and the participants prepare the meals on a rota basis and help with the general domestic shores. Applicants of all nationalities are welcome and a knowledge of French is a great asset. The cost is FF 2440 for 15 days.

Please contact Victorion Stephane at the above address for further details.

Chateau de Saint-Augustin

Chateau sur Allier, 03320 Lurcy-Levis, France; (tel +33 4 70 66 42 01; fax +33 4 70 66 41 34).

A couple of voluntary assistants are needed to give general help in a 35-hectare safari park based around an 18th century chateau. No wages are paid, but board and lodging is provided. The period of work is by arrangement. Applicants must love animals and nature and preferably hold international driving licences: the positions would be ideal for those who wish to perfect their French.

Enquiries to Mme de Montesquieu at the above address.

Club Du Vieux Manoir

10 Rue de la Cossonnerie, 75001 Paris, France (tel +33 1-45 08 80 40).

This non-profit making association is dedicated to the rescue and restoration of endangered monuments and historical sites. Each year 4,000 volunteers contribute to the preservation of France's heritage and at the same time accquire manual and technical skills as well as some knowledge of archaeology and history. Apart from working on a site, club members may take part in research, publication or committee work. There are three permanent sites: at Guise in the province of Aisne, at Argy in Indre and at Pontjoint in Oise.

Volunteers are invited to arrive at any time provided they come equipped with sleeping bag and camp cooking utensils. Special arrangements can be made for groups of scouts, factory employees and children from holiday camps. There are several summer vacation sites throughout the country at which the minimum length of stay is 15 days. Participants must pay 70 francs per day for their board and lodging, which may entail accommodation in the monument itself.

All volunteers must be very fit. Initial membership in the Club de Vieux Manoir costs 90 francs. The minimum age is normally 14; however, at the centre for specialised courses in restoration at the Chateau d'Argy, the minimum age is 17. All nationalities may participate.

Further details may be obtained by sending a stamped self-addressed envelope to Therese Beckelynck, Animatrice Permanente, at the above address.

College Cevenol (International Workcamp)

Le Chambon-sur-Lignon 434000, Haute Loire, France (tel +33 4 71 59 72 52; fax +33 4 71 65 87 38).

This workcamp lasts 17 days in July each year at the College Cevenol International in the Massif Central (Auvergne). The surrounding country is wooded and mountainous and provides an invigorating setting for the camp activities.

The present school at Chambon-sur-Lignon has been partly built by workcamps held at the site, and in fact it is this construction work, landscaping and maintenance with forms the work done in the summer. The camps also offer daily language classes (two hours) for foreigners run by the Collège Cévenol. In the evenings discussion groups meet or those who wish to can use the time for relaxation. Some outings are organized in the area. It will suit those who like a bracing experience, and mixing with young people of all nationalities.

Volunteers should be aged between 16 and 30 years, and in good health. Accommodation is provided at the school itself, food is provided, and all other facilities. The camp is free of charge in exchange for their work campers are given board and lodging. Campers are expected to join in all group activities. All nationalities are welcome. The volunteers may go, at a very reduced price, on the Discovery trip of France organised by the College at the end of the Workcamp.

Application forms can be obtained from Monsieur le Directeur du College Cevenol, Camp International de Travail, at the above address.

Les Compagnons du Cap

Pratcoustals, 30120 Le Vigan Arphy, France (tel +33 4 67 81 82 22).

Les Compagnons du Cap organize the rebuilding and restoration of a small village in France that was abandoned over fifty years ago. Volunteers, from France and abroad, are needed to help with dry-stone walling, rejointing and re-roofing. There are also opportunities for voluntary work in a nearby forest, garden and on the fruit-trees. Volunteers contribute about £10 a day towards the cost of board and lodging. Work lasts about six and a half hours a day plus time for the preparation of meals; weekends are free. Participants can come for more than a fortnight at any time of year but the organised programme runs through July and August. The minimum age is 18.

It would be useful for participants to know some French.

Those interested should write to the above address.

Les Compagnons du Cap was undergoing reorganisation at the time of press and details were not available.

CONFLUENCE — Enfants et Amis de Beauchastel

Montée du Château, 07800 Beauchastel, France (tel +33 4 75 85 30 72).

Workcamp that involves restoring a hilltop fortified village that dates from the Middle Ages. Over many years the village of Beauchastel's inhabitants moved lower down the valley and the village and its castle fell into ruin. In a final attempt to save their patrimony a local association, The Enfants et Amis de

Beauchastel was founded in 1973 with the aim of restoring the picturesque village for future generations. The work involves mainly construction including building stone walls, carpentry, particularly for roofing, tiling, street paving etc.

The village lies on the right bank of the Rhône, not far from Valence in the Ardèche. The workcamp lasts about two weeks in July and the minimum age for volunteers is 18 years. Volunteers work about 30 hours a week with a half day off every two days and a whole day off mid-time. A registration fee of FF500 covers food, lodging and insurance.

Further details from Yves Collet at the above address.

Cotravaux
11 Rue de Clichy, 75009 Paris, France (tel +33 1 48 74 79 20).

Cotravaux is a co-ordinating body for voluntary work organisations in France. It aims to develop the services provided by workcamps, and to find new workcamp opportunities. The kind of work done by the individual organisations covers a wide range including projects in cities, villages, the countryside and wooded areas, help for the homeless, tourism and youth, and intervention when natural disasters occur.

Most workcamps take place during the summer vacations, from the end of June to September. A few workcamps of shorter duration are open during the Easter and Christmas vacations. Most workcamps last three to four weeks. During the summer, teams can succeed each other at the same work site. Organisations with which Cotravaux has links include Concordia, Neige et Merveilles, Service Civil International, Jeunesse et Reconstruction, Alpes de Lumieres, Compagnons Batisseurs, Union REMPART, UNAREC, FUAJ and Solidarities Jeunesses M.C.P.

Conditions for participation, type of accommodation provided, and expenses paid, obviously vary from organisation to organisation. Volunteers should apply to the individual organisations for information: their addresses can be obtained from Cotravaux at the above address.

Les Deux Moulins
Gontard, Dauphin, 04300 Forcalquier, France.

Volunteers are needed to construct new buildings and improve existing amenities at this holiday centre built by and for young people of all nationalities. The minimum age is 18 years and the centre is open throughout the summer. Volunteers pay part of the cost of board and accommodation. The organisation would like to emphasise that volunteers are unpaid but the work is by no means rigid and exacting.

Further details from the above address.

Etudes et Chantiers (UNAREC)
33 rue Campagne Premiere, 75014 Paris, France (tel +33-1 453 89626; fax +33-1 432 28636).

UNAREC is involved in both short-term conservation projects during the school holidays and long-term projects for professional training throughout the year. UNAREC also organizes short-term volunteer exchanges with 30 countries.

About 800 volunteers every year are needed for both short and long term projects, to help with conservation and building work, to lead groups and to take part in international exchanges. Applicants can be of any nationality. Those applying for posts as group leaders need an international driving licence and knowledge of French. Those aged 14 can volunteer for teenage workcamps, for which camp fees have to be paid. Those over 18 years of age can apply to join adult workcamps, for which there are no camp fees. Projects last for two to three weeks. Accommodation and insurance are provided but not pocket money. European volunteers must bring an E111 form. For workcamps in France there is an application fee of 500 francs; 700 francs for workcamps abroad.

For further information please contact Francois Ribaud at the following address: Délégué international, 3 rue des petits gras, 63000 Clermont-Ferrand, France (tel +33 73 31 10 74; fax +33 73 36 46 65).

Groupe Archeologique du Mesmontois
Mairie de Malai n, 21410 Pont de Pany, France (tel +33 3 80 30 05 20 & +33 3 80 23 66 08).

The organisation undertakes archaeological digs and restoration work near Dijon, France. About 40 volunteers are needed to help with tasks which include sketching and photographing the finds, model making and restoration. The digs last from one to eight weeks and are held during July and August.

Volunteers skilled in any of the above areas are especially welcome but no qualifications or skills are obligatory. The minimum age of volunteers accepted is 17 years. Volunteers pay about £10 per week towards the board and lodging provided.

Those interested should apply to M. Roussel at the above address.

Institut d'Histoire
Universite du Mans,Avenue O. Messiaen, 72017 Le Mans, France; (tel +33 2 43 83 31 64; fax +33 1 40 15 77 00/43 83 31 44).

The Laboratoire is undertaking the archaeological excavation of a chateau that belonged to the Counts of Champagne between the tenth and thirteenth centuries. The chateau is situated in Chavot, near Epernay and Reims in Champagne, France. Approximately 20 volunteers per year help with the excavation; the minimum length of stay is three weeks.

Volunteers assist at excavations 8hrs a day, five and a half days a week both with the digging and the recording of archaeological finds (cleaning, numbering and eventually sketching). Applicants of all nationalities are welcome, but knowledge of English or French is essential. Volunteers must also be interested in history and archaeology, as well as being in good health. The minimum age is 18 years. Volunteers are needed throughout July until the beginning of August for three weeks or longer. Free board and accommodation are provided for those with archaeological experience; others must pay for the evening meal. Volunteers from overseas must pay for their own travel to and from France.

Those interested should contact Annie Renoux at the above address.

Jeunesse et Reconstruction
10 rue de Trevise, Paris 9, France.

Volunteers are required to work in camps throughout France. The type of work varies depending on the camp ranging from the construction of community centres to digging drainage ditches in wet areas. Work is unpaid but free board and accommodation are provided. About seven hours work per day is expected, five days a week. Volunteers are likely to come from all over the world.

Applicants should normally be aged 18+ but some camps are open to those aged 17+. Most camps last three weeks. Some longer commitments for three months also pay pocket money.

Applications to the above address.

Ministere de la Culture

Direction de l'Archeologie, 4 Rue d'Aboukir, 75002 Paris, France (tel +33 2 40 15 73 00).

The Ministry compiles an annual list of archaeological excavations requiring volunteers in France. The list is drawn up during spring for that summer season. Around 10,000 volunteers are needed in total, as assistants in all aspects of archaeological excavations for periods of two weeks to one month. The minimum age of volunteers accepted is usually 18 years. No special skills are needed for most teams but some leaders may require experienced volunteers. Accommodation in houses or at campsites is provided.

Write to the Information Scientist of Excavations to receive a copy of the list.

L'Ouvre-Tete

Les Maurels, 04300 Pierrerue, France (tel/fax +33 4 92 75 10 65).

Volunteers aged 17-30 needed in Provence to help with various activities including renovating a sixteenth century farmhouse and creating a horse trekking centre. The location is in an unspoilt area near the Luberon Mountains. Up to a 100 volunteers attend annually. Duties vary but may include: dry stone walling, path making, plumbing and electrical work, carpentry, masonry, grooming, feeding, looking after the horses, organic gardening, cooking and landscaping. The usual duration of stay is two weeks and a knowledge of French is needed (also the willingness to speak it). There is an obligatory contribution of 100 francs a day for food and accommodation (in a dormitory, tent or rooms) and travel and insurance are at the volunteer's expense. The organisers arrange regular French lessons, cultural excursions and group outings for all volunteers. For an information pack, write to Monsieur Remy Garnier at the above address enclosing an International Reply Coupon.

Service Regional de l'Archeologie

6 Rue de Chapitre, 35044 Rennes Cedex, France (tel +33 2 99 84 59 00).

The Service Regional de l'Archeologie organises archaeological excavations in Brittany. Volunteers (10-30 per site) are needed to take part in various excavations throughout Brittany between April and September. Seven-hour day, five or five and a half days a week. Board and accommodation, often on a campsite is usually provided free of charge, but on some sites there is a charge for administration and insurance.The minimum period of work is two weeks and the minimum age 18. No previous experience is necessary, but a basic knowledge of French is required.

For further information on the sites apply to the above address enclosing an International Reply Coupon.

Museum National d'Histoire Naturelle

Institut de Paleontologie Humaine, 1 Rue Rene Panhard, 75013 Paris, France.

The Director of this museum organizes archaeological excavations in France each year from April to August. Volunteers are required to assist with these excavations and they should be prepared to stay for the duration of the camp which is between two weeks and one month. There is a camping site but volunteers must provide their own tents, etc. They must also pay their own travelling expenses although expenses will be paid while at the camp.

Further information can be obtained from Henry de Lumley at the above address.

Neige et Merveilles
Hameau de la Miniere de Vallauria, 06430 Saint Dalmas de Tende, France; (tel +33 4 93 04 62 40).

Neige et Merveilles is an international work camp involved with the reconstruction of a mountain hamlet near the Italian border, one and a half hours north of Nice.

Volunteers should be aged 18+ and the camps generally last three weeks and inscription costs FF500. Longer volunteer stays are also possible for two to six months from March to November for which the inscription is also FF500. Apart from construction work tasks include working in the kitchen, childcare, services and cleaning. The camp is run by a specialist 'animateur'. About 30-50 volunteers are taken on annually from 15th April to 15th October. There are also opportunities to learn French and to explore the region while on the camp.

Pax Christi
58 Avenue de Breteuil, 75007 Paris, France; (tel +33 3 44 49 05 30).

Volunteers are required to run a temporary youth hostel operated over the summer by Pax Christi, the International Catholic Movement for Peace. During the summer months of each year it organises a centre at Lourdes for international encounters. This meeting place, offering bed and breakfast at modest prices, tries to encourage dialogue between different nations, races and religions.

The centre is run by a team of young volunteers who take care of the practical running of the house. In addition to this, however they invite visitors to join them in reflecting, in dialogue and prayer and in exploring Lourdes. The purpose of the centre is to give a living witness that peace is possible. Volunteers are usually between 18 and 30 years old and must speak French fluently. Each team runs the centre for 15 days. Their work demonstrates a very real commitment to peace.

Remy
Les Maurels, 04300 Pierrerue, France; (tel +33 4 92 75 10 65).

Volunteers are needed to help rebuild an 18th century farm in the Provence countryside that will be used as accommodation for people travelling by horse. Many of the jobs to be done need no special skills, but professionals with experience in plumbing, masonry or electrical work would be preferred; otherwise a financial contribution is expected of participants, the amount varying according to the time of year. Food and accommodation are provided. Work is available year round.

For further details write, sending an International Reply Coupon, to the above address.

Restanques et Murets
Mairie, 84210 Venasque, France; (tel +33 4 90 86 36 07).

Environmental work camp held in Provence during July. The camp is open to anyone aged 18+. Work is a basic 30 hours a week and no experience is needed as technical training will be given. There is a programme of leisure activities. Board and lodging are provided and meals are prepared by volunteers on a rota system. Bicycles and musical instruments are welcome. The cost of inscription is FF170 plus FF280 for two weeks.

La Riobe

c/o Miss Genevièe Gleyzes. treasurer, 53, avenue Pasteur, 93260 Les Lilas, France; (tel +33-1 48 97 07 83).

In August La Riobe organises an archaeological dig at a Gallo-Roman site 72 km to the east of Paris. The work to be done includes digging, cleaning and restoring the finds.

Participants should be aged 18 or over, and speak enough French to make themselves understood. They should also possess proof that have had an anti-tetanus injection. They must be available for a minimum of two weeks and pay FF 220 for inscription and insurance, and FF 55 for food per day.

Service Archeologique d'Arras

80 rue Meaulens Prolongèe, 6200 Arras, France (tel +33 3 21 50 86 32).

This organisation carries out archeological research on the sanctuary of Attis and the Byzantine barracks of the ancient town of Nemetacum. About 30 volunteers per year help with the excavations, and with the washing and cataloguing of the archaeological finds.

No special skills and/or qualifications are required. The minimum age limit is 18 years, the maximum is 35. The minimum period for which volunteers are normally recruited is 15 days between July and August. No expenses are paid, and pocket money is not provided. Volunteers will be provided with accommodation. There is an inscription fee of 60 francs payable in cash on arrival for volunteers from abroad.

Those interested should apply to the above address.

Service d'Archéologie du Conseil General de Vaucluse

Hotel Department, BP 318, 84021 Avignon Cedex, France; (tel +33 4 90 86 33 33).

Volunteers are needed to participate in excavations on various sites with the aim of protecting, researching and documenting archaeological sites throughout Vaucluse. Recent excavations have included the prehistoric and medieval sites and the Gallo-Roman towns of Vaison-la-Romaine, Cavaillon, Orange, Apt and Avignon.

Volunteers should be prepared to do hard physical work. 40 hours per week, minimum age 18 years. Some experience is desirable, fluent French is essential. Accommodation, food and insurance are provided. Periods of work are Easter and Summer. Applications should be made to Michel-Edouart Bellet at the above address.

Service Archaeologique du Musee de la Chartreuse

191 Rue St-Aubin, 59500 Douai, France (tel +33 3 27 96 90 60; fax +33 3 27 96 90 75).

This organisation conducts archaeological excavations in the medieval town of Douai. Volunteers are needed to assist with the excavations and drawing of maps. Workcamps generally consist of 50 volunteers for a minimum of 15 days during the months of July and August. All volunteers are welcome provided that they speak English or French and are at least 18 years old. No special skills are necessary but volunteers with experience may be able to obtain a staff position. Innoculation against tetanus is advisable.

Accommodation is provided and staff receive expenses and pocket money. A registration fee of £10 to cover insurance costs must be submitted with the application form.

Contact the Director at the above address for more details.

Service Archéologique du Musée de Douai

191 rue Saint Albin, 59500 Douai, France; (tel +33 96 2 90 60; fax +33 3 27 96 90 75).

Volunteers are needed to assist with archaeological digging and history research in the neighbourhood of Douai in northern France, during summer. A minimum of 15 days is recommended during the excavation season which is generally from 5 July to the beginning of September. Previous relevant experience is an advantage. A knowledge of French is extremely helpful, but English will suffice. The minimum age for volunteers is 18 years. Board and accommodation are provided. The

For further details contact Pierre Demolon, Director of Archaeological Services at the above address.

Service Regional de l'Archaeologie

6 rue de la Manufacture, 45000 Orleans, France; (tel +33 2 38 53 91 38).

Diggers and draughtsmen/women to work on an archaeological dig in Orleans or one of the other digs in central France. Volunteers should have relevant experience: some knowledge of French is desirable. Eight-hour day, five-day week. No salary, but board and lodging are provided free. The minimum period of work is two weeks between June and September. Applications should be sent in April to the above address.

Service Regional de l'Archéologie

Hotel de Blossac, 6 rue du Chapitre, 350044 Rennes Cedex, France; (tel +33 2 99 84 59 00).

Volunteers (ten to 30 per site) needed to assist in various archaeological digs in Brittany between April and September. The work is for seven hours daily, five or five and a half days per week. Board and accommodation (often a campsite) is provided free on some digs; on others there is a charge. There is a charge of £5 per week for insurance. The minimum period of work is two weeks. No previous experience is necessary, but a basic knowledge of French is required. Applications should be sent to the above address in March.

Solidarités Jeunesses

38 rue du Faubourg Saint Denis, 75010 Paris, France; (tel +33 1 48 00 09 05; +33 1 42 42 49 32).

SJ organises international workcamps in France and cooperates with more than 70 organisations in around 55 countries. They exchange volunteers with these organisations. Volunteers are placed on workcamps, projects linked to the environment, renovation, construction or social work. Volunteers are placed in groups of up to 15 people of different nationalities. SJ receives about 1,100 volunteers annually and sends about 500 abroad.

Workcamps (short or long-term) are open to anyone. Volunteers work for five or six hours a day and spend the rest of the time on leisure activities. As well as manual and social work volunteers can also work int eh CJ offfices or local centres.

The camps usually last three weeks and most are during summer though there is a year round programme of projects. Volunteers must be aged 18-30. There is a registration fee which is payable in advance to cover food, accommodation and insurance and the budget for leisure activities. Pocket money and travel costs are at the volunteers' expense. Volunteers who are interested can go on trainin schemes for those who wish to work in developing countries or conflict zones. There are also regular seminars and leader training sessions.

Volunteers from abroad usually apply to a partner organisation in their own country and not to SJ in France. In the UK these include Concordia (see page 50) and UNA (01222-223088).

Union REMP.ART (pour la Rehabilitation et L'Entretien des Monuments et du Patrimonie Artistique)
1 Rue des Guillemites, 75004 Paris, France (tel +33 1-42 71 96 55; fax +33 1 47 71 73 00).

Over 150 workcamps are operated by REMP.ART in every part of France. About 4,000 volunteers are employed each year to restore and maintain châteaux, churches, villages and the old quarters of cities which are of unique historical or cultural value. REMP.ART strives to revivify rather than merely preserve ancient buildings and sites. Another of their aims is to remain sensitive to the temperament and requirements of the local community. Volunteers are accepted for weekend workcamps and for spring and summer vacation projects; the usual minimum length of stay is 15 days.

Participants must pay 40 or 50 francs per day for food and accommodation in cabins or tents. For people whose tastes, studies or professional aspirations have prompted an interest in archaeology, architecture or the history of art and ecology, the association organizes courses which provide an opportunity to learn the practical techniques of restoration.

Volunteers of all nationalities are welcome, although knowledge of some French would be an asset. The minimum age is generally 14, but is set at 16 or 18 for more difficult jobs.

Applications and enquiries should be sent to the above address.

Germany, Switzerland and Austria

British Forces Germany Youth Service
G1 Division, HQ United Kingdom Support Command (Germany), BFPO 140. (tel 2161 473176).

Summer student volunteers are needed to administer and run summer activity programmes set up to meet the needs of dependants of British military families stationed in Germany. The nature of the work may vary slightly depending on whether or not the location has a full-time youth worker. The job however, will already have been established and the job of a summer student volunteer will implemented on a day-to-day basis.

Volunteers receive a weekly pocket money allowance of approximately £54, free flights to Germany and full board and accommodation. Duties consist of ten sessions per week (mornings, afternoons and evenings as required). Volunteers are required for five or six weeks in July and August.

Camphill am Bodensee

Heimsonderschule und Hof Brachenreuthe, 88662 Germany; (tel +49 7551 8007-0; fax +49 7551 8007-50).

The Heimsonderschule Brachenreuthe is a boarding school for about 80 mentally disabled children (ages 4-17) operating in a village-like framework in common with other Camphill villages. The children, staff and their families, the teachers and trainees all live and work together. The work and life there is based on the anthroposophical teachings of Rudolph Steiner. The school also has about ten mentally disabled adults who receive occupational therapy on the farm.

Volunteers should be aged 19+, in good health and with a working knowledge of the German language. Volunteers help with caring for the children (dressing, washing, feeding and organising leisure activities) as well as helping with the housework. A stay of at least six months is preferred though shorter and longer periods are also possible at any time of year except summer (July and August) when the school is closed. A good time to start is from the end of August. to the end of July the following year. Volunteers receive monthly pocket money of DM 350 plus board, accommodation and social security.

EC nationals should apply in writing and state the length of their availability.

Christlicher Friedensdienst Deutscher Zweig e.V.

Rendeler Strasse 9-11, 60385 Frankfurt, Germany (tel +49 69 45 90 72; fax +49 69 46 12 13).

This organisation conducts international work camps on ecological and peace projects in Germany for volunteers. Volunteers work in childrens' centres, on conservation projects, etc. which require light manual work and occasionally campaigning activities. Ample time is provided for the discussion of questions which arise from the work and for leisure activities. Workcamps are from two to three weeks long, and take place from June to September and cater for around 200 volunteers.

No special skills are required but a knowledge of English would be beneficial. Volunteers should be at least 18 years old. Board and lodging are provided but volunteers must pay their own travel expenses.

Interested volunteers from the UK should contact Britis YAP (Youth Action for Peace), Methold House, North Street, Worthing, West Sussex BN1 1DU (01903-528619).

Friedensdorf International (Peace Village International)

Aktion Friedensdorf e.V., Lanterstrasse 21, 46539 Dinslaken, Germany (tel: +49 2 06 44 97 40; fax +49 26 44 97 49 99).

Peace Village International takes up wounded children from war and crisis areas for medical treatment in European hospitals. After the appropriate medical treatment, the children live in the Peace Village institution in Oberhausen for rehabilitation until they return to their native countries and to their families.

Volunteers are required all year round to take care of the children in the Peace Village. Duties include the preparation of meals and working in the Village's educational institution. Applicants of all nationalities are welcome. The command of English is necessary and basic knowledge of the German language would be appreciated. Experience as a social worker is desirable. The minimum placement is three months. Accommodation and board are provided. Other costs have to be borne by the applicants (such as travel costs). The minimum age is 18 years and the volunteer must be in good health and free from infectious illness.

Applications should be sent to Andreas Simon at the above address.

Gruppo Volontari Della Svizzera Italiana
CP 12, 6517 Arbedo, Switzerland (tel +41 77 86 95 30/+41 71 857 45 20).

The GVSI is a voluntary group consisting of adults and young people from the Italian part of Switzerland as well as foreign volunteers, that organizes relief programmes in crisis-struck areas and work camps and activities for the handicapped. In 1994-95 GVSI volunteers were engaged on reconstruction and maintenance work in the mountain areas of Fusio and Peccia in Switzerland.

Volunteers were provided with accommodation in a house in one of the villages and were expected to help with normal tasks within the community such as helping the aged, cutting wood and working in the stables and orchards. Participants also share daily tasks such as cleaning and cooking. Most volunteers stay in workcamps run from the end of June until September; they must be at least 18 years of age, adaptable hardworking,and must pay their own travel costs.

For more information on GVSI write to Mari Federico at the above address.

Heimsonderschule Brachenreuthe
88662 Uberlingen, Germany (tel +49 7551-8007-0; fax +49 7551-8007-50).

This Camphill community-cum-boarding school for mentally disabled children needs volunteers, of any EC (because of work permit) nationality, every year to work with children in the community's homes and to help with household chores. Applicants must have a working knowledge of German and be aged at least 19. Accommodation, board and insurance are all provided as well as DM 350 pocket money per month.

For more information contact the Director at the above address.

Internationale Begegnung in Gemeinschaftsdiensten eV:
Schlosserstrasse 28, D-70180 Stuttgart 1, Germany (tel +41 711-6491128; fax +41 711-6409867).

International workcamps in Germany. Projects include restoring an old castle, environmental protection, children's playschemes and media projects. Each workcamp consists of a group of about 15 people aged 18-30 from all over the world living and working together for the public benefit.

There is a registration fee of approximately £55; food and accommodation are provided free on the camps. The annual programme of camps is published in March.

IJGD (Internationale Jugendgemeinschaftsdienste Bundesverein eV — Gesellschaft fur Internationale und Politische Bildung)
Kaiserstr. 43, 5300, Bonn 1, Germany (tel +49 228-228000; fax +49 228-2280024).

IJGD organises a number of international work camps and workshops in Germany that last between two and four weeks. The projects include renovating educational centres, assisting with city recreational activities and conservation work. They take place around Easter and from June to the end of September.

Around 1,800 volunteers take part in these projects every year. Participants should be aged between 16 and 26, and able to do physical work. Food, accommodation and insurance are provided but participants must cover their own travel expenses.

Those interested should contact the IJGD at the above address.

Involvement Volunteers — Deutschland
Giesbethweg 27, 91056 Erlangen, Germany;(tel/fax +49 91 35 80 75).

Involvement Volunteers enables people to participate in voluntary activities related to conservation, environmental research, archaeology, history or social welfare. Individual placements or Team Task placements run for 2-12 weeks, some with free accommodation and food, others costing up to £34 per week. Volunteers need to understand and speak some English. Individual placements and/or Team Tasks are available in Germany; in addition, German applicants are placed in Australia, California, Fiji, Hawaii, India, New Zealand, Thailand and the Lebanon.

Involvement Volunteers — Deutschland is a non profit organisation which charges a fee of approximately £200 to cover administration costs. For volunteers coming to Germany, this fee includes travel and visa advice, arrival advice for suitable accommodation and transport from the airport, and a communication base for the visit.

For further information please contact K. Werner Mayer at the above address.

Landdienst-Zentralstelle
Mühlegasse 13, Postfach 728, 8025 Zürich, Switzerland; (tel +41 1 261 44 88; fax +41 1 261 44 32).

The Landdienst-Zentralestelle was started over 50 years ago to enable farmers in Switzerland to receive volunteer helpers from Switzerland and abroad to help with busy times like harvests. Every year thousands of young Swiss help on farms throughout Switzerland. The annual total of volunteers from abroad is about 600.

Volunteers should be aged at least 17 and the upper limit is around 30 (but may be flexible). A basic knowledge of German, French or Italian is necessary. It is easier to place volunteers in the German-speaking areas. There is an inscription fee of Sfr.60. Volunteers make their own travel arrangements. The farmers provided board and lodging and an allowance of Sfr. 20 per day. Sundays are free. The minimum period of work is three weeks and the maximum two months anytime from March to October.

Further details can be obtained from the above address.

Norddeutsche Judend im Internationalen Gemeinschaftsdienst) NIG e.V.
Schillerplatz 10, 18055 Rostock, Germany; (tel +49 381 4922914; fax +49 381 4922914).

NIG was started by the students of Rostock University in 1990 for the purpose of supporting important and urgent work for environmental and nature protection, maintenance of monuments and social projects in north-eastern Germany, in cases where local financial, material and personal means are not sufficient. Another aim is to bring together young people from all over the world and offer the chance to learn about different countries and people, their problems and to co-operate. NIG has exchange partners with 40 organisations worldwide.

About 400 volunteers are placed in Germany annually. Camps include archaeology, agriculture, cultural projects, construction, environmental projects, renovation, teenage camps, work with children, mentally and physically disabled and study programmes. The camp-language is English but German is needed for those working in children's summer camps. Camps last about three weeks and food and accommodation are provided.

A full list of camps is published annually and is available from the above address.

Osterreichischer Bauorden
Postfach 149, Hornesgasse 3, 1031 Vienna, Austria.

OB is the Austrian branch of International Building Companions which organises about 15 projects in Austria during July and August such as building homes and community centres for the handicapped, the poor, the young and the old, or constructing sports fields, etc. Projects last between three and four weeks each.

Applicants should be aged 18-30. They should have a basic knowledge of German and be willing to do manual work; previous experience of building work would be useful. Participants are given free board and lodging and insurance is arranged. There is a participation fee of DM110.

Those interested should contact the secretary at the above address for an application form.

PRO International
Bahnhofstr. 26A, 35037 Marburg/Lahn, Germany (tel +49 6421-65277; fax +49 6421-64407).

This organisation seeks to rebuild broken relationships between individuals and peoples by the promotion and encouragement of contact between young people from all over the world. To this end, workcamps, seminars and holiday courses are organized in Germany. About 500 volunteers per year participate in these workcamps. Volunteers may work as child-minders or manual workers, while others take part in activities connected with handicapped children, or the environment.

What actually happens in a work camp is dependent largely on the individual volunteer. Applicants of all nationalities are welcome as the camps are intended to be international. It is advisable, however, that applicants should have knowledge of French, German or English. Volunteers must be aged between 16 and 26, although child-minders must be aged over 18. Camps are held at Easter and between June and October and the minimum length of time for which volunteers are normally required is two to three weeks. The participation fee is 110 DM, but meals and accommodation are free of charge. The Easter and Summer

Programmes, are published in February and April respectively. Applicants should contact a cooperating organisation in their own country, in the UK this is Concordia. Alternatively, send an international reply coupon to the above address.

Vereinigung Junger Freiwilliger eV (VJF)
Müggelstrasse 22a, 10247 Berlin (tel +49 30 588 38 14).

VJF organises international workcamps in the former East Germany, as well as co-ordinating exchanges with 40 partner organisations from more than 30 countries. VJF places 500 international volunteers every year, as well as 500 German volunteers.

Most of the workcamps are social or ecological projects, but there are also special programmes which focus on issues such as the history of Jewish people in Germany. In most cases, volunteers have to do easy manual work on the camps. Special workcamps might demand special skills but such requirements will be outlined in the VJF brochure. Volunteers must be aged between 18 and 30 years. Most workcamps take place between May and September and last for two to four weeks. Accommodation is provided, but no expenses are paid. Travel to the camps must be arranged and paid for by individual volunters and volunteers must pay an application fee of DM200.

Applications should be made with a cooperating organisation in your own country. In the UK these include Concordia, International Voluntary Service and Quaker International Social Projects.

Scandinavia

Atlantis Youth Exchange
Rolfe Hofmosgate 18, 0655 Oslo, Norway (tel +47 22-670043; fax +47-22 68 68 08).

Atlantis is a non-profit making foundation for international youth exchange, recruiting about 500 young people each year to work in Norway on the Working Guest Programme. Working Guests stay with Norwegian families, and although much of the work is agricultural, volunteers may also be involved with the day-to--day running of the household and helping with the children. The programme is quite energetic and there are opportunities for travel to Northern Norway. The minimum stay is four weeks, the maximum three months. Families tend to prefer that the Working Guests stay for at least eight weeks.

Volunteers do not require any special skills, but farm experience is an advantage. If Norwegian is not spoken, the recruit should consider the possible problems of isolation and communication this may cause. However, most Norwegians speak English so knowledge of Norwegian is not compulsory though, of course, it is an advantage. The volunteer should be aged 18 to 30 and will require a medical certificate and references. Board and lodging are provided, and pocket money of Kr 650 a week is paid for the standard 35-hour working week.

Further details and application forms may be obtained from the above address. UK applicants may also apply through Concordia and Americans to Interexchange (161 Sixth Avenue, New York, NY 10013; tel +1 212-924-0446).

Foreningen Staffansgarden
Box 66, Furugatan 1, 82060 Delsbo, Sweden (tel +46 653-16850; fax +46 653-10968).

Foreningen Staffansgarden is a community for mentally disabled adults in Sweden. Between five and ten volunteers work in the community every year. A volunteer can help in many ways, including working in the bakery and the garden, weaving, farming, cooking and cleaning or merely by participating in daily life with the handicapped adults.

Applicants of all nationalities are welcome as long as they have a genuine desire to live communally with other people. The minimum age limit is 19 years and the minimum length of placement is six months, although it would be preferred if volunteers stayed for one year. For the first six months, expenses and pocket money are paid, and after that a small wage is paid. Accommodation is provided.

Applications should be made to Per Iversen at the above address.

Kansainvalinen Vapaaehtoinen Tyoleirijarjestory (KVT: Finnish Branch of Service Civil International)
Rauhanasema, Veturitori, 00520 Helsinki, Finland (tel +358 144 408/144 418).

Through the co-operation of young people, KVT aims to contribute to international peace and friendship and to make people aware of their social responsibilities and act to abolish social injustice. To this end KVT arranges voluntary workcamps for young people of different nationalities, runs meetings, seminars, and discussion groups and keeps in touch with organisations with similar aims in Finland and other countries. It has been the Finnish branch of SCI (Service Civil International) since 1981.

About 300 volunteers are recruited anually by the organisation, of whom two thirds are Finns. Camps last from two to four weeks. The minimum age for most camps is 18 years. A basic knowledge of English is necessary and some camps may need special qualifications. All nationalities are recruited and visas or work permits are not needed. Board and lodging are always provided by KVT or the organisation the work is done for, as is insurance. Travel expenses and pocket money are not paid.

Non-Finnish volunteers should apply to the SCI in their own Country. For the UK the address is IVS, Old Hall, East Bergholt, Colchester, Essex CO7 6TQ (O1206 298215/fax 299043).

Mellemforkeligt Samvirke (MS)
Borgergade 14, 1300 Copenhagen K., Denmark.

Besides arranging for the participation of about 900 Danes in workcamps abroad every year, MS also organizes international workcamps in Denmark and Greenland which are open to foreign volunteers. The main objective of these workcamps is to bring participants into contact with the social problems found in every society. The camps also provide an opportunity for young people from all over the world to live and work together with the local inhabitants.

Camps in Denmark consist of an extensive range of projects such as environmental camps, nature conservation work/study camps, etc. Many camps in Denmark are open to disabled persons. In Greenland, the camps are organized in small settlements where the participants renovate buildings, build new sheep pens, etc.

The minimum age limit for participation is 18 (20 in Finland) and the volunteers must be willing to spend two to three weeks in a camp during July and August. Food, accommodation and insurance are provided but the volunteers must pay their own travelling expenses.

Applications from British people should be made through IVS.

Nansen International Childrens Centre
Barnegarden, Breivold, Nesset, 1433 Vinterbro, Norway; (tel +47 64 94 67 15).

Breivold is a long term relief centre for teenagers ranging in age from 13 to 18 with deep social and emotional needs. It is situated on a renovated farm 25 km from Oslo. Help is needed in all aspects of the centre. Applicants with skills of a practical nature and with initiative to tackle and follow through ideas with the minimum of supervision are needed. Domestic and farm work is also included in the rota and all volunteers take turns with cooking. Cleaning duties and the care of the animals are part of the daily routine at Breivold. There are many opportunities for sports, hobbies, etc. and all the leaders are expected to stimulate the youths in all areas of life. The most important aspect of the work is to motivate the participation of the youths and to prepare them for the future.

Volunteers at Breivold must be prepared to work very hard, the hours being long and very tiring. Volunteers should preferably be over 22 years old, drivers and with some experience of working with young people. Volunteers receive full board and lodging and 500 NKR per week. Applicants are expected to stay for at least six months, preferably for one year. There is also a special summer programme which lasts for six weeks and for this applicants must apply before April.

Send an international reply coupon for all correspondence otherwise a reply cannot be guaranteed. Apply to the Director at the above address.

Stifttelsen Stjärnsund
77071, Stjärnsund, Sweden (tel +46 225 80001; fax +46 225 80301).

Stiftelsen Stjärnsund is a rurally situated centre for spiritual development and for bringing a holistic view of life into reality. It is a non-profit organisation which is completely independent of political and religious oranisations. The community has no leader, but all activity occurs in cooperation and through personal responsibility.

The centre takes full guests who come for a holiday which may include a variety of courses including yoga, tai chi, meditation, music, painting, tarot and healing. Such holiday guests and pay board and accommodation costs. The centre also takes volunteer working guests who take part in the daily life of the centre and who contribute offer four hours of labour daily. The centre has a garden and greenhouses where cultivation takes place for the centre's own needs. Working guests do not pay for meals but pay a small contribution to the centre by agreement and also a fee for being collected from the station.

The Swallows in Denmark
Osterbrogade 49, 2100 Copenhagen O, Denmark (tel +45 35261-747; fax +45 31381746).

The Swallows in Denmark is a non profit organisation which is part of the Emmaus International Community founded by Abbé Pierre. It is also supported by the Danish Agency for Development in India. Swallows provides financial support for grassroot organisations in India and Bangladesh by collecting and selling second hand goods. During the summer, Swallows conducts workcamps for international volunteers to assist with these tasks. The work involves collecting, sorting and selling paper, books, clothes, furniture, electronic and household goods. Participants are organised in teams on a daily rotation basis for leafletting, driving, sorting, cooking, baking etc.

The camp is both a summer income generating activity and an international get-together for young people aimed at increasing understanding by bringing together different nationalities.

Volunteers have to cover their own travel costs and daily spending money, but food and accommodation are provided by Swallows.

Valamo Monastery
79850 Uusi-Valamo, Finland.

About 500 volunteers are taken on annually to help at a Finnish monastery. Volunteers work in the garden, kitchen, cleaning and sometimes with special work according to skills and abilities. Applicants must speak English or German and be aged 18+. The minimum period of service is two weeks at any time of year. Volunteers get free board and lodging.

Applications to Father John at the above address.

World Assembly of Youth (WAY)
Ved Bellahøj 4, 2700 Brønshøj, Denmark (tel +45 3160-7770; fax +45 3160-5797). E-mail way@inform-bbs.dk

WAY is an international coordinating body of national youth councils and organisations. In its continued support of youth development, WAY provided the opportunity for two volunteers at a time to work at its secretariat in Copenhagen. Fluency is required in one of the folowing languages: English, French or Spanish. However, all volunteers should have a strong working knowledge of English. Volunteers should be aged 20-30, have an interest in youth development issues, and be willing to work for six to 12 months. A two-room apartment is provided for the two interns, and 3,000 Danish Kroner each month is paid as pocket money. WAY also reimburses the round-trip travel expenses of its volunteers. All nationalities are encouraged to apply. For further information, please contact the Secretary General at the above address.

Spain, Portugal, Italy and Cyprus

Agape Centro Ecumenico
10060 Prali, Turin, Italy (tel +39 121-80 76 90; fax +39-121-80 75 14)

Agape is an ecumenical conference centre in the Italian Alps for national and international meetings. It was built by an international group of volunteers between 1947 and 1951 as an act of reconciliation after the war, and is sponsored by the World Council of Churches. Each year 12 volunteers help the permanent staff to run the centre which is especially active over the summer. The jobs to be done include working in the kitchen and laundry, cleaning, running the coffee bar and general maintenance work. Volunteers normally work six hours per day, six days per week for periods of at least one month, mostly from June to September, but also at Christmas and Easter.

Applicants must be aged 18+ and would find knowledge of Italian and other languages an advantage. Free board and lodging are provided, but participants must cover their own travel costs to and from the centre.

For further details contact the Secretary at the above address.

Associazione Italiana/Soci Costruttori IBO
Via Smeraldina, 35, 44044 Cassana (FE), Italy; (tel +39 532-730079, fax +39 532-730545)

Associazione Italiana is a branch of International Building Companions and organises construction workcamps in Italy and Europe and takes part in international projects in Peru, Costa d'Avorio, India, Sri Lanka, Albania and Bosnia.

Volunteer vacancies exist year round but workcamps are mainly in summer. Volunteers for workcamps need have no special skills but for international projects technical aptitudes are needed. The minimum age is 18 years. Workcamps usually last 21 days; international projects are of varying lengths.

Workcamp volunteers have to pay all their own travel expenses and insurance. Food and accommodation are provided free. For international projects there is a monthly salary.

Centro Camuno di Studi Preistorici
25044 Capo di Ponte, Brescia, Italy (tel +39 364-42091; fax +39 364-42572).

The Centro is a research institute concentrating on the study of prehistory and primitive art, mainly in Asia and Africa. and run by a non profit making cultural association. Up to ten volunteers a year are needed to participate in the exploration of sites in surrounding Valcamonica and to help with laboratory work, research, mapping bibliographical work and computerising data in the centre both for local research work and for the expeditions abroad. The fieldwork in the Alpine area takes place mostly in the summer, but the centre itself is open around the year.

Volunteers are taken on for an initial period of three months. Board and accommodation are not provided but assistance is given in finding cheap basic accommodation. A few scholarships are available; candidates are selected after the initial trial period of three months. Volunteers must be aged over 18 and be deeply interested in archaeology, primitive art, anthropology or the history of religions, but formal qualifications are not necessary.

Those interested should contact the above address for further details.

Deya Archaeological Museum and Research Centre
Deya, Mallorca, Balleares, Spain (tel/fax +34 71-639001)

DAMARC has been excavating in Mallorca for the past thirty-five years. Volunteers join a team of specialists and other participants from the US and various European countries for two-week sessions. Participants work together in the field and laboratory and live together in the Research Centre.

Accommodation is provided in dormitories of six to eight bunk beds. Meals are home-cooked and participants help in preparation and household chores on a rotational basis. Volunteers must be students of archaeology or mature persons with an interest in expanding their learning and experience in prehistory, especially that of the Balearic Islands. DAMARC is not able to pay for the volunteer's travel costs or room and board. Volunteers must pay £350 to participate in any of the two-week excavations, covering room, board and tuition, and participants should also ensure that they have medical insurance for Spain. Volunteers must also be physically fit.

Those interested should contact William H. Waldren for more information at the above address.

Emmaus Italia
Via Aretina 230, 50136 Florence, Italy; (tel/fax +39 55/6503458).

Emmaus is an international movement of over 230 organisations in 30 countries. The aim of the organisation is to combat suffering in many forms throughout the world. Emmaus works through the formation of communities of which there are eleven in Italy. The Emmaus support groups are comprised of people who share the Emmaus ideals and who contribute part of their own free time from work or studies to Emmaus activities.

Volunteers are needed for two-week work camps in Cuneo and Fiesso Umber-itano (Ferrara) in June and August to help support Emmaus projects abroad through the collection of used materials (paper, metal, clothes, furniture etc). Living conditions are simple and bed and board are provided. It is necessary that volunteers are able to communicate in Italian.

Further details can be obtained from the above address.

Espaço T Association for Support and Social and Community Integration
Rua de Camoes 834, 1°Dto, 4000 Porto, Portugal and C.C. Capitoliolojas 12 & 57, Av de Franca, 4000 Porto, Portugal. (tel +351 2 8302432).

Espaco cares for people with multiple problems: physical, psychological and social, providing them with artistic activities including photography, drama, painting, sculpture, physical education, dance, Tai Chi and so on.
About 50 volunteers are taken on annually to help with these cultural activities. At present volunteers are taken on as needed at any time and for variable periods. There are no funds to pay or house volunteers and so they must be able to fund themselves.

Applicants should speak Portuguese, Spanish or Italian and have some artistic experience. They must have no criminal record, and be in possession of a national passport/identity card and references.

Enquiries should be addressed to the President, at the above address.

Europe Conservation in Italy
Via Tacito 41, 00193 Rome, Italy (tel +39 6-6874028; fax +39 6-6896981).

This organisation arranges archaeological workcamps at sites in Italy. From July to September hundreds of volunteers of any nationality are needed to assist with the excavations. The workcamps are for a minimum of two weeks but the exact period may vary for different sites.

Volunteers experienced in the techniques of excavation work are preferred but unskilled volunteers will be accepted. A certificate of vaccination against tetanus is required upon arrival at the workcamp and volunteers should be at least 16 years old. The fee for attending the camps varies between 400,000 and 500,000 Lire for two weeks which covers board and accommodation, lectures and excursions.

Further information can be obtained from the above address.

Fundación Volver a Casa
Apto. 50, 08180 Moia, Barcelona, Spain (tel/fax +34 72 55 16 33).

The foundation gives emotional support to terminally ill people and their families. The centre provides comfort for those under emotional stress and offers workshops, seminars, meditation retreats, rural tourism and so on. The foundation does not have any religious or philosophical affiliations. Volunteers interested in this kind of work and willing to offer 14 hours of work a week for free rent can apply to Esteban Llobet, at the above address. Types of work available include bricklaying, housekeeping and carpentry. Volunteers pay a goodwill deposit of ptas. 30.000 and should expect to spend the same per week on food and entertainment.

Instituto da Juventude
Av. da Liberdade 194, 1250 Lisbon, Portugal (tel +351 3151955; fax +351 3151960/3143688).

IJ organises around 30 international workcamps in Portugal each summer. About 600 volunteers are needed to assist with construction and reconstruction work, protection of the natural environment and the protection and restoration of Portugal's cultural heritage. The workcamps last for around 2 weeks. No special skills are required to join a workcamp but volunteers must be aged 18-25 years old. Board and lodging are provided.

The workcamps programme is usually issued in February or March. Prospective volunteers should apply to their national branch of International Voluntary Service.

Instituto de la Juventud 'Servicio Voluntario Internacional'
José Orgtega y Gasset 71, 28006 Madrid, Spain; (tel +34 401 66 52).

This organisation arranges summer workcamps in Spain which involve archaeological excavations, the reconstruction of monuments, the preservation of the countryside, building work, nature studies and community work. About 2,000 volunteers take part in the camps each year which last from two to three weeks. There are no restrictions or special skills required. Board and lodging are provided.

Those interested should apply to the address above, or if possible to an affiliated organisation in their own country. These include: Mouvement des Jeunes pour la Paix, 92 rue Stevrin, 1040 Bruxelles, Belgium; Mellemfolkeligt Samvirke, Hejrevej 38, DK 2400 Copenhagen NV, Denmark; Internationale Begegnung in Gemeinschaftsdiensten e V, 7252 Weil der Stadt Marklingen, Haupstrasse 64, Germany; Concordia, 28 Rue du Pont Neuf, 775001 Paris, France; United Nations Association (Wales), Welsh Centre for International Affairs, Temple of Peace, Cathays Park, Cardiff CF1 3AP.

Turkey, Greece and Malta

American Farm School (Summer Work Activities Program)
1133 Broadway 26th Street, New York, NY 10010, USA (tel +1 212-463 8434; fax +1 212-463-8208).

Every summer from early June to July the Farm School organises an international group of about 20 people to help staff the agricultural and maintenance programmes at the school when regular staff and students are on vacation. The work involves a 35 hour week; a small allowance is paid. Other activities include a climb up Mount Olympus, trips into Thessaloniki and the islands, as well as a short stay with a family in a rural village. Accommodation and meals are provided by the school. Participants should be 18 — 26 years of age and are expected to pay their own fare to Thessaloniki.

Further information is available from the Program Co-ordinator at the above address.

Club Paradisus
52 Mannering Gardens, Westcliff-on-Sea, Essex SS0 0BQ (tel 01702-344119).

Volunteers are needed in June, July and August to clean up the local beach and surrounding habitats of the loggerhead turtle near Koroni in the Peloponnese in southern Greece. Duties also include some monitoring of their behaviour and recording of the relevant statistics.

Volunteers pay for their own transport costs and an accommodation charge of £89 for the month. They work for one to three hours a day, five days a week either from mid-June to mid-July or mid/late August to mid/late September. Some leisure activities are organised during the time off. No special experience is necessary. Applicants under 18 years must have parental supervision.

For further details contact Claire Johnson and Darren Dorsett at the above address until late May; after that date contact them c/o Memi Beach Camping, Koroni Messinias, 240 04 Greece (tel +30 72522130) enclosing an International Reply Coupon if writing.

Gençtur-International Voluntary Workcamps
Istiklal Cad. Zambak Sok. 15/A Kat: 5 Taksim 80080 Istanbul, Turkey (tel +90 212 249 25 15; fax +90 212 249 25 54).

Gençtur organises international voluntary workcamps in small villages and towns involving mainly manual work such as constructing schools, village centres, health care houses, teachers' lodgings, digging water trenches, landscaping projects, environmental development projects etc. Gençtur encourages the participants to have contact with the locals for cultural exchange and uses all occasions to create an international, intercultural atmosphere. The language of the Camp is English. Camps last two weeks with free board and lodging and are organised between June and October. The inscription fee is £40. An optional three days' sight-seeing in Istanbul is also organised at extra cost. Those interested should apply to the above address, or the partner workcamp organisation in their home country. For further details please send a SAE and an International Reoly coupon.

Greek Dances Theatre
8 Scholiou Street, Plaka, 10558 Athens, Greece; (tel +30 1 3244395; fax +30 1 3246921).

The 'Dora Stratou' theatre in Athens is an institution in Athens centred around Greek dance. It is both a theatre and a dance company. The theatre, founded in 1953 has 2500 complete traditional Greek costumes, jewellery and other objects and accessories collected from all regions. Its troupe of dancers put on daily displays of dancing and have their own purpose built theatre near the Acropolis.

Volunteers are need for all aspects of theatre and administration all year round for periods of a month or longer. No accommodation or pocket money. Please contact the above address for further information.

Malta Youth Hostels Association
MYHA Head Office, 17 Tal-Borg Street, Pawla PLA 06, Malta (tel/fax +356 693957).

MYHA operates the MYHA Workcamp which gives people the opportunity to learn about the country while spending some of their time doing voluntary work. This involves spending a minimum of 21 hours a week doing office work, building, decorating and administration work in Malta's youth hostels and youth and charitable institutions.

There are no set hours of work, but participants are expected to put in a full daily work session. They will normally work either from the 1st to the 15th or the 16th to the 31st of each month. Applicants may apply for periods of two to 12 weeks. Free accommodation and breakfast are provided. No special qualifications or experience are required, but volunteers are expected to put a reasonable amount of effort into their work.

For further details and an application form send three International Reply Coupons to the above address.

North, Central and South America

ABIC Amazonia
Programa de Intercâmbio e Trabalho Voluntário, Rua BC 12, casa 316, cep 68.914-000 Serra do Navio/AP Brazil (tel/fax +55 96 321 1343) and Rua Espirito Santo, 362 cep 90.010-370 Porto Alegre/RS Brazil tel/fax +55 51 221.9075)

ABIC Amazonia is a non-profit organisation that carries out sustainable development work. This may include work in schools, health care centres, agroforestry, waste recycling campaigns, environmental education etc. Simple food and accommodatin are provided. Applicants must be self motivated, aged at least 18, have a good knowledge of Portuguese and be able to spend at least four months on the projects from March or August onwards. Volunteers should be self-funding and pay a fee of US$100 per month. Applications should be send to the above address before December or June.

ABIC also arranges short-term workcamps (two weeks) in July and August and has a programme for ecotourists upon reservation.

Agropecuaria Balve S.A.
Raizal Colorado de Abangeres, Guancaste, Costa Rica, Central America (tel +506 6780126; fax +506 678 0125); Germany Representative: Amhohlenstein 54, 58802 Balve, Germany (tel +49 2375 2170; fax +49 2375 2190.

Volunteers are needed to help run and co-work a tropical ecological farm in Costa Rica. The number of volunteers needed depends on the season and the length of stay, but six are generally needed at the same time. Work includes: gardening, small scale agriculture, domestic work, construction, carpentry, mechanical and maintenance work and fishing. Relevant skills are always appreciated but not essential, while a basic knowledge of Spanish is recommended. Disabled people are not excluded provided that they are able to make a contribution to the work load. The minimum stay is a month with no maximum.

Volunteers should be self-financing and there is a charge of US$100 per week for accommodation in rooms normally rented to tourists.

Applications can be sent to either the German or Costa Rican addresses. Prospective volunteers will get a brief description of the project, a questionnaire, a map and a description of how to get to the farm. The minimum age accepted is 18 years.

For preference applicants should have an interest in biological farming and ecology. Those wishing to learn Spanish would be particularly suitable. There are opportunities to travel in Costa Rica.

Enquiries to Rudolph Micknass, President, at the above address. Please note that only Spanish-speakers should contact by phone.

Alderson Hospitality House
PO Box 579, Alderson, WV 24910 USA (tel +1 304 445-2980).

The Alderson Hospitality House provides hospitality to people visiting the federal prison for women in Alderson, West Virginia. The small community in the House believes in the importance of visiting prisoners and strives to encourage visitors by meeting their needs. Two volunteers are required to help with general housekeeping duties, gardening and the maintenance of the largeguest room house and its 11 guest rooms. The volunteers are responsible for making the house welcoming and attractive to guests. Assistance may be required from volunteers with the House's work on furthering human rights, writing applications for grants and raising funds.

Volunteers are required, for either periods of from three to six months at any time of year or for twelve months. Board and lodging are provided, along with a small monthly allowance. Applicants must speak English, and a knowledge of Spanish would be helpful; a sense of humour and a warm, outgoing personality are also essential. It is preferable that applicants should be good at house repairs, typing, cooking and working with computers. A driving licence would also be helpful.

Applications should be made to S.J. Sweet at the above address.

American Friends Service Committee
1501 Cherry Street, Philadelphia, Pennsylvania 19102, USA; (tel +1 215-241 7295).

The AFSC is a Quaker organisation supported by individuals who care about peace, social injustice and humanitarian service. Since 1939 it has been operating short term community projects in South America. Approximately fifty volunteers annually work from mid-July to the end of August with rural communities in Mexico. Tasks include construction and maintenance work. Volunteers work in teams of which about half are Latin Americans. There is also a Cuban project during July which involves hard work in the cane fields with study and seminars. There is also a recreational programme. Spanish is essential. Volunteer age limits: 18-26.

On either project, participants live as a group, often in a school or unused building lent by the local community, and all share in the project's work and maintenance tasks. Work can be strenuous, and participants should be prepared to respond positively to the unexpected. For the Cuban Summer Program applicants with community or church activist experience are preferred. The participation fee for the Cuban Program is $400.

For the Mexican Programme, participants must pay $900 which covers orientation, food, lodging, and transportation during the project, plus insurance. For both programmes, volunteers must pay for their own travel costs.

Applications should be sent to the Recruitment Coordinator at the above address.

American Hiking Society Volunteer Programme
PO Box 20160, Washington, DC 20041-2160, USA (tel +1 301 565-6704; fax +1 301 565-6714). E-mail: AMHIKER@aol.com

The American Hiking Society runs a programme for outdoor enthusiasts to help maintain America's public land: Volunteer Vacations. AHS also publishes *Helping in the Outdoors* a directory of 2,500 volunteer opportunities (see 'Further Reading'.

Volunteer Vacations sends teams of ten to 12 volunteers armed with pulaskis, shovels and rakes into some of America's most remote backcountry for one- and two-week vacations to renovate and clear existing trails, and build new ones. Volunteers can spend afternoons exploring the surrounding countryside, photographing wildlife or just relaxing along a mountain stream. The programme offers an inexpensive way to visit a new part of the country, work with your hands and feel good about giving something back. Volunteers should be aged at least 18, in good physical condition and able to hike five miles or more in a day. Volunteers have to provide their own camping equipment (tent, sleeping bag, backpack, personal items) and arrange their own transportation to and from the work site.

A $50 non-refundable registration fee is payable to AHS upon application.

American Jewish Society for Service
15E 26th Street, New York, NY 10010, USA (tel +1 212 683-6178).

The Society conducts voluntary work service camps for teenagers in the United States for several weeks, beginning July 1st. 40-60 volunteers are needed to work as counsellors and to help with the camps' construction work for a period of seven weeks. Volunteers of all nationalities may apply. Accommodation is provided, but pocket money is not; applicants must pay $2,000 plus their travel costs.

Applications should be made to Henry Kohn, Chairman, at the above address.

Amigos de las Americas
5618 Star Lane, Houston, Texas 77057, USA (tel +1 713 782 5209; fax +1 713 782 9267; freephone USA: 800.231 7796).
E-mail: info@amigoslink.org
WWW: http://www.amigoslink.org

Amigos de las Americas is a non-profit organisation established in 1965. It organises summer field programmes for about 700 young adult volunteers from the US and other countries annually. Programmes take place in Brazil, Costa Rica, the Dominican Republic, Honduras, Ecuador, Mexico and Paraguay.

The types of work which volunteers are construction, education and community health and may include:
building latrines, anti-rabies vaccination for animals, fluoride treatment and toothbrush manufacture and distribution, tree-planting, gardening, human immunisation etc.

As well as providing practical help, volunteers learn management skills through a leadership programme which enables them to progress through four levels of responsability. To do this volunteers may return for more than one year. Volunteers pay a participation fee of $3000-$3400. Travel, health insurance, immunisations and document fees are not included. Scholarships are available to those with proven financial need.

Amizade

1334 Dartmouth Lane, Deerfield, IL 60015, United States of America; (tel +1 847 945 9402; fax +1 847 945 5676).

Amizade is the Portuguese for friendship. Amizade is a non-profit organisation dedicated to providing community service and promoting volunteerism. The organisation brings groups of volunteers down to the Brazilian Amazon to participate in service projects with the community. Past projects have included building an orthopedic workshop for disabled children and building a vocational training centre for Brazil's infamous street children.

Volunteers do not need any special skills but they must be aged 18+ and able to fund their own trip. Volunteer projects run from June to August, last about 17 days and cost about US$2,600 which covers board and shared lodging. Volunteers get the chance to work on various projects which have included renovating, tutoring health care workers in English and working on a reforestation project. There will also be a chance to explore the Amazon on a guided hike.

Further details from the above address.

Appalachian Mountain Club Trails Conservation Corps

PO Box 298, Gorham, NH 03581, USA (tel +1 603-4662721; fax +1 603-466 2822).

The Appalachian Mountain Club is a non-profit-making recreation and conservation group which is responsible for over 1,200 miles of trail in the north-east of the United States, including over 350 miles of the Appalachian National Scenic Trail. Every summer the club sponsors three unique weekly volunteer based camps in NH, MA and NY, as well as ten day service projects in Wyoming, Maine and elsewhere. They are are open to individuals, families and other groups. Volunteers work in teams and are given training and tools to enable them to undertake all types of trail, shelter and other work. Over 500 volunteers participate annually.

Volunteers must be at least 18 years old, in good health, willing to learn and work hard with others and have backpacking experience. All volunteers must have their own accident insurance. Room and board are provided but volunteers are charged £25-£30 or more per week towards costs.

For further information contact the Trails Program Director at the above address.

Appalachian Trail Conference

P O Box 807, Harpers Ferry, West Virginia 25425-0807, USA; (tel +1 304 535 6331; fax +1 304 535 2667). E-mail Appalachian Trail@Charities USA.com

The ATC coordinates the management and maintenance of the Appalachian Trail which is a footpath conceived in about 1921, of more than 2,150 miles, which winds through fourteen states from Maine to Georgia in the eastern United States.

Over 200 volunteers are engaged annually to help with trail construction and rehabilitation. Good physical fitness is essential and an ability to work hard, sometimes under adverse weather conditions. Periods of work range from one to six weeks from May to September. Housing and meals are provided for volunteers. An annual membership fee is payable (from US$ 18).

Applicants can be anyone age 18 or older. International volunteers need a 'tourist visa' and need to show that they have personal reasons (i.e. other than to work on the Appalachian trail) for their visit to the USA. A list of U S friends' addresses in the US would help greatly at immigration.

Further information from the above address.

Arborea Project Foundation
Mapache Wilderness Camp, Boca Taboga, Sierpe de Osa, Puntarenas, Costa Rica (tel +506 786 65 65; fax +506 786 63 58).

The Arborea Project Foundation is a private, non-profit organisation whose aims are environmental protection, and the purchase of endangered lands, to protect and reforest if necessary. Volunteer workers are needed for studies on the foundation's lands, aimed at discovering which plants are vital for feeding birds and animals and to increase the presence of flora and fauna. Volunteers are needed for a period of two weeks' fieldwork. Further details from the above address.

L'Arche Mobile
152 Mobile, 151A South Ann Street, Mobile, Alabama 36604, USA (tel +1 334-438-2094; fax +1 334-438 2094).

L'Arche is an International Federation of Communities in which people with a mental disability and those who help them live, work and share their lives together. L'Arche was started in 1964 and there are now over 103 communities in over 26 countries. 12-14 Assistants are needed, annually, at the Mobile community, which consists of four homes and a work/day programme for disabled people.

Duties of assistants include sharing with the manual labour of keeping a home together; cooking, cleaning, yardwork, repairs, etc. Assistants also help people with self-care and community living skills, as well. Shared prayer is a regular part of the life of the Community, although no-one is required to participate. Assistants work in the homes from the rising hour to 10pm, with a three-hour break in the afternoon (at the weekend, only a two-hour break is possible).

Applicants need no special qualifications or professional experience, but they should be aged between 16 and 70 and in reasonably good health. Assistants generally work for three months to a year. Board and lodging are provided. Most assistants have private bedrooms, but otherwise share all the living conditions of the handicapped people. No pocket money is provided, but Medical Insurance is provided after one month of the three-month trial period is completed. Three weeks vacation are given for the first year; one month per year thereafter.

Those interested should apply, at any time of the year, to Marty O'Malley at the above address.

Arcosanti
HC 74, Box 4136, Mayer, Arizona 86333, United States of America; (tel +1 520 632 7135; fax + 1 520 632 6229). E-mail arcosanti@aol.com
wwws http://www.arcosanti.org/

Arcosanti is the a prototype city based on ecological urban design using the principles of architect Paolo Soleri which combine architecture and ecology and utilise solar energy. Student volunteers are invited to take part in a five week Arcosanti Workshop. The first week is an intensive introduction to 'arcology' (architecture and ecology), and the remaining weeks are a hands on experience involving construction, recycling, site maintenance and cultural events and their preparation.

About 10-20 students take part in each workshop of which there are ten throughout the year. The capacity for each workshop is 50 so more volunteers are needed. Volunteers must be aged 18+ and have the relevant experience in architecture and practical skills such as carpentry, building construction, model making, welding, ceramics, landscaping, agriculture etc. The cost is $450 for the seminar, plus $80 per week to cover board and lodging. After the five week workshop volunteers may be considered for additional resident volunteer work for which accommodation will be provided free but volunteers pay for their own meals and a small weekly fee.

Applications to be sent to the above address.

BUSCA (Brigada Universitaria de Servicios Comunitarios Para la Autogestion)
Jose Ma. Vigil 91 C-9, Col. Tacubaya, Mexico D F, 11870 Mexico; (tel/fax +1 525 516 860). E-mail: busca@laneta.apc.org.

Volunteers aged 18-26 years are needed to work with young local people in indigenous communities in Mexico, on development projects concerned with areas such as health, education, human rights, environment, productive options. Volunteers live and work in teams of five or six people, in hardship conditions and in a very different culture. The minimum period of work is seven weeks between 25 June and 20 August. Volunteers must have a good knowledge of Spanish and be willing to share and exchange experiences. They should have initiative, as well as respect for other lifestyles and cultures. No pocket money is paid, and participants pay a fee of US$ 500 towards the cost of food, accommodation and transport inside Mexico. Participants must also pay for their own travel to and from Mexico.

Applications should be sent to the above address from February until 1 May.

Camphill Village Kimberton Hills
PO Box 155, Kimberton, PA 19442, USA (tel +1 215 935-0300).

Kimberton Hills is an international community, primarily agricultural, where about half the adults are mentally retarded; life and work in the community is nourished and inspired by Rudolf Steiner's anthroposophy. All adults residing in the community are volunteers.

Volunteers are needed to help with agricultural work of all kinds, and to work in the craft workshops, farm store, bakery, and coffee shop, as well as with housework. Volunteers trained in office and maintenance work are also needed. Almost all the work is with and alongside mentally retarded adults. Preference is given to volunteers who can stay for a minimum of six months, and volunteers are needed all the year round. Applicants may be of any nationality, but it would help to have some initial knowledge of English, plus lots of good will and enthusiasm. Basic living needs are met by the community including medical and dental coverage after the first six months, as well and board and lodging, and a small amount for pocket money. Travel expenses to and from the community cannot be paid, but vacation expenses will be paid for volunteers staying longer than one year. Help will be given to overseas volunteers in obtaining the necessary visas.

Applicants for the fifteen places available each year should write to the Admissions Group at the above address.

Camphill Village USA Inc.
Camphill Road, Copake, NY 12516, United States; (tel +1 518-329-4851; fax +1 518-329-0377).

There are six Camphill centres in the USA (80 worldwide). The Camphill village in Copake comprises 230 people in a community in which life is shared with 107 adults aged 24 to 82, with mental disabilities. The community lives together as extended families in 20 residences on a property of 700 acres in rural upstate New York. The community has extensive farms, garden and operates eight craft shops including stained glass making, woodworking, candle-making, book binding etc.

About 75-100 volunteers are taken on annually. Volunteers share life with the families. They help care for the adults, with all types of domestic chores in the homes (cooking, cleaning, providing recreational activities for these adults) and help outside the house on the farm, garden, craft shops or in other houses. Tasks become available as the need arises and in realtion to the gifts/skills of the volunteer. The community also runs a four-year training: first year is a foundation/introduction year, and the next three years is a training programme in social therapy.

The community accepts volunteers of any nationality however in practice they are limited by US visa restrictions and the absolute necessity to speak English. The community will provide letters of invitation for J-1 or F-1 visas depending on the circumstances. Age limit is 19+ and the period of service is three months in summer and six to twelve months is preferred for the rest of the year. Applications are acceptable any time of year.

Volunteers receive room and board, medical insurance US$ 75 monthly pocket money and US$440 at the end of a 12-month stay.

Pamphlets about the Camphill communities worldwide and the other Camphill communities in the United States and further details about volunteering from the above address.

Caribbean Volunteer Expeditions
Box 388, Corning, New York 14830, USA (tel +1 607-962 7846).

Caribbean Volunteer Expeditions takes on between 20 and 80 volunteers a year to document, measure and photograph historic buildings in the Caribbean. The tasks normally take one or two weeks at any time of year.

For further details contact the above address.

Casa de los Amigos-Service & Education Project
Ignacio Mariscal 132, 06030 Mexico, DF, Mexico; (tel +52-5 705-0521/705-0646; fax +52-5 705-0771. E-mail: amigos@laneta.apc.org

The Casa de los Amigos is a volunteer-operated Quaker guest house and service centre in Mexico City. Established in 1956, the Casa provided hospitality to people from around the world, many of whom are working on issues of social concern in Latin America. Since its foundation the Casa has maintained a variety of service projects including workcamps in rural Mexico, aiding Central American refugees, post earthquake reconstruction, and an indigenous artisan cooperative, among other projects.

Volunteers are offered a one to two-week experience of work with Mexican communities, combined with field trips, lectures, readings, discussions and reflections. A Project cost of US$35 per day covers food, lodging, local transportation, a donation to the communities the Casa works with and administration.

Volunteers can also apply for full-time work with Mexican social service organisations for 6 months (longer or shorter possible). The work is intense and challenging and includes AIDs hospices, community health clinic, international refugee centre and a shelter for homeless children. Proficient Spanish is required for these and technical skills are helpful but not essential. The volunteer pays a participation fee of US$50 plus US$25 per month to cover administrative costs. Interns should also allow an additional US$150-275 monthly for room, board and personal expenses.

For details and application forms contact Andrew Conning, Project Coordinator, at the above address.

Casa Guatemala

14 Calle, 10-63 Zona 1, Guatemala City, Guatemala (tel +502 25517; fax + 502 319408).

Casa Guatemala is a centre which cares for malnourished, abandoned and orphaned children, providing them with a school, a medical clinic and a farm. The centre needs about 100 volunteers per year to perform many different functions. In particular, the clinic needs two volunteers to act as doctor and nurse. They must be graduates in medicine and able to stay for six months. The farm has two green houses; one grows vegetables hydrophonically, the other uses organic methods. A volunteer with knowledge in these fields will be placed in charge of this project and will be in charge of some of the older children.

The school also needs between two and four volunteers to teach English and other subjects to pupils at early secondary level; the teacher for these pupils must be fluent in Spanish. Many other volunteers with experience in childcare are needed to work as nannies in the orphanage. Even though the main duties of the volunteers are very specific, they are also expected to keep an open mind and become involved in the daily life of the centre and its daily chores. This might include taking care of the chickens, pigs, and fish, or helping with the agricultural programmes. In exchange for their work and enthusiasm, volunteers are provided with a place to sleep and meals. The minimum length of placement is three months. The teachers and agronomist are required for a minimum of one year. Unfortunately, an allowance (of $100 per month) can only be paid to the doctor, teachers and agronomist.

Healthy applicants resident in the UK and over the age of 19 years should contact Michael J Upfield, c/o Caring and Sharing, Market Cottages, Market Street, Hailsham, East Sussex BN27 2AG (tel 01323-846696) for further information. Applicants must meet very strict moral criteria.

Casa Rio Blanco Rainforest Reserve

Apdo. 241-7210, Guapiles, Pococi, Costa Rica; fax +506 710 2652).

Volunteers are invited to take part in volunteer projects ranging from research to hands on projects. These have included building bat houses, gardening, developing educational materials, research, map trails, trail clearing and community service. Projects can be tailored to suit the interests of volunteers. Volunteers who speak Spanish can work in local schools. Volunteers should be aged 18+ and be available for at least four weeks at any time of year. Volunteers pay a monthly charge of $600 for room, board and laundry. Accommodation is in new, modern cabins with hot water and shared bathrooms.

Anyone interested should write to the above address enclosing three international reply coupons.

Coral Cay Conservation Limited

The Ivy Works, 154 Clapham Park Road, London SW4 7DE (tel 0171-498 6248; fax 0171-498 8447). E-mail ccc@coralcay.demon.co.uk

Coral Cay Conservation sends up to thirty fee-paying volunteers per month on expeditions to South Water Cay in Belize. There they learn fish and marine identification in their first week and then participate in two dives a day to carry out survey work. There is no diving on Sundays. The only people sent to Belize to work specifically for CCC, usually on a 6-8 week basis, are Scientific Officers; all other volunteers pay to participate. Volunteers with medical and/or diving experience may be asked to help out as Medical/Diving Officers.

Individuals of all nationalities may apply all year round; all volunteers, whatever their nationality, must attend an interview and have a minimum diving qualification of or equivalent to BS-AC Novice. It is preferable that volunteers should be one of the following; medically trained, students in marine biology or those with marine/tropical biology degrees, carpenters, electricians or builders. All applicants must hold a current and up to date Fitness to Dive certificate or follow guidelines for fitness from a British Sub Aqua Club. Volunteers may stay for one, two or three months. CCC only provide free flight, accommodation and food to Scientific Officers, but accommodation is provided for other volunteers.

Applications to Sally Barnard at the above address.

Crow Canyon Archaeological Center

23390 Road K, Cortez, Colorado 81321, United States of America; (tel 800 422-8975).

Crow Canyon Archaeological Center is a non-profit organisation dedicated to archaeological investigation where lay people volunteer their services and provide a contribution to the cost of research programmes. The volunteer programmes are run from June to October inclusive. Volunteers help with fieldwork and in analysing finds. The minimum period of stay is one week and stays up to the end of the season are possible. Shared accommodation is provided. Fees range from $650 to $800 a week. The price includes room, board and other costs generated by the programme.

Cuba Solidarity Campaign

c/o Red Rose Club, 129 Seven Sisters Road, London N7 7QG; (tel 0171-2636452; fax 0171-561 0191).

The Campaign organises and selects the British contingent of volunteers for the annual 250-strong Jose Marti International Work Brigade in Cuba. The aim of the brigade is to express solidarity with and to learn about the Cuban revolution. Of the three weeks in Cuba, two weeks are spent working alongside Cubans on local construction and agricultural projects for $4\frac{1}{2}$ days a week. The rest of the time is spent visiting schools, hospitals, factories and other organisations and sightseeing to learn about Cuban society and politics. The timing of the brigade varies from year to year.

Only 25 to 30 people living in Britain and who are committed to learning about a socialist society are selected. Volunteers pay a fee of around £600 which covers the cost of accommodation, food and travel. The centre organizes the required visa.

Write to the Brigade Co-ordinator at the above address for an application form and further information by January 31st.

Eco-Escuela de Español

in the USA: Conservation International/Eco-Escuela, 1015 18th Street, NW Suite 1000, Washington DC 2009; tel +1 202-973-2264; fax 202-887 5188; e-mail m.sister@conservation.org. In Guatemala: Eco-Escuela de Español, San Andrés, Petén, Guatemala; tel/fax: +1 502 9 501 370; e-mail ci-guatemala@conservation.org

The Eco-Escuela de Español is a Spanish language school that offers students volunteer opportunities twice a week in the afternoons. It is a project of Conservation International Guatemala (Pro-Petén) and the municipal government and is partly funded by USAID. The mission of the school is to immerse students in the language, culture, and ecology of the Petén region of Guatemala, an area renowned for its tropical forest and ancient Maya ruins.

The projects for volunteering usually involve work with conservation or community development projects in the area. Projects have included: reforestation, the creation of an interpretive forest trail and environmental education in public schools.

A total of 250-300 student/volunteers take part annually. Food and accommodation are provided on a homestay basis with local families in rustic but comfortable accommodation. The fees for tuition (20 hours) are US60 weekly and the homestay $50 weekly. Depending on the country of origin and length of stay, participants may need either a visa or a tourist card to enter Guatemala.

Fenix Language Institute

Apdo. Postal (POB) 155, Centro CP 98000, Zacatecas, Zac., Mexico;(tel +52 492 2-16-43; fax +52 492 2-18-04). E-mail fenixmex@mail.giga.com

Fenix is one of Mexico's oldest and most respected Spanish language and Latin American Studies Institutes. The three different campuses (Cuernavaca, Morelos; Chalchihuites, Zacatecas; and Zacatecas City, Zacatecas) offer volunteers a choice of urban and rural settings in northern and central Mexico.

Approximately 240 volunteers come to these campuses every year to participate in a variety of activities ranging from the administrative to the medical. The only qualification needed is a knowledge of Spanish. Placements are usually for a month at any time of the year, and although accommodation is provided, no other expenses are paid. Volunteers would therefore have to raise finances to cover travel and other costs. Fenix has been praised by universities, professionals and teachers for providing one of the most active and communicative approaches to learning Spanish.

Applicants of all nationalities should contact Ma. Dolores Diaz at the above address or in the USA: Mrs. Christina Espinosa, Fenix Language Institute, POB 3991, Montebello, CA 90640.

Four Corners School of Outdoor Education

P.O. Box 1029, Monticello, Utah 84535 USA (tel +1 801 587-2156; fax +1 801-587-2193). E-mail fcs@igc.apc.org

The Four Corners School, a non-profit making organisation located in Monticello, Utah, provides outdoor education and environmental opportunities within the 160,000 square mile region known as the Colorado Plateau. Its purpose is to increase participants' awareness and sensitivity to the physical and cultural heritage of this rich and varied environment. The School teaches outdoor skills, natural sciences, and land stewardship by creating a community of individuals who share their interests through informal, relaxed, hands-on experiences.

40-50 volunteers take part in these activities every year, assisting at archaeological sites by excavating and cataloguing. Volunteers also help with the counting of Peregrine Falcons on various rivers in Utah. No special qualifications are needed as instruction is given by experts in their field. Volunteers under 14 years of age must be accompanied by an adult. Volunteers stay for seven days, and the wide range of activities run through the summer months to the early autumn. Accommodation is provided in tents, and is included in the cost of the programme. No expenses are paid; participants pay a fee which covers the cost of specialist instruction, food and permits. Travel costs to Utah must also be paid.

Applicants of all nationalities should contact Janet Ross at the above address.

Frontiers Foundation
2615 Danforth Avenue, Suite 203, Toronto, Ontario, Canada, M4C 1L6 (tel +1 416-690 3930; fax +1 416-690 3934).

The Foundation organises workcamps which take place mainly during the summer months. These projects are organised with the cooperation of requesting communities (native or non-native) on low incomes: these can involve native American communities in isolated northern areas. Under the leadership of one of their number, the volunteers live together as a group, and work with the local people on the construction either of housing or community buildings. Volunteers with skills relevant to the construction process are preferred and those with previous social service or child experience for the recreational/educational projects. Volunteers work in teams of 2-8 people.

All applicants must be over 18, and produce a doctor's certificate which states that they are capable of performing manual work in an isolated area. The minimum period of work is 12 weeks. All living and travel expenses inside Canada are paid, and, in addition, pocket money is provided for those who serve for longer than the minimum period. Up to 18 months is possible.

Applicants should write to the Programme Co-ordinator at the above address.

Fundación Golondrinas
Isabel La Catolica 1559, Casilla 1211-Suc. 17-21, attn Maria-Eliza W Manteca, Quito, Ecuador; (tel +593-2-226602; fax +593-2-222390).

The Foundation works both in the conservation of highland cloudforest (the Cerro Golondrinas Cloudforest Conservation Project) and in the implementation of permaculture/agroforestry in deforested areas under agriculture.

The project was established in 1992 on the western slopes of the Andes in the north of the country and is seeking to conserve this area with its exceptionally rich biodiversity and high levels of endemism. Fundación Golondrinas has been implementing small scale activities in several parts of the area; i.e. tree nurseries and three demonstration sites where permaculture and agroforestry techniques are applied in order to teach local farmers sustainable productive methods.

The majority of volunteers (about 80 annually) are short-term. A commitment of at least a month is required. It is important that candidates have a basic knowledge of Spanish, be in good physical shape and be prepared to work and live in primitive conditions. A contribution is required for food and accommodation on the project site: US$ 180 for a month; US$ 155 for a minimum of three months and US$ 95 for a minimum of six months. The type of work is mainly manual labout such as planting trees, cutting weeds, maintenance in the tree nursery and minor building and carpentry tasks. The main location is Gallupe.

Four long-term volunteers are also needed for a minimum of a year to further develop eight acres agro-forestry, permaculture demonstration site (*centro productivo y educativo agroforestal*). Tree nursery, bamboo, fruit and nut trees, nitrogen fixing trees, alley cropping, tree planting. And/or scientists or students (as part of their studies for which credit is granted or as a practice for their career) to assist and carry out research on sustainable agriculture, forest resource management, flora and fauna. Room and board are provided. No salary. Location: Gallupe and the Golondrinas Reserve. Bilingual Spanish necessary. Candidates with agro-forestry/permaculture certificate or degrees and wide knowledge in an environmental science preferred.

Applications to the President of the Foundation, Maria-Eliza W Manteca at the above address.

Genesis II Cloud Forest
Apdo 655, 7050 Cartago, Costa Rica, Central America.

This organisation is responsible for preserving a cloud forest in the mountains of Costa Rica (altitude 2,360 metres) for bird-watching, recreation and academic research. Volunteers are needed to help with the system of trails which are continuously being expanded and improved and other related work. Tasks include trail work, gardening, reforestation, transplanting and fence construction. Volunteers work for six hours per day, five days per week.

Around five volunteers are needed annually for a minimum period of one month. Volunteers must pay a donation to the project of US$150 per week which covers cooking, sleeping and laundry facilities. Volunteers of all nationalities are welcome but a knowledge of Spanish is useful and preference is given to people experienced in construction or ecological work. Since conditions are rugged and work takes place at high altitudes, applicants should be in good physical condition with all senses intact. Accommodation is provided.

For more details contact the Co-Owner at the above address. Applicants should note that competition for places is very tough, with many places filled by March and most places filled by May. Enclose three international reply coupons with any correspondence.

Hospice Dwelling Place
5784 Occohannock Neck Road, P O Box 127, Jamesville, Virginia, USA 23398, United States of America; (tel +1 804 442 5354; fax +1 804 442 2902).

The Hospice is a home for persons in the terminal stage of cancer or AIDS and is an all volunteer, non-profit ministry providing a warm, caring home for four people at a time. The hospice needs six volunteers daily, two for each twelve-hour shift. Placements are for a minimum of one month and up to a year. Volunteers can be any nationality but must be over 20 years old and speak English well. Full board and lodging are provided.

In addition to providing the guests with personal care, volunteers are required to cook, housekeep, garden and keep the grounds maintained, work in the office (computer skills needed) and much more. No prior training is needed, initial and ongoing professional training is provided. The philosophy of the Hospice is to create an environment where loving care that can be fostered to make the end of others' lives the best they can be. In the process, the carers' lives can also be transformed.

Applicants for this very demanding work should apply to the above address. The hospice can write to the consulate to request the appropriate visa for voluntary service work.

Human Service Alliance (HSA)

3983 Old Greensboro Road, Winston-Salem North Carolina 27101, U.S.A. (tel +1 910-761 8745; fax +1 910-722-7822). E-mail 72634.1002@compuserve.com.

Human Service Alliance represents the idea that ordinary human beings with jobs and families, can do extraordinary things when they work together as a group in service to others. HSA is a non-profit organisation comprised completely of volunteers. There are no paid staff and all services are provided free of charge. Located at the above address, HSA is nonetheless a reproducible model. It is based on principles and methods which can be taught to people of goodwill, anywhere on earth.

HSA offers a full-time, live-in volunteer programme. Volunteers who commit to a specific time and period of service receive board and accommodation free of charge. HSA has four operational projects inluding Care for the Terminally Ill which offers a homely setting where guests live out their lives in a caring and supporting environment. Round the clock care is provided by trained volunteers from all over the world who volunteer for a minimum of three weeks. No previous experience is needed as full training and supervision are provided.

HSA offers a wide variety of opportunities for people interested in full-time, live-in volunteer service. In addition to direct care of the terminally ill, duties can include caring for children with developmental disabilities, cooking, housekeeping, gardening and grounds maintenance, carpentry, general building maintenance and office work.

Those interested in volunteering should contact the above address.

Institute for International Co-operation and Development

PO Box 103, Williamstown, MA 01267, USA (tel +1 413 458-9828; fax +1 413 458-3323). E-mail iicdl@berkshire.net
Web site: http://www.berkshire.net/iicdl

The IICD was founded as a private non-profit organisation in 1986. The Institute runs 'Global Education Programs' which last for between six and 18 months in Angola, Brazil, Mozambique, Zimbabwe and Nicaragua. Programmes include training and follow-up periods in the US. 70-80 volunteers take part in the various programmes every year.

Volunteers work in the following projects: Mozambique-teaching youth and families in rural villages; Zimbabwe-teaching in a school for troubled youth and community construction work; Angola-planting trees, teaching in primary and secondary schools, leading pre-school activities and taking part in community health projects; Nicaragua and Brazil-community construction work.

The programme fee is $3,400-4,600 which covers training, room, board, international insurance and airfare. Fundraising ideas and some financial aid are available. The minimum age for participants is 18 years.

For further information please write to Josefin Jonsson, Administrative Director, at the above address.

Jubilee Partners

Box 68, Comer, GA 30629, USA (tel +1 706 783-5131; fax +1 706 783-5134).

Jubilee Partners is a Christian community based in Georgia, USA, dedicated to serving poor and oppressed people. The community's work includes several areas of service; resettling refugees, peace-making, some prison work, fund raising for Nicaraguan amputees and working against the death penalty. Approximately 10 volunteers per session are required (about 30 per year). Volunteers are involved in a wide variety of work, such as teaching English as a second language, doing childcare, construction/maintenance of the buildings, gardening, office work, library work, etc. It is important that volunteers are flexible and willing to contribute wherever they are needed. Applicants may be of any nationality, but they must be fluent in English. Applicants with construction and/or mechanic skills are always welcome.

Volunteers must be over 19 years of age. Although Jubilee is a Christian community volunteers do not have to be Christian, but should be individuals who are searching in their spiritual life and are open to dialogue. Volunteers are expected to enter wholeheartedly into the life of the community. There are two different volunteer sessions per year: January-May and June to December. Board and accommodation, as well as a community allowance of $10 per week are all provided.

Those interested should contact Sue Byler Ortman, Volunteer Co-ordinator, at the above address.

Koinonia Partners Farm

1324 Georgia Highway, 49 South Americus, Georgia 31709, United States of America. (tel +1 912-924 0391; fax +1 912 924-6504). E-MAIL: koinonia@habit-at.org

Koinonia Partners is a non-profit Christian organisation working in the rural south to combat all apects of poverty and racism. Koinonia attempts to promote self-sufficiency for low-income neighbourhoods and to fight inequality in this region.

Koinonia operates a large farm and bakery under predominantly African American management. All income from the operation is used to fund community programmes including youth education and housing. The aim is to make the neighbourhood a model of self-sufficiency and interacialness and to empower the community.

Volunteers support full-time staff in many different areas: the farm, garden, youth programme, office, Child Development Centre, maintenance, bakery, and products business. Volunteers also share four weekly study sessions that focus on justice, racism, environmentalism, community and issues of faith.

Koinonia supports volunteers with housing, fresh garden and farm produce, access to field trips, social events, and transportation, and stipends for food and extra costs. Applicants must speak English and volunteers must obtain a tourist visa.

For more information contact the Volunteer Coordinator, at the above address.

Latin Link (STEP Office)

38-40 Kennington Park Road, London SE11 4RS; tel 0171-582 4952; fax 0171-793 1023). E-mail: latinlink@solo.pipex.com

The STEP (Short Term Experience Projects) programme provides volunteers with the opportunity to carry out voluntary practical work in teams of ten to twelve people in Latin American countries including Argentina, Brazil, Bolivia, Ecuador, Peru and Nicaragua each year. Most projects are community based both in rural and urban areas.

Over 150 volunteers are part of the STEP programme each year, carrying out practical work in teams in the above areas. The wide range of projects includes building and/or refurbishing schools, extending orphanages' facilities, working alongside deprived children, building/extending churches, bible schools and community/health centres. All are Christian based projects run by Latin American Christians and all applicants must be Christians.

Applicants of all nationalities are welcome, although most of Latin Link's volunteers come from the UK. However, Latin Link is happy to include any nationalities as long as visas are obtainable for them. UK citizens do not need visas to enter any of the countries listed above. 'Steppers' are not allowed to drive in Latin America. Knowledge of Spanish and/or Portuguese would be an advantage, as would any drama, music and first aid skills. Unskilled volunteers are also very welcome.

Volunteers must be aged at least 17; volunteers have been as old as 60 years, but most are under 35. As long as a volunteer is happy to fit in with a team of people from varied backgrounds, they are very welcome. There are few health restrictions, although it is best for asthmatics to work in lower altitudes on non-dusty projects.

The summer projects run from mid-July to early September, and Spring projects run from March to July. Medical electives can be fixed up all year round if plenty of notice is given. Volunteers have to provide all their own expenses. Summer teams must pay £1,340, while Spring teams must pay £1,620 approx. This sum includes pocket money, food, accommodation, flights and insurance but not essential inoculations. Accommodation can be fairly basic as Latin Link believes in living to a standard similar to that of the Latin American hosts. Latin Link can also provide information on long-term work and 2 year placements.

Short-term applicants should contact the Step Office; long-term enquiries to Miss Janet Quarry, both at the above address.

Los Medicos Voladores

P O Box 445, Los Gatos, CA 95031-0445; (tel 800 585-4568 in CA only; otherwise +1 415 967-4137).

Los Medicos Voladores organises medical, dental and optometrical services to remote villages in northern Mexico. Up to six volunteers from September to June are flown in small aircraft to different areas for four-day stints to provide professional health care services to rural inhabitants of Mexico. Volunteers who are health care professionals, pilots, those bilingual in Spanish and educators are especially welcome.

Volunteers are lodged locally sometimes in private homes. There is a volunteers annual membership fee of $35 and $200 for airplane costs. Living expenses are also borne by the volunteers.

Los Niños

9765 Marconi Drive, Suite 105, San Ysidro, CA 92173, United States of America; (tel +1 619-426-9110).

Los Niños is a charitable foundation started in 1974, to provide food, clothing, shelter and education to children in orphanages and poor communities in the

Mexican border town of Tijuana. Volunteers are mainly high school or college students who take part in weekend or two-week educational workshops throughout the year or a six-week summer programme in July and August. Volunteer work covers nutrition, construction, education, youth counselling or other areas of community development. Some volunteers stay for up to a year. The minimum age is 16 for short-term projects and for longer term 18+. Short term volunteers receive accommodation but must pay a participation fee. Longer-term volunteers receive free board and lodging and a small amount of monthly pocket money and should be skilled in one of the above and have a driver's licence.

Applicants should be mature, cross-culturally aware and sensitive to the Mexican culture. All applicants should be fluent in Spanish.

Those interested should contact the above address.

Lubbock Lake Landmark

The Museum of Texas Tech. University, Lubbock, Texas 79409-3191, USA (tel +1 806-742-2481 museum office; +1 806-742-1117 Landmark office; fax +1 806-742-1136). E-mail mxegi@ttacs.ttu.edu

The Lubbock Lake National Historic and State Archaeological Landmark is an archaeological preserve on the outskirts of Lubbock. The aims and activities of the Landmark are orientated toward the excavation of data and the interpretation of that data for the public through a number of public education courses. Around 50 volunteers a year are required to help with the excavation programme.

Volunteers must be able to read, write and speak English and are required to act as field and laboratory crew members during the excavations, collections workers for the care of the collections in the museum, or as leaders on tour programmes.

The minimum age for prospective volunteers is 18 years, and the period of participation is from six weeks to three months between June and August. Volunteers must pay for their own travelling and incidental expenses but receive free board and lodging in the field camp.

For further details contact the Director at the above address.

Mar de Jade

In Mexico: contact Mar de Jade, A.P. 81, Las Varas, Nayarit 63715; tel/fax: +52 327-20184.

In the US: Mar de Jade, P O Box 423353, San Francisco, CA 94142; tel 95 415-281-0164.

Mar de Jade, a tropical, ocean-front retreat centre in a beautiful unspoiled fishing village near Puerto Vallarta, offers unique volunteer opportunities in a 21-day work/study programme. Volunteers work in a farmers' health clinic, in local construction, in cottage industries, or teaching. No prior knowledge of Spanish is required. Most volunteers study Spanish and practise their Spanish while working. Classes are taught in small groups by native speakers. In their free time, volunteers relax and enjoy great swimming, kayaking, hiking, boating, horseback riding and meditation. The programme is offered year-round to people of all ages. The cost for the 21-day programme is US$865, and includes shared room, board, 12 hours of Spanish per week and 15 hours of community work. A longer resident programme is available at a reduced weekly cost.

For more information, contact Mar de Jade at the above address.

Modoc National Forest
441 North Main Street, Alturas CA 96101, Unites States of America.

The National Forest Service of the United Stated Department of Agriculture needs volunteers to work in the Californian National Forests. Volunteers with and without experience are accepted. Accommodation is provided free but a contribution of about £8 a day towards meals is required. Volunteers' duties include assisting with archaeological excavations, both historic and prehistoric (recording, sketching, cataloguing, oral interviewing and research).

Nicaragua Solidarity Campaign
129 Seven Sisters Road, London N7 7QG (tel 0171-272 9619; fax 0171-272 5476). E-mail nsc@gn.apc.org

The Nicaragua Solidarity Campaign (NSC) organises work brigades to do environmental work in Nicaragua. There are two brigades per year, each lasting for one month: one over the Christmas/New Year period and one in the summer. The brigades work for three weeks and spend the fourth week on a programme of talks and visits to organisations in Managua and around the area where the brigade is working. The programme can be varied according to the interests of the group.

Volunteers must be fit, adaptable and prepared to get involved in the work of NSC and ENN in Britain on their return from Nicaragua. The total cost including air fares, living expenses and transport in Nicaragua is approximately £1,100.

For further details contact the above address.

Nicaragua — United States Friendship Office
225 Pennsylvania Ave, SE, 3rd Floor, Washington, DC 20003 USA (tel +1 202 546-0915; fax +1 202 546-0935).

This organisation is a support group for other organisations which operate in solidarity with Nicaragua. Its Technical Assistance Program, organised in conjunction with FUNDECI, enables people to do voluntary work in Nicaragua. About 75 volunteers, of all nationalities, join this program every year. Volunteers with particular skills will be assigned to a Nicaraguan community or project in those skill areas. FUNDECI will set up work assignments with ongoing Nicaraguan projects for those who have limited experience or skills. These projects usually take the form of construction. Almost all skills are needed in Nicaragua; while the mainstay of the program are the technical skills typically lacking in the third world such as hydrology, engineering, architecture and planning, some volunteers become involved in jobs as diverse as massage therapy and video production. A knowledge of Spanish is advisable, if not essential; a volunteer's overall experience in Nicaragua will certainly be enriched if he/she can be self-reliant in terms of language.

The programme operates around the year and there is no limit on how long a volunteer can work under the programme; it is the volunteer's decision as to how long to stay. However, one month is the usual minimum. The average is three months, while some volunteers stay for as long as one year. Volunteers usually live with a Nicaraguan family, although on some occasions volunteers may live together in a house. The programme fee is $300, while monthly expenses in Nicaragua should cost a maximum of $400 per month; this covers basic expenses, as well as room and partial board with a Nicaraguan family.

Applicants of any nationality are welcome to apply. For further information, or an application form contact Stephen Poethke at the above address.

One World Workforce (OWW)
Rt 4, Box 963A, Flagstaff, Arizona 86001, USA; (tel/fax +1 520-779-3639). E-mail one.world@racebbs.com

One World Workforce offers trips for the general public to visit and volunteer at conservation projects in Mexico. At present six trips are offered: sea turtle conservation in Baja and Jalisco, Mexico, crocodile conservation, ornithology, agriculture and environmental education.

Thirty to sixty volunteers are taken on annually and undertake all aspects of work at the camps: data collection, beach patrols, beach cleaning, environmental education, construction and maintenance, releasing sea turtle hatchlings. Any nationality of volunteer is welcome but a knowledge of English or Spanish is an advantage. No previous experience is required. The minimum age is 14 years if accompanied by an adult and good health is essential. Volunteers can work for a week or longer in general between May and December.

Volunteers cover all their own expenses including travel and fees of $300-$600 a week for all food, accommodation and local travel, boat rental etc. Accommodation is in large wall tents with cots, showers and latrines. Meals are prepared and guides are provided.

Anyone interested should apply to the above address.

Parks Canada-Yoho National Park
Box 99, Field B.C. VOA IGO Canada; (tel +1 604 343 6324; fax +1 604 343 6758). E-mail http:/www.worldweb.com/ParksCanada-Yoho/

Parks Canada is the government agency entrusted with preserving and protecting Canada's 36 national parks. Parks Canada organises Research Adventures where those interested in the environment can join a study team headed by one of the parks' environmental education coordinators. The research adventures projects monitor the the health of the environment. Participants can choose from a range of alternative projects including tracking wolf packs, checking bluebird nesting success and measuring mountain forest diversity. Projects last from six to ten days. Accommodation and meals are provided in rustic lodges, warden cabins and field camps. Volunteers must be fit as research days are spent outdoors working. Projects often involve hiking, flatwater paddling, or in winter snowshoeing and skiing. No previous scientific experience is necessary as training will be given in the field and research equipment and safety gear are provided. Participation fees cover lodging, food and local transportation and range from $80 to $170 per day.

Plenty International
P O Box 394, Summertown, Tennessee 38483, USA; (tel/fax +1 615 964 4864).

Plenty is a relief and development organisation founded in 1974. It works with native peoples from Central and South America and Africa as well as within the USA. Projects have included sustainable agriculture, primary health care, ecotourism, alternative energy and other low impact technologies. Volunteers stay for one to three months and fund themselves. Plenty will give advice on fundraising activities.

Sierra Club

730 Polk Street, San Francisco, CA 94109, USA (tel +1 415 776-211; fax 415-776-0350).

The Sierra Club is one of the oldest US environmental campaigning organisations having been founded in 1892. It subsidises trips which combine wilderness outings with preservation projects in North America, although occasionally one or two trips are held in Europe. Between 1,000 and 1,200 volunteers are needed annually. Volunteers use their own camping equipment and camp out while helping to build or repair trails and restoring damaged wilderness areas. The trips last from one week to ten days with most of the trips being held in summer although some are conducted in spring and autumn, and all trips incorporate days free from work.

Volunteers must be physically fit and usually aged at least 18 years. No special skills are required but medical doctors may have their trip cost waived if they act as a staff doctor on an expedition. A typical trip costs around US$275 which includes food but not transportation.

Contact the Outing Manager at the above address for further information.

Sioux Indian YMCAs

Box 218, Dupree, South Dakota 57623, USA.

The Sioux YMCAs annually recruit volunteers as counsellors for their summer residence camp. The Leslie Marrowbone Memorial Camp is on the shores of the Missouri River. It is a primitive summer camp without electricity or running water. The campers are from the Cheyenne River Reservation and other reservations in South Dakota.

Volunteers must like working with children. They must also be sensitive and mature and able to relate to children of other cultures. All skills are welcome, especially those connected with water safety, first aid, creative arts and crafts, games and sports. Those interested in summer camp should have previous experience of camp life.

Volunteers should be in good mental and physical health and aged over 18. Board and lodging are provided, but volunteers ar responsible for their own travel and personal expenses.

Applications should be made to the Programme Director at the above address.

St. Jude's Ranch for Children

PO Box 60100, Boulder City, Nevada 89006-0100, USA (tel +1 702 293-3131; fax +1 702 293-7864).

St. Jude's Ranch for Children is a non-profit, non-sectarian residential child-care facility founded in 1967. It serves boys and girls aged six to 18,(admitted only before they are 14) who are neglected, abused or homeless or who have had difficulty functioning satisfactorily while living at home. The Ranch does not accept the physically or mentally handicapped or severely emotionally disturbed. Children live in cottages of six where they are supervised by 'cottage parents' and attend the local public schools. The director of 24 years, Fr Herbert A Ward, is an Episcopal priest and conducts services according to the Episcopal tradition. The Ranch is financially supported in part by Episcopalians, and through special grants and many generous donors.

St Jude's needs summer volunteers with life-saving certification to assist with their swimming and recreation programmes (including camping, arts and crafts, music and dramatics). Other full-time positions may be available for volunteers with specific education and/or experience dealing with emotionally disturbed or behaviourally disordered children.

Volunteers must be mature, responsible and take strong initiative. They are expected to act at all times as role models in behavious, manners, speech and values. No alcohol, drugs,heavy metal music, or inappropriate posters are permitted. Attendance at religious services is required. Service students are considered part of the staff, and are expected to accept the judgment and follow directions of the professional staff as to what is an appropriate response to children, their problems and behaviour. An orientation, weekly staff meetings, and opportunities for daily discussion with supervisors guide the students in their work.

Applications to the Volunteer Coordinator at the above address.

Student Conservation Association
PO Box 550, Charlestown, NH 03603, USA (tel +1 603 543-1700; fax +1 603 543 1828). E-mail mel@sca-inc.org

This Association offers internships for students and adults to work in national parks, forests and wildlife refuges across the United States, including Alaska and Hawaii.The High School (HS) Programme enables 500 students between 16 and 18 years of age to work on labour-intensive projects such as trail construction and ecological restoration in groups of six to ten students. In the Resource Assistant (RA) Programme around 1,300 older students and adults work in a professional capacity alongside other staff in resource management agencies. Placements are for four or five weeks during the summer for the HS Program, or for ten to twelve weeks at any time of year in the RA Program.

All volunteers should be in good health and overseas applicants must pay for their travel to the United States. No special skills are needed for the HS Program but participants must pay for their personal equipment and transportation to the site. Financial aid may be available. The RA positions require either a specific academic background or an interest in conservation and an enthusiasm for performing this type of work. RA volunteers must be at least 18 years old and out of high school. They are paid for their travel expenses within the United States and receive accommodation and a food allowance.

For further information contact the Program Director in Recruitment at the above address.

Third World Opportunities
1363 Somermont Drive, El Cajo, CA 92021, United States America; (tel +1 619 449-9381).

Third World Opportunities works with Habitat for Humanity in providing volunteer house-building tasks in Tijuana, Mexico, mainly during the spring and summer months. These projects are six-day events in which volunteers live and work with people in Tijuana who are in need of low-income housing.

About 250 volunteers are taken on in summer. Volunteers work with experienced *maestros* in doing all of the tasks necessary to building houses that are 20x4, two-bedroom, wood and stucco construction. No previous experience is necessary as on-the-job training will be provided. However, volunteers with some understanding of building work will be especially welcome. The minimum age for volunteers is 15 years and a knowledge of Spanish would be helpful. The volunteer pays a contribution of $190 towards food and simple dormitory accommodation, plus the cost of getting there. Bible study and integrated worship (Lutheran) are a part of the camp.

Applications to the above address.

United Church Board for Homeland Ministries
700 Prospect Avenue, Cleveland OH 4415, USA (tel +1 216 736-3266).

This Church administers three voluntary programmes which are located in the United States and Puerto Rico. Volunteers may undertake short term, summer or one year voluntary service programmes. Tasks include undertaking community service, assisting with emergency shelters, helping with programmes concerned with peace and justice, etc. Of the 90 volunteers needed each year, up to 15 of these are from overseas.

Volunteers must be at least 21 years old, English-speaking and willing to be placed by a Christian church organisation. Some projects may have specific health, professional or driving licence requirements. Overseas volunteers must pay their full round trip transportation costs and have a J-1 visa. Summer service volunteers receive room and board while one-year volunteers also receive an allowance.

Those interested should apply to the Secretary for Volunteer Services at the above address.

University Research Expeditions Program (UREP)
University of California, Berkeley, CA 94720-7050, USA (tel +1 510 642-6586; fax +1 510 642 6791).

UREP provides opportunities for people to participate in scientific discoveries by acting as field assistants on a University of California research expedition. Research topics offered in a large number of countries include animal behaviour, archaeology, anthropology, sociology, art, music, botany, ecology and marine studies. Over 200 volunteers are needed each year for over 20 different projects. Most projects are offered from February to September and last around two or three weeks.

Volunteers must be in good health, at least 16 years old, have a desire to learn, enthusiasm and be willing to undertake team work. Specific skills or experiences are not essential but may be an advantage. Volunteers pay an equal share to cover the project's costs, which may be anything from about £350 to about £800 depending on the logistics of the expedition. This contribution covers research equipment and supplies, preparatory materials, camping and field gear, ground transportation and meals and accommodation. Travel to the site is not included.

For more information contact the Secretary at the above address.

US Department of Agriculture-Forest Service (USDA)
P O Box 96090, Room 1010 RPE/HRP, Washington, DC 20090-6090, USA (tel +1 703 235-8855).

Volunteers for the Forest Service have been organised formally since 1972. Typical volunteer jobs include maintaining trails, campground hosting, wildlife conservation and timber management. They are also required to help with recreation, range activities, office work, interpretation and the visitor information services. There are almost no restrictions on the type of volunteers required and the organisation attempts to tailor jobs to match the volunteers' skills. Volunteers must, however, be able to speak English, and be in good physical condition although the organisation tries to accommodate disabled applicants.

The length of time for which volunteers are required varies, but the longer commitment (preferably between six and eight weeks) a person can make the better the chance of obtaining a placement. Volunteers are mostly required on a seasonal basis although there are some limited year-round opportunities. Food and incidental expenses are reimbursed, and lodging is provided for long-term full-time volunteers only.

Those interested should contact the above address for details of the regional Forest Service offices.

Volunteers for Peace Inc
International Workcamps, 43 Tiffany Road, Belmont VT 05730, USA (tel +1 802 259-2759; fax +1 802 259-2922).

VFP offers over 800 short-term voluntary service projects in 60 different countries. These programmes are an opportunity to complete meaningful community service while living and interacting in an international environment. VFP places about 400 North American volunteers in foreign workcamps each year, plus about 400 foreign volunteers in US workcamps. Participants live and work with an international group for two to three weeks, providing a diverses cultural exchange with the other volunteers as well as the local hostss.

Work projects include: construction/renovation of low-income housing or community buildings, historic preservation, archaeology; environmental education, wildlife surveying, park maintenance, organic farming; social services, working with children, the elderly, physically or mentally handicapped, refugees, minority groups, drug/alcohol recovery, AIDS education; arts projects, festivals...

Most workcamps are for those aged 18+; a few are for those aged 15+. The main workcamp season is from May to September. A few camps operate year round. Volunteers provide their own transportation to the workcamp site and pay a US$175 registration fee per camp. Non-North American residents must apply through a partner organisation in their own country. In the UK this is: International Voluntary Service (IVS), Old Hall, East Bergholt, Colchester, Essex C07 5TQ; tel 01206-298215; fax 01206-29904).

Vosh International
RR £1, Box 86J, Wentworth, SD 57075; United States of America; (tel +1 605 256-6236).

Vosh International is a health care providing organisation with programmes around the world though mainly in Central and South America and Mexico. Qualified optometrists and opthalmologists are preferred. Volunteers pay their own transportation costs and accommodation costs where necessary.

Further details from Dr. Phil Hottel, Secretary, 132 So. 1st Ave. Iowa City, IA 52245, United States of America.

The Winant-Clayton Volunteers
Davenant Centre, 179 Whitechapel Road, London E1 IDU. (tel 0171-375 0547).

This Association organizes an annual exchange between the United Kingdom and the eastern states of the United States of America for a group of 20 volunteers. Selected volunteers work on community projects which include visiting house-bound people , working with children of all ages, psychiatric rehabilitation/HIV/AIDS and the elderly. The exchange lasts for three months, the last month being free for individual travel, between June and September.

In order to be selected to travel to the United States, volunteers must be resident in the UK or Eire and over 18 years old. The average age of volunteers is between 22 and 28 years old but individual volunteers may be much older. Volunteers must have some experience of community or group work, an interest in people, a sense of humour, flexibility, stamina and a satisfactory way of dealing with stress.

The Association obtains the special work permit required and provides pocket money and accommodation for the two months of work. No other expenses are paid. Interviews are held each February.

Applications should be made to the Co-ordinator at the above address.

Israel, Palestinian-ruled Territories & Egypt

The Church's Ministry among Jewish People
30c Clarence Road, St Albans, Herts AL1 4JJ (tel 01727-833114; fax 01727 848312). E-mail CMJ — ST — ALBANS@compuserve.com

Every year the Church requires about 30 volunteers to work in its hostel in Tel Aviv, guest house in Jerusalem and conference centre on Mount Carmel for periods of three to 12 months. The work usually consists of the preparation and serving of meals for guests, housework and maintenance of the grounds and buildings. No special skills are required and volunteers may be of any nationalilty provided they are over 17 years old and in good health.

Volunteers must pay for their own travel expenses and medical insurance but receive full board and lodging and pocket money. Visas are arranged in Israel.

Further details can be obtained from the General Director at the above address.

Edinburgh Medical Missionary Society
7 Washington Lane, Edinburgh EH11 2HA (tel 0131-313 3828; fax 0131-313 4662).

This Society assists the Nazareth Hospital in Nazareth, Israel, to obtain volunteers for occasional medical, nursing, para-medical and general maintenance vacancies. Vacancies occur irregularly at any time of year. Volunteers may be of any nationality provided that they are in good health and have appropriate qualifications or experience in the relevant area. At least three volunteers a year are required for placements of one to two months, but longer stays are possible. Simple accommodation and the appropriate work visa are provided by the hospital. Travel expenses are not paid.

Write to EMMS for an application form or directly to Mr Kamal Abdo, The Nazareth Hospital, EMMS, PO Box 11, 16100 Nazareth, Israel, for further information.

Ein Yael Living Museum
PO Box 9679, Jerusalem 91094, Israel (tel +972 2-4132571).

The Ein Yael Living Museum is situated in the Rephaim Valley of Jerusalem. The project combines experimentation in the techniques of traditional agriculture with crafts such as pottery, weaving, mosaic, basketry, paper making and construction, as practised in various historical periods. The research in these fields is an attempt to understand the way ancient man interacted with his environment. Volunteers are needed for the building of workshops, to act as guides for child visitors,and to help with research. The participants will be guided by the staff and archaeologists of the institution.

Volunteers are welcome all year round provided that they are at least 16 years old and in good health. No previous experience is needed but volunteers must be prepared to work five days a week for a period of two weeks or more.

For further information wite to Gershon Edelstein, Director, at the above address.

Friends of Israel Educational Trust
25 Lyndale Avenue, London NW2 2QB (tel 0171-435 6803; fax 0171-794 0291). E-mail FOI — ASG@MSN.COM

The Trust has three basic functions. It runs the Bridge in Britain Scheme which is a school-leavers' award scheme; twelve travel awards are granted competitively each year; each Bridge group spends six months working in Israel. Travel to and from Israel and basic living expenses are provided, but not pocket money. It also organizes the Bessy Emanuel Award. One or two travel grants each year are awarded to school, undergraduate or postgraduate students planning a personal research project in Israel. Any project idea can be submitted to the academic adjudication panel. The Trust also offers placements in Israel for young artists, farmers and horticulturalists/botanists.

Further details from the Director at the above address.

Hebrew Union College — Jewish Institute of Religion
One West 4th Street, New York, NY 10012, USA (tel + 1 212-674 5300).

The Nelson Glueck School of Biblical Archaeology in Jerusalem, in co-operation with the Israel Department of Antiquities and the Semitic Museum of Harvard, has a long term ongoing programme of excavations at Tel Dan,Gilat and Shiqmim, Israel.

Around 50 volunteers per season are needed to assist with the excavation process during summer. Volunteers must be at least 18 years old with an interest in archaeology but no special skills are required. The minimum placement is two weeks and all volunteers must submit a completed medical form. The cost of around £800 excludes travel but includes room and board.

Applications to Dr Paul M Steinberg, Director, American Office, at the above address.

Institute of Archaeology, Tel Aviv University
PO Box 39040, Ramat Aviv 69978, Tel Aviv, Israel (tel +972 3-6409703; fax +972 3-6407237).

The Institute is involved with archaeological excavations in a scholastic setting. Lectures, field trips and other recreational activities are also organised outside working hours. About 300 volunteers are taken on every year, drawn from many different countries. Volunteers are mostly students or individuals interested in Biblical archaeology, field archaeology or the historical geography of Israel. There is also the possibility of work for graphic artists, surveyors and pottery restorers. Most work involves digging.

No experience is necessary, but the applicant must be in good health. English and Hebrew are the basic languages, however groups may come with an interpreter. Excavations are generally carried out in the summer months and anyone over 18 who is capable of working in outdoor conditions may apply. The minimum stay is two weeks, going up to six weeks.

Accommodation is provided in camps or in a kibbutz. Three full meals and several breaks are also provided five days a week. Expenses above this are the responsibility of the individual volunteer.

Those interested should apply to the above address.

Israel Antiquities Authority
P.O. Box 586, Rockefeller Museum Building, Jerusalem 91004, Israel; (fax +972-2-292628). E-mail harriet@israntique.org.il

Israel is a country rich in history, and possessing archaeological remains from every period since prehistoric times. A number of excavations in Israel accept volunteers each year. Details of most of them cannot be given very far ahead as final plans are not usually drawn up before spring. If applicants write to the Authority early in the year they will be sent a detailed list of proposed excavations.

The minimum age for prospective volunteers is 18 years, and the minimum period of participation is usually two weeks. Volunteers must be willing and able to do any work connected with the excavation. Accommodation and food are provided by the expedition, but full or part payment may be asked for this, especially if archaeological tuition is involved.

Kibbutz Program Center
Volunteer Department, Takam-Artzi, 18 Frischman Street (3rd floor, apartment 6); corner of Ben Yehuda, Tel Aviv 61030; Israel; Postal address: PO Box 3167, Tel Aviv, Israel (tel +972 3 527 8874; +972 3 524 6156; fax +972 3 523 9966).

This organisation accepts visitors, both as individuals and groups, as temporary workers on a kibbutz for a period of at least nine months. A basic knowledge of English is necessary for participation, and the age limits are 18-32 years. A working visitor on a kibbutz works an eight hour day, six days a week. Apart from Saturday, which is usually the day of rest, the visitor receives three extra days per month. As a rule, working visitors must be prepared to do any kind of work allotted to them by the work manager.

The kind of work involved is of a very diversified nature, and depends on the type of kibbutz that the volunteer is sent to. It is still mainly agricultural, but increasingly tends to be industrial as well. As the kibbutz is a self supporting community, with its own services, quite a proportion of volunteers also go into essential services. The kibbutz provides rooms (for two to three persons), meals in the dining hall, laundry service, work clothes, medical care, entertainment and pocket money. Travel expenses are not paid.

The best way to ensure a place on a kibbutz is by applying to a placement organisation such as Kibbutz Representatives in one's own country. For the UK their address is: 1A Accommodation Road, Golders Green, London NW11 8EP (tel 071-458 9235). For the U.S.A.: 27 West 20th Street, New York, NY 10011 (tel 212-255 1338). Alternatively, volunteers who are already in Israel may apply directly to the offices at the above address, but in this case a place on a kibbutz cannot be guaranteed.

Kibbutz Representatives
1A Accommodation Road, Golders Green, London NW11 8ED (tel 0181-458 9235; fax 0181-455 7930). E-Mail enquiries@kibbutz.org.uk

Each year working holidays on kibbutzim in Israel are organized for about 3,000 people aged 18 — 32 and in good health. The work may involve physical labour in the fields, orchards, fish ponds, cowsheds and gardens; or work in the kitchens, laundry, general services or factory. Applicants must pay for their own travelling expenses and insurance for their stay lasting from two to three months with the option of extending it up to six months. A special work visa is needed and this will be arranged at the Kibbutz Representatives office. They will then receive free board and accommodation, leisure and entertainment facilities and occasional excursions, plus a small amount of pocket money.

All nationalities are welcome, except those which do not hold diplomatic relations with Israel. One can arrange to travel either as an individual or with a group of around ten people, which will be organized by Kibbutz Representatives. Prospective participants are all interviewed by Kibbutz Representatives and kibbutz life is fully explained. Kibbutz Representatives is the only official organisation which represents all the kibbutzim in Israel.

Enquiries to the above address.

The Moshav Movement Volunteer Centre
19 Leonardo da Vinci Street, Tel Aviv 64733, Israel (tel +972 3-6968335; 03-6951954; fax +972 3-6960139).

Moshavim are agricultural communities where almost all farms and homes are privately owned. There are about 450 Moshavim in Israel, and over 100 of these participate in the Moshav volunteers scheme. Volunteers must be aged between 18 and 35 with a clean bill of health and prepared to work for at least two months. Accommodation varies from moshav to moshav, but there is generally a self-catering volunteers' house next to the farmer's home with a shower, cooking facilities, etc. There is also a club for the volunteers with facilities for sport and social activities. The minimum period of work is two months.

The working week is eight hours per day, six days per week with one day off extra per month. Any overtime is paid over and above the minimum monthly wage which works out at about a £1 an hour (1995). For volunteers who stay for the whole winter season (four months) there should be a bonus worth up to two months' wages. Volunteers must pay their own air fares. Unlike kibbutz work, moshav work is mainly agricultural.

For more information contact the above address.

Neve Shalom/Wahat al-Salam
Doar Na Shimshon, 99761 Israel; (tel +972 29912222; fax +972 2 9912098). E-mail 100320.611@compuserve.com

NS/WAS is a Jewish/Palestinian village with educational institutions intended to contribute to understanding and tolerance between these two peoples. The Community also has a guest house. Volunteers assist in the nursery, kindergarten, school and guesthouse doing simple, unskilled work. There are five to six volunteers working at NS/WAS at any one time. It is preferred that applicants speak fluent English. Volunteers tend to fall within the age range of 19-30 but there are no strict age limits. Volunteers are expected to stay at least six months and preferably twelve months at any time of year. Pocket money and accommodation are provided free.

Further information can be obtained on the internet home page (HTTP:// OURWORLD.COMPUSERVE.COM/home pages/nswas).

Anyone interested should contact the Volunteer Recruiter at the above address.

Project 67
10 Hatton Garden, London EC1N 8AH (tel 0171-831 7626; fax 0171-404 5588).

Project is a commercial organisation that has been organising working holidays in Israel since 1967. Project arranges for over 2,000 people a year to go on two types of working holiday, on a 'package holiday' basis; these are as kibbutz volunteers who work for keep only, and moshav volunteers who receive a small wage. The minimum period is two months. Departures take place around the year, with placement guaranteed on arrival in Tel Aviv.

Project cooperates with two Kibbutz movements and volunteers receive free accommodation, meals, laundry, pocket money, recreational facilities and occasional trips in exchange for working an eight-hour, six-day week. Age limits are 18-32.

On a moshav working holiday age limits are 21-35. Work is mainly agricultural. Free accommodation is provided (usually self-contained). In exchange for their work volunteers receive a monthly salary which may be increased if overtime is worked.

Project 67 has its own office in Tel Aviv which is easily accessible to volunteers while they are in Israel. The Tel-Aviv office can arrange return flights, a change of kibbutz or moshav, insurance extensions and offer general advice. It can also be used as a forwarding address and baggage store and travel agent for trips to Egypt, Jordan and onward travel and excursions throughout Israel and the Mediterranean.

For more details those interested can visit Project's London office to watch a video about volunteering, or telephone or send a sae for a brochure .

Religious Kibbutz Movement
7 Dubnov Street, Tel Aviv, Israel (tel +972 3-6957231).

The Movement accepts a limited number of volunteers to work on its kibbutzim which are situated in many parts of Israel, including the Beit Sh'ean Valley, Ashdod, Ashkelon, and the Jerusalem and Tel Aviv areas. It should be noted however that only Jewish young people who are ready to follow an orthodox way of life are taken on as volunteers by the Movement. The minimum period of stay is two months. The volunteer works at least eight and a half hours each day, most of the work being seasonal and agricultural. The Movement also runs four Kibbutz-Ulpan programmes (five months in duration), which combine formal instruction in Hebrew with voluntary work in a Kibbutz. These programmes take place throughout the year.

Volunteers must be at least 18 years of age, and in good health. No special qualifications are needed, but people with diplomas in life-saving are appreciated. All nationalities are welcome. Accommodation and food are provided, and moderate pocket money is paid. Expenses are not paid, including those arising from travel. A tourist visa is required but no work permit is needed.

Applications should be sent to: Bnei Akiva, 2 Hallswell Road, London, NW11 0DJ or to Kibbutz Representatives, 1a Accommodation Road, London NW11 8EP.

Shatil: Support Project for Voluntary Organisations
P O Box 53395, Jerusalem 91533, Israel; (tel +972 2 723597).

Founded over fifteen years ago by the New Israel Fund of Great Britain, Shatil operates throughout Israel providing technical and organisational assistance and support to non profit and social change organisations. Volunteers can be placed in various types of work including teaching English and preparing TEFL materials, working with the disabled, special research projects (e.g. legal). Other possibilities exist depending on the individual volunteer's abilities and experience. A minimum of four months' commitment is preferred. Working hours range from a few hours a week to full-time. Board and lodging can be provided in rural villages. No wages or other costs are paid unless working on the placement involves travel expenses.

Volunteers with previous experience of Israel are preferred. The ability to speak Hebrew or Arabic is essential. Communicators/writers, teachers, community organisers, IT experts and medics are particularly needed.

Applications can be sent direct to the above address or the New Israel Fund, Craven House, 121 Kingsway, London WC2 6NX.

Transonic Travel
3 Phoenix Street, London WC2H 8PW; (tel 0171-240 9909; fax 0171-240 8909).

Transonic is a commercial organisation that recruits paid volunteers for moshavim and volunteers for kibbutzim in Israel. About 650 volunteer places are arranged annually. On kibbutzim, jobs can be agricultural, kitchen, or helping out in guesthouses and small-scale factories. On moshavim a small wage is paid for agricultural labour, usually crop picking. Age limits are 18-32 years old and the minimum work period is two months up to a year maximum. Kibbutz volunteers work eight hours a day, six days a week; there is usually a lot of overtime on moshavim. Volunteers are needed all year round and volunteer visas are arranged once the volunteer has arrived in Israel. Board and lodging are provided. Transportation to Israel and the kibbutz/moshav is at the volunteers' expense and can be arranged through Transonic.

Universities' Educational Trust For Palestinians (UNIPAL)
CMEIS, South Road, Durham, DH1 3TG. (tel/fax 0191-386 7124).

UNIPAL is the Universities' Trust for educational exchange with Palestinians. It sends volunteers each year to work on short-term projects during July and August in the Palestinian territories of the West Bank and Gaza Strip and with Palestinian communities in Israel and Jordan. Most projects involve teaching English or work with children. There are also opportunities to teach English for a minimum of one year. TEFL qualifications, experience of teaching English or working with children is essential.

Short-term volunteers are provided with food and accommodation but pay their own air fares and insurance. Long-term volunteers receive pocket money and may be given assistance in paying fares etc.

Send SAE for application form which must be returned before the end of February. Interviews normally take place in March with a briefing in June for those selected.

Wind Sand & Stars
2 Arkwright Road, Hampstead, London NW3 6AD (tel 0171-433 3684; fax 0171-431 3247).

Volunteer Expedition members are needed to participate in a 2-week summer environmental expedition to the high desert mountain area of Sinai around Mt. Sinai and St. Catherine's Monastery. Participants will help clean up the areas worst affected by increasing numbers of visitors to the Monastery, Mt. Sinai and the surrounding mountains. The growing amounts of rubbish threaten this unique and beautiful region. Participants will also help assess the impact of the waste ont he fragile eco-system. Participants will work closely with the local Bedouin and the monks at the Monastery. The expedition is part subsidised; participants are required to contribute towards food, accommodation and transport.
Enquiries to the above address.

Africa

Les Amis des Chantiers Internationaux de Meknes
BP 08, 50001 Meknes, Morocco.

ACIM runs three-week summer camps in Meknes in July and August. It also arranges voluntary exchanges between other countries and recruits Moroccans for voluntary placements abroad. For the summer camps, ACIM takes international volunteers to work with children and to do some ecological, agricultural and building work. Applicants must be aged 17+. Working hours are normally 30-35 weekly with afternoons and weekends free. Volunteers receive board and lodging and insurance. All other expenses are borne by the volunteers.
For more information on the summer camps, contact the above address enclosing an international reply coupon.

The Centre for Alternative Development Strategies (CADS)
5 Frazer-Davies Drives, off King Street, PMB 1290 Freetown, Sierra Leone, West Africa (tel +232 22 230964; fax +232 22 232258).

CADS runs a international volunteer exchange programme that works on projects emphasising cooperation, where volunteers from all over the world can work together in sharing resources, ideas and solutions. Volunteers pay a registration fee of US$750 or the equivalent once month in advance of arrival. This covers registration certificates, reading materials and an audio-visual documentary on Sierra Leone sent prior to arrival. Volunteer fees are paid in cash in US dollars or equivalent on arrival in Freetown. There are two durations of stay: Short term: the minimum stay is one week and the maximum four weeks and costs US$4,895; longer term is for five to 12 weeks and costs US$7,950.
The CADS range of activities covers reconciliation, reconstruction and rehabilitation programmes, community based projects, agricultural projects, earth rescue programmes, overseas exchanges and academic guidance programmes.

Chantiers Jeunesse Maroc
BP 1351, Rabat R.P. 10001, Morocco (fax +212 7 72 66 58).

CJM organises workcamps in Morocco which concentrate on projects intended to benefit the local community. It also sends Moroccan volunteers abroad.

Volunteers may work on construction, restoration of buildings, painting and working with abandoned children, spending two or three weeks of the summer on the sites with fellow workers from many European and African countries.

Applicants should be between 18 and 30 years old, and in good health. Food and accommodation are provided, but volunteers are responsible for all their own personal expenses.

Those interested can either apply through their national branch of the CCIVS (which is IVS in Britain), or directly to the President at the above address or if American through the Council on International Educational Exchange.

Chantiers Sociaux Marocains
P O Box 456, Rabat, Morocco (tel +212 7-79 13 70).

CSM organises workcamps in Morocco which focus on projects aimed at benefiting the local community. About 300 international volunteers a year are recruited for two to three weeks at a time. The age limits for applicant is 18-30 years old and good health is essential. Accommodation and board is provided but all other expenses are the volunteers' own responsability.

Applicants should apply through a cooperating organisation in their own country; in the UK this is the United Nations Association Youth Service or IVS.

Development Aid from People to People (DAPP)
Box 2630 Tastrup, Denmark (tel +45 40 94 92 22; fax +45 43 99 59 82).

Volunteers are needed for human development projects in Angola after the ravages of the 30-year war there. Volunteers need no special qualifications and will be given six months' training at the Travelling Folk High School, Norway including fundraising for Africa in Finland, Sweden and Norway. Placements in Angola last six months and projects include: teaching street children in a 'children's town', building latrines, watercleaning systems and fire-saving stoves. Also, teaching young Angolan women agriculture, buisness and health skills. After completion of the project period in Angola there is a two-month project evaluation at the school.

Volunteers are entirely self-financing. Starting dates are in November and June.

For further details contact the Information Secretary at the above address.

Eclaireuses et Eclaireurs du Senegal
5 rue Pierre Millon, BP 744 Dakkar, Senegal (tel +221 21 73 67; fax +221 22 88 73).

This organisation needs volunteers to help on the following projects. They are needed to carry out a survey in Senegal on health problems and to work both in the national headquarters and at local or district level. Volunteers are needed to lead training courses for scouts' unit leaders and other commissioners, and to train young people in agriculture, mechanics, wood craft and to give sex education and advice to adolescents. A voluntary Deputy Director is also needed for a community Development Project in a rural area, who will be able to oversee an agricultural training programme.

Applicants may be of any nationality, but it would be preferable if applicants were able to speak French. Applications are welcome at any time of the year; the length of placements depends on the availability of volunteers. Accommodation is available in both urban and rural areas, but volunteers must make a financial contribution towards costs. Pocket money is not provided and volunteers must pay for their own travel expenses to and from Senegal.

Those interested should apply to the National Commissioner for Administration at the above address.

FOCUS, Inc.

Department of Opthalmology, Loyola University Medical Centre, 2160 South First Avenue, Maywood, Illinois 60153, USA (tel +1 708-216 3408; fax +1 708/216-3557).

FOCUS recruits opthalmologists as short term volunteers for eye clinics in Nigeria where they provide medical and surgical eye care services. Around 15 volunteers are needed for placements of three weeks or longer, all year round.

Applicants must be certified opthalmologists and need to obtain a Nigerian visa. Usually a US medical licence is required but this would be waived for UK opthalmologists. Board, lodging, laundry services and transportation within Nigeria are provided but volunteers pay for their own international travel.

Write to the President of FOCUS at the above address for more details.

Greenforce Africa — Conservation Through Research

Applications Department, 7 Gloucester Mews, London W2 3HE (tel/fax 0171-402 6387).

Greenforce needs volunteer researchers to join varied aid projects for ten to twelve weeks. Project work includes: threatened mammal surveys, biodiversity work, tribal study and management, flora and fauna analysis and educational work. No specific experience is required but volunteers must be resourceful as field conditions are basic. Taking part can be viewed as a start to an environmental career. After completing a volunteer research project researchers can then apply for staff positions including Ph.D funding.

Volunteers have to pay their own costs (about £2,650 in total) which includes: fundraising and information packs, a briefing weekend, flights, in-country training, accommodation and food, insurance, visas and transport.

Health Projects Abroad

PO Box 24, Bakewell, Derbyshire DE45 1ZW; tel 01629-640052; fax 01629 640054).

HPA offers young people in the UK opportunities to spend time living and working in Africa as part of long-term development projects. The volunteer programme is aimed at anyone aged 18-28. No special skills are required. The programme involves three months in Tanzania plus three UK-based briefing weekends. In Tanzania, volunteers work alongside the local villagers on small construction projects, such as building new village health centres, or improving water storage facilities.

Volunteers are chosen on the basis of an application form and a selection weekend. They should be open individuals able to benefit from the experience and sensitive to host communities and to other members of the team. Over 120 volunteers will take part in the programme in 1997, in small groups of ten.

Currently, overseas phases start in May, July and September. Each participant is required to raise £2,700 (1995/96) towards the cost of their involvement (including travel, food and insurance) and project costs. Advice and support with fundraising is given through the briefing weekends.

For an application pack, contact HPA at the above address. A 36p stamp towards mailing costs would be appreciated.

International Association of Dental Students
c/o Executive Director, FD1-World Dental Federation, 7 Carlisle Street, London W1V 5RG.

IADS was founded in 1951. Its aims are to stimulate the interest of dental students in the advancement of dental science and to promote cultural and social contact between dental students and dental student organisations worldwide. The voluntary work programme involves students and young qualified dentists to countries where dental aid is needed. So far the programmes have been in African countries though other continents may be included in the future.

Mouvement Twiza
BP 77 Khemisset, Morocco; (tel +212 7 55 30 68).

Mouvement Twiza organizes weekend and summer work camps for volunteers in Morocco. It recruits about 500 volunteers per year to participate in a range of programmes including, development, socio-cultural activities and environmental.
    Applicants of any nationality are accepted, but volunteers must speak French and English, and preferably be outgoing and sociable. The minimum age limit is 18 years of age, and applicants must be healthy, willing and able. Volunteers are required in the summer for a maximum of three weeks. Accommodation is provided but pocket money is not.
    Those interested should contact Lahcen Azeddou, President, at the above address.

Pa Santigie Conteh Farmer's Association (PASCOFAAS)
PMB 686 Freetown, Republic of Sierra Leone, West Africa; (tel +232 22 228568; fax +232 22 224439).

PASCOFAAS is centred around Makarie and over 20 neighbouring villages in the Bombali district, and was founded in 1982 to promote increased agricultural productivity for food production and income generation in order to improve the living conditions of its approximately 2,000 members with special attention to women, children and young people.
    Activities undertaken include agriculture, the planting of rice and trees, construction of houses, roads and so on. Opportunities open to volunteers include secretarial work in the head office, agricultural and construction work and training local people in different skills.
    All nationalities may apply as long as they speak English. They are required all year round for periods of two weeks to two years. Up to 20 international volunteers are taken on at a time. Preference will be given to volunteers who are willing to help programmes either financially or with materials. The minimum age is 17. Expenses and pocket money are not paid but accommodation is provided.
    The Association also supplies information to anyone interested in farming in rural areas of Sierra Leone. For further details about this or the voluntary work, contact Andrew Conteh, the Director, at the above address.

Pensee et Chantiers
B.P. 1423, Rabat R P, Morocco (tel +212 7-69 83 38).

Pensee et Chantiers organize international work camps in Morocco for international volunteers. The work camps last for three weeks days during July and August and projects include forest management, gardening, construction and maintenance work. Volunteers need no special skills but the minimum age accepted is 17 years. Sleeping bags and tools are necessary during the projects.

Volunteers must pay a registration fee of around $US 80 and pay for their own travel expenses. Generally food and accommodation are proviede.

For further information write to the Secretary General at the above address in April of each year and send two international reply coupons.

Right Hand Trust
Gelligason, Llanfair Caereinion, Montgomeryshire SY21 9HE (tel/fax 01938-810215).

Each year the Trust places around 50 young Christian people in their gap year between school and university or university and work, on Anglican missions in Zimbabwe, Kenya, The Gambia, Swaziland, the Windward Isles and Uganda. The positions normally involve teaching and parish work, but there are occasional paramedical placements. The placements are usually from January to August. Training is given in the UK before departure.

For details contact the above address.

Saint David's (Africa) Trust
St. David's House, Rectory Road, Crickhowell, Powys NP8 IDW; (tel 01873-81061; fax 01873-810665). Internet: http://www.gibnet.gi/stdavids

Saint David's Africa Trust is registered as a charity by the Charity Commissioners in Gibraltar and arranges educational visits to Africa (Ghana and Morocco) for those taking a year off between school and university or after graduation. About 30 volunteers are taken on annually. The visits combine language studies in Arabic and French and voluntary work with disabled, orphaned and blind children in Morocco. Men can also work with animals in Morocco. In Ghana there is voluntary work with children. Applicants for Morocco must have GCSE French and be able to swim 100 metres in sea water. Candidates with some experience with disabled children are preferred. Age limits are 18-25 years and good health is essential. The posts last from January to June (6 months) and September to December (3 months).

Applications to David Denison Director, at the above address.

Uganda Voluntary Workcamps Association
G P O Box 3367, Kampala, Uganda; (tel +256 41 270904).

Started over 30 years ago, the UVWA is a non-governmental, voluntary organisation that promotes practical self-help projects throughout Uganda. Volunteers are needed to participate in two-week programmes during April, August and December to coincide with Ugandan school holidays. Volunteers work an eight-hour, six-day week assisting with construction of community buildings and roads.

Applicants should be students, and preferably able to speak both English and French. Volunteer age limits are 18-30. Board and accommodation are provided free but all other expenses are the volunteers' own including travel to and back from Uganda.

Further details from the above address.

Union Marocaine Des Associations De Chantiers (UMAC)

BP 455, Rabat, Morocco (correspondence); or 37 Rue Al Hind, Immeuble Chandouri Maison No.; 3, Rabat, Morocco.

Morocco is a country with a young population: three out of four Moroccans are under 30 years of age. Workcamp organisations have come to play an important part in mobilizing the energies of Moroccan youth, and encouraging a positive attitude to the problems of a developing country. The Moroccan workcamp movement grew out of local organisations and the first major project the latter undertook was helping with the construction of 'La Route de l'Unité' joining the North and South of the country. This was shortly after independence. In 1960 six regional organisations were founded in Meknes, Rabat, Fez, Sale, and Safi. Then a national co-ordination committee was founded in 1961, which became UMAC in 1963.

UMAC organises weekend camps throughout the year and about 15 summer camps lasting three weeks to a month in July and August. About 500 volunteers are recruited each year.

The summer camps are international, and all nationalities are welcome. No special qualifications are needed. Volunteers should however speak Arabic, French or English, and enjoy good health. The age limits are 18 — 35. A participation fee of about £40 is payable. Board and lodging are free and work insurance is provided. No pocket money is paid, however, and volunteers pay their own travel expenses.

Applications should be made to the individual organisations directly. Some of these are: Amis des Chantiers Internationaux de Meknes, BP 8, Meknes, RP; Association des Chantiers de Jeunes, BP 171, Sale; Jeunesse et Co-operation, BP 19, Safi; Chantiers Sociaux Marocains, BP 1423, Rabat; Mouvement Twisa, BP 77, Khemisset; Association de Travail Volontaire et Culturel, BP 4537, Casablanca, Morocco.

Voluntary Workcamps Association of Ghana (VOLU)

PO Box 1540, Accra, Ghana (tel +233 21 663486; fax +233-21-663486).

VOLU organises international workcamps in the rural areas of Ghana for international volunteers. Tasks involve mainly manual work; construction projects, working on farm and agro-forestry projects, tree planting, harvesting cocoa and foodstuffs, working with mentally disabled people, teaching, etc., Around 1,500 volunteers are needed for workcamps at Easter, Christmas, and from June to October. Volunteers can stay throughout each period.

No special skills or experience are required but volunteers should be over 16 years old and fit to undertake manual labour. Volunteers pay their own travelling costs and a £200 registration fee but accommodation and food are provided at the camps. VOLU supplies offical invitations to enable volunteers to acquire visas before leaving for Ghana.

Those interested should apply either through Service Civil Internationnal member organisations in their own country or directly to the National Organising Secretary at the above address.

Voluntary Workcamps Association of Nigeria
PO Box 2189, Lagos, Nigeria (tel +234 1-961290/821568).

VWAN organises workcamps centred around community projects for youths of different cultural backgrounds and nationalities throughout Nigeria. Between 120 and 150 volunteers per year participate in the workcamps; the work is mainly unskilled manual labour, but can also include bricklaying, carpentry, sport, games, excursions, debates and discussions.

Applicants of any nationality are welcome, but a knowledge of English is required. Volunteers must also be physically fit. The usual length of placement is between one and two months between July and September. Volunteers must pay a registration fee of $100 and provide for their own upkeep apart from board and lodging.

Applications should be made to the Secretary General at the above address.

WWOOF Togo
Boite Postale 25, Agou Nyogbo, Togo, West Africa.

The Togo branch of Willing Workers on Organic Farms needs volunteers and contacts to support organic farming including horticulture, aquaculture, agriculture, bee-keeping, fruit growing etc. Sponsorship also needed. A knowledge of French and horticultural/agricultural experience helpful. For an application form write to Prosper, at the above address.

Asia and Australia

Australian Trust for Conservation Volunteers (ATCV)
PO Box 423, Ballarat, Victoria 3353, Australia (tel +61 53-331 483; fax +61 53-332290; freecall in Australia 1800 032 501).
E-mail atcv@peg.ape.org

ATCV is a non-profit, non-political, community based organisation undertaking practical conservation projects all year round in all States and Territories. Typical projects include tree-planting, erosian and salinity control, collection of native seed, habitat restoration, endangered flora/fauna survey and monitoring, noxious weed eradication and heritage projects. Projects are supervised by ATCV Team Leaders, and take place on private land (e.g. farms), public land (e.g. Council/Shire projects, rivers, creeks, coastal areas etc.) and national and State Parks (sometimes including World Heritage Areas).

Volunteers must be aged 18+, be reasonably fit and willing to live and work with a team of six to ten people from several nations. A sound knowledge of English is essential for safety reasons. ATCV organises packages for volunteers including the Banksia Package which costs 560 Australian dollars for four weeks and the Echidna Pakcage at 840 AUD$ for six weeks. Food, accommodation and travel while working with the Trust is provided (it does not cover the fare to Australia). All packages commence from State and Territory capital cities.

For further information and an application form, please write to the Executive Director at the above address enclosing an international reply coupon,.

Bharat Sevak Samaj
Nehru Seva Kendra, Gugoan By-pass Road, Mehrauli, New Delhi 30, India (tel +91 11 6852215/6967609/6969743).

The Samaj was founded by Shri Jawaharlal Nehru, the first Prime Minister of India, as a non-political national platform for mobilizing people's spare time, energy and resources for national reconstruction as a part of the first Five Year Plan. It has a network of branches all over the country, with a membership of over 750,000, 10,000 members working on projects, and about 50 foreign volunteers helping each year. Any person who offers his services for a minimum of two hours a week can become a member of the Samaj.

Its normal programme includes the organisation of urban community centres in slum areas, night shelters, child welfare centres, nursery schools, training camps for national reconstruction work, family planning camps and clinics, and publicity centres for the Plans. The work also encompasses relief and reconstruction work after natural calamities, such as famine, drought, cyclones and earthquakes as well as the construction of houses for the Schedule Caste (lowest caste) and tribes and low cost latrines in villages.

Both skilled and unskilled workers are welcomed. Foreign volunteers, who can serve for between 15 days and three months, should be prepared to live in simple accommodation and respect local customs and traditions. They must finance their own stay, and it is preferred that they speak English.

Applicants should contact the General Secretary at the above address for further details.

Calcutta Rescue Fund
PO Box 52, Brentford, Middlesex TW8 0TF (tel 0171 701-2765).

The Fund recruits suitable volunteers from the UK to work exclusively at the Calcutta clinics for destitute people founded by Dr Jack Preger. Volunteers help with the day to day running of two street clinics. Duties include diagnosis and treatment of patients, record keeping, accounting, general administrative tasks, the ordering and administering of medication and the regular dressing of wounds.

No experience is essential, but preference will be given to those with medical, administrative and accounting knowledge. There is no age limit but it is important that applicants are in good health; it is advisable that all volunteers obtain all the recommended vaccinations as well as an adequate supply of malaria tablets. Volunteers stay for a minimum of two months. The maximum stay is usually six months due to visa restrictions. It must be emphasised that participants must pay for their travel expenses. Accommodation is not provided but cheap accommodation is readily available in the area.

Applicants may apply all the year round for the 150 places available each year. Those interested should write to Jane Higgins at the above address.

Christian Workcamps Australia
P O Box K164, Haymarket, NSW 2000, Australia.

Volunteers are needed to take part in work camps lasting two to four weeks in January and July. The camps are currently held in New South Wales, the Northern Territory and Far North Queensland. Volunteers must pay camp registration fees of approximately £23. Additional expenses may include food and accommodation for about £25 per week. Volunteers are responsible for their own travel costs.

Enquiries to the above address enclosing an International Reply Coupon.

Dakshinayan

F-1169, 2nd Floor, Chittaranjan Park, New Delhi-110019; (tel/fax +91 11 6484468). E-mail sid@dax.unv.ernet.in

Dakshinayan is a non-profit, non-religious organisation which promotes international and intercultural solidarity and a better understanding of the myth and reality of 'third world poverty' through its Development Education Programme.

Under this programme self-supporting volunteers are placed on grassroots development projects throughout north India. This provides them with an opportunity to observe and experience the culture of rural India; study the problems of disadvantaged communities and participate in development efforts.

The programme is open to both skilled and unskilled participants aged 18+. Participants are expected to cover all their expenses (travel, food, accommodation and other personal expenses). On the projects they have to contribute three to five US dollars a day for food and accommodation in order not to be a burden on the project's resources. Dakshinayan charges a nominal fee of US$20 towards administration expenses. Volunteers should stay a minimum of two weeks up to a maximum of six months at any time of year.

Applications should be sent to Siddharth Sanyal, at the above address.

Friendship Club Nepal (FCN)

P O Box 11276, Dillibazar, Kathmandu, Nepal; (tel +977-1 410856; +977-1 421518. 411642).

Friendship Club Nepal is a non-profit organisation that aims to improve the lot of very poor people in rural Nepal. Volunteers are needed throughout the year and although most volunteers stay a few months or weeks there are possiblitities to stay for longer. Volunteers are self funding.

Volunteers are needed for the following:

Teachers to teach English in a school/campus or college for three to five hours daily per six-day week. Volunteers should have at least a BA.

Secretaries to work in the FCN headquarters in Kathmandu or FCN office in Chitwan same hours as above. Relevant qualifications and experience needed.

Project Experts to visit less developed rural areas to prepare project proposals or action plans. FCN provides Rs 1000 pocket money. Should have appropriate qualifications.

Volunteers pay £75 per month. Basic accommodation will be provided.

Grahung Kalika

Walling Village Development Committee, Bartung, Ward 2, Syngja, Western Nepal.

The above organisation is non-governmental and was established in 1996 to improve the teaching of English to primary school children in a remote area of Nepal. The organisation consists of local people working within their communities. The project requires volunteer teachers of English for long and short-term appointments (the minimum is two weeks) to work in primary schools. Although no teaching experience is required, volunteers must adopt a practical and creative approach to the placement and demonstrate a willingness to participate in the local community. Volunteers are offered low-cost accommodation with local families and are expected to be entirely self funding. Further information can be obtained from Mark Scrotton, 125 Trowell Road, Nottingham NG8 2EN.

India Development Group (UK)
68 Downlands Road, Purley, Surrey CR8 4JF; (tel 0181-668 3161; 0181-660 8541).

IDG (UK) works in India to alleviate poverty and improve the employment situation and quality of life in rural and backward areas of India and to arrest the migration of the rural poor to city slums by offering training in appropriate technology, primary health care and social forestry at the Schumacher Institute in Lucknow, northern India.

Five to ten volunteers are taken on annually in India to help with the above programmes for six months at a time, preferably November to March/April. IDG can arrange reasonably priced accommodation at the organisation's boarding house or with a family. Volunteers should be 20-45 years old and should be capable of withstanding the rigours of the Indian climatic and health and hygiene situation. A knowledge of English is essential and UK and other nationalities will need a visa.

The UK office also needs some volunteer office staff.

Indian Volunteers for Community Service
12 Eastleigh Avenue, Harrow, Middlesex HA2 0UF (tel 0181-864 4740).

This organisation offers a learning opportunity to anyone over the age of 18 who is keen to go to India and learn about Indian culture and rural development work. Each year, between September and March, people are sent to a rural project in North India for two weeks' acclimatisation and then on to other projects where they may stay for longer periods of time, provided that they are able to make themselves useful. Project Visitors as they are called, must pay all their own expenses, including airfares, personal and sightseeing expenses and basic board and lodging in the projects.

No skills are required. Project Visitors are going primarily to learn, to have a unique and rewarding experience and to see a different way of life.

For more details, contact the General Secretary at the above address.

Insight Nepal
PO Box 6760, Kathmandu, Nepal; (tel +977-1-418-964, fax +977-1-416144).

Insight Nepal's 'Placement for Volunteer Service Work' is a programme which arranges work places for volunteers interested in teaching English in school, or to help community development projects in the rural and urban area of Nepal. Participants pass through four different phases of the programme: orientation, placement, village excursion and a recreational tour. Each placement lasts three to four months and 12 volunteers are taken on a year. Volunteers must be aged 18 to 60 years with at least A-level education (High School Diploma US). The programmes begin three times a year in February, April and August but other times can be arranged on request. Two meals a day and accommodation will be provided. The programme costs US$20 application fee plus US$600 programme fee which covers all four phases of the programme.

Further details from the above address.

Interserve
325 Kennington Road, London SE11 4QH (tel 0171-735 8227; fax 0171-587 5362).

Each year approximately 30 volunteers participate in the On Track Programme in Pakistan, India, Nepal and the Middle East. Generally volunteers become involved in medical, educational and technical projects which last from three months to a year. This is a self-financing scheme.

Volunteers must be committed Christians who have a desire to share their faith as well as their skills.

Further information may be obtained from the Personnel Director at the above address.

Jaffe International Education Service
Kunnuparambil Buildings, Kurichy, Kottayam 686 549, Kerala, India; (tel +91-4826-470; fax +91-481-561 190).

Voluntary positions are available to young and experienced teachers interested in teaching at English medium high schools, hotel management colleges, teacher education colleges, language schools, vocational training institutes etc. in Kerala state, southern India. Positions are available from July to March every year and duration ranges from two weeks to three months.

No salary is offered but volunteers will be provided with free transportation from the nearest airport and free homestay with English-speaking native families. Assistance will also be given for visiting places of interest in Kerala.

Volunteers should be motivated to share and experience the life and culture of the people of Kerala through living and working with them.

For more information contact the above address or fax enquiries.

Joint Assistance Centre
G 17/3 DLF Qutab Enclave, Phase I, Gurgaon, Haryana, 122002 India; (tel +91 11 835 2141; fax +91 11 463 2517).

The JAC is a voluntary group concerned with disaster preparedness. Volunteers from abroad can help by participating in workcamps held all over India. Jobs undertaken include: office and library work, editing, developing useful training resource materials. Workcamp projects may involve road repair, construction of community centres, replanting forests and conservation projects, etc. About 100 volunteers are needed each year, all year round although workcamps are held intermittently. Placements vary from four to 26 weeks duration. Volunteers must be aged 18+ and English-speaking. Very basic accommodation with elementary facilities is provided and volunteers are asked to contribute about £80 a month towards the cost of their stay.

For further information contact JAC at the above addess enclosing four international reply coupons. Applicants in the Americas can apply to: Friends of JAC, c/o Krishna Gopolan, POB 14481, Santa Rosa, California 95402, United States.

Lanka Jatika Sarvodaya Shramadana Sangamaya (Inc)
98 Rawatawatta Road, Moratuwa, Republic of Sri Lanka (tel +94-1 647159; +94-1 645255; fax +94-1 647084).

The ideals on which this organisation is based are contained in its name: 'Sarvodaya' means the awakening of all, and 'Shramadana' means the sharing of labour. For about 40 years the movement has sought to improve the quality of life of those who live in the most deprived areas of Sri Lanka, placing as much stress on the spiritual and cultural elements of life as on purely material development. Construction work is undertaken in 8,000 villages around the country with about 30,000 volunteers lending their services every year. Small numbers of helpers are taken from those countries with which Sri Lanka has diplomatic relations, and those with qualifications in tropical agriculture and technological skills are preferred. Any familiarity with the fields of health, nutrition, education, and social welfare would also be useful.

Volunteers should be aged 21+ and in good health. They should get the recommendation of a recognised organisation/institution in their respective countries. The usual period of service is three to six months but it depends on the visa extensions given by the authorities concerned. No expenses are paid. Limited accommodation is available in dormitories. Volunteers are recruited according to the availability of vacancies.

Those interested should write to the Co-ordinator, International Division.

The Leprosy Mission
Goldhay Way, Orton Goldhay, Peterborough PE2 5GZ; (tel 01733-370505; fax 01733-370960).

The Mission sponsors about ten medical students, and occasionally other health professional students (physiotherapists, occupational therapists and chiropodists) each year to spend an elective period of a minimum of eight weeks at one of its centres in Southern Asia. They receive a substantial grant towards travelling costs and free board and lodging at the centre, but no pocket money. Students must be in their final year of training, in good health, and practising members of one of the Christian churches.

Applications should be made to the Executive Director at the above address.

The Nepal Trust
Cullerne House, Forres, Moray IV36 OYY; (tel/fax 01309-691994).

The Nepal Trust is a registered charity with offices in Scotland and Nepal. It was started in 1993 by a group of people with a long association with Nepal. The aims of the Trust are to offer medical, educational and technical assistance, help with eco-tourism and promote student and cultural exchanges. It is the Trust's philosophy to ask the Nepalese people what they want by way of assistance. The projects are low cost, community-based and sustainable.

Projects for the future or underway include: providing tourist treks to fund health in the community, providing medicines and training for local women and foreign volunteers (nurses, doctors and midwives) to share their skills, and promoting the link-up by computers of Durbar School students to others throughout the planet.

Four to six volunteers are engaged annually. These can be doctors, nurses or midwives who would like to spend two to three months (perhaps up to six months) at a remote health post in Humla supporting the local healthworker. Also experienced trek leaders/guides with knowledge of Nepal to lead 'treks to build health and community'. Also, computer teachers for a course at Durbar High School.

Applicants need to be able to speak English. A knowledge of Nepali would be an advantage. Other qualification should be relevant to the post being applied for. The project work is mostly in spring and autumn (compute project is during school terms).

The Nepal Trust does not have the resources to pay for flights or other expenses and so volunteers must fund themselves or find sponsors. A video *Bridging the Gap* about the trek to build health and community can be hired for £5 or bought for £15.

For further details contact Elizabeth Donovan, Trust Director at the above address.

Rural Organisation for Social Elevation (ROSE)
SAC Kanda, PO Kanda District Almora, Uttar Pradesh, India.

Kanda is a small village on China Hill in northern Uttar Pradesh. The objective of ROSE is to improve the plight of the poorest people through education and the raising of social awareness. This is done through ROSE's school for pupils aged five to 12 years. ROSE is funded locally and from donations and visitor resources. The types of activities which volunteers from abroad can take part in include: helping teach English in the school, administrative duties, cultural activities, visiting women's community groups, working on an organic agriculture farm, trekking and walking, planting trees, writing project reports, local path making, construction and environmental work.

It is preferred that volunteers come in organised groups for two week work-camps and work five hours daily.

Further details from Jeevan Lal Verma, Director at the above address.

Shin Shizen Juku (New Nature School)
Tsurui-mura, Akan-gun, Hokkaido 085-12, Japan; (tel +81 154 64-2821).

SSJ needs volunteers to help teach English to both adults and children. In summer there is also manual labour on nearby farms. Volunteers usually stay two to three months, but many have stayed as long as six to twelve months. Volunteers are welcome at any time of year. There are usually about six volunteers working at the school at any one time. A knowledge of Japanese is a great help, but not essential. An international driver's licence would be useful. As the work is voluntary, a tourist visa is sufficient. Food and accommodation only are provided in return for work, but occasionally, at the end of the month a small amount of pocket money is given.

Anyone interested should contact Hiroshi Mine, Manager, at the above address.

Teaching Abroad
46 Beach View, Angmering, Sussex, BN16 4DE; (01903 249888/859527; fax 01903-785779). E-mail 100533.26240 compuserve.com

Teaching Abroad aims to help teach English (mainly spoken) in India in local schools. Teaching volunteers do not need a TEFL or teaching qualification. Teaching Abroad charges from £445 for the placement, food and accommodation during the stay which can be from two weeks up to a year; a typical length is three months. Volunteers may also be asked to help with sports and cultural activities in the schools. The minimum age is 18.

There is also a business placement programme in India, Business Abroad which is for students.

For further information on Teaching Abroad or Business Abroad, contact the above address.

Trek-Aid
2 Somerset Cottages, Stoke Village, Plymouth, Devon PL3 4AZ; (01752-567617).

Trek-Aid is a charity that runs small-scale direct aid initiatives to help Tibetan Refugees in Nepal and India. The aim is to assist the Tibetans' cultural, physical, medical, educational and community needs. All the charity's officials, committee members and volunteers absorb their own office costs, fax, phone and postal charges.

Volunteers are needed to help for periods of one to three months to share skills with the refugees to help their development; applicants should be doctors, nurses, teachers, horticulturalists, roofing/building workers, tailors, dentists, opthalmic opticians etc. The costs (self-funded) are from £600 to £1200. For further details contact the above address with the following: a large SAE, two copies of a full cv, employment/character references, a covering letter about yourself, experiences, previous Third World travel (if any) and reasons why you would like to help refugees. Applicants must be adaptable and enthusiastic and if selected are required to raise their placement cost through sponsorship and fundraising. Flights, accommodation, living allowances, pre-fieldwork briefings included.

Trekforce Expeditions
134 Buckingham Palace Road, London SW1W 9SA; (tel 0171-824 8890; fax 0171-824 8892). E-mail Trekforce@dial.pipex.com

Trekforce is the expeditionary arm of the International Scientific Support Trust, a UK registered charity. Expeditions to Indonesia and Belize provide assistance to scientists undertaking biogeographical and ecological research in general conservation and the regeneration of the rainforest, as well as giving trekkers the opportunity for adventure and exploration in remote parts of these countries.

Recent expeditions have travelled to the islands of Java, Borneo, Seram and Sumatra, working on projects ranging from building a natural laboratory and a light railway for scientists to mapping remote rainforest areas, and working with the Sumatran Tiger Project. Trekforce has also carried out extensive work upgrading the Orang-u-tan Rehabilitation Centre in Kalimantan.

The expeditions last six weeks and there is an opportunity to stay for another two weeks on the visa fained on entry to Indonesia. In Belize there are no restrictions. Expeditions run throughout the year and each volunteer has to raise £2,700 towards the International Scientific Support Trust's work once selected to join an expedition. Help and advice are given throughout the with fundraising. The ISST cover the costs of all air flights, health insurance, food, accommodation permits, staffing the running of the project and any material needed, casualty evacuation and jungle-training at the start of the expedition.

Applicants do not need any scientific training or knowledge but they should be enthusiastic, keen to discover a wider world and welcoming challenge. All applicants for an expedition are invited to attend an introduction weekend. This provides an excellent opportunity to learn more about Trekforce and what an expedition involves. The weekends are enjoyable and a chance to meet past trekkers as well as learning more about jungle skills, expedition preparation and fundraising techniques.

Please contact Andrew Beer or Zoe Kalis at the above address for further information.

VADHU
Joshi Bhawan, Abkari, Ranikhet 263648, Distt. Almora, Himalayan Hills, India; (tel +91 5966-2806/2506; fax +91 5966-2403/2451.

VADHU is a non-governmental organisation that is working on a watershed management project covering 14 mountain villages. The project comprises environmental awareness, conservation, appropriate technology, community organisation, agriculture and so on. Additionally VADHU also works for NGO networking in the nine hill districts of Uttar Pradesh State. There are 38 small NGO's in these regions. Winter is extremely cold throughout, but from April to December is reasonable.

Volunteers are needed for: secretarial work at centre office, documentation and compilation, nursery raising, agro-forestry and library upkeep.

Volunteers are welcome any time but should be prepared to stay for a minimum of six months. Volunteers have to fund themselves as regards travel and food, but simple accommodation will be provided. It is also essential to able to cope with the cold weather and be used to trekking. With its many contacts in the nine hill districts VADHU has the ability to enable volunteers to work in a variety of disciplines.

For further information contact The Secretary, at the above address.

World Travellers Network
14 Wentworth Avenue, Sydney, NSW, Australia (tel +61 2 9264-1201; fax +61-2-9264-1445; e-mail wtn@ozemail.com.au

The World Travellers Network is the official overseas representative of the Australian Trust for Conservation Volunteers and can arrange for participants to spend a period of six weeks with the ACTV in an area of their choice (i.e. based in any Australian state capital.

WTN offer two options:

The Australian Conservation Programme: volunteers pay Aus$ 1,045 to cover all meals, accommodation, phonecard, YHA membership, Sydney Harbour Cruise (Sydney arrivals only), plus access to WTN services.

The Basic Echidna Package: volunteers pay Aus$ 895 for all meals, accommo-dation and transportation while on the task, plus WTN services.

Departures are on an individual basis and anyone is eligible to join the programme. For further details contact WTN at the address above or:

WTN North American Office: 7350 North Broadway, Denver, Colorado 80221 USA (tel 0303-426 0141/tollfree (USA) 1800-252 2012; fax 0303-426 1270.

WTN European Administration Office: c/o Travel Active Programmes, Postbus 107, 5800 AC Venray, The Netherlands (tel 0478-58 8074; fax 0478-51 1557).

Other Short Term Opportunities

The following organisations are mostly concerned with long term voluntary work, but they also cater to some extent for volunteers for periods of under a year. They will be found listed in the *Long Term* chapter above.

Alderson Hospitality House
ATD Fourth World Voluntariat
Escuela de Enfermeria Stella Maris
Habitat for Humanity
Human Services Alliance
International Liaison of Lay
Volunteers In Mission
Missions to Seaman
Peace Brigades International
Christian Welfare and Social Relief
    Organisation

Daneford Trust
Boys Hope/Girls Hope
International Health Exchange
Benediction Lay Volunteers
Casa Guatemala
Catholic Medical Mission Board
Centro Studi Terzo Mondo
Christians Abroad
Project Ladywood
Visions In Action

PART TWO

Non-Residential Work in the United Kingdom

Glancing over some of the headings in this non-residential section: *The Sick and Disabled, Elderly People, Prisons and Probation*, or *Hospitals*, may give the impression that government cuts have meant that volunteers are now needed to perform tasks formerly undertaken by the welfare state. Tempting though some would find it to make such an assertion, this would not be wholly accurate: few, if any, of the voluntary opportunities described below involve doing work formerly done by paid professionals.

It is rather the case that volunteers can be of most use when they are complementing existing statutory services, not replacing or competing with them. One of the volunteer's greatest assets is that they are volunteers, that it to say, they are doing whatever their chosen task may be because they want to, not because it is their job. One of the most extreme examples of this is in the case of working with prisoners: it can make all the difference to a prisoner to know that whoever they are speaking to is there because they genuinely desire to help, not because they are part of 'The system'. Volunteers are also able to devote a period of time to helping and befriending an individual, whether it involves visiting an old person or going shopping with someone with learning difficulties, that would be prohibitively expensive were they doing so as paid professionals.

Another advantage possessed by the voluntary sector is that it can react to events in a far quicker manner than the statutory authorities, which may have to drag a new idea through levels of bureaucracy before it can take a new course of action. The most conspicuous example of this involves AIDS: the Terrence Higgins Trust, a charity, was using volunteers to take positive action to help sufferers from AIDS long before the Social Services had adjusted to its existence.

Volunteers are also, of course, able to involve themselves in activities that most people would accept are not the responsibility of the state; examples in this book range from promoting vegetarianism to campaigning against nuclear weapons. People can also pursue their own interests through voluntary work; dog lovers can work in an animal sanctuary run by the National Canine Defence League, or those with equine interests can help the Riding for the Disabled Association.

The work listed in this section may often be pursued on a full-time basis, but since few of us are lucky enough to have no other commitments, the majority of opportunities described below are more of a part-time nature. Some of these part-time duties involve a fairly large time commitment of several hours a week; others merely require a degree of regularity or consistency. Some may continue for several years; others may last only for a weekend or for a couple of weeks during the summer.

In attempting to categorise the different types of voluntary work available in the UK, it has not been possible to draw distinct dividing lines, although it is to be hoped that the classification system we have used will act as a useful guide. There are obvious overlaps, for instance between the section on *Disease and Disability* and the sections of *Children* and *The Elderly*. At the beginning of several sections, an attempt is made to cross-refer readers to other relevant sections, but it is assumed that the general areas of overlap will be easily deduced from a glance at the table of contents. It should also be mentioned that several sections, notably National and Local Volunteer Organisations, Community Projects and Fund Raising and Office Work describe organisations that cut across the general classifications system.

National and Local Volunteer Organisations

Unbeknown to the general public, the UK's voluntary resources are carefully monitored by several complex and overlapping networks of official and semi-official organisations. At the national level, these organisations are concerned with collecting and interpreting data, and producing new plans and programmes in response to both national and local needs. The local offices are in charge of implementing these plans, and acting as recruitment and referral agencies on behalf of the prospective volunteers, and of the local bodies that require volunteers.

As far as individual applicants are concerned, the national offices that are described below are of little practical value, other than as a source of information and referral to the appropriate local office. Local branches — whatever title they adopt — act more or less in the same way as labour exchanges. However, they vary a great deal in their policies, and some are more actively involved in recruitment than others. All can at least offer information on local volunteer needs, and can refer enquiries to the appropriate local organisations.

The people who run local volunteer bureaux should be in touch with all nearby organisations and institutions concerned with voluntary work, and be aware of the type of help that they need. For example, a conservation group may need people with a knowledge of architecture, an old people's home may want car drivers with their own cars, or a youth club may require a bricklayer to help build a new clubhouse.

There is normally a short informal interview before a volunteer is sent on to an agency. This is to make sure that the volunteer will be used in a situation where his or her interests and abilities will be put to the greatest use, and to tell him or her what exactly their job will entail. There is a big difference between vaguely wanting to 'do something useful', and being prepared, for example, to give up every Monday evening for an indefinite period in order to drive people to and from a hospital. Of course, not all voluntary work involves a regular commitment of time, but there are many cases, especially those which concern befriending people, where some degree of regularity is essential.

National Associations

National Association of Volunteer Bureaux
New Oxford House, Waterloo Street, Birmingham B2 5UG; (tel 0121-633 4555; fax 0121-633 4043). E-mail navbteam@waveridet.co.uk

NAVB is a democratic membership network of self-determining local volunteer bureaux. It is not a headquarters organisation with local volunteer bureaux branches.

The aim of NAVB is to provide a consultancy and advice service to volunteer bureaux on organisational and management issues and on issues relating to volunteer development. NAVB encourages communication and the exchange of information, experiences and skills between volunteer bureaux. Regional Development Groups facilitate this work at regional level.

NAVB helps volunteer bureaux to help volunteers by promoting volunteer work to individuals seeking volunteer opportunities.

NAVB also provides training for new VB managers and organises training for VB staff through its annual National Conference.

National Council for Voluntary Organisations
8 Regents Wharf, All Saints Street, London N1 9RL; (tel 0171-713 6161).

NCVO was established in 1919 as the representative body of the voluntary sector. It is a membership-based organisation, including some 600 national voluntary organisations. Through its wide-reaching activities, NCVO is also in touch with thousands of other voluntary bodies and groups, and has formed close links with government departments, local authorities, the European community, statutory and public bodies and the business sector.

NCVO can provide prospective volunteers with information sheets on employment opportuniuties in the voluntary sector, both paid and unpaid. It also produces factsheets listing the major national voluntary organisations which work in the Uk and overseas.

For any of the above please contact the Publicity and Enquiries Officer at the above address.

National Youth Agency
17-23 Albion Street, Leicester LE1 6DG (tel 0116-2856789).

The National Youth Agency provides information and support for all those concerned with the informal and social education of young people. It provides information about voluntary work opportunities for young people in England and Wales. This list of voluntary work placements is available from the Agency's Information Services, price 50p.

The Volunteer Centre UK
Carriage Row, 183 Eversholt Street, London NW1 1BU; (tel 0171-388 9888; fax 0171 383 0448).

The Volunteer Centre UK is a national agency looking critically and constructively at current practice in volunteer involvement. It gives information and advice to people working with volunteers in both voluntary and statutory sectors. The Centre is an independent charity funded by the Voluntary Services Unit of the Home Office and by charitable trusts.

The Volunteer Centre UK operates an enquiry service (there is an information bank of 10,000 items on volunteering and a weekly selection is shown on BBC2 Ceefax), a consultancy service, runs training courses, and produces publications and case studies on the policy, theory and practice of volunteering, plus regular publications including a quarterly journal. These services are aimed not only at voluntary service co-ordinators, but also paid workers working alongside volunteers (for example, social workers, nurses, teachers) and policymakers and managers in central and local government and voluntary organisations.

If you wish to get involved in voluntary work locally, contact your volunteer bureau, or contact the Centre's information unit at the above address.

Volunteer Development Scotland (VDS)
80 Murray Place, Stirling, FK8 2BX; (tel 01786-479593; fax 01786-447148).

VDS is the national resource agency for volunteering in Scotland. Although its main brief is to provide support to the various agencies and organisations that use volunteers it can also be a useful starting point for anyone wanting voluntary work in Scotland because of its comprehensive information resources on all the organisations using volunteers in Scotland.

Local Volunteer Bureaux and Councils

Prospective volunteers are recommended to consult one of their local volunteer associations or councils for advice on voluntary work opportunities within their area. Not all local associations are actively involved in recruiting volunteers, but all should be prepared to at least refer applicants to an appropriate local recruiting body.

A few of the more active local volunteer bureaux and councils are described below, but it must be emphasised that these are only included as examples, and their activities are typical of many such bureaux up and down the country. The Volunteer Centre UK (entry above) should be able to advise you of your nearest bureau or council.

Gwent Association of Voluntary Organisations
8 Pentonville, Newport, Gwent (tel 01633-213229).

This Bureau recruits, places and provides support for volunteers in Gwent. There are around 200 mostly non-residential positions offered each year. The minimum age for volunteers is usually about 15 years. Special or useful skills such as having a driving licence may be required for some jobs, but are not necessary for most. The length of time for which volunteers are required varies widely.

Those interested should contact GAVO at the above address.

Leicester Volunteer Bureau
20 Belvoir Street, Leicester LE1 6QH; (tel 0116 2553333; fax 0116-2558032).

Leicester Volunteer Bureau recruits for both statutory and voluntary organisations in the Leicester City area. Opportunities are available during the daytime, evenings and weekends and are both long and short term. As with other Volunteer Bureaux there is a wide variety of openings available, ranging from helping with children in playschemes through to elderly people at Lunch Clubs, or to local groups on outings and holidays. Practical help is also needed from drivers with their own cars, people to help with basic woodwork, metalwork or painting at a workshop or to serve in charity shops and so on.

Special qualifications may be needed for some opportunities, but not for most. The minimum age is normally 18 but there are some opportunities for younger people as well. Organisations recruiting volunteers are encouraged to pay expenses. The length of time for which volunteers are required varies widely.

NEWVOL (formerly Clwyd Voluntary Services Council)
North East Wales Voluntary Services Council, Station Road, Ruthin, Denbighshire, North Wales, LL15 1BP; (tel 01824-702441).

NEWVOL collects information about the opportunities available for volunteers within the area of North East Wales. Potential volunteers are provided with advice and information before being referred to appropriate organisations.

Volunteers are recruited to help support vulnerable people, holiday play projects, and/or undertake environmental/conservation work, clerical work, driving etc.

Those interested should contact the Volunteer Bureau Organiser at the above address.

Rochdale Voluntary Action
158 Drake Street, Rochdale, Greater Manchester OL16 1PX (tel 01706-31291).

The Council for Voluntary Service for Rochdale Metropolitan Borough supports the work of over 360 local organisations involved in voluntary activities with disabled, elderly, young or disadvantaged people, etc. It also represents the interests of the voluntary sector with the local authorityand seeks to develop new initiatives in voluntary work.

RVA has an extensive library, and provides a limited duplicating, typing and DTP service for member organisations.

Further information may be obtained from the Manager at the above address.

Scottish Community Education Council
Rosebery House, 9 Haymarket Terrace, Edinburgh EH12 5EZ; (tel 0131-313 2488; fax 0131-313 6800). E-mail maureen — quinn@cosnet.dircon.co.uk

The Scottish Community Education Council aims to provide a national focus point for community education in Scotland. It provides an information service on topics related to community education and refers volunteers to appropriate agencies and organisations. The council also issues an annual information sheet *Summer Opportunities* which lists addresses of voluntary work programmes in Scotland.

For more information or referral, contact the Information Officer at the above address.

Service 9-Bristol's Volunteer Bureau
66 Gloucester Road, Bishopston, Bristol BS7 8BH (tel 0117-9247929).

The aim of Service 9 is to promote, support and develop opportunities for people to become involved in their community through voluntary work. Service 9 advertises and recruits for approximately 150 organisations throughout Bristol by keeping on file details of the work they do and their requirements for volunteers.

For more information contact the above address.

Voluntary Service Belfast
70-72 Lisburn Road, Belfast BT9 6AF, Northern Ireland (tel 01232-329499; fax 01232-321797).

VSB only operates in the Belfast area and it recruits and places 320 volunteers every year in all types of voluntary work including child care, work with the elderly or disabled, befriending, counselling, clerical work, fund-raising, decorating, horticultural work and mechanics. In addition, VSB refunds out-of-pocket expenses, and provides training and support to all volunteers. The length of time for which volunteers are normally required depends on the type of voluntary work chosen.

Those interested should contact the Volunteer Organiser at the above address.

West Kent Voluntary Services Unit
The Jukebox, c/o Tunbridge Wells Girls Grammar School, Southfield Road, Tunbridge Wells, Kent TN4 9UJ (tel 01892-531584).

VSU recruits volunteers aged between 14 and 18 in the West Kent area and aims to give them the opportunity to initiate, organize and implement projects and activities with the elderly, disabled, children, conservation, fund raising, etc.
Those interested should contact the above address for further information.

Other Nationwide Organisations

The organisations listed and described above, whether at the national or local level, are all inter-related through official and semi-official networks. The entries below refer to organisations and schemes that are nationwide in their scope and also cover such a wide spectrum of voluntary work opportunities that they defy classification elsewhere. Other national bodies that are more specific in their activities and volunteer needs will be found under the other divisions of this chapter.

Association for Jewish Youth (AJY)
AJY House, 128 East Lane, Wembley, Middlesex HA0 3NL; (tel 0181-908 4747; fax 0181-904 4323). E-mail ajy@ort.org

The AJY can give young people details of the services and possibilities open to young Jewish people. It may also be able to help with grants for specific purposes and also has an apprentice sheme for young people who want to work as volunteer youth leaders in youth clubs.

British Association of Settlements and Social Action Centres (BASSAC)
1st Floor, Winchester House,11 Cranmer Road, London SW9 6EJ; (tel 0171-735 1075; fax 0171-735 0840).E-mail bussac@mcr1.poptel.org.uk

This Association unites 63 member organisations around the country doing many types of local community work. These need volunteers to work with young people, the mentally and physically handicapped and the elderly.
A list of the member organisations can be obtained from the above address and applications should be made direct to them.

Christian Service Centre
Holloway Street West, Lower Gornal, Dudley, West Midlands DY3 2DZ (tel 01902-882836; fax 01902 881099).

The Christian Service Centre acts as an information centre and advisory service for people wishing to undertake voluntary work ,whether short or long-term, with Christian organisations and missionary societies both in Britain and abroad. Among its various publications it produces *The STS Directory*, a catalogue of short-term opportunities with over 80 different Christian organisations.
For more information contact the above address.

Family Service Units
National Office: 207 Old Marylebone Road, London NW1 5QP (tel 0171-402 5175/6).

The aims of Family Service Units are to undertake intensive and comprehensive welfare work among families who require special assistance, and to develop community resources. The contribution of voluntary workers has had a far-reaching influence on the work of Family Service Units, as the genesis for the organisation was the activities of a group of volunteers during the Second World War. Today there are at least three times as many volunteers, including committee members, as paid staff in the 20 Units in England and Scotland.

There are five broad categories of volunteers working in the units: (1) committee members who manage local and national business; (2) those who provide services to clients, such as transport to clinics or holiday homes, running children's groups, playschemes and mothers' groups; (3) those who bring practical skills such as fund raising or decorating, and who usually are not in direct contact with clients; (4) those who give free advice to Unit committees and staff, based on their professional experience, e.g. teachers, doctors, psychiatrists and social workers; (5) clients and ex-clients who are able to offer practical help to either a Unit or to other clients.

Those who would like to help should contact their local Unit; the address should be in the telephone directory.

League of Jewish Women
4th Floor, 24-32 Stephenson Way, London NW1 2JW; (tel 0171-387 7688; 0171-387 2110).

The League of Jewish Women is the leading national Jewish Women's Voluntary Service organisation in the UK. It provides all types of service to the whole community regardless of race, colour or religion. Membership is approximately 6,000 and almost 75% of these actually carry out voluntary work such as working with the young, in hospitals, for the physically and mentally disabled, the elderly, and with and for other organisations including the WRVS, the Red Cross, Adult Literacy, Relate, and the Council of Christians and Jews.

Membership is open to all Jewish women resident in the UK who are over 15 for a minimal annual subscription. There are groups throughout the UK which meet regularly. No special skills are required, all are welcome and expenses are paid where necessary.

Applications for membership should be made to the General Secretary at the above address and will be forwarded to the relevant Group Secretary.

National Federation of City Farms (NFCF)
The Green House, Hereford Street, Bedminster, Bristol BS3 4NA; (tel 0117-923 1800).

NFCF is the national organisation which supports and advises those who wish to set up and operate smallholdings and farms in city areas. A list of city farms which you can become involved with either on a volunteer basis or as a full-time worker can be obtained from the above address.

REACH
Bear Wharf, 27 Bankside, London SE1 9ET (tel 0171-928 0452; fax 0171-928 0798).

REACH finds part-time, expenses-only jobs for retired business or other professional men and women who want to use their skills to help voluntary organisations with charitable aims. This free service is available for jobs anywhere in Britain.

For further information contact Jill Munday, the Director, at the above address.

Women's Royal Voluntary Service

234-244 Stockwell Road, London SW9 9SP (tel 0171-416 0146; fax 0171 416 0148).

The WRVS assists Government Departments, Local Authorities and other voluntary bodies in organising and carrying out welfare and emergency work for the community on a nationwide network operated through area, county, district and London Borough organizers.

Activities include work for elderly and disabled people: residential/day clubs, meals on wheels, books on wheels, visiting schemes; for young families: children's holidays, playgroups, mother and baby clubs; for offenders and their families; non-medical work in hospitals including shops/canteens and trolley services; clothing stores which provide clothing for distribution to the needy; drivers for rural transport; welfare work for HM Forces and for Service families; trained members to assist local authorities in emergencies including food, rest centres and information services.

Women and men of all ages, who can provide a few regular hours of help are welcomed. Local office addresses are in telephone directories, or for further information write to the above address.

Advice and Counselling

Below are listed several organisations that need help from volunteers to offer the general public advice and support with their problems. To offer direct help the volunteer needs more than a sympathetic ear and a liking for the sound of their own voice; they need to be mature enough to cope with serious problems, intelligent enough to offer appropriate advice, and discreet enough to respect their clients' confidence. Of course, no organisation will place a volunteer in a position of responsibility without giving them during due preparation: for example RELATE (the former Marriage Guidance Council) gives its advisors full training, and in exchange expects them to give a regular commitment of their time for at least five years.

Those who are not willing to become so deeply involved can still be of use by helping with the administration and office work involved with running such large national organisations. Obviously those who know how to type or have experience of office procedure can be of the greatest use here, but there may still be scope for those whose main qualification is enthusiasm.

Blackliners

Eurolink Business Centre, 49 Effra Road, London SW2 1BZ (tel 0171 738-5274).

Blackliners provide counselling, advice, information, buddying/befriending, housing advice and a drop-in centre for black people of African, Asian and Caribbean descent in South London who are HIV positive. Volunteers, who must be black (the definition is quite wide), are needed to staff the drop-in centre and the Helpline, to do 'outreach' work and to help with the buddying/befriending scheme. Blackliners also provide domiciliary care for which volunteers are also needed.

Those interested should contact The Volunteer Coordinator at the above address.

CARA

178 Lancaster Road, London W11 1QU (tel 0171-792 8299; fax 0171-792 8004).

CARA is a pastoral ministry offering care and resources for people affected by HIV/AIDS. CARA also visits religious organisations and orders, helping to inform, educate and increase awareness of the issue of HIV/AIDS.

Volunteers are needed all year round to help for one day per week with an assortment of jobs including catering, hospitality, office work and word processing. After training, volunteers can help with home and hospital visiting, and also massage and alternative therapies. Applicants of all nationalities are welcome to apply, but all applicants must have knowledge of the issues surrounding HIV and AIDS. Travel fares will be paid, and a meal will be provided after five hours' work.

Applicants can apply for the 40 places by contacting the Volunteer Co-ordinator at the above address.

CRUSE-Bereavement Care

Cruse House, 126 Sheen Road, Richmond, Surrey TW9 1UR (tel 0181-940 4818; fax 0181-940 7638; helpline 0181-332 7227).

Founded in 1959, Cruse Bereavement Care offers help to all bereaved people. It provides counselling support by trained and selected counsellors, advice on practical issues and the opportunity for social contact. It also provides training courses for professionals and those caring for the bereaved.

There are branches throughout the UK and a publications list is available on request.

For details contact your local branch or contact Cruse House at the above address.

Emergency Services Trauma Counsellors

6 Wellgreen Close, Saffron Walden, Essex CB11 4BA (tel 01799-526112; fax 01424 890498).

The ESTC provides critical incident debriefing and counselling to all emergency services departments and to members of the armed services and the public. Counsels only if the individual requests such. About 50 volunteers are taken on annually to act as a 'listening ear' until debriefer-counsellors can get to individuals. With greater awareness of the need for the service ESTC provides, this organisation is expanding and volunteers can if they wish become trained in the skills needed for this kind of work if they are not trained already.

To become a volunteer no previous experience is needed but all skills are welcome, particularly languages; a driving licence is also an asset.

For further information contact the Secretary at the above address.

Family Planning Association

2-12 Pentonville Road, London NW 9FP; (tel 0171-636 7866).

The FPA is a charity whose role is to promote sexual health and family planning through information, research, education and training and publicity. Expenses and training are provided.

The FPA welcomes volunteers who would like to work in any of the four centres in the UK which are in London, Glasgow, Cardiff and Belfast.

Further details from the above address.

FWA (The Family Welfare Association)

501-505 Kingsland Road, Dalston, London E8 4AU (tel 0171-254 6251).

FWA is a national charity that offers emotional and practical support to families and individuals living in poverty. Volunteers are needed both to offer assistance to social workers in local projects and also to take part in fundraising activities. Volunteers are also needed to staff the FWA telephone information and helpline. Expenses are paid.

Further information from the above address.

Lesbian and Gay Switchboard

PO Box 7324 London N1 9QS; (tel 0171-837 7324).

Lesbian and Gay Switchboard provides a 24 hour telephone information, advice and support service for gay men and women. As well as having detailed information on clubs, pubs, discos, befriending and counselling organisations in London and UK (including information on specialist groups such as disabled and married gays); they also operate an accommodation service for those gay people seeking somewhere to live as well as those wishing to let, within the Greater London Area. They have about 160 volunteers to answer the telephone lines, produce publicity, carry out fund raising, administration and training.

Volunteers are of either sex and are welcomed on the basis of being lesbian or gay and willing to undertake a short, supervised training aimed at expanding their knowledge of the London gay scene, AIDS and the law. Travelling expenses are reimbursed for unemployed volunteers.

Applications initially to the Training Group at the above address.

Marriage Counselling Service

24 Grafton Street, Dublin 2, Ireland; (tel +253 1 8720341 Monday to Friday 9.30am to 9pm).

Marriage Counselling is non-denominational and has been in existence since 1962. It offers service to couples, both married and unmarried, in relationship counselling, psychsexual therapy, separation counselling, mediation and teen between.

The education and training department of MCS provides courses in relationship skills, pre-marriage preparation and basic counselling skills. Many of the professionals who deliver their services do so voluntarily. This means the client cost is negotiable and nobody is refused counselling through inability to pay.

For futher details constact the Chief Executive, Ruth Barror at the above address.

National Association of Citizens Advice Bureaux

115/123 Pentonville Road, London N1.

The Association is the central servicing body for the 1,727 Citizens Information and Advice Bureaux outlets throughout the UK. These provide free, independent, impartial and confidential advice to any individual on any subject. Many Bureaux have special legal and/or financial advice sessions with specialists on hand. Over 90% of the 27,000 people working in the CAB service are volunteers. Some of these have special skills, such as legal or financial knowledge or experience of administration or social work, but they should all be mature, understanding and sympathetic. The range of jobs to be done include interviewing, tribunal work, secretarial, clerical, filing and organizing. Each interviewer is asked to work for at least four hours a week.

Skills are developed by training and in-bureau experience. All new workers are required to undergo a ten week course of information sessions, practical work and visits for one day a week which should provide a basic knowledge of procedure. After this course trainees are generally offered a three month probationary attachment to a bureau. Training is a continuing process and all workers are expected to attend courses for experienced workers, refresher courses, training on new legislation, and special courses on particular topics. The service expects an equal quality of work from paid and unpaid workers. Any travelling or personal expenses incurred by voluntary workers in attending courses are reimbursed.

Those interested in offering their services should contact their local bureau: the address should be under 'C' in the telephone directory.

RELATE, National Marriage Guidance
Little Church Street, Rugby, Warwickshire CV21 3AP (tel 01788-573241).

Men and women who would like to volunteer as relationship counsellors are required to undertake a selection and training programme and commit at least seven hours a week of their time, for forty weeks a year. RELATE looks for an informal commitment from their volunteers for five years. Volunteers are normally over the age of 25   Out-of-pocket expenses are paid, some RELATE centres pay counsellors who work substantially more than the basic voluntary commitment.

Local RELATE centres are always happy to hear from interested people and are listed under 'RELATE' or 'Marriage Guidance'.

Children and Youth

Voluntary work with young people can mean far more than working with those who are from disadvantaged backgrounds or suffer from some physical disability. For example, the hundreds of thousands of members of the Guide Association depend upon the assistance of thousands of adult volunteers to keep the movement going, not only to act as leaders but also to provide transport, deal with paperwork and so on.

Indeed, many of the opportunities in this section are to do with helping young people to make constructive use of their time, which can also be of great assistance to hard-pressed mothers, who have their offspring taken off their hands for a while. Not listed here, however, are the untold number of children's playschemes operated by local authorities during the school holidays which keep children aged up to thirteen occupied during the week while their parents are at work. These playschemes are normally staffed by paid workers but additional assistance from volunteers will normally be greatly appreciated, whether it is offered on a regular or irregular basis. People with artistic, musical or sporting abilities will normally be especially appreciated. For further information contact the Recreation Department of your local authority, which will be co-ordinating playschemes in the area.

The subject of child abuse has been made of in recent years and continues to be the subject of much media focus and attention. At the time of going to press a government White Paper on whether or not a UK register of paedophiles should be compiled is imminent. In the meantime any prospective volunteer applying for a job which involves direct contact with children should be prepared to undergo a thorough vetting by the prospective employer before being accepted. For example the Social Services departments around the UK will have candidates' names run through the police computer to check for a criminal record. If the volunteers are from abroad they will be asked to provide a Certificate of Good Conduct. Generally speaking, students and others working for short periods during their holidays or for work experience will not be subject to such checks.

Other voluntary opportunities connected with child care and youth work will be found under *The Sick and Disabled, Hospitals* and *Education.*

Army Cadet Force Association
E Block, Duke of York's Headquarters, London SW3 4RR (tel 0171-730 9733; fax 0171-730 8264).

The ACF is a national Voluntary Youth Organisation committed to developing confidence, self-discipline, self-respect and health in 13-18 year olds so that they can gain employment and take their place in society as responsible, contributing young citizens. It achieves this through a challenging structured programme of military, adventurous, sporting and citizenship training. Adult volunteers are needed to conduct this training. They should be in good health, aged between 18 and 55 and British citizens. Training is given to them at the Cadet Training Centre in Surrey.

Those interested should contact the General Secretary at the above address.

Barnardo's
Tanners Lane, Barkingside, Ilford, Essex 1G6 1QG (tel 0181-550 8822; fax 0181-551 6870).

Barnardo's, the UK's biggest children's charity, works with 26,500 children, young people and families a year. Two hundred projects provide a range of services from under fives day care to work with young people with severe physical and learning disabilities. Volunteers are needed for both child care work and fund raising activities.

Those interested in child care should contact their nearest Divisional Office, while those interested in fund raising their nearest Regional Office:
Divisional Director, London Division or Regional Field Manager, London and East Anglia Region, Tanners Lane, Barkingside, Ilford, Essex 1G6 1QG (tel 0181-551 0011 (Child Care) or 0181-550 8822 (Appeals)).
Regional Field Officer, Southern England Region, Lynnem House, Victoria Way, Burgess Hill, W Sussex RH15 9NF; tel 01444-871643.
Divisional Director, Midlands Division or Regional Field Manager, Midlands Region, Brooklands, Great Cornbow, Halesowen, West Midlands B63 3AB (tel 0121-550 5271/6).
Divisional Director, North East Division, Orchard House, Fenwick Terrace, Jesmond, Newcastle-upon-Tyne NE2 2JQ (tel 0191-281 5024).
Regional Field Officer, North East England Region, Four Gables, Clarence Road, Horsforth, Leeds LS18 4LB (tel 0113-2591070).

Divisional Director, North West Division, 7 Lineside Close, Liverpool L25 2UD (tel 0151-487 5313).

Regional Field Officer, North West England Region, Golden Hill, Leyland, Preston, Lancs. PR5 2NN (tel 01772-453929).

Divisional Director, Yorkshire Division, Four Gables, Clarence Road, Horsforth, Leeds, West Yorkshire LS18 4LB (tel 0113-259 1070).

Director, South Wales/South West England Division or Regional Field Manager, Wales and the West Country Region, 11-15 Columbus Walk, Brigantine Place, Atlantic Wharf, Cardiff CF1 5BZ (tel 01222-493387).

Divisional Director, Scottish Division or Regional Field Manager, Scottish Region, 235 Corstorphine Road, Edinburgh EH12 7AR (tel 0131-334 9893).

Divisional Director, Northern Ireland Division, 542-544 Upper Newtownwards Road, Belfast BT4 3HE; (tel 01232-672366).

Bristol Association for Neighbourhood Daycare

81 St Nicholas Road, St Pauls, Bristol BS2 9JJ; (tel 0117-954 2128; fax 0117 954 1694).

BAND was formed in January 1978 with three member groups. These groups arose in response to the Finer Joint Action Committee Report (1976) which recognized that one of the most fundamental needs of a working single parent was a facility for school age children during holidays, and after school. Such a facility would enable parents to work full-time and the family unit to become stable and financially independent. BAND currently has 50 member groups. Volunteers are needed to help the above groups carry out their aim.

For further information contact the above address.

Children's Country Holidays Fund (Inc.)

42-43 Lower Marsh, London SE1 7RG (tel 0171-928 6522; fax 0171-401 3961).

Every year the Fund provides holidays in the country, at the seaside, in private homes or established camps, for almost 3,000 disadvantaged London children. The arrangements for the children's holidays are undertaken by voluntary workers, under the umbrella of a small administrative staff in Head Office. Volunteers are also needed to act as train marshals supervising the children's travel to and from London.

There are no special requirements for camp supervisors, beyond a minimum age of 18, good health, and the ability to supervise children aged between nine and 12 years. The holiday periods vary between ten to fourteen days, and holidays always take place during the six weeks of the school summer holidays. The Fund much regrets that it can no longer accept applications from outside the UK.

Those interested should write to the Director at the above address to find out how they can help.

Children North East

1a Claremont Street, Newcastle Upon Tyne NE2 4AH (tel 0191-2323741; fax 0191-2323741).

The organisation was founded in 1891 and its main concern is the welfare of children (and their parents) in Northumberland, Tyne and Wear and Co Durham. It runs seven home visiting schemes with more than 200 trained volunteer parents who befriend families in their own homes, a Family Centre, supported accommodation for young care-leavers and a playbus/toy library which visits isolated villages in Tynedale.

Any volunteers interested in helping with these activities should apply to the Director at the above address.

The Children's Society
Edward Rudolf House, Margery Street, London WC1X OJL (tel 0171-837 4299; fax 0171-837 0211).

Established in 1881, The Children's Society is one of Britain's leading child care charities. They work with some of the country's most vulnerable children and young people in over 90 projects throughout England and Wales. Work includes support for children with disabilities and their families, young runaways, young homeless people and families experiencing difficulties.

The Children's Society relies on the support of the public to carry out this important work and so volunteer fundraisers are always welcome, as are volunteers able to to work alongside trained social workers in selected projects.

For more information contact the Children's Society for details of your local office.

City of Bradford Playscheme Association
c/o Community Recreation Office, Baildon Recreation Centre, Green Lane, Baildon, Bradford, W. Yorks (tel 01274-593234).

At present the Association organizes playschemes throughout the whole of the Bradford district which operate during the summer holidays for children aged between 6 and 15. There are about 90 schemes in operation, many of which include children from different racial backgrounds. Most of the schemes run for around three weeks. Volunteers must be 16 or over, and like hard work and children. A small sum is usually paid to cover expenses.

Applicants should write to John Bedford, Community Recreation Officer, at the above address.

Community Links
Canning Town Public Hall, 105 Barking Road, London E16 4HQ; tel 0171-473 2270; fax 0171-473 6671).

Community Links runs a social action centre for the purpose of encouraging groups and individuals to deal with their problems through self awareness and self help. There is a very large children's and youth work programme which covers a vast range of activities. The organisation is run by a permanent staff of 300 volunteers but thousands of part-time, short-term volunteers are needed every year to help run holiday playschemes, camping holidays and clubs and to assist with children at risk of going into care.

For further information, please contact the above address.

Contact a Family
170 Tottenham Court Road, London W1P OHA; tel 0171-383 3555; fax 0171-383 0259).

Contact a Family is a national charity which supports families who have children with disabilities or special needs. It brings families with a disabled child together through local mutual support and self-help groups. It advises parents who wish to start a group in their neighbourhood for parents of children with disabilities and offers nationwide support to families where the child has a rare syndrome or handicap.

For more information contact Harry Marsh at the above address.

Deaf Education Through Listening and Talking (DELTA)
P.O. Box 20, Haverhill, Suffolk, CB9 7BD; (tel/fax 01440 783689).

Delta is a nationwide support group of teachers and parents of deaf children. Delta provides support ranging from information and advice to guide parents in helping their children develop normal speech and to live independently within a hearing society. Volunteers are always needed. There are regional branches which hold regular meetings and conferences. DELTA also runs courses for parents and families including summer schools for parents with hearing-impaired children. While the children enjoy themselves, their parents attend lectures, workshops and discussion groups.

For further information contact Wendy Barnes at the above address.

Duke of Edinburgh's Award
Gulliver House, Madeira Walk, Windsor, Berkshire SL4 1EI (tel 01753-810753).

The Award is a programme of adventurous, cultural and practical activities undertaken voluntarily by young people; it is now operating in over 50 countries. All participants are required to complete a Service Section which is intended to encourage them to realise that as members of a community they have a responsibility to others and that their help is needed. This Service Section involves practical work in one of the following fields (after some initial training): first aid; coastguard service or mountain rescue; work with the WRVS; or care of the mentally handicapped. For the Gold Award this participant must give practical service over a minimum period of 12 months, as well as reaching the required standard in the course of instruction and the service to which it is related. The scheme relies on an estimated 40,000 adults in the UK, who assist as leaders, organizers, instructors, fund raisers and committee members.

The Award programme is open to all young people between the ages of 14 and 25. Adults who help as instructors and assessors must be suitably experienced or qualified persons nominated by the appropriate bodies.

Applications should be made to the Operations Officer at the above address, who will pass them on to the appropriate Regional Officer.

Endeavour Training
Sheepbridge Centre, Sheepbridge Lane, Chesterfield S41 9RX (tel 01246-454957; fax 01246-261865).

Endeavour runs courses and programmes to support its network of Local Volunteer Groups around the country. The training opportunities and Local Groups provide opportunities for personal development and enjoyment. Endeavour takes up where traditional education leaves off, by drawing out untapped reserves of personal resource. As a culmination to a person's progression through Endeavour's developmental curriculum opportunities for expeditioning are provided combining adventure with service to the host country/ community.

Volunteers can work alongside or become part of a Local Endeavour Group and join in whatever community service is being undertaken. Endeavour's 'target' group are 16-26 year olds from disadvantaged backgrounds or who are considered to be at risk. Volunteers are required for a week at a time to help run summer camps for disadvantaged 8-14 year olds. Those wishing to take up the Endeavour challenge can be associated for as long as they wish. Applicants can be of any nationality but they should be resident within the UK at the time they wish to participate in the programme. The minimum age limit is 16 years. Accommodation is provided for volunteers helping on the summer camps. Expenses may be paid; this is looked at on a case by case basis.

Applicants should contact Endeavours Voluntary and Community Services Team, at the above address.

Friends for Young Deaf People (FYD)
East Court Mansion, College Lane, East Grinstead, West Sussex RH19 3LT; (tel 01342-323444 & 312639; fax 01342-410232).

FYD aims to promote an active partnership between deaf and hearing people which will enable young deaf people to develop themselves and become active members of society.

Volunteers are needed all year round to work on projects and there is also a training programme. Reasonable travel expenses or agreed expenses will be paid. Useful publications include *Signpost*.

For further details, please contact the above address.

Gingerbread: The Association for One Parent Families
16-17 Clerkenwell Close, London EC1R OAA; (tel 0171 336 8183; fax 0171-336 8185). E-mail ginger@lonepar.demon.co.uk

Gingerbread was founded in 1970 by a woman who was experiencing difficulties in keeping a home together for her sons and herself. The authorities told her that the boys should be taken into care whilst she found a home, which would not only have been far more expensive for the state, but would also have broken up the family. The organisation grew as a result of the initial publicity, and there are now more than 300 self-help groups operating throughout England and Wales, with separate organisations covering Scotland and Ireland.

Although the organisation runs largely on a self-help basis, volunteers are also needed, especially to assist with child care. This ranges from baby sitting for individuals to running full and part-time holiday playschemes and after school care for 5 — 11 year olds. Help may also be needed by lone parents who are ill and therefore unable to take their children to school, go shopping, or perform household jobs.

Those interested should contact the national office at the above address, who will put them in touch with their local branch.

The Guide Association
17-19 Buckingham Palace Road, London SW1W OPT (tel 0171-834 6242; fax 0171-828 8317).

The Guide Association is the UK's largest voluntary youth organisation for girls and young women with some 750,000 members. It aims to enable girls to mature into confident, capable and caring women determined as individuals, to realise their potential in their career, home and personal life and willing to contribute to their community and the wider world.

The Guide Association believes that it can best develop these qualities in a mutually supportive, female structure within an environment of fun, friendship and adventure underpinned by moral and spiritual and moral values. The association creates programmes to fulfil these aims and to attract and inspire women leaders to provide Guiding wherever it is wanted. Within this framework, the Guide Association will grow and contribute to the advancement of girls and women.

Membership is open to any girl over five years. Activities are divided by age group into Rainbows (5-7 years), Brownies (7-10 years), Guides (10-14 years) and Rangers and Young Leaders (14-25 years).

The Guide Association is dependent on over 80,000 adult volunteers who are involved in many aspects: as Unit Guiders working with groups of young women to apply the Guiding method, in administration, fund-raising and in advisory roles.

For further information about Guiding in your area contact the Public Relations Department at the above address.

Great Ormond Street Hospital for Sick Children NHS Trust
Great Ormond Street, London WC1N 3JH (tel 0171-829 8861, ext. 5528)

GOSH NHS Trust needs volunteer helpers who are aged a minimum of 18 years and are able to offer a commitment of one day per week for at least six months. For further details, please contact the Voluntary Services Organiser at the above address.

Handicapped Adventure Playground Association Ltd
Fulham Palace, Bishop's Avenue, London SW6 (tel 0171-736 4443).

There are five adventure playgrounds for disabled children in London maintained by this association. Each has four full-time paid playleaders with extra temporary workers in the Easter and Summer holidays. Volunteers are also welcomed to help both with caring for the children and the playground. A charity shop in Fulham, run entirely by volunteers raises money for the playgrounds. Volunteers can also help with administration, office work, etc. They are needed all the year round and all skills and experience can be put to good use. Travelling expenses are given to regular volunteers if necessary.

Those interested should apply to the Administrator at the above address.

Hawksworth Hall School — SCOPE
Guiseley, Leeds, West Yorkshire, LS20 8NU. (tel 01943-870058; fax 01943 870038).

Hawksworth is a residential school for severely disabled children with multiple learning difficulties which uses many part-time volunteers each year for care and classroom work and taking the children on outings. Volunteers are needed all the year round except in the main school holidays, and there are no restrictions except that they should be in good health and physically strong.

Those interested should write to the Headteacher at the above address.

Holicare (North Bournemouth)
c/o Mrs Brenda Gritt, 36 Glamis Avenue, Bournemouth BH10 6DP (tel 01202-578715).

Holicare is a holiday playscheme for children from five to twelve approximately with working parents that is operated during all school holidays in North Bournemouth.

It provides supervised activities in groups of approximately 20-25 with a varied programme that includes craft work, games, outings, swimming and trips to the beach in summer.

One or two volunteers are needed to help run each playscheme. The schemes operate from 8.45am to 3.45pm Monday to Friday. Applicants must be aged over 18. For further details contact Mrs Brenda Gritt, at the above address.

National Playbus Association/Mobile Projects Association
93 Whitby Road, Brislington, Bristol BS4 3QF; tel 0117-977 5375; fax 0117-9721838).

Playbuses and mobile community resources are any vehicle, normally double decker buses, which provides a range of services in isolated areas, both rural and urban. These resources include playgroups for the under fives, holiday playschemes and afterschool work, youth club work, exhibition and welfare rights work, education and health projects and work with pensioners. The Association provides information, publications and support services to the 500 projects operating in the United Kingdom.

Anyone interested in helping with one in their area or seeking advice on how to organize one should contact the headquarters at the above address.

Off the Record
75a Murray Place, Stirling, FK8 1AU (tel 01786-450518).

Off the Record provides information, advice and counselling for the under 25s and is open four afternoons a week. New Volunteers are always needed for the centre and for a variety of groups run by Off the Record. Please telephone for further details.

Play Matters (National Association of Toy & Leisure Libraries)
68 Churchway, London NW1 1LT (tel 0171-387 9592; fax 0171-383 2714).

Play Matters is the parent body for over 1,000 toy libraries in the United Kingdom; it is a registered charity. The first toy libraries were set up by parents to loan toys to children with physical and/or mental handicaps. Now a growing number of toy libraries (over 50%) are open to all children in the community. Many toy libraries are run wholly by volunteers; those which have a paid organiser are also dependent on voluntary help. There are toy libraries in schools — nursery, infants' and junior — attached to public libraries and some loan to groups such as childminders and play groups. They offer a befriending, supportive service to parents and carers. Leisure libraries also offer a similar service to people who are mentally and/or physically handicapped and to their carers.

Each toy/leisure library is autonomous and the need for voluntary help can vary from one to another. Anyone wishing to offer their services should contact Play Matters who will put them in touch with the nearest toy/leisure library. if there is not a toy/leisure library in your area, help and advice is available to anyone wanting to start one. Please contact the above address. A SAE would be appreciated.

The Prince's Trust Volunteers
18 Park Square East, London NW1 4LH (tel 0171-543 1234; fax 0171-543 1367).WWW: http://www.princes-trust.org.uk

The Prince's Trust Volunteers was founded at the instigation of the Prince of Wales. It offers a personal development programme for 16-25-year olds in community work across the UK, both as individuals and as part of a team. Tasks are both caring and environmental. About 6,000 volunteers participate in the scheme annually. Participants may be employed or unemployed. Most tasks are in the volunteers' own local area so accommodation is not provided.

For the team task the Trust provides a 60-day development programme for volunteers who are placed in teams of 12-15 people under the guidance of a team leader. A major part of the programme is a 40-day placment where the team provides voluntary assistance; this may involve community care or environmental work.

For individuals the usual period of commitment is about 12 weeks at any time of year.

Anyone interested should first call freephone (0800 842 842) and ask where their nearest Prince's Trust Volunteers programme is; then call there.

The Rathbone Community Industry
Head Office, 1st Floor, The Excalibur Building, 77 Whitworth Street, Manchester M1 6EZ; (tel 0161-236 5358; fax 0161 236 4539.)

Founded at the beginning of the century by Elfrida Rathbone, to benefit educationally deprived people, the Rathbone CI is now a national charity with centres throughout Britain. Their aim is to improve opportunities for people who have limited access to services; many of whom have learning difficulties and other special needs. The range of services provided include: training and employment, residential and independent living centres; work with families and children, vocational education projects and a National Information Line. In addition, Rathbone CI produces a range of publications and reports, commissions research and where possible seeks to influence the policies of central and local government insofar as these affect people who have been denied the opportunity to realise their full potential.

Volunteers are seen as having a unique contribution to make and are needed all year round, to give one-to-one support in social and communication skills and literacy and numeracy. Only a few hours a week are needed, but a regular commitment is important. Enquiries regarding volunteering opportunities can be made to the National Development Manager at the above address.

Sailors' Families Society
Newland, Hull HU6 7RJ (tel 01482-342331/2).

The Society cares for the children of seafarers from all parts of the country. A further 550 are supported with their widowed mothers in their own homes in different areas around the country. As well as its work for children the Society provides or supports homes for aged seafarers or their widows in Hull. The Society has a number of fund raising committees in various parts of the country, staffed by voluntary helpers.

Those interested in helping should contact the Fundraising Manager at the above address.

Saturday Venture Association
66 Clarendon Road, London W11 2HP (answer phone 0171-727 0670).

This association is concerned with the provision of activities for deprived, disabled or terminally ill children. It works with councils to ensure that the most is made of entertainment and sports centre facilities and supports Saturday clubs for the children and their friends. The Saturday Venture Association supports various charities and furniture projects. Volunteers are needed to assist with the various projects; surveying areas to establish local needs and then setting up autonomous clubs, working in the charity furniture shops, helping with Saturday activities in the clubs and helping on holiday projects which occur during Easter, Christmas and summer vacations. Any commitment, from one month to 12 months will be accepted.

Volunteers should be non-smokers and preferably have a driving licence. Typing and other skills are useful. Depending on the project accommodation may be provided but pocket money is always paid.

Those interested should contact the Chairman at the above address.

St Basil's Centre
Heath Mill Lane, Deritend, Birmingham B9 4AX (tel 0121-772 2483).

This youth organisation based in the city centre of Birmingham needs volunteers to help in the running of its fifteen residential projects, hostels and information centres. Most of the young people who seek assistance are aged 16-25, and come from backgrounds of tension, frustration, fear and violence. They need to be helped in finding accommodation, and in learning to adjust to a more stable environment through acquiring appropriate social skills.

Applicants of all races and nationalities are welcome, provided they speak fluent English and are over 23 years of age. Experience of working with youths in informal settings would be an asset, although not essential.

Enquiries and applications may be sent to The Volunteer Coordinator, at the above address.

Scout Association
Baden-Powell House, Queen's Gate, London SW7 5JS (tel 0171-584 7030; fax 0171-590 5103).

The Scout Association aims to prepare young people to take a constructive place in society by providing interesting and enjoyable activities under voluntary adult leadership. Scouting began in 1907 based upon Lord Baden-Powell's ideas and book, *Scouting for Boys*. The Movement quickly spread and the world Scout population is now 16 million in 150 countries. In the UK there are some 648,000 members including Beaver Scouts (boys and girls aged six to eight years, Cub Scouts (boys and girls aged eight to ten and a half), Scouts (boys and girls aged ten and a half to $15\frac{1}{2}$ years) and Venture Scouts (aged $15\frac{1}{2}$ to 20 years). All offer a progressive training scheme which encourages personal development as well as collective and individual achievement. There is an emphasis upon outdoor activities. Scouting in the UK is committed to offering its services to young people in ethnic communities and in remote and inner-city areas.

Long-term voluntary opportunities are available with Scout Groups throughout the country and there is the possibility of occasional paid jobs at activity centres during the summer. Similar opportunities are also available in some other countries, notably the USA and Switzerland, for suitably qualified and experienced adults.

Further information can be obtained from the above address.

Sea Ranger Association (SRA)
HQTS 'Lord Amory', Dollar Bay, 631 Manchester Road, London E14 9NU.

As well as providing opportunities for women and girls to learn how to sail and operate other kinds of water craft, learn first-aid etc. the SRA also enables them to do community-based voluntary work in hospitals and children's homes.

Details of the nearest Sea Ranger contact can be obtained from the above address.

Surrey Docks Play Association
Trident Street, London SE16 (tel 0171-232 0846)

The Play Association offers safe play facilities, both indoors and outside, for able-bodied and disabled children aged up to 19 years old in south-east London. There is a wide range of activities open to volunteers including fundraising, arts and crafts workshops with the children, working on a one-to-one basis with children, driving the mini-bus and carpentry. Applicants of all nationalities are welcome.

Volunteers are recruited for an unlimited period of time if they prove satisfactory. A small amount of pocket money per week is paid.

Applications should be made all the year round to the Volunteer Co-ordinator, at the above address.

Youth Clubs UK
11 St. Bride Street, London EC4A 4AS; tel 0171-353 2366).

Youth Clubs UK (formerly the National Association of Youth Clubs) provides a range of services to support youth club work throughout the UK. There are over 45,000 youth workers including part-time workers and volunteers, involved in over 7,500 affiliated clubs. Volunteers are welcome, whether they bring a specific practical skill or simply enjoy working creatively with young people.

Prospective volunteers should contact their local youth club or Local Association of Youth Clubs, or the Youth Work Manager at the above address.

Community Projects

Community projects can take many forms and have many functions: they may exist to run a drop-in centre for local unemployed people or elderly people, to provide a local base for arts and crafts, or to run a toddlers playgroup. What they all have in common is that they are all run by the community for the community. Sometimes local authorities may provide some funds or premises to assist a community project, but most depend for their existence on the time and energy of volunteers.

Anyone thinking of starting a community project in their own area should first contact the National Federation of Community Organisations (see entry below). The first problem will be finding suitable premises from which to operate, preferably with a telephone. With the right array of talents, skills and enthusiasm, it should be possible to start and run a successful community project. Most projects find that, after slow beginnings, their schemes snowball and their range of activities multiplies. Publicity is one of the keys to the success of this type of project: once a scheme is established and proves to be useful, it will generate its own publicity. Local press coverage and distribution of leaflets in public places (libraries, information centres, citizens advice bureaux, etc.) are invaluable in the early stages.

Many community projects exist in towns and cities up and down the country but they need not be solely in urban areas: for example. residents of country villages isolated by reductions in bus services may now legally pool their resources and share car journeys, on an organised basis, for example. The best community projects depend on an individual spotting some local need, then setting out to meet it.

Community Matters
8/9 Upper Street, Islington, London N1 OPQ (tel 0171-226 0189).

Community Matters exists to provide advice and information to local community organisations on running voluntary organisations, managing community centres, identifying and meeting community needs, working with statutory authorities and other voluntary organisations, etc. Help is needed from volunteers who are able to conduct research, do general clerical work or provide legal advice.

Some volunteers give regular help perhaps once a week, others just occasionally to help with specific jobs such as mailings. Expenses are covered where necessary.

Applications should be sent to the Administration Officer at the above address, who can also advise on the addresses of community organisations around the country.

Free Form Arts Trust
38 Dalston Lane, London E8 3AZ (tel 0171-249 3394).

Free Form is a registered charity which uniquely combines the skills of artists and architects on large scale projects which involve local communities; demonstrating the art of urban regeneration and improving the environment both socially and pysically. Work may be either interior or exterior and examples include mosaic wall panels, landscaping, street furniture and planting. Free Form is organised as a practice, with artists and architects working together in teams, with the involvement of local communities throughout the design process. In addition, 15-20 trainees and a number of volunteers are annually offered skills training through the Trust's projects, enabling many of them to move on to further education or enter directly into full employment. Anyone who is interested in finding out more should write to the above address.

SCADU-The National Centre for Student Volunteering in the Community
Oxford House, Derbyshire Street, London E2 6HG (tel 0171-739 4565; answer phone 0171-739 0198).

The Unit encourages, promotes and develops the voluntary community work of students through approximately 130 local Student Community Action Groups in the United Kingdom. Altogether there are over 15,000 volunteers involved with these autonomous local groups which have different priorities including people with mental health problems, disabled children and adults, young people, welfare rights, women's centres, etc.

These groups are not volunteer bureaux; most members are students who become involved with the groups attached to their place of study and who state the level of involvement they are able to give to its activities over the academic year. There is no payment for this voluntary work; arrangements for travel expenses, board and lodging will depend upon the individual groups.

Those interested should send a stamped addressed envelope for a list of Student Community Action Groups in Britain.

Conservation, the Environment & Heritage

Since the first edition of this book was published over a decade ago there has been a massive increase in public awareness of environmental matters. Concern for the environment was once regarded by many as the preserve of cranks: now it has become a selling point in car advertising.

The organisations in this section share the goal of preserving the environment against the ravages of progress. They have different objectives, and use voluntary help in many different ways: for example, the Henry Doubleday Research Association needs knowledgeable guides for its organic gardens in Coventry and Kent while the Commonwork Land Trust needs voluntary assistance for hands-on conservation work on 500 acres of land, including coppicing and bridge building.

The largest voluntary body concerned with nature conservation is the RSNC Wildlife Trusts Partnership which consists of 47 Wildlife Trusts and 50 Urban Wildlife Groups in the UK. The Partnership's national office itself has only a limited need for volunteers, to perform clerical and administrative work in its offices at The Green, Witham Park, Lincoln LN5 7JR. The regional Wildlife Trusts, however, have wide needs for skilled and unskilled volunteers to perform practical conservation work on nature reserves and other land of conservation interest, to work as wardens on the reserves and to help with their office work. Each Trust recruits its own volunteers, and needs may vary from region to region: contact names and addresses for individual Wildlife Trusts and Urban Groups are available from the national office (tel 01522 544400).

Those who find that voluntary work in this area whets their appetite for environmental work can consult *Working With the Environment* published by Vacation Work in 1996 (£9.99) and *The Environmental Careers Handbook*, published by Trotman & Co., (12-14 Hill Rise, Richmond, Surrey TW10 6UA).

Anglesey Sea Zoo
Brynsiencyn, Isle of Anglesey, North Wales, LL61 6TQ; (tel 01248-430411; fax 01248-430411). E-mail: FISHANDFUN@SEAZ00.demon.co.uk

Anglesey Sea Zoo operates with a base of volunteers, mainly marine biologists who help generally in the zoo, caring for the fish and communicating with the public and helping them to understand more about marine life. The zoo has a breeding and conservation policy and volunteers should be familiar with the range of specimens, species and habitats on display. Training courses may be deemed necessary by the management. Up to 14 volunteers are taken on annually and mostly stay for the season, but volunteers are welcome at any time. Volunteers from abroad are accepted if their English is good. A reasonable degree of fitness is essential and a driving licence as the zoo is quite remote. No accommodation is provided but up to £5 daily expenses are paid.

Beale Park
The Child-Beale Trust, Lower Basildon, Reading, Berkshire RG8 9NH; (tel 01734-845172; fax 01734-845171).

Beale Park is a charity dedicated to the conservation of the land it owns and rare breeds of animals and birds. It is open to the public in the form of a natural world theme park of 300 acres which includes ancient water meadows and 45 acres of woodland. Animals graze the meadows while birds are housed in spacious bird enclosures which are part of a captive breeding programme. Peacocks, golden pheasants, owls are amongst the birds kept and llamas and highland cattle are amongst the free grazing animals.

20-30 volunteers per year work at Beale Park helping with animal and bird care and maintenance, the gardens, grounds, organic farm, education (environmental) and administration.

Volunteers can be taken on for a few days, weeks or all year. Expenses and pocket money are paid but accommodation is not readily available.

Anyone interested should contact the Beale Park office at the above address.

The Barn Owl Trust
Waterleat, Ashburton, Devon TQ13 7HU; (tel 01364-653026; fax 01364-654392 phone first).

The Barn Owl Trust operates mostly in south-west England and uses volunteers for a range of tasks. There are office-based volunteers who word process, file, design, enter data and construct nestboxes. Outdoors volunteers install nestboxes and carry out survey work. Volunteers can be taken on for various periods but a year's commitment is usual. The Trust needs volunteers all year round except during August. A small contribution is made towards petrol.

The Trust publishes 29 free information leaflets on Barn Owls and various research projects and a publication *Barn Owls on Site-a Guide for Developers and Planners* for £5 mail order.

Anyone interested in helping out should contact D Ramsden at the above address.

BBONT-The local Wildlife Trust for Berkshire, Buckinghamshire and Oxford-shire
3 Church Road, Cowley, Oxford (tel 01865-775476).

BBONT Wildlife Trust is one of 47 county-based Wildlife Trusts in the UK concerned with all aspects of local wildlife protection. BBONT's objective is to protect the future of wildlife and to create a greater appreciation of and involvement in wildlife and wildlife sites and to generate more opportunities for all to enjoy our wildlife heritage and develop a better understanding of the environment as a whole.

As an integral part of its aims, BBONT encourages active participation by volunteers. Volunteer work falls into three areas:

Practical conservation work which comprises roving, mid-week teams who carry out work on a variety of sites, regular work parties on nature reserves and reserve wardens. Wardens need to be able to commit on a consistent basis. Other work involves species recording and habitat monitoring. No experience is necessary though specific skills will be utilised.

Sales and fundraising and public relations and education volunteers, help with stalls at events, write walkers' leaflets and local newsletters. Volunteers are also needed for the Wildlife Shop in Wallingford and to assist the Education Officer.

Office administration which includes filing, computing and data base work in a busy membership office.

Anyone interested in any of the above should contact the Information Officer at the above address.

Bridport Museum Service
South Street, Bridport, Dorset DT6 3NR; (tel 01308-422116; fax 01308-458105).

Bridport Museum Service comprises two museums, a local history centre, and education service, two stores and twelve collections. Volunteers are needed to assist with a variety of museum work, including reception, guided walks, research and displays and exhibitions. The work would suit people with an interest in local history, museums and heritage who are keen to develop museum skills and acquire experience. The varied range of services provided by the above means that most volunteers find the the work worthwhile.

Applicants should be aged 18+ and be able to work for a minimum of one month between the beginning of August and the end of September. All applicants should be available to attend an interview. Applicants from abroad with museum experience and good English are welcome to apply.

Enquiries from July to the Museums Officer at the above address.

British Naturalists' Association
1 Bracken Mews, Chingford, London E4 7UT.

The Association was founded in 1905 (as the British Empire Naturalists' Association) in order to bring nature lovers in all parts of the UK and from overseas into contact with each other. It encourages and supports schemes and legislation for the protection of the country's natural resources, and organizes meetings, field weeks, lectures and exhibitions to extend and popularise the study of nature. The Association does not supplement the activities of local and regional bodies, some 50 of which are at present affiliated to it.

Volunteers who wish to offer practical help on such projects as clearing a village pond should join their local branch, if possible. These are at present operative in the following areas: Buckinghamshire, Dorset, Essex, Hampshire, Hertfordshire, Kent, Lancashire, London, Greater Manchester, and Devon.

The subscription rate for members is variable: £12 (£10 for senior citizens). It includes six issues of the Association's Journal *Country Side*, and the *British Naturalist*, which provides details of branch activities.

Applications for membership should be sent to the Hon. Membership Secretary at the above address.

Canterbury Oast Trust
South of England Rare Breeds Centre, Highlands Farm, Woodchurch, Ashford, Kent TN26 3RJ (tel 01233-861494).

The Trust offers work for 20-30 volunteers throughout the year at the Centre, which is a commercial tourist attraction run by a charity for adults with learning disabilities. Jobs are open to volunteers in various areas. In the restaurant, servers are needed and volunteers are needed to work in the kitchen. Car park supervisors are required, as are volunteers to help in the shop and entrance kiosk. On the farm, volunteers are needed for a variety of jobs ranging from general farm work and basic maintenance to tractor-driving.

Applicants can be of all nationalities, but they must speak English and have their own transport. It is essential that they are capable of working with disabled adults. The minimum age is 16, and applicants must be in good health. Disabled applicants are welcome to apply, although individual cases would have to be discussed.

Volunteers are required all the year round, but demand is highest in the summer when the minimum stay would be one month. Accommodation is not provided, but camping space may be available. No pocket money can be paid. Enquiries and applications should be sent to the Volunteers Co-ordinator at the above address.

Commonwork Land Trust
Commonwork, Bore Place, Chiddingstone, Edenbridge, Kent TN8 7AR (tel 01732-463255; fax 01732-740264).

Commonwork requires conservation volunteers to work on 500 acres of the Kent Weald at Bore Place. Activities open to volunteers include coppicing, bridge building, field trail maintenance and gardening. Volunteers are required to fit the specific volunteer days offered by Commonwork. Applicants of any nationality may apply, but accommodation and pocket money are not provided.

To apply, or for a copy of Commonwork's annual Broadsheet, please contact John Waller at the above address.

Council for the Protection of Rural England
25 Buckingham Palace Road, London SW1W 0PP (tel 0171-976 6433; fax 0171-976 6373).

CPRE fights for a living and beautiful countryside. It is active locally, nationally and internationally. As a registered charity, CPRE relies upon volunteers for the achievements of its objectives. Membership is open to all.

Enquiries to the above address.

Didcot Railway Centre
Didcot, Oxon OX11 7NJ; (tel 01235-817200).

Didcot Railway Centre is famous for its collection of bygone railway engines and rolling stock much of it restored, under restoration, or in working condition. Volunteers are needed in several departments: casual catering assistants are needed from May to the end of September; voluntary clerical assistants are needed to staff the office, switchboard and other office tasks; gardeners to maintain gardens and lawns; volunteer stewards to see people on and off the trains (mainly weekends and Wednesdays in August). Volunteers are also needed all year round to work on the restoration of locomotives.

Anyone interested should contact the Manager at the above address.

Dumfries Museum
The Observatory, Dumfries DG2 7PW; (tel 01387-253374); fax 01387-265081).

The museum needs four volunteers to work as curatorial assistants. The hours are 10am to 1pm and 2pm to 5pm, two to five days per week. No accommodation is available. The minimum period of work is two months.

Applicants should be graduates with specialism in a section of the museum's collections (archaeology, natural history or Scottish history). The work could be a valuable experience for those wishing to make a career in this field.

Applications should be addressed to the Museums Manager at the above address.

The Earth Centre
Kilner's Bridge, Doncaster Road, Denary Main, South Yorkshire DN12 4DY; (tel 01709-770566; fax 01709-861727).

The Earth Centre is a new environmental centre. Volunteers are needed to work as interpreters, rangers and project assistants. Interpreters should be educated preferably to degree level. Rangers should have previous experience and be aged 18+. Volunteers work directly with the public and should be available for a minimum of one month. Limited board and lodging is available for £25 per week. The period of work is between April and September. Experience with children and an understanding of sustainability are essential. Some practical conservation work is also involved.

Applications should be sent to The Chief Executive, at the above address.

Henry Doubleday Research Association
Ryton Organic Gardens, Coventry CV8 3L9 (tel 01203-303517; fax 01203-639229).

The Gardens, which are open to the public, need about 15 volunteer guides each year. At present, these are mostly needed in Ryton Organic Gardens, but there may also be a similar need in Yalding Organic Gardens in Kent. These organic and environmentally friendly gardens are designed to educate and give pleasure. There might also be opportunities for volunteers in the organic café/shop and also to help in the office. Applicants of all nationalities are welcome, but some knowledge of gardening, conservation, organic growth and the environment is needed. Volunteers are required to work on a part-time basis, usually all the year round. Expenses will be paid.

Those interested should apply to the Executive Director at the above adress.

Ironbridge Gorge Museum
The Wharfage, Ironbridge, Telford, Shropshire TF8 7AN (tel 01952-433522; fax 01952-432204).

The Ironbridge Gorge Museum is widely regarded as one of Britain's premier museums. Set amongst the beautiful Shropshire countryside, it is an independent educational charity providing enjoyment to hundreds of thousands of visitors each year. The Museum was founded in 1967 with the aims of conserving, restoring and interpreting the unique heritage of the Gorge.

Approximately 30 local volunteers help at the Museum complex every year. Volunteers are required to help with a huge variety of activities in all the different sections of the Museum. Most opportunities for volunteers are with the Blists Hill Open Air Museum. Demonstrators, clad in Victorian style costume, are required to work in exhibits, explaining the site and its shops, works and houses, to visitors, including school parties. The opportunity also exists for volunteers to learn and use traditional skills within the exhibits. Good communication skills and an ability to speak English are essential. There is also the opportunity to research and present street activity of the period. Good communication skills and the ability to work partly unsupervised are needed.

Volunteers are also required to assist with general site maintenance and with the making, repairing and maintenance of the period style clothes worn at the Open Air Museum. Volunteers are required to help with research and documentation. Applicants must be graduates or undergraduates with an interest in social and industrial history, possessing neatness, patience and accuracy.

At the Coalport China Museum volunteer demonstrators are needed to work in a ceramic workshop making and painting porcelain flowers. The possibility also exists for work with historic printing and manufacturing equipment. In the pottery workshop, volunteers can have the opportunity to make, decorate and fire earthenware items, or help with school parties. Good communication skills and an ability to speak English are essential.

Voluntary researchers are needed at the Long Warehouse, Coalbrookdale where a variety of research, cataloguing and interesting projects are always waiting to be undertaken. A knowledge of library and archive procedures would be a distinct advantage, as well as an interest in history. Volunteers are also required to assist with documentation; the ability to type and to do a repetitive job is essential. Computer skills and a good command of the English language would also be useful.

At the Jackfield Tile Museum demonstrators are required in the Tile Works, explaining and practising the art of decoration and glazing. There would be opportunities to work as a guide or with school parties.

Local volunteers assist at the Museum for an indefinite period, while volunteers needing accommodation are requested to stay a minimum of two weeks between March and October. The basic self-catering volunteer accommodation on the Blists Hill site provides carpeted dormitories fitted with bunk beds, a kitchen/dining area, washing facilities and toilets, at a cost of £1.15 per night. As space is limited, please book in advance. No expenses are paid but a main course meal is provided at lunch-time, and hot drinks are provided at any time of day. Applicants may be of any nationality, but the ability to speak good English and to work well with the general public are essential. Training, costume, equipment and supervision are all provided as appropriate.

For an application form please contact Jan Jennings at the above address.

London Canal Museum
12/13 New Wharf Road, Kings Cross, London N1 9RT; tel 0171-713 0836.

Two or three volunteer museum assistants with a sense of humour are required annually. The museum is open Tuesday to Sunday from 10am to 4.30pm. Local travel expenses are reimbursed.

London Wildlife Trust
80 York Way, London N1 9AG (tel 0171 278-6612/3; fax 0171 837-8060).

The Trust was founded in 1981. It is an independent voluntary organisation with charitable status which operates throughout the Greater London area and is affiliated to the national network of Wildlife Trusts. The LWT has the following aims and objectives; to positively promote an interest in wildlife to members of the public to encourage them to support the work of the Trust as members or supporters, to protect identified sites of wildlife interest, to promote positive management of those sites, thereby conserving or enhancing the wildlife interest of those sites and to encourage local community involvement and volunteer support.

Approximately 500 volunteers per year help the Trust with practical conservation work, wardening, educational activities, publicity, campaigning, local group work, monitoring and surveying wildlife and visitors to reserves. Volunteers of any nationality will be accepted but fluent English is essential. It would also be useful if volunteers have had previous experience in any of the above areas, especially in ecological surveying. Volunteers must also be reasonably fit. The length of time for which volunteers are recruited is dependent on the project, but the usual minimum commitment is 2 months, although this is not necessarily on a full-time basis. Lunch and travel expenses are available.

Those interested should contact Graham Turnbull, the Director, at the above address.

Marine Conservation Society

9 Gloucester Road, Ross-on-Wye, Herefordshire HR9 5BU (tel 01989-566017; fax 01989-567815).E-mail mcsuk@gn.apc.org

The Marine Conservation Society is the only environmental organisation which works exclusively to safeguard the marine environment across the whole range of conservation issues. The Society is a registered charity with an expanding membership which encourages members to take part in projects to help provide a sound research base for campaigns. The Society is a limited company and has two associated companies which support its work. One deals with the sales of MCS goods and related products and the other with marine biological consultancy.

Volunteers assist with beach surveys and clean-ups, measuring the impact of human activity and waste by surveying and recording specific marine animals. Volunteer divers are also needed to help with underwater surveys of coastal waters. Volunteers may also be needed to assist at shows and exhibitions. Applicants of any nationality may apply and no special qualifications are needed, except for the diving-related activities. The length of time for which volunteers are recruited depends on the task, but volunteers are usually required between May and October every year. Applicants should note that no accommodation is provided for volunteers, and no expenses are paid.

For further information contact the Society at the above address.

The Merthyr Tydfil Heritage Trust

Ynysfach Engine House, Ynysfach Road, Merthyr Tydfil, Mid-Glamorgan CF48 1AG; (tel 01685-721858; fax 01685-721858).

Volunteers are required to carry out research and field work at Ynysfach Iron Heritage Centre and Drenewydd Museum, both important heritage attractions in South Wales. Hours are 9am to 5pm, five days a week. No accommodation is provided but assistance can be given in finding some. Volunteers should be aged 18+. Posts would suit those who study or have an interest in history, archaeology or tourism. The minimum period of work is two weeks. Volunteers are required all year round.

As the posts involve research and text writing, overseas applicants must prove they have very good written English. All applicants have to attend an informal interview. Applications at any time to the above address.

North York Moors National Park
The Old Vicarage, Bongate, Helmsley, York YO6 5BP (tel 01439-770657; 01439-770691).

The North York Moors National Park covers 554 square miles in North York-shire. Between Easter and October of each year, 150 volunteers are needed to act as rangers throughout the park. Tasks include providing information to visitors, patrolling the park and carrying out both conservation work and improvements to the public rights-of-way network. Weekend and day-long training sessions for prospective rangers are held during winter. Voluntary rangers are required to work a minimum of 12 sessions each lasting for six hours between 10am and 5pm during the opening season.

Volunteers should be between 18 and 65 years old, able to get on well with people and reasonably fit. Applicants with a knowledge of the area and driving licences are preferred. No accommodation is available but a mileage allowance is paid.

Applicants should apply to the Principal Assistant in Land Management at the above address.

North Yorkshire Moors Railway
Pickering Station, Pickering, North Yorkshire YO18 7AJ.

Volunteers needed for all aspects of the operation and maintenance of a busy 18-mile stretch of steam railway running from Brosmont (near Whitby) to Pickering. Work includes train running, sales, catering, engineering (both civil and mechanical). Volunteer work is available all year round for both skilled and unskilled people aged 16+ who are reasonably fit. Basic accommodation is available.

Applicants should contact John Bruce, Volunteer Liaison Officer, North York Moors Historical Railway Trust, 15 Lincoln Court, Darlington, DL1 2XN.

Peak Park Conservation Volunteers
Peak National Park Office, Aldern House, Baslow Road, Bakewell DE45 1AE (tel 01629-815185; fax 01629-815045).

Each year thousands of volunteers help to protect the wildlife habitats and areas of outstanding natural beauty in the Peak District National Park over weekends, bank holidays and during school and college holidays around the year. Types of work to be done include building and repairing footpaths, stiles, steps, foot-bridges, fencing, walling, hedgelaying and tree planting, pond clearance and collecting litter.

No specific requirements are expected of volunteers except that they be between 14 and 65 years old. No accommodation is available so applications from local volunteers are preferred; but tools, materials, training and drinks are provided. Individuals outside the UK should not apply until they are in the country and have accommodation arranged.

Those interested should contact the Volunteers Organiser at the above address.

River Thames Society
Side House, Middle Assendon, Henley-On-Thames, Oxon RG9 6AP (tel 01491- 571476).

This registered charity has, over its 30 years existence, assumed the role of the guardian of the whole river. The Society has been active in protecting the

Thames as a public amenity, for effective commercial use, an area of conservation and natural beauty. Using volunteers the Society has been very successful in surveillance of such matters as planning consents, pollution and navigation while undertaking surveys of banks and paths. In association with local authorities and organisations such as the Thames Heritage Trust, the Society actively manages restoration projects.

In the first instance applications should be made to the Administrator at the above address giving personal details and suggested availability and type of work sought.

Rutland Railway Museum

Ashwell Road, Cottesmore, Oakham, Leicestershire LE15 7BX; (tel 01780-813203 for site; 01780-55380 for information).

The Rutland Railway Museum is a registered educational charity. Volunteers are required for various duties, consisting mainly of locomotive restoration and servicing, coach/wagon painting and woodworking, and also site development and maintenance. Volunteers work at weekends only. No accommodation is provided on site, but bed and breakfast is available locally. Applications welcome at any time to the Honorary Secretary at the above address.

Tree Council

51, Catherine Place, London SW1E 6DY; 35 Belgrave Square, London SW1X 8QN; (tel 0171-828 9928; fax 0171-828 9060).

The Tree Council promotes and co-ordinates the Tree Warden Scheme, sponsored by British Gas, which was launched in September 1990. The Scheme is a national initiative to enable people to play an active role in conserving and enhancing their local trees and woods. Between 6,000 and 7,000 volunteers per year act as tree wardens and gather information about their local trees, give advice on tree matters, protect threatened trees and encourage local projects to do with trees and woods. Trees are a precious part of the national heritage and action must be taken now if future generations are to enjoy the beauty and variety of British landscapes. To be most effective, this action should be taken by people on the spot; the people who know their own localities intimately and have most to gain from the protection and enhancement of their immediate environment. The Tree Council is working closely with local authorities and voluntary organisations to set up schemes in town and country throughout the British Isles.

Anyone can become a Tree Warden as long as they are enthusiastic about trees; volunteers are needed all the year round. Tree Wardening can often happily be combined with other activities such as taking the children to school, exercising dogs and family walks. Some wardens have demanding jobs; others are unemployed or retired.

Applications to the above address will be forwarded to the relevant local organisations, or write for a list of these organisations.

Yorkshire Carriage Museum

Aysgarth Falls, Wensleydale, North Yorks DL8 3SR (tel 01969-663399; fax 01969-663699).

Volunteers needed to carry out a variety of jobs on a three-storey, Grade II listed building housing a collection of Victorian carriages. The restoration of the building is an ongoing project governed by a charitable trust. Help required includes landscaping, carriage cleaning, stone cleaning and plaster removing. Also needed are skilled volunteers with stonewall, brick/stone work and pointing experience.

Those interested should contact Ann Kiely at the above address or telephone number.

Zion Community & Health Resource Centre
Zion Crescent, Hulme, Manchester M15 5BY; (tel 0161-226 5412).

ZCHRC believes that caring for the environment is one of the best ways to further health. The organisation is committed to operating in an ecologically friendly way. To do this it runs a variety of projects based at the Centre that respect the fact that the earth has limited resources and aims to counteract the impact of pollution on health.

Volunteers are needed to further organise and develop recycling and other initiatives, to organise monthly meetings. to liaise with cleaners and administrations to compare prices of green products with non-green ones, to monitor whether green products are as genuinely green, and to raise awareness locally of environmental issues and much more.

Anyone interested in volunteering their services please contact Milan Ghosh, at the above address.

Education

For one reason or another large numbers of people in Britain manage to slip through the state education system without managing to learn basic skills: it is estimated that there are two million adults who can barely read, and half a million who are totally illiterate. There are many more who do not reach their full potential in the education system, and volunteers can provide invaluable help in amending this situation by acting as tutors with, for example, the Marine Society, which helps seafarers to continue their education to secondary and tertiary levels.

There is also a large number of immigrants living in ethnic minority communities around Britain who have little or no knowledge of English, which can lead to immense problems in coping with day to day life. Volunteers are greatly needed to act as language teachers with them: the job requires patience and a sympathetic approach, but no formal qualifications.

This section also includes details of ways in which volunteers can help other organisations whose aims are educational, although not necessarily to do with fundamentals such as literacy or speaking English.

The Africa Centre
38 King Street, Covent Garden, London WC2E 8JT (tel 0171-836 1973; fax 0171-836 1975).

The Africa Centre functions as an education centre, which gives information about Africa and its culture. The Centre requires 10 volunteers per year to work mainly as administrative and secretarial assistants in its office, but also as Programme assistants, who will help in the running of a variety of activities from Film Festivals to workshops on African culture.

Volunteers, of any nationality, are required all the year round and can work for up to twelve months. Volunteers can be of any age, and no special qualifications or experience are needed. Although the Centre does not provide accommodation for its volunteers, it will pay for any travel expenses.

Applications should be made to the Director, Adotey Bing, at the above address.

Commission for Racial Equality
Elliot House, 10/12 Allington Street, London SW1E 5EH (tel 0171-828 7022; fax 0171-630 7605).

There are over 100 Racial Equality Councils in the UK, many of which can use voluntary help in such areas as running projects and assisting with general administrative duties of the organisation as well as with publicity.

The needs of Councils vary from area to area; prospective volunteers should contact their local Councils directly, either by finding their address from the phone book or through the Information Officer at the above address.

GLOSA Education Organisation (GEO)
PO Box 18, Richmond, Surrey TW9 2AU (tel 0181 948-8417).E-Mail glosauk@-cix.compulink.co.uk7

GLOSA's aim is the organisation of 1,000 international Latin and Greek roots into an expressive and euphonious International Auxiliary Language (IAL). GEO aims to publicize this language, to provide information about it among the public, pupils and educationalists and promote the teaching of GLOSA as a second language in schools worldwide.

GLOSA is already taught as a second language in the US, Asia, and Africa and there are now more than 100 volunteers in different countries helping with the above aims. Volunteers mainly working from home, are urgently neededed worldwide to help publicise GLOSA via the writing of articles for journals and newspapers. Voluntary translators are needed to translate many GLOSA publications, especially the central vocabulary, as are people to teach GLOSA either in their school etc via letters and cassettes or small groups/individuals in their own town. Applicants of all nationalities accepted. Knowledge of a second language is preferable, but motivation is the main qualification as GLOSA can be mastered in just a few days. Volunteers are needed all the time, and can help for as long or short a time as they want. Funds are limited but paper/ink expenses can sometimes be paid. Free literature about GLOSA is provided.

Those interested should write to Wendy Ashby at the above address.

The Hornsby International Dyslexia Centre
Glenshee Lodge, 261 Trinity Road, London SW18 3SN (tel 0181-874 1844; fax 0181-877 9737).

The Centre runs courses, primarily for teachers, in the skills and techniques needed to teach those with Specific Learning Difficulties/Dyslexia. Courses are run at the Centre but there is also a distance learning version with students in over fifty countries. The Centre is also a registered charity.

Volunteers are needed for clerical and secretarial duties and if they are computer users, to update data bases. British undergraduates living in London are preferred. A small amount of pocket money and a contribution towards travel expenses is paid by the centre.

Those interested should contact Colonel Tony Benett, Chief Executive at the above address.

The Marine Society
202 Lambeth Road, London SE1 7JW (tel 0171-261 9535; fax 0171-401 2537).

The Marine Society, as the oldest maritime charity in the world, provides several operations in support of professional seafarers/ Among these is the College of the Sea and Seafarers Libraries.

The latter offers an exchange library service to merchant ships and offshore platforms, and to individuals book lending, finding and selling.

The College of the Sea offers comprehensive educational support, facilitating seafarers to continue their education while serving at sea. Distance-led supported self-study in non-vocational education, from remedial literacy and numeracy through GCSEs and A Levels, is provided by means of a network of mainly voluntary tutors and equally important, an educational advice service on any matter of concern.

Offers of volunteer help always welcome. Enquiries to the Head of Education.

Elderly People

As standards of medical care and nutrition have steadily increased over the course of this century so has life expectancy, and Britain now has a rapidly growing number of octogenarians. Parallel with this has been an increase in the average age of the population as products of the post World War Two 'baby boom' grow older without having replaced themselves with equal numbers of children. The result of these factors is growing pressure on the stretched resources of the social services to cope with the frailties of an increasingly large proportion of the population, and the activities of the voluntary organisations described below are becoming more and more needed. Although the state can take care of an old person's physical needs, volunteers can be of invaluable assistance in helping their mental well-being.

It can make an immense difference to the life of an elderly person if they are visited by a volunteer, even if it is for only an hour a week. There are many simple practical jobs which a volunteer can do to improve the quality of life of an old person, from shopping, gardening or going to the library, to simply changing a light bulb, but the most important job that the volunteer can do is simply to provide companionship, whether the old person lives alone or in a home or hospital: this is a job at which the young are particulaly successful. For many housebound people the volunteer may their only visitor, someone to talk to over a cup of tea, and someone who is there because they care, not because they are just doing their job.

There are many ways of entering this field of voluntary work: Age Concern, the British Red Rross and the WRVS are the principal national organisations which are active on a local scale. If none of the opportunities listed in this section appeal you can simply phone up the officer in charge of a local old people's home and ask if you can help in any way.

Apart from the entries below, other voluntary work concerning elderly people is discussed in the sections on *The Sick and Disabled* and *Hospitals.*

Abbeyfield Society

Abbeyfield House, 53 Victoria Street, St Albans, Herts AL1 3UW; tel 01727-857536; fax 01727 846168).

The Abbeyfield Society is a federation of local, autonomous societies set up and run by local voluntary workers throughout the UK. The national support office staff and some regional staff, guide and advise volunteers as they acquire, build, develop, maintain and run houses for older people no longer willing or able to live alone. The aim is to provide care and companionship for such older people within the setting of a small household. The average age of residents is 85.

Residents furnish their own rooms, and each house is self-supporting; the aim being to achieve a family setting while preserving the privacy and independence of each resident. Every house has well-equiped bathrooms, some with special adaptations for people with disabilities. Increasingly, societies are offering rooms with en suite facilities. There are around 600 local societies and some 1,000 houses. In addition, Abbeyfield Societies run 50 registered residential care houses for those who, through frailty, need personal care.

Ordinary domestic properties may be purpose-built or converted to provide communal facilities and 8-12 living spaces. A resident housekeeper typically cooks and serves two main meals daily. Members of local societies, except the housekeeper are volunteers.

Abbeyfield societies need a wide range of skills from volunteers in order to function effectively. Executive committees usually have a solicitor, an accountant and a doctor to liaise with the medical profession and advise on medical matters generally. People with property development experience, such as estate agents or chartered surveyors are valuable. A committee would also need several members who are available during the day to be responsible for the day-to-day operational administration of the houses. Besides these voluntary committee members, whose responsabilities require fairly specific amounts of time, there is always a need for volunteers whose time cannot be given on such a regular basis. These contributions may take the form of visiting, taking residents on outings, gardening, handiwork, organising events or coffee mornings, or deputising for the housekeeper on their days off.

Those interested should contact the Chief Executive at the above address for the address of their nearest local society.

Age Concern England

Astral House, 1268 London Road, London SW16 4ER (tel 0181-679 8000; fax 0181-679 6069).

The Age Concern movement is a confederation of over 90 national and 1100 regional and local UK organisations which exists to promote the well-being of older people, helping to make later life a fulfilling and enjoyable experience. Established in 1940 as the National Council on Ageing, Age Concern England is a central co-ordinating body for those other organisations concerned with older people and our ageing society.

The 1,100 regional and local Age Concern organisations rely upon over 180,000 volunteers to provide a wide and varying range of services and opportunities appropriate to the needs of older people in their area. These can include running day centres, lunch clubs, transport schemes, home visiting, and providing practical advice and assistance, and can extend to the provision of intensive care for mentally and physically frail elderly people in some areas. The time and skills of volunteers are highly valued; everyone should have something to offer their local Age Concern organisation.

Details of the nearest Age Concern Group can be discovered from the telephone directory.

Age Exchange Theatre Trust Limited

The Reminiscence Centre, 11 Blackheath Village, London SE3 9LA (tel 0181 318-9105; fax 0181 319-0060).

Age Exchange aims to improve the quality of life for older people by emphasising the value of their reminiscences for old and young. To this end the Reminiscence Centre was founded in 1987 to provide creative activities for older people. 30-50 volunteers are recruited annually to staff the Centre and to help in the Café. This is done on a rota of morning and afternoon sessions.

Duties are varied, ranging from clerical work to welcoming visitors to the Centre. Applicants can be of any nationality, but must be able to speak good English. Pocket money is not provided, but some expenses can be reimbursed.

Apply to the Administrator, at the above address.

Counsel and Care

16 Bonny Street, London NW1 9PG (tel 0171-485 1550; advice line 10.30am-4pm 0171-485 1556).

Counsel and Care is a registered charity providing a nationwide service for older people and their carers.

The organisation runs a free advisory service and provides advice on a wide range of issues such as welfare benefits, accommodation, residential care, community care, and hospital discharge, backed up by a series of well-researched and regularly up-dated fact sheets.

C&C administer a number of trust funds for single payments, are able to allocate limited grants themselves, and advise on other charities who may be able to provide financial assistance.

C&C holds an extensive Home Care database to advise on private and voluntary Home Care and Nursing Agencies throughout the country and a database of Nursing Homes in the Greater London area from which they are able to make appropriate suggestions to enquirers.

Volunteers are needed to carry out a wide variety of activities, from responding to requests for information to assisting in project work, depending on individual interests.

that offers a free advisory service, particularly concerning care, for those of pensionable age who are facing problems, and provides advice on finding and paying for care in a registered home.

Some help is available for single needs payments for people living in their own homes for items such as telephone installation, clothing, etc. Volunteers help to send out factsheets.

Enquiries to the above address.

Help the Aged

St James's Walk, Clerkenwell Green, London EC1R OBE (tel 0171-253 0253).

Help the Aged offers a variety of opportunities for voluntary work:

Shops

There are over 300 Help the Aged shops in the UK. They are open from 9am to 5pm, Monday to Saturday, and are run by paid shop managers and teams of volunteers. You can become involved in all aspects of shop work, from sorting and pricing items for sale, to window dressing, operating the till and serving customers. Full training is provided, and a friendly atmosphere guaranteed. Anyone unable to help in their local shop can set up a 'Friends' group attached to a particular shop. The group could raise money by holding various events such as jumble sales.

Local Committees
Help the Aged committees are groups of volunteers in a County or Region who organise high profile fundraising events and agree with Help the Aged, on how the money raised will be spent on local projects working with older people.

Volunteers can be involved with their local committee by helping with the practical side of organising an event, being a secretary or a treasurer or even setting up a new committee for your area.

Other opportunities
These include research work, home-based secretarial and clerical work and helping with administration at Head Office or one of the three Regional offices.

For further information please contact the Volunteer Co-ordinator at the above address.

Jewish Care
Stuart Young House, 221 Golders Green Road, London NW11 9DQ (tel 0181-458 3282; fax 0181-455 7185).

For over 125 years Jewish Care (formerly the Jewish Welfare Board), a voluntary organisation, has served the Jewish Community in London and South England. Their objective is to meet the needs of elderly people and their families by maintaining elderly people in the community, supporting and encouraging families and the community to care for their elderly, reducing isolation and loneliness, and helping people prepare for and adjust to old age.

Volunteers are needed to assist Social Workers by providing a back-up service, which involves visiting and befriending people in their own homes. Other ways of being of service include driving, escorting and shopping. There are no recruitment restrictions; however volunteers of the Jewish faith will be preferred.

Enquiries may be sent to the Voluntary Services Co-ordinator, at the above address.

Tooting Neighbourhood Centre
28 Glenburnie Road, Tooting, London SW17; (tel 0181-767 1619).

The Centre runs a luncheon club for the elderly on Tuesdays, Wednesdays and Thursdays, a community care for the elderly project and a youth club. 30-40 volunteers are engaged annually by the Centre; there is a wide range of activities open to them including preparing meals and work in the luncheon club, visiting housebound, frail and isolated elderly people in their homes and providing recreational activities for the young people. Volunteers can also work on the playscheme, attend regular meetings, escort the elderly to and from the Centre and accompany them to the doctor, shops or on outings.

Applicants of any nationality are welcome as long as they speak English. They must also be aged over 18 years and in fairly good health. The length of time for which volunteers are recruited varies from three months to as much as three years. Volunteers are needed all the year round, although the playscheme operates on a seasonal basis. Lunch money and, sometimes, travel expenses are paid.

Those interested should contact Rose Powell at the above address.

Westminster Pensioners Association
284 Harrow Road, London W2 5ES (tel 0171-289 1849).

Pensioners who are frail or differently abled and living alone often have to rely on volunteers for even very simple odd jobs. These may include gardening, decorating or doing small repairs. Westminster Pensioners Association organizes volunteers to do these jobs for pensioners living in Westminster. A drop-in centre is also open three days a week for friendship and information.

Outings, always need plenty of support from volunteers. This challenging work with an equal opportunities collective can be very rewarding. Out of pocket expenses are paid.

Enquiries to the above address.

Fund Raising and Office Work

Fund raising has always been one of the most important activities of any charity or voluntary body, but in the past it has tended to suffer from a less than glamorous image; people have tended to associate it with rattling collection boxes in the high street on damp Saturday afternoons. This has in recent years changed with the help of the media: both one-off events like Live Aid or annual appeals like the BBC's Children in Need have added a veneer of show-business to this essential activity. Such media-generated appeals are not, however, covered in this section, as the regular ones tend to be seasonal in their operation and they generate their own publicity at the appropriate time.

There is hardly an organisation in this book that would turn down an offer of either money or administrative help from a volunteer. The organisations in this section have many different specific objectives, but all have in common the fact that their greatest need for voluntary help is with raising money and doing office work.

It must be stressed that the list of organisations requiring this type of help is almost endless, and the few entries below are merely given as examples. If a volunteer wishes to help a specific organisation, then he should find the address of the local branch from the phone book and offer his services. Alternatively, many organisations advertise in local and national newspapers for help with some specific project; for example the British Legion appeal for poppy sellers in early autumn. Most good causes have some established machinery for fund raising, such as flag days or jumble sales, but they should also welcome new ideas, such as an offer from a school to organise a sponsored swim. The most dramatic fund raising schemes, such as wind surfing around Britain or running across the Himalayas, are normally the result of individual enterprise, someone feeling that he or she has some special way of attracting the attention of the public. It is always advisable to contact the relevant organisation before arranging any project, as it may be possible to link it with some publicity material such as leaflets or T-shirts to increase its impact.

Clerical and administrative work are equally essential in any organisation whether commercially or voluntarily run. The examples of office work included below range from routine filing and letter-writing to organizing complete surveys and investigative research studies. Although it may seem mundane, it is work that must be done if the organisation's overall aims are to be successful.

Action Aid
Hamlyn House, McDonald Road, Archway, London N19 5PG; (tel 0171-281 4101).

This charity aims to improve the quality of life in some of the poorest parts of the world. Although Action Aid does not operate an overseas voluntary programme, volunteers are required all year round at the London office. UK. Volunteers are also needed at Action Aid's Chard office in Somerset to do administrative work. Applicants can be of any nationality, but they must speak English. Pocket money is not provided, but Action Aid may pay for travel to the Chard Office if volunteers live outside the immediate Chard area.

   Those interested should apply to the above office or if interested in volunteer work at the Chard office should apply to Mrs Felicity Rowe, Chataway House, Leach Road, Chard TA20 IFA.

Akina Mama Wa Afrika
London Women's Centre, 4 Wild Court, London WC2B 5AV (tel 0171 405-0678; fax 0171 831-3947).

Akina Mama wa Afrika means 'Solidarity among African women'; AMWA is a voluntary development organisation for African women based in the UK, providing support services. This includes advice, information, counselling, advocacy services, the publication of a journal called *African Women*, and a project for African women in prison. Up to thirty volunteers, preferably black African women, are required all the year round to help with a wide variety of tasks such as filing, mailing, typing, research, prison visiting and helping in reception. Volunteers are welcome for any length of time, and travel expenses will be paid.

   Volunteers should apply to Bisi Adeleye-Fayemi at the above address.

Aklowa
Takeley House, Brewers End, Takeley, Bishops Stortford, Herts (tel 01279-871062; fax 01279-871256)

Aklowa is a charitable organisation established in 1977 with the overall aim of promoting understanding of African culture and society through the study and participation in the music, dance and the arts of Africa, all in the setting of an 'African Traditional Heritage Village'. A voluntary receptionist and volunteers with secretarial skills are needed to help at Aklowa.

   Applications to the above address.

Anti-Slavery International
The Stable Yard, Broomgrove Road, London SW9 9TL; (tel 0171-924 9555). E-mail antislavery@gn.apc.org

Anti-Slavery International campaigns against slavery in all its forms throughout the world including child labour, human rights abuses, forced prostitution, the plight of domestic workers in Britain and so on. Volunteers are required only for the London office to carry out anything from basic administration to research and internships.   Office duties include photocopying, data inputing, media related work and small mutually beneficial research projects. Volunteers may be working under conditions of confidentiality so good references are essential. The minimum period of service is normally three months and volunteers are provided with lunch and travel expenses. Other services provided by ASI include exhibitions, video and library loans and a range of publications on the above and other instances of slavery.

Anyone interested in volunteering should contact the above address.

Art & Commerce for a Healthy World

Eurolife Building, Suite 2C, 1 Corral Road, P O Box 627, Gibraltar.

Art and Commerce for a Healthy World launched, in May 1996, a Painting and Fact Finding Road Tour of Europe including Belgium, France, Germany, Hungary, Austria, Holland, the UK, Ireland, Denmark, Norway, Sweden, Finland, Italy, Greece, Spain and Portugal which it is intended will take about five years to complete. The 'team' includes a resident artist, a researcher, computer buff, an export/import agent and an administrator. This field team will be travelling in two Internet /WWW linked auto caravans. During the tour, the artist will be painting about 88 water colour paintings per year from which Art and Commerce intends to make a range of art prints, greeting cards and so on which will be distributed through an art print club. The aim of the the group is to raise extra capital to not only finance the Road Tour but also a computerised information help line (internet/www linked) providing both on and off line information on the location world wide of holistic and alternative medicine centres. The ultimate aim is to buy land in Europe to build a holistic health centre and adjoining organic farm. The Help-Line is intended also to contain information on many aspects of green living such as alternative energy, land, air and water purification and a list of financial institutions who provide funds for health and green projects.

The group is open to any voluntary or professional help that can be provided regarding any aspect of the above project. All volunteers and helpers will automatically become honorary subscriber/sponsors.

For further information contact the secretary at the above address or fax +350 42 701.

Association of Medical Research Charities

29-35 Farringdon Road, London EC1M 3JB; (tel 0171-404 6454; fax 0171-404-6448).

The Association's aims are the advancement of medical research in the UK and, in particular, the advancement of the collective effectiveness of those charities for which a principal activity is medical research. The Association aims to represent charities supportive of medical research through membership organisations. One volunteer is needed for approximately one day per month to do payroll and pensions and assist with book keeping; experience in all the above areas is essential. Applicants of all nationalities are welcome, but it must be emphasised that this is a long-term commitment. The Association will pay for any expenses.

Those interested should apply to Diana Garnham, General Secretary, at the above address.

The Balmore Trust
Viewfield, Balmore, Torrance, Glasgow G64 4AE (tel 01360 620 742).

The Balmore Trust is a small grant-giving Trust funded largely by its shop, The Coach House Charity Craft Shop, which is run by volunteers. Related activities include a branch of Tools for Self-Reliance and occasional hyperactivity in 'material aid' both in Glasgow and also in the shipment of hospital and educational supplies to parts of the Third World.

Volunteers are needed to work in the shop, to help with work servicing the shop (especially baking), to refurbish tools for export to developing countries and also to help with the collection and distribution of goods as 'material aid'. Applicants of all nationalities will be accepted, but accommodation and expenses cannot be provided except in special circumstances.

Those interested should contact Rosalind Jarvis at the above address.

Birth Control Trust
16 Mortimer Street, London W1N 7RD (tel 0171-580 9360; fax 0171-637 1378). E-mail bct@birthcontroltrust.org.uk

The principal aim of the Trust is to advance medical and sociological research into contraception, sterilization and legal abortion and to publish the results of this research. Volunteers normally help at the above address, filing and sorting press cuttings, once per week or per fortnight.

Applications should be made to the Information Officer at the above address.

Books Abroad
Richmond Avenue, Rhynie, Huntly, Aberdeenshire AB54 4HJ; (tel/fax 01464-861446).

Books Abroad is a registered charity which sends carefully chosen 5kg parcels of books direct to the places of greatest need worldwide. It was started in 1982 with the aim of joining the battle against illiteracy in needy parts of the world. Volunteers work in their HQ in Scotland helping with book sorting and selection, and performing general clerical tasks. Applicants of any nationality are welcome. Knowledge of school text book requirements and the ability to lift boxes of books would be useful. Expenses may be negotiable. Applications should be sent to Christine Cullingworth at the above address.

Book Aid International.
39-41 Coldharbour Lane, London SE5 9NR (tel 0171-733 3577; fax 0171-978 8006;). E-mail rls@gn.apc.org

Book Aid international sorts and processes books to be sent to schools, libraries and institutions in the Third World. They have between 15 and 20 volunteers helping with packing, sorting and stamping of books in their warehouse in London. They also require volunteers to carry out administrative duties, as well as assisting fundraising and projects. The length of time for which volunteers are normally recruited varies, but they are required all year round. Travel expenses are paid.

If you are interested please contact Rob Sarjant/Nayla Islam at the above address.

The British Association of the Experiment in International Living
Otesaga, West Malvern Road, Malvern, Worcs. (tel 01684-562577; fax 01684-562212).

The Association exists to promote understanding between people of different cultures and countries throughout the world. It does this by enabling anyone over the age of 17 to stay as a member of another family in over 45 countries. In becoming part of that family they learn something of the customs and culture of that country. Host families are volunteers as are the local representatives who administer the programmes in each country. The National Office with 11 paid staff recruits volunteers during busy periods. In addition, volunteers are always needed to meet Experimenters arriving in this country at a variety of airports, and to act as advisors on how to recruit outbound participators.

There are no restrictions or special requirements and the period for which volunteers are recruited depends upon the job. Host families receive expenses as do local representatives. Travelling and out of pocket expenses are provided for London work and generous expenses are given to recruiters of outbound participants.

Further information can be obtained from the National Director at the above address.

British Heart Foundation Appeal
14 Fitzhardinge Street, London W1H 4DN (tel 0171-935 0185; fax 0171-488 5820).

Volunteers are always needed to help with fundraising events throughout the United Kingdom and in the Distribution Section of the Head Office above .

Enquiries should be made to the nearest Regional Office which is listed in all telephone directories or to Melanie Glanville on 0171-935 4370.

BUFORA (British UFO Research Association)
BM BUFORA, London WC1N 3XX; (tel/fax 01924-444049).

BUFORA depends entirely on the voluntary participation of its members for its research, investigations and administrative activities. The association, founded in 1964, aims to encourage, promote and conduct unbiased scientific research of UFO phenomena in the UK. It also co-operates with other researchers throughout the world. The research findings and theories are published in the bi-monthly *UFO Times* and presented in a series of monthly lectures in London.

Volunteers who are both sufficiently interested and informed are needed to carry out, collate and document research. Voluntary help is also required in editing reports, summarising news, writing articles, translating relevant foreign journals and letters, and interviewing eye-witnesses, where the qualities of tact, perseverance, initiative and common sense are essential. BUFORA publishes an Investigator's Manual for instruction in researching and interviewing techniques. Some form of transport is usually needed by volunteers, since sightings can be reported in remote areas of the country. Sometimes expenses are reimbursed, although the majority of investigators bear their own expenses.

Enquiries, enclosing a medium-sized self-addressed envelope, may be sent to the Honorary Secretary at the above address.

Cancer Research Campaign
Cambridge House 6-10, Cambridge Terrace, Regents Park, London NW1 4JL (tel 0171-224 1333).

As the largest single supporter of research into forms of cancer, including leukaemia, in the UK, the Cancer Research Campaign needs an unlimited amount of help with fundraising activities. There are 1,000 local committees throughout the UK who co-ordinate the efforts of several thousand volunteers every year. The money they raise is used to support over 700 projects in universities, medical schools, and hospitals throughout the country. It is impossible to do more than generalize about the range of fundraising activities which are organized, as volunteers are encouraged to use their initiative to find original means of attracting money.

Any questions please contact Sharon Reeves, Personnel, at the above address.

CARE International UK
36-38 Southampton Street, London WC2E 7AF (tel 0171-379 5247; fax 0171-379 0543).

CARE International UK is a Third World development agency operating in 65 countries but voluntary positions are only available within the London office. Volunteers are used whenever there is a requirment such as during fund-raising campaigns etc.

Volunteers are normally recruited for periods of one to four weeks, all year round. No special skills are required and volunteers may be of any nationality. Reasonable travel expenses within London and lunch are provided.

Those interested should contact the Personnel Officer at the above address.

The Cats Protection League
17 Kings Road, Horsham, West Sussex RH13 5PN (tel 01403-261947).

The objects of the League are to rescue stray, unwanted and neglected cats, to provide information on the care of cats and kittens, and to encourage the neutering of all cats not required for breeding. The practical work of the League and fund raising are carried out by voluntary workers through a system of over 240 local branches and groups, with some 45,000 members.

For further information those interested should contact the above address.

CHANGE
PO Box 824. London SE24 9JX (tel/fax 0171-277 6187).

CHANGE researches and publishes reports on the condition and status of women all over the world and organizes exhibitions, international meetings, training workshops, book stalls, and other events.

Around six volunteers are needed to help with all aspects of this work; basic administration, data entry, media work, organizing meetings, exhibitions, book stalls, Parliamentary lobbying and research. The duration of particular projects can vary from one month to one year. Volunteers of any nationality with skills in any of the above areas are welcome.

Contact the Director at the above address for more information.

Commonwealth Institute
Kensington High Street, London W8 6NO (tel 0171 603-4535; fax 0171 602-7374).

The Institute is a London based education and cultural exhibition centre with the objective of increasing knowledge and understanding of the British Commonwealth, its nations and people. A variety of activities are open to volunteers, linked to marketing and publicity, exhibitions, events and the performing arts, visual arts and administration. Applicants of any nationality are accepted as long as they possess the capacity to 'do the job' and can speak and write English. Short and long term placements are available, but the Institute's needs vary. There is no pocket money, but travel expenses within the London area only might be paid.

Applications should be sent at any time of the year to Paul Kennedy at the above address.

Dial UK
Park Lodge, St Catharine's Hospital, Tickhill Road, Balby, Doncaster, South Yorkshire DN4 8QN (tel 01302-310123; fax 01302-310404).

Dial UK is the national organisation for DIAL network of over 100 disability information and advice services. DIAL groups are run by people with direct experience of disability. They give free, independent, impartial advice to disabled people, carers and professionals.

Dial UK provides a number of services to disability advice centres, including a reference information service, training and management support

Approximately 1,000 volunteers work for Dial UK, both at the Doncaster headquarters and with local DIAL groups, every year, engaged in a variety of functions including writing, clerical work, information officers and disability advice workers. Applicants may be of any nationality, but good English is essential and volunteers must have direct experience of disability. Volunteers are required to work full and part-time all year round and the usual length of placement is one year. Local travelling expenses are normally paid.

Those interested should contact Mrs D. McGahan, Information Manager, at the above address.

Dian Fossey Gorilla Fund
110 Gloucester Avenue, Primrose Hill, London NW1 8JA; (0171-483 2681).

Dian Fossey was sent to Africa in the 1960's by the Anglo-American archaeologist Louis Leakey to undertake a study of the last remaining mountain gorillas. She founded the Karisoke Research Centre over 25 years ago and pioneered the way animals are studied in the wild. Her researches were constantly impeded by the activities of poachers who are high on the list of factors that threaten the survival of the mountain gorillas. Dian Fossey herself died in mysterious circumstances at the Karisoke Centre in 1985. Her life and work were the subject of the cinema film 'Gorillas in the Mist' which starred Sigourney Weaver who is also honourary president of the Fund.

The high profile of the Dian Fossey Gorilla Fund helps in its efforts to protect the last 650 mountain gorillas in Central Africa but the effort needs to be constant and sustained. About 75 volunteers work annually in the UK in office administration and fund-raising activities. The Fund will pay travel expenses.

Environmental Investigation Agency
15 Bowling Green Lane, London EC1R OBD; tel 0171-490 7040; fax 0171 490 0436). E-mail daniel@gn.apc.org

EIA, founded in 1984, is an independent non-profit group working to protect the natural environment and the species that inhabit it. The Agency has a very small but dedicated team of staff and volunteers. Dubbed the 'Animal Detectives' by the press, EIA has built up a reputation for in-depth research and undercover investigations. EIA teams gather unique film footage, interviews and information from across the world, often at considerable personal risk. The results of EIA's research are used for their campaigns and to brief other conservation and animal welfare organisations, as well as governments and intergovernmental organisations. EIA works through international conventions to develop workable and effective solutions to environmental abuses, and to implement changes which will protect exploited species.

Regular volunteers are required mainly to help in EIA's London office. Duties may include opening the post, computer input onto a Paradox database, posting merchandise, replying to queries from members, banking cheques, organisation of press cuttings and releases, working with staff on various projects such as fundraising, corporate sponsorship, PR, membership, office management and accounts. EIA has room for, and need of, many volunteers. All volunteers will be trained in the relevant areas. Applicants are required for anything from a few hours per day to full time all year, or longer. Travel expenses are paid after the volunteer has been into the office twice. Applicants should note that there is no wheelchair access to the office.

Those interested should contact Gill Copeland at the above address.

Feed The Children
82 Caversham Road, Reading, Berks

Feed the Children is an international humanitarian relief organisation, dedicated to children, which delivers aid through its own in-country teams directly to children and their carers. Areas of work include: Bosnia, Albania, Rwanda, the Caucasus, Georgia, Armenia, Haiti and northern Iraq.

About 150-300 volunteers are engaged at any one time. Volunteers are needed to help in the above office (reception, project work, filling envelopes, p c work. Also to help in the aid supply centre, sorting and packing aid (for Bosnia and Albania at the time of press). Volunteers are also needed on a national basis, to be involved in Community Support Groups, raising funds, aid and awareness of Feed the Children.

Period of commitment can be anything from a week or long term. Reasonable travel expenses can be reimbursed.

Anyone interested in volunteering their services should contact the above address.

Global Partnership
P O Box 1001, London SE24 9NU (tel 0171 924-0974; fax 0171 738 4559).

Global Partnership works to increase public awareness of the Third World, environment and human rights through annual events held in cities throughout the UK including London. A variable number of volunteers are needed to work in the London based office at intervals throughout the year and also at the regional and London events. Volunteers are needed in the office to help with tasks such as direct mailing, research, PR and coordination of conferences. At the events, volunteers act as stewards, ticket sellers, and work with school children and in the crèche etc.

Applications to Benny Dembitzer at the above address.

The Haemophilia Society

123 Westminster Bridge Road, London SE1 7HR (tel 071-928 2020; fax 0171-620 1416; 0171-620 1416).

The Society was established in 1950 to serve the needs of people with haemophilia and similar blood disorders. The Society represents the interests of people with haemophilia by providing help, information and advice to them and their families. Volunteers serve the Society at all levels (the Executive Committee, Chairman and Vice-Chairman are all volunteers) and all its 26 local Groups are all staffed and run by volunteers. Volunteers of all nationalities are welcome to serve the Society in any way they can whenever they can spare the time.

For a complete and up-to-date contact list for local groups please write to the above address.

HEADWAY: National Head Injuries Association

7 King Edward Court, King Edward Street, Nottingham NG1 1EW (tel 0115-9240800; fax 0115-9240432).

HEADWAY offers advice and support to individuals who suffer the devastating effects of accquired brain damage following head injury, and helps families to come to terms with the enormous responsibility of home care and rehabilitation. HEADWAY is very much involved in fund-raising to enable this work to continue.

The Nottingham central office also recruits for almost 112 local HEADWAY support groups and 40 HEADWAY day care centres throughout the UK. The Nottingham central office has about 3 or 4 volunteers working at any one time. Locally, there are unlimited opportunities for volunteers, according to local need. In the central office, volunteers are required to give general assistance or to work on specific projects related to office administration, fund-raising, groups and membership or information and services. Overseas volunteers are welcome, but special skills or qualifications may be needed for various jobs. Volunteers are required all year round; placements will be by negotiation. Out-of-pocket expenses will be reimbursed.

Those interested should contact Ian Garrow, Executive Director at the above address.

Heritage Ceramics

Unit B18, Charles House, Bridge Road, Southall, Middlesex UB2 4BD (tel 0181-843 9281; fax 0181-813 8387).

Heritage Ceramics, founded in 1984, is a small collective of artists who work in the area of ceramics and pottery with the aim of exploring and producing work with themes that spring from the African experience. The UK based organisation provides basic and advanced training in all aspects of ceramics and pottery, as well as providing input in arts and crafts education in schools through outreach workshops.

Six volunteers work with Heritage every year mainly contributing to and assisting in administrative management, but also in technical/practical operations in the workshop. Applicants may be of any nationality and no special qualifications are necessary apart from a basic command of the English language. Volunteers usually work for one year on a full or part-time basis. In most cases Heritage pays for travel and subsistence.

For further information contact Mr Tony Ogogo at the above address.

Imperial Cancer Research Fund
PO Box 123, Lincoln's Inn Fields, London WC2A 3PX (tel 0171-242 0200).

The Imperial Cancer Research Fund is dedicated to preventing cancer, finding cures and saving lives. The Fund operates throughout the United Kingdom and recruits volunteers to help with all aspects of fundraising amd running their network of High Street charity shops. Volunteers of all nationalities are needed all the year round for varying lengths of time. Those interested should contact their nearest Regional Centre.

Index on Censorship
Writers and Scholars Educational Trust, 33 Islington High Street, London N1 9LH; tel 0171 278 2313; fax 0171-278 1878).

The Trust is a charity that publishes manuscripts that have been banned and gives details of writing that has been censored anywhere in the world. There is a constant need for help in the office both with research and general clerical work. Volunteers are needed to work on a regular basis even if only for half a day per week.

For further details contact the editor at the above address.

International Institute for Environment and Development
3 Endsleigh Street, London WC1H 0DD (tel 0171 388-2117; fax 0171 388-2826).

This organisation is a policy research institute working on Third World environment issues in development. Volunteers are required to help with general office work and administration, to work in reception and to do any odd jobs. Applicants may be of any nationality, but they must have had previous experience of office work. They must also be in good health, as provisions for disabled people are limited. Volunteers would be needed for a few days per week, or more, all the year round. Travel and lunch expenses will be paid.

Those interested should contact the Personnel Officer at the above address.

Jewish Child's Day
Fifth Floor, 707 High Road, London N12 0BT (tel 0181-446 8804; fax 0181-446 7370).

This organisation needs occasional clerical help with its fund raising. With the money it raises it provides equipment for a wide variety of children's houses, mostly in Israel, but also in the UK, France, Yugoslavia, Morocco and Tunisia.

Applications should be sent to the Director at the above address.

Kids' Clubs Network
Bellerive House, 3 Muirfield Crescent, London E14 9SZ; (tel 0171-512 2100; fax 0171 512 2010).

Kid's Club Network is the only national UK charity which supports and promotes school age children before and after school and during school holidays. Volunteers have the opportunity to help at an administrative level or the organisation can put them in touch with clubs that are members of Kids' Clubs Network.

Volunteers can help in the London office assisting with general administrative duties including photocopying, word processing, mail outs, filing and assisting with the Information Helpline, as well as helping with the preparation for training events and seminars. Applicants may be of any nationality but they should speak fluent English. The London office is accessible to wheelchair users. All volunteers must abide by an Equal Opportunities policy. Volunteers will be expected to work for KCN on a fairly flexible basis; the office needs help all year round. Expenses will be paid subject to negotiation with the volunteer.

Those interested should contact Mike Rich at the above address.

Kurdish Cultural Centre
14 Stannary Street, London SE11 4AA (tel 0171 735-0918; fax 0171 582-8894).

The Centre gives assistance to Kurdish refugeees and asylum seekers in the UK, promotes Kurdish culture and is involved in relief work in Kurdistan.

Approximately 100 volunteers of all nationalities work for the Centre every year, helping with office work, translation, relief work, and work with refugees in London. Help is needed all the year round and volunteers are welcome to work with the Centre as much as possible. Travel and lunch expenses are paid.

Those interested should apply to Sarbast Aram at the above address.

Life Education Centres
115-123 Baynham Street, London NW1 0AG (tel 071 267-2516; fax 071 267-2044).

Life Education Centres provide positive and innovative drug prevention programmes for children and young people aged from three to fifteen via mobile classrooms which travel to schools throughout a region. The 11 mobiles are equipped with audio-visual and advanced teaching aids and the programmes are run by specialist educators. Life Education also produce materials for use in following up the messages of the programmes for schools.

Three or four volunteers are engaged by the organisation each year. Volunteers are usually sporadically involved in fund-raising or awareness raising events in London, although the organisation does have a part-time volunteer accountant and there may be occasions when a suitably qualified volunteer might become involved in educational work with children. Usually, no qualifications or skills are needed but volunteers must have had either teaching qualifications or experience if they are to be involved in any education-based activities. Out-of-pocket expenses are usually reimbursed.

Applications to Jane Goodwin at the above address.

Live Music Now!
4 Lower Belgrave Street, London SW1W OLJ (tel 0171-730 2205; fax 0171-730 3641).

Live Music Now is dedicated to taking live music to disabled and disadvantaged people throughout the UK. There are over 250 of the finest young professional musicians taking part, performing almost 2000 concerts annually. Volunteers are needed for a variety of different tasks. For more information please contact Virginia Renshaw or Katherine Potter at the above address.

National Asthma Campaign
Providence House, Providence Place, Islington, London (tel 0171-226 2260; fax 0171-704 0740).

The National Asthma Campaign is the major charity in the UK funding research into asthma and allergy in hospitals and university departments throughout the country; it strives to improve the treatment and management of asthma and ultimately to find a cure. The Campaign also provides information for doctors and nurses, sponsors activity holidays for children and provides help and advice for all people with asthma and their families.

About 12 volunteers per year are needed to help in the London office with clerical work, data entry and typing and filing, etc. Volunteers of all nationalities are accepted; it would be useful if applicants have knowledge and/or experience of asthma. The office is without disabled access. Volunteers are needed for any length of time all the year round. No expenses are paid.

Applications should be made to Lynne Elliot, Voluntary Personnel Officer, at the above address.

National Canine Defence League
17 Wakely Street, London EC1C 7LT; (tel 0171-837 0006; fax 0171-833 2701).

Although volunteers are needed at rescue centres for mistreated and abandoned dogs throughout the country to help with the exercising of the dogs their help is especially needed to help raise funds to keep the centres open, running coffee mornings and stalls at local venues, etc. In addition, clerical help is always welcomed at the head office in London. Volunteers should be at least 18 years of age.

A list of centres is available from the above address.

National Society for the Prevention of Cruelty to Children
42 Curtain Road, London EC2A 3NH. (tel 0171-825 2500; fax 0171-825 2525).

Although the society's active work is conducted only by professionally qualified staff, volunteers are always needed to start fund raising groups or join in existing groups. The society has around 4,000 branch and district committees that raise money through house to house collections, organizing events and flag days, etc. Many individuals and groups of people help by running their own fun activities in aid of the Society.

Those willing to help should contact the Appeals Dept. at the above address.

One Village
Charlbury, Oxford OX7 3SQ (tel/fax 01608-811811; fax 01608-811911).

One Village works with craft producers' co-operatives in Africa, Asia, South America, and sells their products in the UK. There are opportunities for volunteers in One Village shops in the UK, particularly in Oxford; these take the form of both long-term commitments and temporary holiday-time jobs. Other posts can also sometimes be filled by volunteers. The length of time for which volunteers are recruited varies. Expenses are sometimes paid

Applicants, of any nationality, should contact Roy Scott at the above address.

OXFAM
Oxfam House, 274 Banbury Road, Oxford OX2 7DZ (tel 01865-311311).

OXFAM volunteers work in the UK and Republic of Ireland to help OXFAM carry out its objective of relieving poverty, distress and suffering in any part of the world. As well as raising funds, this involves campaigning and educating the public in order to help tackle the causes of poverty. OXFAM is committed to an Equal Opportunities Policy and welcomes offers of help from people of all backgrounds and abilities.

OXFAM does not send volunteers overseas but many thousands of volunteers are involved in OXFAM's work throughout the UK and Ireland. They run over 800 shops and work in regional offices throughout the UK and Ireland. Some help organize fundraising events, others are involved in campaigning and educational work. In the regional offices, help with clerical and administrative work is often needed too. People with special skills such as book-keeping, design and typing can often put their talents to good use with OXFAM, but there are lots of opportunities for people without any particular qualifications.

In the Oxford headquarters over 100 volunteers work with 450 staff on a range of duties from routine packing and mailing through to research projects. Oxfam cannot provide accommodation or pocket money, but does reimburse travel expenses and meals, depending on the number of hours the volunteer works each day. Some regions offer a local one-day 'knowledge of Oxfam' course as an introduction to the organisation. A pamphlet, *Volunteer for a Fairer World*, gives more details about volunteering opportunities in OXFAM.

For further information, look up your local OXFAM office or shop in the telephone book, or for work in Oxford contact the Management Service Division Personnel Officer at the above address.

PLAN International (UK)
5/6 Underhill Street, Camden, London NW1 7HS (tel 0171-485 6612; fax 0171-485 2107)

PLAN International is a long-term development agency helping over 680,000 children, their families and communities in 30 countries around the world. The areas covered include Asia, the Far East, Africa and S. America, and the majority of fund-raising is done through child sponsorship.

Volunteers are needed in the small and friendly London Office to help support the work of about 30 paid staff. There is a base of over twenty daytime and twenty evening volunteers, with a full-time volunteer co-ordinator to support them. The volunteer work includes a wide range of basic administrative tasks, including computer work and processing the communications from the children. Every effort is made to match the skills of the volunteers to the work available, and applicants of any nationality are welcome. Full training is given on all tasks. The usual minimum commitment is two days per week, but there are also regular volunteer evenings for those in full-time work. Travel expenses are reimbursed.

Those interested should contact the Volunteer Coordinator, Lynne Gillett at the above address.

Population Concern
178-202 Great Portland Street, London W1N 5TB; (tel 0171-631-1546).

Population Concern raises funds for overseas population and development programmes, provides an information service and campaigns on population and related issues in schools and amongst the public. Projects are being undertaken in many developing countries in Africa, the Caribbean and Asia, but volunteers are only required in the London office. Volunteers may work on a regular basis or just for short intensive periods, all year round. The work available depends on the applicant's interests and skills but includes such areas of work as information, education, fund raising and occasional project work.

Special skills such as typing, word processing and artwork designing are desirable but not essential. Students or recent graduates in Demography and related disciplines are very welcome. Payment of travelling expenses is negotiable but accommodation is not provided.

Those interested should apply to the Information Officer at the above address.

Psychiatry Research Trust

De Crespigny Park, Denmark Hill, London SE5 8AF (tel 0171-703 6217; fax 0171-703 5796).

The Trust raises funds for research into mental illness, brain disease and mental disability at the Institute of Psychiatry. Approximately 50 volunteers around the country are engaged by the Trust as fundraisers who work from home organising activities that will generate contributions for the trust. There are no restrictions on the type of volunteer required by the Trust.

For further information please contact Sandra Refault at the above address.

Royal National Lifeboat Institution

West Quay Road, Poole, Dorset BH15 1HZ (tel 01202-671133).

The operator of the lifeboat service throughout the United Kingdom and the Republic of Ireland, the RNLI is supported entirely by voluntary contributions. It is impossible to estimate the number of volunteers who assist the service; most of the crews of the life boats run from the 215 lifeboat stations are unpaid, and there are also some 2,000 fund raising branches around the UK.

There is an important distinction between these two forms of voluntary work; while anyone who is willing to help with fund-raising will be welcomed, only those who pass a medical, can swim, meet age requirements and live in the vicinity of a lifeboat station can be accepted as crew members.

It is preferred that those interested should apply to their local branch of the RNLI, but if there is any difficulty about obtaining the relevant address, please contact the Public Relations Department at the above address.

Save the Children Fund (SCF)

17 Grove Lane, Camberwell, London SE5 8RD; (tel 0171-703 5400; fax 0171-703 2278).

SCF is the UK's largest international voluntary organisation that deals with the welfare of children worldwide. As well as running large scale programmes in more than 50 oveseas countries, SCF also has a network of projects in the UK. Its activities are supported by funds from the public and volunteers are needed to help in over 700 fund-raising groups nationwide.

Contact the above address for details of your nearest group.

St. James's House

108 Hampstead Road, London NW1 2LS (tel 0171-388 2588; fax 0171-387 1553).E-mail 100703.2073@compuserve.com

St. James's House provides work and training for people with mental health problems in London. A drop-in service is run, together with some structured activities which benefit enormously from the support of volunteers. Volunteers do some work directly with clients, as well as administrative and secretarial work. Volunteers are required to assist with research and development and they could also become involved in outreach work, such as buddying.

Projects open to volunteers might include feasibility studies and fundraising events, and longer-term volunteers might be needed for specific tasks. There are no restrictions on the type of volunteer required other than people living legally in the UK, able to communicate effectively in English. Volunteers are required all year round for an indefinite amount of time. Travelling expenses are paid.

Those interested should contact Graeme Jones at the above address.

Soil Association

The Organic Food and Farming Centre, 86 Colston Street, Bristol B51 5BB (tel 0117-9290661; fax 0117-925 2504). E-mail soilassoc@gn.apc.org

The Soil Association is dedicated to the promotion of organic food and farming in the UK. The number of volunteers engaged annually varies enormously; there are usually two or three volunteers in the office at any one time, but some have been regular volunteers for years.

Volunteers assist with general office and administrative work, as well as being involved with special projects. Applicants of all nationalities are accepted as long as they have good written and spoken English. Office and keyboard skills would be useful. There is no age limit and volunteers must be in good health. The length of time for which they are recruited varies but it would help if volunteers can come to the office on a regular basis. Lunch and local travel expenses are paid.

Applications should be made to Alison Ollis at the above address.

Survival International

11-15 Emerald Street, London WC1N 3QL; (tel 0171-242 1441; fax 0171-242 1771).

Survival International is a worldwide organisation supporting tribal peoples. It stands for their right to decide their own future and helps them to protect their lives, lands and human rights. Survival works for threatened tribal peoples in the Americas, Africa, Asia and Australasia. Survival lobbies international organisations, governments and multi-national companies, works to raise awareness of the situation of tribal peoples and supports practical realistic field projects with the aim of assisting the survival and self-determination of tribal peoples.

Volunteers are required in the London office to assist with clerical and secretarial work, library duties, visual aid materials and fund-raising activities. A commitment of anything from half a day to five days a week for a minimum of three months is required. Those interested should contact the London office.

Teaching Aids At Low Cost (TALC)

PO Box 49, St Albans, Herts AL1 4AX (tel 01727-853869; fax 01727-846852).

This registered charity distributes health and medical teaching materials worldwide. One to two volunteers are needed to sell TALC materials and respond to customer enquiries at the TALC outlet in London for one or two days a week. This TALC outlet is located in the Resource Centre of the Institute of Child Health in London. Volunteers may be of any nationality but must speak fluent English and have a good knowledge of Third World health issues. Although there is no fixed length of time for this volunteer placement, we prefer volunteers who can regularly commit to one or two days a week for at least one year. Health or medical experience in a developing country is desirable. A small expense allowance is paid. Applications to Indira Biswas-Benbow at the above address.

The Tibetan Community in Britain/The Tibetan Refugee Charitable Trust
1 Culworth Street, London NW8; (tel 0181-458 6174).

The Tibetan Community in Britain is the association of all Tibetans living in the United Kingdom, formed in 1970 to establish a formal organisation to inform the people and government of Britain of the plight and suffering of the Tibetan people under the occupation of the Chinese Communists. Anyone interested in the struggle of Tibetans to regain their independence and preserve their unique culture is welcome to become involved. The Community organizes public events in the UK and sends donations to the Tibetan administration in India towards their various projects for Tibetan refugees and sponsoring Tibetan children's education.

There are over 200 supportive members who participate in the Community's functions and raise funds for its work for the Tibetan cause. Anyone who subscribes to the Community's objectives and pays an annual subscription is welcome to join as a supportive member. Most of these volunteers work to publicise monthly events but there is no fixed job description. Most of the Community's activities are related to fundraising and the promotion of a greater awareness of Tibetan issues. Any skills in publicity and fundraising are therefore very welcome, as would be anyone with a driving licence. There are no age limits.

Those interested should contact the secretary Mr Tsering Thundup, at the above address or phone the above number (evenings).

Tidy Britain Group
The Pier, Wigan WN3 4EX (tel 01942-824620; fax 01942-824778).

This organisation is a government agency dedicated to the control of litter and environmental improvement. Volunteers are needed all the year round to help with general office work in local offices throughout the UK. Expenses are sometimes paid.

For further information please contact Dee Bingham at the above address.

Uganda Society for Disabled Children (USDC)
Chichester House, 145A London Road, Kingston-upon-Thames, Surrey KT2 6NH. (tel 0181-541 3736; fax 0181-296 9826).

USDC is a development agency established in 1985 specifically to operate in Uganda. Its mission is to provide resources and opportunities for children with disabilities to achieve their potential and lead fulfilling lives.

The focus of its activities is on the individual child living at home with his/her parents and other family members, who are the principal carers. It follows a community-based approach, using local and appropriate resources. Promoting public awareness of disability issues and challenging negative attitudes are also accorded high priority. It collaborates with the Government of Uganda and other partners to strengthen service provision through professional, technical and material support.

Two full-time employees are based in the UK. There are opportunities for volunteers to become involved in publicity and fundraising activities both in the office and elsewhere; for example distributing leaflets to family, friends and colleagues; collecting on Children's Day; helping on stalls at local events; preparing envelopes for a mailing; organising a small fundraising event. Travel costs would be covered for an office volunteer.

In Uganda thirty national staff are headed by Country Representative and Deputy Country Representative. Placements would be considered on a case by case basis for professionals with appropriate skills and experience and the necessary financial support.

Please contact the Fundraising Officer for further information.

War On Want
37-39 Great Guildford Street, London SE1 OES (tel 0171-620 1111; fax 0171-261 9291).

This organisation undertakes development and relief work to alleviate famine in the Third World. A national network of groups throughout the United Kingdom raise funds and campaign in their local areas. Volunteers are needed to join these local groups and volunteers are required annually for office and administrative work in the head office in London. Work continues all year round and volunteers give whatever time they can.

Any special skills that volunteers have will be utilized but none are essential. All volunteers are welcome but there is no access for disabled people at the London office. London office volunteers have their travelling expenses within London paid and receive a £2.50 lunch allowance per day. Local groups make their own arrangements.

Those interested in obtaining a list of local groups or wishing to work in the London office should contact the Volunteer Co-ordinator at the above address.

WOMANKIND (Worldwide)
3 Albion Place, Galena Road, London W6 OLT (tel 0181-563 8607/8; fax 0171-563 8611).

This is a small development charity dedicated to helping women in developing countries to help themselves to overcome poverty, ill-health and disadvantage. Volunteers are not recruited for overseas work. Five or six volunteers at any one time are needed in London to help with office work, fundraising, events and sometimes, research. What the volunteer actually does depends very much on what skills the applicant has and the time she or he can offer. Applicants of more than one nationality are accepted. Volunteers are needed all the year round, but the length of time for which they are recruited depends on the individual. Travel and lunch expenses are paid.

Those interested should contact the above address.

The Women's Environmental Network (WEN)
Aberdeen Studios, 22 Highbury Grove, London N5 2EA (tel 0171-354 8823; fax 0171-354 0464).

WEN is dedicated to informing and educating women who care about the environment. 20 volunteers are needed at any one time to assist with general office tasks and fundraising. Volunteers might find themselves involved in research, campaigning, PR, financial administration or dealing with the media. Applicants of any nationality are welcome as long as they have commitment and motivation. The length of time for which volunteers are normally recruited varies but help is needed all year round. Travel expenses are paid and lunch is provided.

Those interested should send their CV to Diana Cripps at the above address.

Women's Therapy Centre

6-9 Manor Gardens, London N7 6LA (tel 0171-263 6200; fax 0171-281 7879).

The Centre was founded by Louise Eichenbaum and Susie Orbach to provide a psychotherapeutic service for women by women, and to develop and promote an understanding of women's psychology. Several volunteers work at the Centre in fund-raising and adminsitration, although limited space restricts the number of volunteers the Centre can take. Vacancies occasionally arise to undertake specific pieces of fundraising research. Applicants must be women only, of any nationality and a minimum age of 18 years. Enthusiasm and a commitment to women's issues are essential. Fares to work and lunch will be provided.

If interested, please contact Gill Coleman at the above address.

World Vision UK

599 Aveburby Boulevard, Milton Keynes MK9 3PG; (tel 01908-841000; fax 01908-841014).

World Vision UK offers office work in Milton Keynes only. About 30 volunteers help out in any one year doing clerical and administration work. Volunteers can be taken on at any time and for any period. Expenses are paid. Most volunteers live in Milton Keynes. Overseas volunteers have to meet their own expenses and no accommodation is arranged.

World Vision also has occasional volunteer opportunities overseas (see shortterm work worldwide).

World Vision publish a free quarterly magazine.

WWF-UK

Panda House, Weyside Park, Godalming, Surrey GU7 1XR (tel 01483-426444; fax 01483-426409).

WWF fundraises and campaigns partly through a network of around 300 voluntary supporters' groups in the UK. Scientific research could be carried out by volunteers who can finance themselves and with appropriate degrees. Volunteers can also assist with fundraising in the UK. Accommodation cannot be offered.

Volunteers within the UK should write to the above address to obtain a list of regional WWF groups; international volunteers can apply to WWF International, 1196 Gland, Switzerland.

Writers In Prison Committee of International PEN

9-10 Charterhouse Buildings, Goswell Road, London EC1M 7AT (tel 0171-253 3226; fax 0171-253 5711). E-mail intpen@gn.apc.org

This organisation researches and campaigns on behalf of writers, journalists, publishers, poets, editors, etc. who have been arrested, killed or attacked because of their views. It deals with all cases in all countries. Volunteers of all nationalities are needed to help with photocopying, filing and general correspondence. Other tasks might be open to volunteers according to their skills.

Volunteers should have typing skills, and knowledge of languages other than

English, French or Spanish would be useful. The office is situated up eight flights of stairs and there is no lift which makes it unsuitable for disabled applicants. Volunteers should be able to make a commitment of one day per week for at least two months. Help is needed all year round. Local travel costs are paid.

Hospitals

There is much that volunteers can do to help the hard-pressed professional staff of a hospital to make a patient's stay more comfortable. It must be stressed, however, that the range of activities a volunteer can do is strictly limited, as they must not encroach upon the professional's preserve, and in many cases the number of hours a volunteer can help will be limited.

For example, it is permitted to drive a patient's relatives to and from hospital, but driving an out-patient home would encroach on the work of the ambulance service so may not be permitted. Nearly all of the work involving hospitals is concerned with direct contact with the patients and their families. The range of services provided by volunteers includes running shops, canteens, libraries and telephone lines, befriending and escorting patients, and arranging outings, flower arranging, hairdressing and writing letters for them. They may also be of help in preparing the homes of patients for their return.

The majority of hospitals either have their voluntary work organised by a League of Hospital Friends (see the entry for the National Association of Leagues of Hospital Friends below) or employ their own Voluntary Services Co-ordinator; the voluntary services of the remaining hospitals may be run by another organisation such as the Red Cross or the WRVS. However, the incessant commercial pressure on the NHS trusts to exact the best financial advantage from any aspect of healthcare means that that the services traditionally provided by volunteers are increasingly likely to be contracted to professional profit-makers. Trolleys and tea-bars are being replaced by well-known retail outlets located within hospital premises and paying market rents. The League of Friends contribute their profits towards improving patient facilities and this can include the purchase of medical equipment. The NHS trusts now have to balance such contributions against the profits from contracting out. The Leagues of Hospital Friends have thus received a serious challenge to their virtual monopoly of service providing.

A simple telephone call to a local hospital should enable you to find out who to contact if you wish to offer your services there. The individual hospitals listed below are given only as examples of the needs of hospitals up and down the country.

Other work involving hospitals and hospital patients will be found in the sections on *Sick and Disabled People*, *Mental Health*, *Children and Youth* and *Elderly People*.

Amandus Club
Atkinson Morley's Hospital, Copse Hill, Wimbledon SW20 0NE (tel 0181-946 7711, ext. 41048).

Volunteers are needed to assist in a small workshop twice a week engaged in recycling greeting cards, printing, knitting, making toys, etc. and to provide a hot midday meal for those who attend the workshop and tea and coffee for visitors. Some secretarial help is also needed.

Anyone interested in helping should contact the Secretary at the above address; please note that the office is staffed on Tuesdays and Thursdays only.

Ida Darwin Hospital
Fulbourn, Cambridge, CB1 5EE (tel 01223-884059).

The Ida Darwin Hospital is home for some 68 adults with profound learning disabilities, many of whom are also physically handicapped. Many volunteers, both short and long term, join with trained staff to improve the residents' quality of life, primarily in developing their leisure opportunities.

The hospital is due to close by 1998 and the residents are gradually being resettled into the community.

Volunteers do not need any special qualifications but it would be helpful if applicants had some experience of working with people with learning disabilities. Volunteers should be at least 18 years old.

Anyone interested should contact the leisure and voluntary co-ordinator at the above address.

National Association of Leagues of Hospital Friends
2nd Floor, Fairfax House, Causton Road, Colchester CO1 1RJ (tel 01206-761227).

The National Association acts as a support, resource and advice centre to some 1,214 Leagues of Friends in England, Scotland and Wales. Together these have 270,000 members and 50,000 volunteers who give about $6\frac{1}{2}$ million hours of voluntary time to their Leagues. About £31 million pounds is raised each year of which £26 million is spent on patient comforts and medical equipment needed by the hospitals.

The aim of the charity is to improve the life of patients and ex-patients from hospitals and health care establishments by offering service and support facilities. The work of the volunteer is very varied and can stretch from patient befriending, through help in canteens, shops or ward trolleys to chaperoning on patient outings, etc. The emphasis is now also changing to help within community care homes.

The work can be rewarding and interesting with as much variety as the individual volunteer wants. For more details ask at the local hospital for the League of Friends contact or write direct to the National Association at the above address.

Richmond Twickenham & Roehampton Healthcare NHS Trust
Roehampton House, Queen Mary's University Hospital, Roehampton Lane, London SW15 5PN (tel 0181-789 6611 ext. 2038; fax 081-780 1089).

The Trust welcomes volunteers of all nationalities to assist with the provision of care to patients at hospital and clinic sites within an integrated NHS Trust. The voluntary opportunities are extensive and varied, ranging from talking to patients to working on the main reception, from working as a volunteer driver to helping maintain ward gardens or assisting with the provision of administrative support to wards and departments. In this way volunteers can improve the quality of a patient's stay simply by giving up a little of their time. Recruitment is as flexible as possible. The Trust can offer a variety of opportunities to suit the volunteer's available time. Anyone wishing to work for the Trust while in the UK on holiday, please contact the Trust in advance of their arrival to avoid disappointment. Opportunities are available all year round.

Applicants should be between the ages of 18 and 65, and must have a reasonable command of the English language. No accommodation or travel allowances are paid but lunch is provided for those working five hours or more per day.

Those interested should contact Craig Dixon, Portering and Administration Manager, at the above address.

St Pancras Hospital Voluntary Help Department
4 St. Pancras Way, London NW1 (tel 0171-387 4411 ext. 368).

The range of jobs for volunteers at St Pancras Hospital is very varied: chatting to patients, writing letters, helping with arts, crafts and pottery, doing the shopping for patients, accompanying wheelchair patients to parks or on other outings and other activities run by the Activities Organizer, helping with the trolley ship and entertainment afternoons.There is a well organized voluntary programme for the large number of helpers under the direction of a full time Voluntary Help Organiser. The patients at St. Pancras are primarily geriatrics, but there are also psychiatric and tropical diseases wards and two Day Hospitals (Psychiatric and Elderly). Volunteers are also needed from time to time in these areas to assist in groups. Many of the patients have been in hospital for a long time and are in particular need of contact with ordinary people leading ordinary lives. Personal attention to lonely patients, whether in the capacity of listener or entertainer, is invaluable.

Volunteers are provided with overalls and free meals, but no accommodation. All volunteers must commit themselves to three hours per week for at least eight weeks. Volunteers of any nationality over 18 years of age can bring pleasure to a person in hospital. The most important requirement is the possession of a cheerful and relaxed personality.

Applications may be submitted to the Voluntary Help Organiser at the Hospital.

University College London Hospitals NHS Trust
Voluntary Services Department
Rockefeller Nurses Home, Huntley Street, London WC1 6DE; (tel 0171-380 9828; fax 0171-380 9977).

The Department co-ordinates a wide variety of patient-orientated activities in several hospitals within the Trust. It is always looking for responsible and reliable people to join its regular team of just under 200 people who offer their time and support for the well-being of patients.

Volunteers do not need any special skills, other than good spoken English and a genuine interest in people. Volunteers are offered meal vouchers and local travelling expenses but not accommodation.

Enquiries should be made to the Voluntary Services manager at the above address.

Pressure Groups

Most charities and voluntary organisations would like to change public knowledge of and interest in their chosen area, whether it is research into heart disease or care for the mentally handicapped. Pressure groups go further than this and are working for long term defined changes not just in public perception, but in real terms.

Those groups listed in this chapter have many different objectives, from abolishing blood sports to fighting for the human rights of prisoners of conscience abroad.Clearly, a prospective volunteer is required to share the views of the organisation he would like to help. Involvement with an organisation such as Hunt Saboteurs Association may call for conviction deep enough to motivate someone to risk physical danger or arrest and so people should examine their motives carefully before becoming involved in the more controversial organisations. We have not included organisations that are protesting against specific local developments, such as the extension of a motorway, or the closing of a village school, because such groups normally receive full coverage in the local media.

Alcohol Concern
Waterbridge House, 32-36 Loman Street, London SE1 OEE; (tel 0171-928 7377).

There are many local alcohol advice agencies which train and use volunteers as alcohol counsellors to give individual help to those who come to them with problems. Alcohol Concern operates a scheme called VACTS (Volunteer Alcohol Counsellors Training Scheme) which is a national initiative set up to ensure minimum standards in the training and on-going supervision of volunteer counsellors. Local alcohol agencies whose courses meet the agreed minimum standards are granted official recognition and any counsellors who undertake the recognized course of training and supervision are eligible for formal accreditation.

For further details on the scheme and information on which agencies train volunteers to the VACTS standard, contact the VACTS Training and Development Officer at the above address.

Amnesty International
UK Section, 99-119 Rosebery Avenue, London EC1R 4RE; (tel 0171-814 6200; fax 0171 833 1510).

Amnesty International won the Nobel Peace Prize in 1977. It works for the release of prisoners of conscience. These are people detained anywhere for their beliefs or because of their ethnic origin, sex, colour or language; who have not used or advocated violence. It campaigns to ensure fair and prompt trials for political prisoners and to abolish the death penalty, torture and other cruel treatment of prisoners. It also campaigns to end extra-judicial executions and 'disappearances'.

Between 50 and 100 volunteers are needed to do routine clerical work: envelope stuffing, typing, wrapping parcels etc. Travelling expenses are reimbursed for office helpers and commercial luncheon vouchers are provided.

Enquiries should be sent to the Personnel Office, Amnesty International, at the above address.

Animal Aid
The Old Chapel, Bradford Street, Tonbridge, Kent TN9 1AW (tel 01732-364546; fax 01732-366533).

This UK based organisation campaigns against all animal abuse (including vivsection, factory farming, the fur trade and circuses), and promotes living without cruelty as an alternative. Ten volunteers are needed for one to four weeks all the year round to assist with general office duties at Tonbridge. Applicants may be of any nationality.

Applications should be made to Iain Green at the above address.

ASH (Action on Smoking and Health)
109 Gloucester Place, London W1H 4EJ (tel 0171-935 3519)

ASH is an information campaign which aims to prevent the disability and death caused by smoking. It needs volunteers in its office to help service the thousands of requests for information received each year and to assist with projects on the many different aspects of smoking control, including smoking in public places, children and smoking, and passive smoking. Volunteers are paid travelling expenses and £1 to cover lunch.

Anyone interested should contact the Volunteer Co-ordinator at the above address.

Campaign Against the Arms Trade
11 Goodwin Street, London N4 3HQ; (tel 0171-281 0297; 0171-281 4369).E-mail caat@gn.apc.org

CAAT operates in the UK and needs volunteers for all sorts of office work in London. About 12 volunteers work at any one time; some have been with CAAT for many years, others offer their services for a few weeks. Tasks are varied depending on the work period and can include writing briefing, data entering, organising events and lots of envelope stuffing. Volunteers are paid travel expenses of up to £5 per day and lunch is provided. The organisation publishes 'CAAT News' bi-monthly. The organisation also provides a library information service.

Anyone interested in volunteering should contact the Joint Co-ordinator, at the above address.

Campaign for Nuclear Disarmament (CND)
162 Holloway Road, London N7 8DQ; (tel 0171-700 2393; fax 0171-700-2357.) E-mail cnd@gn.apc.org

The aim of CND is to persuade the Government to abandon nuclear weapons, and all foreign policy based on their use. The membership of 50,000 is distributed among about 300 local groups which collect signatures for petitions against nuclear warfare, hold meetings, and recruit people to join in nationally organized marches and demonstrations, and help organize them. Specific weapons recently campaigned against include Trident, Britain's nuclear weapons system and French nuclear testing in the Pacific. Membership is optional: any supporter is welcome to join in the activities of the organisation.

Those interested should apply to the organisation at the above address to find out the address of their local group. There is also a youth CND section at the same address (see under *Youth Campaign for Nuclear Disarmament* below).

Child Poverty Action Group (CPAG)
1-5 Bath Street, London EC1V GPY (tel 0171-253 3406)

CPAG works to draw attention to the problems of the impoverished and to provide these people with advice concerning their rights. They accomplish this by publishing research pamphlets, such as *The National Welfare Benefits Handbook* and *The Rights Guide to Non-Means-Tested Benefits*. Volunteers are needed to carry out the clerical work of sending out the literature. Travelling expenses are paid and an allowance is given for lunch.

Enquiries may be addressed to the Publications Distribution Worker at the above address.

Farmers' World Network
The Arthur Rank Centre, National Agriculture Centre, Stoneleigh Park, Warks CV8 2LZ (tel 01203-696969 ext. 338; fax 01203-696900).

The Farmers' World Network is a group of farmers and people with agricultural connections which seeks to promote awareness among the United Kingdom farming community of the problems of developing countries and the relationship between European and Third World agriculture. Volunteers are needed to join local groups which have specific action committees, assist volunteers going to Third World countries and host farmers and students from overseas on their farms. Volunteers are also needed to carry out basic administration in the office at the above address.

Volunteers need a knowledge of agriculture or food production but no other restrictions apply.

Those interested should contact the Co-ordinator at the above address.

Friends of the Earth
26-28 Underwood Street, London W1 1JQ (tel 0171-490 1555; fax 0171 490 0881).E-mail info@foe.co.uk

For over 20 years FOE has led the way in putting forward positive solutions to many of the environmental problems which threaten this planet. FOE campaigns locally, nationally and internationally in order to get politicians, industry and individuals to take action to protect the environment. It is one of the UK's leading environmental pressure groups and campaigns on more issues than any other environmental organisation.

FOE is committed to empowering local communities and individuals to get actively involved in the debate to protect the environment. We strongly believe that pressure for change is most effective when people have access to the facts and we devote considerable resources to research, information and education activities and to publishing and distributing innovative environmental materials.

FOE employs over 100 staff, based mainly at the national office in north London. There is also a Supporters Services Unit in Luton and regional offices comprising one full-time staff member and volunteer helpers in: Belfast, Birmingham, Bristol, Cambridge, Cardiff and Leeds.

Volunteering Opportunities
Volunteers play a vital role in the success of the organisation. There are usually over 50 volunteers helping at the London office, about 20 in the regional offices and over 2,300 people working on a voluntary basis in local network groups throughout England, Wales and Northern Ireland.

The London and Regional Offices: Anyone interested in pursuing a career in environmental campaigning or administration within the voluntary/environmental sector, volunteering at FOE offers an opportunity to gain valuable work experience. Volunteers carry out a variety of administrative support work from helping with mailouts and sorting incoming post to assisting with research and information gathering work. For further details and an application form send a SAE to the Volunteer Coordinator at the London address.

Volunteering in your local area: Anyone living outside reasonable travelling distance from London or the regional offices can get involved with FOE through local groups.

FOE has a network of over 250 local voluntary groups. As a member of a local group there are opportunities to get involved with a range of activities: organising fund-raising events, and helping to distribute leaflets and newsletters. Local groups meet on average one evening a month. For further details please contact the London office for the name and address of the co-ordinator of your nearest group.

The Green Alliance

49 Wellington Street, London WC2E 7BN (tel 0171 836-0341; fax 0171 240-9205). E-mail gralliance@gn.apc.org
WWW http://www.gn.apc.org/gralliance/

The Green Alliance is a London based environmental policy organisation. Its central aim is to raise the prominence of the environment on the agendas of the key policy-making institutions of the UK and in so doing to help improve their environmental performance across the board in Britain and throughout the world.

One or two volunteers are needed to assist with general duties in the London office. Applicants can be of any nationality but they must have a work permit and be able to speak English; specialist office skills would also be useful. Volunteers would only be needed intermittently all year round. Expenses will be paid.

Please apply to K. Crane at the above address.

Greenpeace

Canonbury Villas, London N1 2PN (tel 0171 354-5100; fax 0171 696-0013).

The UK-based administrative office of the international environmental pressure group engages approximately 50 volunteers to help with fund-raising and routine office work every year. Volunteers are required all the year round for a minimum period of three months. Travel expenses will be reimbursed.

Those interested should contact Personnel, at the above address.

Hunt Saboteurs Association

PO Box 1, Carlton, Nottingham NG4 2JY (tel/fax 0115 959037).E-mail hsa@gn.apc.org
www http://envirolink.org/arrs/MSA/hsu.html.

This unique organisation was formed in 1963 and is engaged in a continuing campaign on non-violent direct action style campaigning which both saves the lives of hunted animals and brings to the public's attention the atrocities inflicted upon wild animals in the name of sport. The HSA is an animal rights organisation and is opposed as much to angling and shooting as it is to hunting deer, hare, mink and fox with hounds.

The HSA has nearly 5,000 members of which nearly 1,000 are active on a once weekly basis, normally Saturdays, throughout the winter months. Less activity takes place during the summer months. The Association will advise on the tactics to be employed in the saving of lives and welcomes enquiries from interested people.

The HSA employs no staff and has a decentralized structure. Volunteers may offer their services for as long as they like; it is preferable that active members are over 16 years of age. The annual membership fee is £8 for the waged and £5 for the unwaged.

Further details are obtainable from the above address.

International Broadcasting Trust
2 Ferdinand Place, London NW1 8EE; (tel 0171-482 2847; fax 0171-284 3374).

International Broadcasting Trust is a television production organisation which specialises in the making of programmes on Third World, human rights, development and environmental issues. The Trust's aim is to promote a wider understanding of these issues through the use of the media. Volunteers are occasionally needed to complete very basic office duties such as telephone answering and photocopying. Travelling expenses (London area only) and lunch allowance are paid.

Those interested should apply to the Volunteer Co-ordinator at the above address.

Liberty (National Council for Civil Liberties)
21 Tabard Street, London SE1 4LA (tel 0171-403 3888).

Liberty is a pressure group which works to defend and extend civil liberties throughout the UK. Volunteers at the London office help prepare publications, assist with research or perform routine administrative tasks/ Volunteer lawyers assist with legal casework. A luncheon allowance is provided for volunteers and travelling expenses are paid inside London.

Enquiries should be sent to the Office Manager at the above address.

Minority Rights Group
379 Brixton Road, London SW9 7DE (tel 0171-978 9498; fax 0171-738 6265).E-mail minorityright@mrg.sprint.com

MRG is concerned with the research and publication and advocacy of human rights about minority groups around the world. Although space restrictions mean that MRG is able to accept only a small number of volunteers, it is happy to consider applications from individuals who wish to apply. Members from ethnic minority communities and refugees are especially welcome. Work is likely to involve the following: information collecting and filing, general office work, assisting members of staff, helping with mailing, etc. Travelling expenses within London are paid.

Enquiries to the above address.

National Peace Council
88 Islington High Street, London N1 8EG (tel 0171-354 5200; fax 0171-354 0033).

The National Peace Council is at the centre of a network of over 250 peace organisations and related movements, including trade unions and religious peace associations. The council's task is to provide an exchange of information between its member organisations to facilitate co-operation among them. It also acts as a pressure group on behalf of its affiliates. A small number of volunteers are needed to look after the correspondence and mailing services, and to do continuing research into current events which pertain to disarmament issues. Typing, some computer experience and general office experience would be an asset for those volunteers wishing to apply.

Enquiries may be sent to Lib Peck, Co-ordinator, at the above address.

One World Week
PO Box 100, London SE1 7RT (tel 0171-620 4444; fax 0171-620 0719).

One World Week in October of each year is a chance for churches and other groups to get together, celebrate and learn about issues of justice, peace, the environment and development. Offices in London, Edinburgh and Cardiff provide support for this by supplying study materials and suggestions for activities and providing local contacts. Volunteers are needed to help existing groups celebrate the week or to organize their own activities. Fundraising is not encouraged.

Those interested should contact a Programme Worker at the above address for more information.

Prisoners Abroad
82 Rosebery Avenue, London EC1R 4RR (tel 0171-833 3467).

Formerly, the National Council for the Welfare of Prisoners Abroad, this charity works for the welfare of British prisoners in foreign jails. The specific work done for individual prisoners varies enormously; dealing with foreign and British lawyers, and prison and other authorities, writing personally to prisoners and organising penpals, providing funds for prisoners to buy essentials like blankets and medicines, etc. Around 20 volunteers are needed all year round to help with all office activities; typing and other clerical work, answering both telephone and postal queries, word processing and writing letters to prisoners. Volunteers normally help for three months or more on a regular basis, with full days of work being preferred to half days.

Volunteers of all nationalities are welcome. Good communication skills are important and languages are an advantage but not essential. All other skills will be put to good use. As the office is located on the second floor of the building with no lift it is regretted that disabled people will find access difficult. Travelling expenses and a lunch allowance are paid.

Volunteers should apply to the Director at the above address.

Railway Development Society
2 Clematis Cottage, Hopton Bank, Cleobury Mortimer, Kidderminster DY14 OHF; (tel 01584-890807).

The RDS was formed in 1978 by an amalgamation of earlier societies. It is a national pressure group, with a network of local branches, fighting for the improvement of Britain's railway system as a vital environmental issue. It maintains regular contact with Railtrack, the Rail Franchising Director, Train Operating Companies, freight customers, ministers, MP's and local authorities. It produces reports, leaflets, a quarterly journal and branch newsletters.

It requires over 100 volunteers a year to help with its activities. Involvement can be at a national or local level. There are no restrictions on applicants and no special qualifications are required.

Enquiries to the Administrative Officer at the above address.

Survival International
11-15 Emerald Street, London WC1N 3QL (tel 0171 242 1441; fax 0171-242 1771).

Survival International is a world wide organisation supporting tribal peoples, standing for their right to decide their own future and helps them protect their lives, lands and human rights. Survival works for threatened tribal peoples in the Americas, Africa, Asia and Australasia. Survival lobbies international organisations, governments and multi-national companies, works to raise awareness of the situation of tribal peoples and supports practical realistic field projects with the aim of assisting the survival and self-determination of tribal peoples.

Volunteers are required in the London office to assist with clerical and secretarial work, library duties, visual aid materials and fundraising activities. A commitment of anything from half a day to five days per week for a minimum of three months is required.

Those interested should contact the London office.

Teetotal Support Groups
'Jordans', 1c Grassington Road, Eastbourne, East Sussex BN20 7BP (tel 0323-638 234).

Teetotal Support Groups aim to offer support to anyone who wishes to totally abstain from alcohol. Social contact with others on the nationwide Teetotallers' Register or local support groups will be encouraged, especially for members who move to other areas.

Help is needed to form new groups in different localities. Groups may choose to launch a juice bar, or coffee shop project run by volunteers and based in a school, community house or spare room of a local church.

Anyone interested in joining or forming a local group should write or telephone to the above address for advice and addresses.

Tools for Self Reliance
Ringwood Road, Netley Marsh, Southampton SO40 7GY (tel 01703-869697).

Tools for Self Reliance is a charity which aims to help people in Africa and Central America obtain tools. To this end they operate a tool-making and tool sending programme. In the tool sending programme basic hand tools are collected, refurbished and then send to partner organisations in priority countries for distribution to local artisan groups. Volunteers are needed to help with all aspects of this work: refurbishing and packing tools, office work, building maintenance, gardening and general site work at the Head Office in Netley Marsh. TFSR also has a network of local groups throughout Britain and hosts three workcamps a year, which are organised through IVS and QUISP. For further information on Netley Marsh work contact Tim Young; for local groups contact Judith Barrett (0116-2540957), and for workcamps either IVS or QUISP.

The Vegetarian Society
Parkdale, Dunham Road, Altringham, Cheshire WA14 4QG (tel 0161-928 0793; fax 0161-928 0798). E-mail vegsoc@vegsocdemon.co.UK

The Society's aim is to increase the numbers of vegetarians in the UK in order to save animals, benefit human health and protect the environment and world food resources. Volunteers are needed each year to help at their headquarters.

Tasks include administrative duties and answering children's letters. Volunteers give whatever time they can. Those interested should contact the Campaigns Director at the above address.

World Development Movement
25 Beehive Place, Brixton SW9 7QR (tel 0171-737 6215; fax 0171-274 8232).

The World Development Movement (WDM) is dedicated to tackling the root causes of poverty. WDM works together with people in the Third World. WDM is aligned to no political party but influences all. WDM is a democratic network of members, groups and campaigners. Volunteers are needed in the London office. No accommodation is provided but travel expenses to and from the office and a lunch allowance of £2.50 are paid. Apply to the volunteers Coordinator. Volunteers can also join in campaigning through a local action group. Contact the Groups Officer at the above address for details.

World Disarmament Campaign
45-47 Blythe Street, London E2 6LX (tel 0171-729 2523).

This UK based organisation campaigns for nuclear and conventional disarmament, third world development and environmental protection on the basis of resolutions agreed by the UN. A few full-time volunteers assist with general office duties in London. Applicants of any nationality are welcome as long as they have knowledge of English. Volunteers are required all the year round apart from at the height of summer. Expenses will be paid.

Those interested should contact The Treasurer, at WDC HQ at the above address.

Youth Campaign for Nuclear Disarmament (YCND)
162 Holloway Road, London N7 8DQ; (tel 0171-607 3616; fax 0171 700 2357). E-mail cnd@gn.apc.org

CND campaigns for nuclear disarmament worldwide. Youth CND is run by young members for other young members. Members receive the quarterly magazine *CND Today* as well as special youth publications and publicity material for schools. New members and campaigners are always welcome. There are separate national offices for Scotland (6 Dalcross Pass, Glasgow G11 5RE) and Wales (9 Idris Terrace, Swansea SA9 OJY).

Prisons and Probation

There is a strong historical link between volunteers and prisons: indeed, the statutory Probation Service itself was begun when the authorities realised how successful voluntary involvement had been in re-integrating prisoners into society. The special value of volunteers in this work lies in the fact that they are not a formal part of 'the system', and so offenders respond more readily and openly to them than they would to paid and officially appointed officers.

By visiting a convicted prisoner, a volunteer can be of use either by simply providing companionship, or by maintaining a link with the prisoner's family, as a period of imprisonment can prove a strain on marriages. The need for the help of a volunteer does not end with the release of an offender; the support of a known and trusted volunteer can be of great help in finding a job and somewhere to live. This is especially valuable in time of high unemployment, as prisoners will experience more difficulty than most people in finding work. The organisations listed below show the many ways in which a volunteer can be of use to a prisoner both before and after release.

The Bourne Trust

Lincoln House, 1-3 Brixton Road, London, SW9 6DE; (tel 0171-582 1313/6699; fax 0171 735 6077).

The Bourne Trust aims to support prisoners and the families of prisoners through the inevitable problems that accompany imprisonment. Projects based in London are: professional counselling for remand prisoners, professional counselling for family members of prisoners. Volunteer groups visiting prisoners are based in Wakefield, Channings Wood and Holloway Prisons. Volunteers supporting families work in Hewell Grange (Redditch). The Trust runs a playscheme in visits at Wormwood Scrubs and Independent Visitors' Centres at Wormwood Scrubs and Belmarsh prisons. The Trust also welcomes individual requests for advice and support from across England and Wales through letters or telephone contact.

Inner London Probation and After-Care Service

71/73 Great Peter Street, London SW1P 2BN (tel 0171-222 5656; fax 0171-222 0473).

The Service undertakes a wide range of activities with voluntary helpers within the 12 Inner London boroughs. These relate to most aspects of the Probation Service's work and would entail, for example, one-to-one contact with clients, group work, adventure activities, or practical help on a regular or single task basis.

Applicants should be at least 18 years old and under most circumstances it would be helpful if they could offer their services for at least 12 months. The personal qualities needed are sound common sense, tolerance and kindness. Applicants must also be prepared to work closely with supervising Probation Officers.

Those interested should, in the first instance, contact Mr John Godfrey (SPO), ILPS/SOVA Thoroughcare Partnership, 90 Clapham Road, London SW9 OJT (0171-793 0834).

National Association for the Care and Resettlement of Offenders (NACRO)

169 Clapham Road, London SW9 OPU (tel 0171-582 6500).

NACRO runs housing, employment, youth training, education and advice projects for offenders and others; provides research, information and training services for people concerned about crime and offenders; and contributes to the development of crime policy and the prevention of crime. Over 1,000 staff work in some 150 projects and other services throughout England and Wales.

Opportunities for voluntary work are limited to a small number of projects providing education for unemployed adults and activities for young people, which are organized on a local basis. NACRO aims to be an equal opportunities employer and to eliminate unfair descrimination against anyone in its selection process.

For further information, contact NACRO's Communications Department at the above address.

National Association of Prison Visitors
46B Hartington Street, Bedford (tel 01234-359763).

In the UK prison visitors are officially appointed. Normally they make an appointment to see the govenor of the prison nearest them. If this interview passes satisfactorily they are accepted for a probationary period of three months. After this they must be appointed by the Home Office. It is important that people in prison (and in other penal institutions) should not lose contact with the outside world. Prison staff and visiting probation officers have a part to play, but the prison visitor has a unique contribution to offer, working alongside this team rather than as a member of it. Although appointed by the Home Office and subject to the regulations of the prisons, he or she is a volunteer, not an 'official' and this independent status has an appeal to the prisoner. The main role of the visitor is to establish a one-to-one , impartial, non-authoritarian relationship with the prisoner. There are 1400 visitors in the UK and 8-10% of prisoners have prison visitors. The Association wishes to expand its activities and new recruits will be welcome. Prison visitors should not be confused with Voluntary Associates, who work in co-operation with the Probation and After-care service.

Visitors must be at least 21 and not over 70, and are normally expected to retire at 75. To be of value, visits must be made at frequent intervals, normally weekly or fortnightly, early in the evening, and at weekends. Both men and women are taken on, and women visitors can visit men's prisons. Visitors usually visit their nearest prison.

Those interested should apply to the Governor of their nearest prison.

The New Bridge
27a Medway Street, London SW1P 2BD; (tel 0171-976 0779; 0171-976 0767).

The New Bridge operates a nationwide befriending scheme for people who are in prison, parenting classes for young offenders in institutions in the South West, Feltham and Manchester and a Foreign Nationals initiative to help ameliorate the isolation of foreign prisoners held in British prisons. Some 250 volunteers lend their time to the organisation, of whom the majority are involved in the befriending scheme. This entails the volunteer keeping in touch with the prisoner through letters and visits while he or she is in prison and offering encouragement in starting a new life on their release. Volunteers should be aged 18+ good listeners, non-judgmental, mature in outlook and have an ability to cope. For parenting classes, experience of parenting, group work, working with offenders, or teaching is required, and for work with foreign nationals, fluency in at least one other language besides English is desirable. Expenses may be reclaimed, and those interested should write to the above address.

Society of Voluntary Associates (SOVA)
350 Kennington Road, London SE11 4LH; (tel 0171-793 0404; fax 0171-735 4410).

SOVA recruits and trains volunteers to work with offenders, their families and young people at risk across England and Wales. About 749 volunteers are employed at any one time. The types of work volunteers are involved in include teaching basic skills, helping people on probation with a range of practical problems, housing, benefits, employment, substance abuse etc. and befriending young offenders (10-17 year-olds).

To be eligible volunteers need to have a minimum of two hours available each week during the daytime (9am to 5pm), aged over 17 and if an ex-offender themselves to have been out of prison for at least two years. Volunteers are needed all year round and receive expenses.

Anyone interested should contact Keith Knight at the above address.

Problems, Emergencies and Housing

If the stereotypical image of the last decade was the yuppie wheeler-dealer, that of the current decade is the all too-familiar one of the homeless person bedding down for the night in a cardboard box on a city street. There are many people trapped in a vicious circle of unemployment and homelessness, and the social services find it hard to cope. The following organisations illustrate how the individual can help to alleviate homelessness and other housing-related problems.

Many of the organisations listed below deal with individuals who are facing a rapid succession of linked problems, such as bereavement, poverty, homelessness, unemployment and hopelessness. Without some assistance many such cases may end up with suicide or crime. Often all that is needed is a friendly voice for someone to speak to: it is significant that the suicide rate has dropped since the Samaritans began operating. In other cases skilled help is needed, to liaise with council housing departments, for example.

Some of the organisations listed under *Sick and Disabled People, Children and Youth, Elderly People* and *Prisons and Probation* also contain provisions for dealing with crises within their respective areas of activity.

Catholic Housing Aid Society (CHAS)
209 Old Marylebone Road, London NW1 5QT; (tel 0171-723 7273; fax 0171-723 5943).

The Society has 13 branches throughout the country. It helps anyone with a housing problem. The branches advise on landlord-tenant questions, council housing arrangements and problems with purchasing. The time at which advisory services are open varies from branch to branch, although most operate in the evenings. Volunteers are needed to work in the advice centres, to do administrative office work and to help with research work; Those working in the advisory centres need to offer a couple of evenings a month and the Society runs a number of in-service training programmes.

Those interested should apply to the above address or to their local branch.

Centrepoint Off The Streets
54 Dean Street, London W1 (tel 0171-434 2861; fax 0171 287 0622).

This is an emergency night shelter for up to 12 homeless people who are living on and around the streets of London or are felt to be at risk in the West End. Volunteers work as part of a team of about six, one night a week under the supervision of a full-time worker. Their main function is to provide a welcoming atmosphere for clients and a sympathetic ear when required, as well as helping with practical chores such as cooking and washing.

All nationalities are welcome but applicants should be able to speak English, and preferably be aged over 18. It is preferred also if volunteers can make a long term commitment, i.e. for at least six months.

For further information and application forms contact the Volunteer Administrator.

Salvation Army

105-109 Judd Street, King's Cross, London WC1H 9TS (tel 0171-383 4230).

The Salvation Army performs a greater variety and volume of social service than any other voluntary organisation in the world. It has 25,000 Officers in 84 countries who have dedicated their lives to the service of God in the Army; but their work is made even more effective by the support of individuals who give voluntary help in hostels, homes and centres. In Britain alone the Army has nearly 1,000 centres of worship, evangelism, and community activity, as well as 125 social centres, all of which operate varying programmes for helping others.

There now exists in Britain a nationwide network of homes, hostels and other centres caring for people in physical and moral need. Although much of the work is done by Officers, volunteers can provide valuable ancillary services.

For further details contact the Personnel Secretary, Social Services, at the above address.

The Samaritans

10 The Grove, Slough SL1 1QP (tel 01753-532713; fax 01753-819004).

The Samaritans is a registered charity, founded in 1953. The Samaritans' service is available 24-hours to provide confidential and emotional support to anyone passing through crisis and at risk of suicide. The Samaritans aims to provide society with a better understanding of suicide and the value of expressing feelings that may lead to suicide.

Volunteers must be over 17 and feel that they are able to listen to others who may be despairing and suicidal, without judgement. If you think you can do this, contact the local Samaritans' branch (in the phone book) and they will send an application form and invite you to an introduction evening. The Samaritans welcome volunteers from all cultures and backgrounds. Training is normally spread over six weeks (six evenings and one full day). Volunteers are expected to do two or three shifts per month which will include an overnight shift.

Alternatively, the Samaritans always welcome applications from volunteers to raise funds through Friends of the Samaritans groups (details from your local branch).

SHELTER, National Campaign for the Homeless

88 Old Street, London EC1V 9HU (tel 0171-253 0202; fax 0171-608 3325).

Shelter helps provide a housing aid service and aims to improve housing conditions all over the country, as well as offering telephone advice direct to London's homeless people. Volunteers work in the national headquarters and in the regional offices around the country. The type of work that they do depends on their personal skills; for example, some may be able to type, which is always useful, while others may have a specialized knowledge of housing or campaigning. But enthusiasm and conscientiousness can make a volunteer equally useful. In addition, many people help to finance the organisation with fund raising events. All are welcome to join local groups or become members of the campaign.

The amount of help which is given to Shelter depends on the volunteer her/himself. Some people have helped for years, while others only do so for a week or two. Travel expenses are reimbursed.

Applicants should contact the Personnel Assistant at the above address for further information.

Women's Aid Ltd
P.O.Box 791, Dublin 1, Ireland (tel +353 1-8745302/8745303; fax +353 8745525).

Women's Aid is an organisation which provides advice, support and accommodation to women and children suffering physical, emotional, sexual and financial abuse in their own homes. Women's Aid also provides training to other groups who come into contact with women and children who are suffering from domestic violence.

The aims of Women's Aid include:

Providing education and awareness to groups in order to increase levels of awareness about the issue.

Lobbying government and state agencies on social and legal reform.

Initiating research and compiling statistics on the extent of domestic violence in Ireland.

Volunteers can assist with work in areas such as the crisis helpline, women's refuge, Education and Awareness group.

There are no special requirements, but the ability to show empathy, concern and a non-judgmental attitude is essential for all voluntary work with Women's Aid. Workers on the helpline are required to undergo the helpline training which includes a feminist analysis of the issues provided by the organisation.

Sick and Disabled People

In these cost-conscious times The National Health Service is unable to provide full support for all those who have chronic illnesses or permanent disabilities. The organisations in this section are able to help fill this gap because they have specialized knowledge of the condition and can provide appropriate support.

Volunteers can help these organisations in a wide variety of ways, whether directly, perhaps by helping with swimming therapy, or indirectly, such as by walking puppies for future training as guide dogs for the blind. In cases such as Arthritis Care (below) there is a particular need for volunteers with the relevant disabilities or injuries. In other cases, able-bodied volunteers prove more useful.

Other sections dealing specifically with the sick and disabled include *Hospitals*, *Children and Youth* and *The Elderly*.

Arthritis Care
18 Stephenson Way, London NW1 2HD (tel 0171-916 1500).

Arthritis Care was founded in 1948 by a young person with arthritis who wished to help and encourage others. There are at present about 600 branches around the country (all the branch officers and helpers are volunteers) and around 60,000 members. Active branch members render indispensable help in running the branch meetings, which may be a housebound member's only contact with the outside world. Any assistance which can be given with transport is much appreciated. Volunteers are needed to visit the housebound on a regular basis.

Those interested in joining should contact the Secretary at the above address to be put in touch with their local branch.

Birmingham Tapes for the Handicapped Association
20 Middleton Hall Road, Kings Norton, Birmingham B30 1BY (tel 0121-628 3656).

The Association sends a monthly tape recorded sound magazine to handicapped people around the country. It also has a tape library which is free to members.

Those interested in helping should contact Mr Derek L Hunt, Honorary Secretary, at the above address.

Body Positive (London)
51B Philbeach Gardens, Earls Court, London SW5 9EB (tel 0171-835 1045; fax 0171-373 5237).

This is a drop-in centre based in London for people affected by HIV/AIDS, offering external support groups for such people. Around 200 volunteers help at Body Positive each year. In the Centre itself practical help is needed such as laying tables, washing up and welcoming its users. Volunteers are also required to visit people in hospitals in the London area, and drive people to and from the Centre and other groups. Applicants of any nationality are welcome. Each applicant must complete an induction/training program. The length of placement depends on the volunteer; volunteers are needed all the year round. Expenses are paid for public transport on Body Positive business only.

Those interested should contact Roger Gustafson at the above address.

Bristol Cancer Help Centre
Grove House, Cornwallis Grove, Clifton, Bristol BS8 4PG (tel 0117-973 0500).

Opened in 1980, the Centre offers programmes which complement orthodox medical treatment for cancer patients. The patient receives medical supervision and counselling on nutrition, lifestyle and relaxation and meditation methods, as treatment is based on the principle that the whole person rather than just the disease should be treated. Approximately 20 volunteers are needed all year round to assist with postal queries (often the first contact patients have with the Centre), gardening, fund raising and clerical duties. Ideally volunteers work for a half or full day per week on an on-going basis.

Volunteers should be reliable, over 17 years old, and have a caring but humourous personality. A driving licence is an advantage but not essential. Only in special circumstances will travelling expenses be paid.

Those interested should contact the Volunteer Coordinator at the above address.

British Limbless Ex-Servicemen's Association (BLESMA)
185-187 High Road, Chadwell Heath, Romford, Essex RM6 6NA (tel 0181-590 1124; fax 0181-599 2932).

BLESMA operates two residential homes and a welfare service to make sure that limbless ex-servicemen and women (including widows) do not suffer hardship. The Association operates a regular Welfare Visiting Service through its branches across the country. Organized social activities are arranged and a general information and advice service is provided.

The Association is now in need of some 200 volunteers to help branches with committee work, welfare visits and fundraising. Individuals may undertake any or all of these tasks. The amount of time given is at the discretion of the individuals concerned. Possession of a driving licence would be advantageous and a motor mileage allowance can be paid.

For further details contact the General Secretary at the above address.

The British Retinitis Pigmentosa Society
Pond House, Lillingstone Dayrell, Bucks MK18 5AS (tel 01280 860363; fax 01280-860515).

The Society was formed in 1975 and it aims to give relief to sufferers of RP in any way which may help them to live with, or overcome, their handicap, and to pursue measures towards finding the cause of RP and means of its treatment and cure.

For further details of how volunteers can help with this please contact the Honorary Secretary at the above address.

The Chalfont Centre for Epilepsy
Chalfont St Peter, Gerrards Cross, Bucks SL9 ORJ (tel 01494-873991; fax 01494-871927).

The Centre, run by the National Society for Epilepsy, welcomes volunteers to assist their work with the care and rehabilitation of people with epilepsy. Volunteers are needed to provide caring assistance, raise funds, provide transport and act as escorts for outings, help at social events, help with sporting activities. Help is useful at any time, but especially during holiday periods. Volunteers may stay for any length of time. No qualifications are necessary. Travelling expenses to and from the Centre are not paid, but outings and holidays are paid for.

Applications to Colonel D W Eking, Chief Executive, at the above address.

Cope Foundation
Bonnington, Montenotte, Cork, Eire (tel +353 21-507131).

The Association operates a number of services for the mentally handicapped in Cork city and County, including care units, schools, training centres, hostels and a sheltered workshop. Voluntary help is needed in all of these areas, especially during the school holidays.

For further details contact the Personnel Officer at the above address.

Cystic Fibrosis Research Trust
Alexandra House, 5 Blyth Road, Bromley, Kent BR1 3RS (tel 0181-464 7211; fax 0181-313 0472).

The Trust has branches throughout Britain which give support to patients and their families. Volunteers are generally already familiar with cystic fibrosis and its problems, due to prior experience of the disease; however, outside volunteers within the local community may be of service.

Enquiries may be sent to the Director, at the above address.

Eating Disorders Association
Sackville Place, 44 Magdalen Street, Norwich, Norfolk NR3 1JU; (tel 01603-619090).

The Eating Disorders Association (EDA) is a national charity which offers information and help to people with anorexia or bulimia nervosa, their families, friends and professionals involved in the treatment of eating disorders. Its main services include a membership scheme, a network of self help groups, telephone helplines, information about treatment and a professional journal. Volunteers are needed to work on the National Helpline which is based in Norwich. The organisation offers training in listening skills to volunteers selected for this work.

Anyone interested in working as a helpline volunteer should contact Alison Black at the above address.

Enable
6th Floor, 7 Buchanan Street, Glasgow G1 3HL; tel 0141-226 4541; 0141-204 4398).

Enable is the largest voluntary organisation for people with learning disabilities in Scotland. It uses volunteers in several ways in its work. There are 75 local Enable branches in different parts of Scotland. Most run social clubs and outings and welcome volunteers able to give up some time on a regular basis.

Volunteers are also needed over the summer by Enable's holiday department to help at camps or to accompany holidaymakers with learning disabilities for a week or a weekend at a time. Other volunteer opportunities are within the fundraising department where help is always welcome at events, public collections or in the office stuffing envelopes. Enable Homes, the housing organisation, is looking for people who would be willing to spend time socialising with the organisation's tenants, all of whom have profound or complex disabilities, either in their home or by taking them out to use local facilities. No particular knowledge is necessary but people able to give a regular and sustained commitment in most of the above areas are preferred. Expenses are paid. Please note that there are seldom opportunities for paid vacational employment. For initial information please contact the Information Service at the above address.

The Guide Dogs for the Blind Association
Hillfields, Burghfield Common, Reading RG7 3YG (tel 01734-835555; fax 01734-835433).

Help is needed by the Association in rearing its puppies for one year until they are ready to be taken back for training. Anyone interested in becoming a puppy-walker should live near Bolton, Exeter, Forfar, Leamington, Middlesbrough, Redbridge or Wokingham. The Association pays a feeding allowance, meets vet's bills and offers regular support and advice from puppy-walking supervisors. Most of the Association's brood bitches also live with families and there are occasional opportunities to help in this way.

Fund-raising for the Association is organised through over 450 local branches that have been formed by volunteer supporters. Those who would like to help in these activities should contact the offices near Reading.

Hertfordshire Association for the Disabled
Woodside Centre, The Commons, Welwyn Garden City, Herts. AL8 7HG; (tel 01707-324581; 01707-371297).

Volunteers at the rate of six per fortnight are needed to help with holidays for people with disabilities at Hertford House, Clacton. Helpers work on a rota basis, aiding the mobility of guests, to give companionship and assist them in dressing, transferring from wheelchair to bed/bath/toilet, pushing guests in wheelchairs to shops, church, the seafront etc. and escorting them on outings in the hotel minibus.

Free return transport to the hotel from Welwyn Garden City is provided. Volunteers are needed all year round. The minimum age is 20 years. Experience of working with disabled people would be helpful.

Enquiries with a SAE to the above address.

Kith and Kids
c/o The Irish Centre, Pretoria Road, London N17 8DX; (tel 0181-801 7432)

Kith and Kids is a self-help organisation which provides support for the families of chldren with a physical or learning disability. Volunteers are needed to take part in social training schemes working on a two-to-one basis with learning disabled children and young people, helping them with everyday skills and helping to integrate them into the community. Volunteers must be aged a minimum of 16 years. No experience is necessary, but lots of enthusiasm is essential. Volunteers work a minimum of two consecutive weeks during August or a week at Christmas and Easter from 9.30am to 5pm daily. Lunch and travel expenses within the Greater London Area are provided. There is also a preparatory three-day training course before each project. There is no accommodation so volunteers should be based locally. Kith and Kids also organises a one-week camping holiday in August with accommodation for volunteers provided.

For further details contact the volunteer organiser at the above address.

MIND (National Association for Mental Health)
15-19 Broadway, London E15 4BQ; (tel 0181-519 2122; fax 0181 522 1725).

MIND is the leading mental health charity in England and Wales. Working for a better life for everyone experiencing mental distress. Mind campaigns for their right to lead an active and valued life in the community and is an influential voice on mental health issues. Drawing on the experience and skills of providers and users of mental health services, MIND has become the largest charitable provider of quality community care.

Local Associations
Mind's network of 218 local associations throughout England and Wales offers a range of services including supported accommodation, drop-in and day centres, befriending, counselling, advocacy and employment schemes and cannot operate without substantial help from volunteers.

Minds Matter
Mind's trading arm runs a network of charity shops around the country, marketing selected Mind products, also available through mail order. Volunteers are vital to help run these shops.

Mindinfo Line
Mind's infoline (0181-522 1728 London; 0345-660 163 outside London) is open Monday to Friday from 9.15am-4.45pm except Tuesday, open from 2pm-2.45pm. The infoline offers callers confidential information on the range of mental health problems, from their headquarters in East London. To cope with increasing demand, an expansion programme is underway, training volunteers to work ont the information line.

Further information can also be obtained from the following regional MIND offices:

North West Mind: 21 Ribblesdale Place, Preston PR1 3NA; tel 01772-821734.

Northern Mind: 158 Durham Road, Gateshead, NE8 4EL; tel 0191 490 0109.

South West Mind: 9th Floor, Tower House, Fairfax Street, Bristol BS1 3BN; tel 0117-9250961.

Trent & Yorkshire Mind: 44 Howard Street, Sheffield S1 2LA; 0114-2721742.

Wales Mind: 23 St Mary Street, Cardiff CF1 2AA; tel 01222-395123.

South East Mind: 1st Floor, Kemp House, 152-160 City Road, London EC1V 2NP; tel 0171-608 0881.

West Midlands Mind: 20/21 Cleveland Street, Wolverhampton WV1 3HT; tel 01902 24404.

Mobility Trust
50 High Street, Hungerford, Berkshire RG17 ONE; (tel 01488-686335; fax 01488-686336.

Mobility Trust is a registered charity run on an entirely voluntary basis. The office of the Trust is open Monday to Thursday from 10am to 4pm. The Trust will provide to beneficiaries who may be either physically or mentally disabled, use of a particular piece of mobility equipment inclusive of the first year's insurance, after which the beneficiaries become responsible for the cost of cover and maintenance.

Volunteers are needed to work with disabled people, including offering advice and counselling. A driving licence is an advantage, but is not essential. Most volunteers work for two to three months and sometimes longer. Expenses will be paid. Applications to Brian Geering at the above address.

Multiple Sclerosis Society of Great Britain and Northern Ireland
25 Effie Road, London SW6 1EE (tel 0171-610 7171; fax 0171-736 9861).

The Society is the largest national organisation dedicated to supporting people living with MS. Its main roles include raising public awareness of MS and its consequences, campaigning to enable people with MS to participate fully in all areas of society, funding research into the causes of and treatments for MS and providing practical and financial support to people with MS and their families/carers.

It is a volunteer-based organisation, depending heavily on volunteers for the management of its national leadership structures. It also depends on volunteers to provide a range of local support services.

Enquiries should be sent to the Director of Development at the above address who will forward them to the appropriate Branch.

Muscular Dystrophy Group of Great Britain and Northern Ireland
7-11 Prescott Place, London SW4 6BS (tel 0171-720 8055; fax 0171-498 0670).

The Muscular Dystrophy Group raises funds for medical research into neuro-muscular conditions and offers practical advice and support to those people (and those families) affected by it. There are over 450 branches and representatives throughout the UK and Northern Ireland, all of whom are anxious for local volunteers helpers to assist in their fundraising and other activities i.e. office work, and envelope drops etc.

Write to the Branch Services Manager at the above address for the details of local branches.

National Deaf-Blind League

18 Rainbow Court, Paston Ridings, Peterborough PE4 6UP (tel 01733- 573511; fax 01733-325353).

The National Deaf-Blind League offers hope and support to those with a dual sensory impairment to live full and active lives despite their disability. Part of this is achieved by teaching and encouraging touch-based communication systems and raising awareness of deafblindness in the caring professions and amongst the wider public, and to ensure that the needs of of deafblind people are appropriately met in health/community care planning.

The League's activities include visiting/assessing deafblind individuals; participation in national developmental/lobbying groups; contributing to individual community care plans. Information and advice on dual sensory loss; social activities for deafblind people; rehabilitation services; holiday flats; independent living accommodation; linking deafblind people through magazines and newspapers and touch-based media. International representations.

Anyone with a genuine concern for people with the double handicap of deafness and blindness, and time and energy to spare to help promote these activities, should contact the Chief Executive at the above address.

National Eczema Society

163 Eversholt Street, London NW1 1BU; (tel 0171-388 4800).

This Society aims to promote mutual support for individuals and families coping with eczema. Volunteers are required to assist with the day to day running of the National Office and they may find themselves working within any of the Society's departments. Help is required all the year round. Both travel and lunch expenses are paid.

Those interested should contact Julie Braithwaite, Information Officer at the above address.

National Society for Epilepsy

Chalfont St Peter, Gerrards Cross, Buckinghamshire SL9 ORJ (01494 873991; fax 01494 871927).

The NSE welcomes volunteers to assist their work caring for and rehabilitating people with epilepsy. Volunteers are needed to raise funds, provide caring assistance, provide transport and act as escorts for outings, help at social events and sporting activities.

Help is needed at any time, but especially during the holiday periods. Volunteers may stay for any length of time. No qualifications are necessary. Travelling expenses to and from the Society are not paid, but holidays and outings are paid for.

Applications to Kathy McLoughlin, Volunteer Coordinator at the above address.

Phab

12-14 London Road, Croydon CRO 2TA (tel 0181-667 9443).

Phab works through social clubs and activities in which physically disabled and able bodied people work together on an equal basis on membership, management and programme issues. Phab also provides holidays and courses in which physically disabled and able bodied people live, work and play together. Volunteers can help with all aspects of these programmes by joining a local club.

For further information and details of local clubs contact the secretary of the Chief Executive at the above address.

Parkinson's Disease Society of the United Kingdon Ltd

22 Upper Woburn Place, London WC1H 0RA (tel 0171-383 3513; fax 0171-383 5754).

The aims of the society are threefold: to help patients and their relatives with the problems arising from Parkinson's Disease; to collect and disseminate information on the disease; and to encourage and provide funds for research into it. Voluntary workers provide vital assistance in the achievement of these aims; they assist at the national headquarters and run about 230 local branches. Helpers are especially desirable if they can assist in the setting up of new branches, as at present many voluntary workers are relatives of sufferers from the disease who already have many demands on their time. Drivers are always welcome at local branches, and fuel costs are reimbursed where appropriate.

Enquiries should either be directed to the Office Manager at the above address, or to the Honorary Secretary of the local branch of the applicant.

Riding for the Disabled Association

Avenue 'R', National Agricultural Centre, Kenilworth, Warwickshire CV8 2LY (tel 01203-696510; fax 01203 696532).

The aim of the Association is to provide the opportunity of riding to disabled people who might benefit in their general health and well-being. There are Member groups throughout the UK, whose voluntary helpers are drawn from many sources: Pony Clubs, Riding Clubs, the British Red Cross Society, Rotary Clubs, the Police Force, older school children, or simply responsible members of the community.

Prospective volunteers should contact a local Member Group directly. The list of Member Groups and a leaflet about the activities of the Association are available from the Director at the above address.

Royal Association in Aid of Deaf People (RAD)

27 Old Oak Road, Acton, London W3 7HN (tel 0181-743 6187; fax 0181-740 6551).

RAD is a charity committed to meeing the individual needs of people affected by deafness through its centres south east England. RAD provides services which include: advocacy, chaplaincy, counselling, information, interpreting, leisure facilities and support groups.

RAD has specialist knowledge and influence which give deaf people the opportunity to lead confident, effective and independent lives.

Volunteers help with special one-day excursion and longer holidays.

The Royal Association for Disability and Rehabilitation (RADAR)

12 City Forum, 250 City Road, London EC1V 8AF; tel 0171-250 3222; fax 0171-250 0212).

RADAR is the national disability organisation that campaigns for disabled people's rights and their full integration into society. RADAR operates nationally with an affiliated network of around 500 local and national organisations.

The Association does not recruit volunteers directly, but can assist with information. Among its activities is the publication of a list of organisations which seek volunteers to help with holidays for disabled people.

Those interested should write to RADAR at the above address enclosing a large stamped addressed envelope.

Royal National Institute for the Blind (RNIB)
224 Great Portland Street, London W1N 6AA (tel 0171-388 1266; fax 0171-388 2034).

RNIB is Britain's largest organisation helping blind and partially sighted people, and needs volunteers in many different areas of its work. For instance, in fundraising, by organizing or helping at local events in co-operation with your local appeals organizer. The schools need qualified or experienced help with swimming, riding, outings, etc. The cassette library needs volunteer readers to record books at home or in the RNIB studios. Volunteers are also needed to read books to students at university or at home. Talking books are recorded by professional readers, but volunteers are needed to service the playback machines loaned to members. No great technical knowledge is necessary. Volunteers are recruited for an indefinite period of time. Expenses are paid.

Applications should be sent to the Director General at the above address.

RNIB Schools
RNIB Sunshine House Schools (nursery/primary) are at 33 Dene Road, North-
    wood, Middlesex HA6 1DD (01923-822538); 2 Oxford Road, Birkdale, South-
    port, Merseyside PR8 2JT; (01704-67174; Dunnings Road, East Grinstead,
    West Sussex RH19 4ND; (01342-323141).
RNIB Rushton Hall School (junior): Rushton, nr Kettering, Northants NN14
    1RR (01536-710506).
RNIB Condover Hall School (secondary) incorporating Pathways Deafblind
    Unit, Condover, Nr. Shrewsbury, Shropshire SY5 7AH (01743-872320).
RNIB New College Worcester (secondary), Whittington Road, Worcester WR5
    2JX (01905-763933).

Royal National Institute for Deaf People
19-20 Featherstone Road, Street, London EC1Y 8SL; (tel 0171-296 8000; fax 0171-296 8199).

The RNID is the major service providing organisation for deaf people in the UK. Most of its work is highly specialised. However, approaches by volunteers with administrative or office skills are welcomed in national and local offices in London, Bath, Birmingham, Salford, Sunderland, Belfast and Glasgow. Offers of voluntary fundraising support are always appreciated. Volunteers hoping to work directly with deaf people should contact their local deaf club, details of which can be obtained from the RNID.

St John Ambulance
1 Grosvenor Crescent, London SW1 7EF (tel 0171-235 5231).

The St John Ambulance Brigade is a body of 250,000 volunteers worldwide who give millions of hours of unpaid service every year providing first aid cover at public events and undertaking a variety of welfare work in the local community. Recruits are always welcome; the UK membership now numbers over 80,000.

Children aged between 6 and 10 can join St John Ambulance as Badgers, and become Cadets from the age of 10 to 16 and thereafter adult members.

For further information about the Brigade, contact the local county office (details in local telephone directory) or the address above.

SCODA — The Standing Conference on Drug Abuse
Waterbridge House, 32-36 Loman Street, London SE1 OEE; (tel 0171-928 9500).

SCODA is the national co-ordinating body for the drug abuse treatment field. As such it has information on local agencies which may need volunteers to work in the area of combatting drug abuse. Anyone interested in such work should contact the above address for information of local agencies which may need volunteer helpers.

Terrence Higgins Trust
52-54 Gray's Inn Road, London WC12 8JU (tel 0171-831 0330; fax 0171-242 0121).

The Terrence Higgins Trust is the UK's largest AIDS charity and continues to expand to meet the many demands which AIDS and HIV infection present to all. There are currently over 1300 volunteers who provide help, advice, information, support and training not only to people with HIV and AIDS, but also to anyone concerned about this health crisis. The Trust provides direct services in Greater London as well as sharing information and its expertise throughout the UK and Europe.

Approximately 50 new volunteers join each month to help with a wide range of services. Most volunteers work locally in the befriending scheme as a 'buddy'. Volunteers are also needed to do practical work for the Helper Cell, work on the Helpline, in the advice centre, counselling and administrating. Special skills may be needed, but training is provided. Volunteers must be over 18 years and London-based. The Trust pays travel expenses and office-based volunteers will receive luncheon vouchers.

Those interested should contact the Volunteer Coordinator at the above address.

Umbrella
St James House, 108 Hampstead Road, London NW1 2LS (tel 0171-387 2026; fax 0171-383 5177).

Umbrella is a special needs housing project which provides a variety of accommodation with different levels of care and support to people with long-term mental health problems. All its projects are a short distance from the head office at the above address and, as a specific community care organisation, it operates only in that particular locality.

About 10 volunteers help at Umbrella at any one time with each having their own allocated supervisor from amongst the paid staff. Volunteers can get involved in direct client work in many different ways; as befrienders, social facilitators, teachers of daily living skills, providers, facilitators of access to community facilities, etc. There are also volunteer opportunities in the finance department and in the administration of the organisation as a whole, with opportunities to learn computer skills. This type of work can cover anything from photocopying, filing, typing and wordprocessing to spreadsheets and super calc, depending on the volunteer's ability, willingness to learn and particular interests. Work with clients is possible in three different areas distinguished by the particular needs of clients; housing and social care, nursing care and residential care.

Applicants may be of any nationality, but a reasonable command of the English language is essential. Any previous criminal convictions must be disclosed and the organisation rejects the right to reject candidates with particular convictions. Minimum period of work is at least a few months; this is not necessarily on a full-time basis. Volunteers are needed all the year round. All expenses incurred while on Umbrella business will be paid. Volunteers who can commit themselves to a minimum of 35 hours work per week also qualify for one day or £50 worth of training to be decided in consultation with their supervisor.

For further details, or for a copy of a Volunteer Information Pack, contact Annie Ward at the above address.

Unity Centre of South London
2-4 Ravenstone Road, Balham, London SW12 9SS (tel 0181-673 0793; fax 0181 673 5486).

The Centre runs a telephone Helpline for those suffering from, or at risk of developing, mental illness and also a day centre with rehabilitation facilities for those recovering from mental ill-health. Applicants of any nationality are welcome. All volunteers will receive appropriate training. Volunteers are needed all the year round, and the length of placement is flexible. Expenses are paid.

Those interested should contact Rev. Harry Kudiabor at the above address.

OTHER NON-RESIDENTIAL OPPORTUNITIES

The following organisations have been included in the Short Term Residential chapter but they also welcome non residential support.

Conservation Volunteers —
  Northern Ireland
Festiniog Railway Company
National Autistic Society
National Trust — Northern Ireland
Otto Schiff Housing Association
Upper Nene Archaeological Society

Queen Elizabeth's Foundation for the
  Disabled
Ritchie Russell House Young
  Disabled Unit
The Scottish Conservation Projects Trust
The Simon Community (UK)
Stallcombe House

The Volunteer
and the Job Seeker's Allowance

One of the basic principles behind the payment of the Job Seeker's Allowance in the United Kingdom is that it must only be given to those who are actively looking for work and are free to take up a job if one becomes available. The official line used to be that if someone was doing voluntary work then they were not available for work, and so should not receive any allowance. The official attitude has changed in recent years, as it has been realised that in times of high unemployment it does not achieve anything to bar those who have little chance of finding work, especially if they have no work experience of any kind, from making constructive use of their time and in the process acquiring potentially valuable experience. Ultimately, what is permitted is at the discretion of the individual's Benefit Office, so people are advised to consult the publications listed below for full details of their entitlement.

The situation now is that volunteers can claim the Job Seeker's Allowance , provided they meet a few basic conditions. They must remain available either for a job interview or to begin work at 24 hours notice, and be actively seeking work. They are allowed to receive reasonable expenses, such as the payment of bus fares to wherever they will be helping and a small amount of pocket money.

People who are unemployed can also continue to receive the Allowance if they take part in a voluntary workcamp lasting for up to fourteen days as long as they give their Benefit Office advance warning and the camp is run by either a charity or a local authority. The situation is less clear for those wanting to join a work camp abroad, as it is at the discretion of their Benefit Officer whether or not they will be allowed to continue claiming.

The same basic principles as those listed above apply for people claiming income support. Further information on volunteers and welfare benefits can be found in various booklets including *Volunteers and the Council Tax, Volunteers and Welfare Benefits* and *Volunteers' welfare benefits and taxation* which cost £1-£2.50 each from the Volunteer Centre UK, Publications, Carriage Row, 183 Eversholt Street, London NW1 1BU (tel 0171-388 9888; fax 0171-383 0448; E-mail: voluk@mcr1.geonet.de)

Further Reading

Please note that many other organisations featured in this book also produce their own literature: do not hesitate to contact them if you would like further information about their activities.

American Hiking Society Volunteer Programme: PO Box 20160, Washington, DC 20041-2160, USA (tel +1 301 565-6704; fax 301 565-6714). E-mail: AMHIKER@aol.com. Publishes *Helping Out in the Outdoors* ($10) is a directory of volunteer opportunities and internships on public lands including national and state parks and forests, nature reserves and environmental centres. Opportunities include campground hosting, backcountry patrolling, wildlife assistants and visitor centre receptionists. Ages from 16. Although many posts are seasonal, opportunities are available for year round, full-time jobs. Some agencies provide housing, reimbursement for travel and food expenses. Enquiries to the above address.

Archaeology Abroad: 31-34 Gordon Square, London WC1H OPY. produces three information bulletins a year on archaeological opportunities abroad for its members: send a stamped addressed envelope for details of membership.

Central Bureau for Educational Visits and Exchanges: 10 Spring Gardens, London SW1A 2BN. (0171-389 4931; fax 389 4140). Publish *Volunteer Work*, a guidebook to organisations recruiting for medium and long-term voluntary service in Britain abroad. Available in bookshops, price £8.99, or by post from the above address (add £1.50 for postage).

Christians Abroad (World Service Enquiry): 1 Stockwell Green, London SW9 9HP. Produce a comprehensive free information guide on how and where to begin a search for unskilled voluntary opportunities overseas. Send a stamped addressed envelope for details.

Christian Service Centre: Holloway Street West, Lower Gornal, Dudley, West Midlands DY3 2DZ. (tel 01902-882836). Publishes *Jobs Abroad* twice a year that contains details of current long-term opportunities abroad of interest to Christians. Send £2.99 plus 64p for postage and packing (per issue). Also publishes a book entitled *Short-Term Service Directory* available at the end of each year. It costs £3.99 plus 75p postage and packing.

Commission on Voluntary Service and Action: (P O Box 117-19, New York, NY 10009, USA) published a catalogue *Invest Yourself* which is a list of openings in voluntary work in America and worldwide.

Co-ordinating Committee for International Voluntary Service: 1, Rue Miollis, 75732 Paris Cedex 15, France (tel +33 1 46 68 27 31; fax +33 1 42 73 06 21; E-mail: ccivs@zytek.fr). Produces a list of UK organisations offering opportunities abroad (send an international reply coupon). Booklets giving organisations in Europe/North America or Asia/Africa are also available (send 6 international reply coupons for each or £2 each of UK stamps also acceptable).

Council for British Archaeology: Bowes Morrell House, 111 Walmgate, York Y01 2UA (tel 01904 671417; fax 01904 671384; E-mail: 100271.456@compuserve.com) Publishes *British Archaeological News* and its information supplement (called *CBA Briefing*) which carries advertisements for volunteer help on archaeological sites in Britain. *British Archaeology* is published ten times a year, with *CBA Briefing* appearing every other month (on the first Friday in March, May, July, September and November). The annual subscription is £17 for Europe (including the UK); £22 (US$38) for surface mail outside Europe; $29 (US$50) for airmail outside Europe. Send an International Reply Coupon for details.

Council on International Educational Exchange: USA address: 205 East 42nd Street, New York, NY 10017; UK address: 52 Poland Street, London W1V 4JQ (tel 0171-478 2000; fax 0171-734 7322; E-mail cieeuk@easynet.co.uk) publishes a paperback entitled *Volunteer* that gives details of short and medium term voluntary projects in the US and around the world. Published every two years; next edition 1997. UK price £12.95 including postage and packing.

Israel Antiquities Authority: P.O.Box 586, Rockefeller Museum Bldg, Jerusalem 91004, Israel; (fax +972-2 292628; e-mail: harriet@israntique.org.il). Publishes an annual guide (in mid-winter) to archaeological digs in Israel requiring help from volunteers: send an international reply coupon to the above address.

The National Youth Agency: 17-23 Albion Street, Leicester LE1 6GD (tel 0116-285 6789). Publishes a range of literature dealing with voluntary work placements for young people in England and Wales. Contact the above address for a free catalogue.

Returned Volunteer Action: 1 Amwell Street, London EC1R 1UL; (0171-278 0804). Publishes an information pack *Thinking about Volunteering and Overseas Development: a Guide to Opportunities* which costs £3.50 plus 36p postage and packing.

The Royal Association for Disability and Rehabilitation (Radar): 12 City Forum, 250 City Road, London EC1V 8AF (tel 0171-250 3222). Publishes a factsheet on organizations which seek volunteers to help with holidays for disabled people. Send an A5 SAE to the above address.

The Third World Directory (1996) Lucy Stubbs price £12.95 plus £2.50 postage, published by the Directory of Social Change, 24 Stephenson Way, London NW1 2DP; (tel 0171-209 5151; fax 0171-209 5049). A comprehensive guide to over 200 development organisations based in the UK and their volunteer requirements. Also includes details of funds available from the EC and the ODA and how to apply for them.

The Universities and Colleges Christian Fellowship for Evangelical Unions 38 Dr. Montford Street, Leicester LE1 7GP produce a booklet *Jobs Abroad* in which they list overseas vacancies.

Vacation Work Publications: 9 Park End Street, Oxford OX1 1HJ; (tel. 01865 241978). Publish a range of books covering both voluntary and paid work in Britain and around the world, including: *The Directory of Jobs and Careers Abroad, The Directory of Work and Study in Developing Countries, Kibbutz Volunteer, The Directory of Summer Jobs Abroad, The Directory of Summer Jobs in Britain* and *Work Your Way Around the World.* Send a stamped addressed envelope to the above address for a list of books and an order form.

Index of Organisations